Intended Consequences

Other works by the author:

With Us Always: Private Charity and Public Welfare (co-editor) (1998)

Studebaker: Life and Death of an American Corporation (1996)

The Politics of Abortion and Birth Control in Historical Perspective (editor) (1996)

A History of the United States, I-V, (in Polish) (co-editor) (1995)

America!: A Concise History (1994)

Poverty and Public Policy in Modern America (co-editor) (1989)

Federal Social Policy: The Historical Dimension (co-editor) (1989)

Socialism in the Heartland: The Midwestern Experience (editor) (1986)

The Brookings Institution, 1916–1952: Expertise and the Public Interest in a Democratic Society (1985)

Intended Consequences

Birth Control, Abortion,
and the Federal Government
in Modern America

Donald T. Critchlow

New York   Oxford
OXFORD UNIVERSITY PRESS
1999

OXFORD UNIVERSITY PRESS

Oxford   New York

Athens   Auckland   Bangkok   Bogotá   Buenos Aires
Calcutta   Cape Town   Chennai   Dar es Salaam   Delhi   Florence
Hong Kong   Istanbul   Karachi   Kuala Lumpur   Madrid   Melbourne
Mexico City   Mumbai   Nairobi   Paris   São Paulo   Singapore
Taipei   Tokyo   Toronto   Warsaw

and associated companies in
Berlin   Ibadan

Published by Oxford University Press, Inc.
198 Madison Avenue, New York, New York 10016

Oxford is a registered trademark of Oxford University Press

Library of Congress Cataloging-in-Publication Data

Critchlow, Donald T.
Intended consequences : birth control, abortion, and the federal government in
modern America / Donald T. Critchlow.
p.   cm.
Includes index.
ISBN 0-19-504657-9
1. Birth control—Government policy—United States.   2. Abortion—
Government policy—United States.   3. United States—Social policy.
4. United States—Politics and government.   I. Title.
HQ763.6.U5C75   1999
363.9'6'0973—dc21   98-13691

Printing (last digit) 9 8 7 6 5 4 3 2 1
Printed in the United States of America
on acid-free paper

With love and devotion to my wife, Patricia,
and our family, Magda, Agnieszka, and Andrew

Contents

Acknowledgments

―――――――

I owe a great debt to many people and institutions that supported the writing of this book. A fellowship in 1996–97 at the Woodrow Wilson International Center for Scholars in Washington, D.C., allowed me to complete this project in an ideal environment. I want to thank the staff at the Wilson Center, especially Michael Lacey, director of the United States Studies Division, and his able former assistant, George Wagner, for their encouragement and intellectual stimulation. The center provided me with a number of research assistants during the course of the year whose enthusiasm for the project was evidenced in their willingness to ferret information from the Library of Congress, the National Archives, and organizations located in Washington, D.C. These research assistants deserve recognition: Dayspring Brock, Misty Brown, Nina Choi, and Bernice Lee. Throughout the course of the year, other Wilson fellows challenged my thinking about federal family planning policy. Henry Munson shared with me his interest and insights into religious fundamentalism in the United States and the Middle East. Anne Feldhaus, Richard Grassby, Robert Lerner, Seymour Lipset, William O'Neill, and John Stone provided valuable comments on two seminar presentations I made at the center. Temma Kaplan and Dorothy Ross read a preliminary draft of a chapter that concerned the women's movement and offered sharp criticism as feminist historians interested in social and intellectual history. In Washington, Clyde Wilcox and Patrick Fagan shared survey data drawn from their work on abortion and social values.

I want to thank a small group of my friends who read the manuscript in its entirety including James Fisher, Wilfred McClay, and William Rorabaugh. James Reed and James Hitchcock, although having different perspectives and levels of expertise concerning the subject, offered criticisms that inform this book. Mark Neely and Philip Gleason deserve particular praise for their detailed line-by-line reading of an earlier draft that led to a radical revision of the manuscript—stylistically, organizationally, and intellectually. They illustrate scholarship and friendship at its best.

Numerous archivists facilitated primary research at their institutions including the Alan Guttmacher Institute (Washington, D.C.), American

Philosophical Society Archives, Catholic University of America, Federation of Americans for Immigration Reform, the Ford Foundation, the Library of Congress, the National Archives, Princeton University, Smith College, the University of Notre Dame, and the various presidential libraries cited in the notes. In this regard, I especially want to thank Thomas Rosenbaum who guided me through the immense documentary record at the Rockefeller Archives. He directed me to recently opened and still unprocessed papers of John D. Rockefeller 3rd, the Population Council, and Joan Dunlop. A research grant from the Rockefeller Archives provided time to conduct research over the course of two summers.

While in Washington, D.C., Frank and Teresa Wagner provided a room in their Georgetown house in July 1997 when my lease expired in "staid" Chevy Chase, Maryland. Their hospitality allowed the additional time to put the finishing touches on the first draft of the manuscript. At Hong Kong University, the staff of the Department of History, especially Ng Wai Man, solved a major problem when my computer crashed, shortly after my arrival as a visiting professor for the academic year, 1997–98. My good friend at Hong Kong University, Kerrie McPherson, while introducing me to the richness of Chinese history and the implications of the turnover of Hong Kong to mainland China, provided insightful comments from her reading of the introduction and conclusion before it was sent to press. At Oxford University Press, my editor Thomas LeBien, who replaced Sheldon Meyer in overseeing this project, upheld the high standards of the press.

Finally, I want to thank my wife, Patricia, who helped to research this book. Once again, as I did in my previous study on the Studebaker Corporation, I asked her to list her name as the coauthor of this book, but in typical modesty she once again refused this invitation. Nonetheless, this book is as much hers as it is mine.

Intended Consequences

Introduction

In the years between 1965 and 1974, the federal government's role in family planning policy underwent a dramatic shift from nonintervention to active involvement. This change occurred with the support of both political parties, Republican and Democratic, under the administrations of Lyndon Baines Johnson and Richard M. Nixon. Initially federal family planning meant artificial contraception and sterilization, but after 1973 it included abortion. Although the legalization of abortion by the Supreme Court in *Roe v. Wade* (1973) led to the emergence of an antiabortion movement and fierce political debate, federal involvement in family planning remained established policy, even though Congress placed restrictions on funding for abortion services. By 1997 federal and state funding for family planning, including contraception, sterilization, and therapeutic abortion, reached over $700 million annually. This book explores the transformation of federal family planning policy in modern America since 1945. By examining federal family planning within the context of policy history, this book follows the development of this policy through a process of innovation, legislative enactment and administration imposition, program implementation, reappraisal, and politicization.

The modern family planning movement in the United States emerged from two distinct concerns—overpopulation and the rights of women to legalized birth control. While the advocacy of contraception as a mechanism for liberating women from the arbitrary controls of a male-dominated society remained an important source of support for federal family planning, the movement for federally supported contraceptive programs that emerged in the immediate aftermath of the Second World War drew to its ranks a wide variety of people. Many of them remained indifferent to the issue of women's rights, treating it in perfunctory fashion or ignoring it completely. As a consequence, the primary impetus for federal family planning policy came initially from those who believed that overpopulation threatened political, economic, and social stability in the United States and the world.

These policy experts and activists who lobbied policy makers in Washington to initiate federally funded contraceptive programs saw family planning as a means of controlling the burgeoning global population and the rise in the birthrate in America following the war. These policy actors were organized into a loosely knit coalition of organizations, including philanthropic foundations such as the Population Council and the Ford Foundation and activist organizations such as the Population Crisis Committee and Planned Parenthood Federation of America. Although they were divided over strategy and the urgency of the population problem, these organizations cooperated in an intense lobbying effort to involve the federal government in family planning. Initially, these groups focused their attention on establishing international family planning programs. Their emphasis turned to domestic federal family planning with Johnson's Great Society, as federal involvement in family planning became an instrument to alleviate problems of poverty, welfare costs, and out-of-wedlock births.

In the aftermath of the Second World War, population control advocates, promulgating a neo-Malthusian vision of the world, assumed a prominent place in the family planning movement. Proponents of population control differed among themselves, however, over strategies for addressing this perceived population problem. From the outset, some of the hard-liners on population control such as Hugh Moore, the founder of the Population Crisis Committee, believed that more coercive measures were needed to control the rate of population growth. After actively contributing to Planned Parenthood in the late 1940s, he withdrew from the organization in the belief that it was concerned too much with individual and women's rights and not enough with overpopulation as a general social problem with ramifications beyond personal rights. Others, especially social science experts, found Moore "hysterical" and often a detriment to the movement.

While differences within family planning circles manifested themselves as the movement took shape, one man proved pivotal in bringing the movement together and orchestrating the campaign to change federal policy on this issue—John D. Rockefeller 3rd, the grandson of the oil tycoon John D. Rockefeller. When the Rockefeller Foundation turned down his proposal to initiate a population program, Rockefeller 3rd organized the Population Council in 1952 to support medical research into reproduction and to train demographers and population experts who could be employed in the developing nations of the world. He envisioned the Population Council as a way of providing leadership to a movement that was dominated by those he considered "alarmists," such as Moore. Under the leadership of its first chairman, Frederick Osborn, the Population Council sponsored demographic training and medical research into the population problem. While the council avoided public controversy by identifying itself as a neutral, scientific organization, from the outset it was policy oriented. Joined by the Ford Foundation, the Population Council played a principal role in establishing an international network of experts who shared a set of assumptions about overpopulation and technical intervention.

Shortly after Rockefeller organized the Population Council, Hugh Moore undertook a campaign to educate the American public about the impending "population explosion." Moore had become interested initially in the population question as a peace issue. Prior to the Second World War, he had played a central role in the National Peace Conference, a group that called for international disarmament. After the war, he became active in the Atlantic Union and the World Federalists. Influenced deeply by William Vogt, research director at Planned Parenthood of America, Moore became convinced that world peace would not be possible without population control. As a consequence, he devoted his life and his fortune to the population problem. In 1965 he organized the Population Crisis Committee, a lobbying organization based in Washington, D.C.

At the same time, the Planned Parenthood Federation of America, under Alan Guttmacher and Cass Canfield, continued to advocate birth control, primarily as a women's rights issue. Within Planned Parenthood, however, population control advocates found a prominent place. Thus, Planned Parenthood maintained its mission of promoting birth control as a woman's right, but it joined other groups in lobbying for family planning as a means of controlling the rate of population growth.

These individuals and organizations formed a policy network that became the basis of the population movement. Although tensions existed between these individuals and organizations, they shared a belief in this early period that the limitation of population growth was necessary for economic growth, international stability, and domestic tranquillity. While population control advocates disagreed among themselves on a number of points, there was a consensus among the policy experts that population intervention offered a technical solution to larger structural problems. In terms of domestic policy, social scientists and population activists believed that population stability was essential to an array of social problems, including poverty, welfare, crime, urban decay, and pollution. The population lobby actively sought to shift American policy toward family planning assistance domestically and internationally.

In the 1950s, as the population lobby was taking shape, American policy makers carefully avoided involvement in population policy for fear of the political consequences. Only late in the Eisenhower administration did the issue arise, when a presidential commission headed by William Draper recommended that population control programs in developing countries be funded through the military assistance program. When the U.S. Catholic bishops publicly condemned the recommendations, Eisenhower backed down and declared that population problems of other countries were not the concern of the United States. (After leaving office, Eisenhower would endorse federal family planning as a means of addressing rising out-of-wedlock births in America.)

Yet, if Eisenhower skirted the population question while in office, the Democrats were equally worried about becoming too quickly immersed in a potentially explosive political issue. Population activists met quietly with Kennedy administration officials in the State Department, the National Institutes of Health, the Department of Health, Education, and Welfare (HEW), and the White House staff to press for gradual changes in U.S. foreign aid and domestic health policy.

The advent of the Johnson administration furthered this quiet revolution. Worried about a backlash from Catholic voters, as well as accusations within the African-American community that family planning targeted only poor blacks, Johnson remained cautious in supporting congressional legislation that would have mandated family planning on a state level. Instead, federal agencies established family planning through administrative channels. By 1967, however, the administration was ready to press the population issue further. A review of the HEW family planning programs by Frederick Jaffe (Planned Parenthood) and Oscar Harkavy (Ford Foundation) led to the creation of a new position of deputy assistant secretary for population, headed by Katherine Oettinger, formerly of the Children's Bureau.

Although executive agencies resisted legislative changes as unnecessary and unmanageable, Congress aggressively pursued legislation that expanded federal family planning through the Foreign Assistance Act (1967), which earmarked funds for family planning. The Social Security amendments (1967), proposed by Congressmen George Bush (R-Texas) and Herman Schneebeli (R-Pennsylvania), allowed the federal government to fund family planning programs through state agencies and private organizations. As a consequence, family planning became closely linked to the War on Poverty. To implement family planning programs, the federal government, through OEO and other HEW agencies, relied on Planned Parenthood, the Population Council, and the Ford Foundation to set up family planning clinics and demonstration programs.

President Nixon extended family planning policy. In 1970 the Family Planning Services and Population Research Act was passed. Expenditures for family planning programs increased dramatically in the first years of the Nixon administration. The implementation of these programs, however, proved difficult in a system that relied on various federal and state agencies, as well as private organizations.

In 1972, Nixon shifted his support for family planning. Pursuing what the White House called the "Catholic Strategy," designed to lure Catholic voters to the Republican party, Nixon distanced himself from his own presidential commission headed by Rockefeller. At the same time, his policy of "creative federalism" lumped family planning funds into welfare and health care funds. The Supreme Court's decision in *Roe v. Wade* (1973) only intensified growing polarization over the abortion issue. In the process, family planning, which became linked with the abortion issue, was converted from a nonpartisan issue into a political issue that divided politicians, political parties, and the electorate along ideological lines. Moreover, abortion transformed the discussion into a "rights" debate, with the proponents of legalized abortion upholding the rights of women and antiabortion activists proclaiming the rights of the fetus. In the process, overpopulation became less important as a policy concern, although it never fell completely off the policy agenda.

At the same time legalized abortion emerged as a prominent political issue, many population experts raised doubts about the efficiency of traditional family planning programs. Within the population movement in the United States, many activists felt that voluntary family planning had failed to retard the rate of population growth. Others, especially social science experts, believed that family planning programs needed to consider economic development and the status of women if they were going to succeed in addressing population problems, especially in developing countries. Such criticism of traditional family planning programs became evident in the United Nations World Population Conference, held in Bucharest, in 1974. At the same time, social scientists became increasingly critical of linking population control to economic development without addressing larger social and economic questions.

After Bucharest, the Population Council underwent significant administrative and programmatic restructuring. In undertaking this new course, the Population Council was influenced by the Ford Foundation's decision to withdraw from direct family planning service projects and to focus instead on social development projects concerned with education and improving the status of women, as well as primary reproductive medical research. At the same time the Population Council, after much discussion, endorsed abortion as a birth control measure. Until this time leadership in the council had not seen abortion as an important tool of family planning.

Although a number of the council's early projects provided abortion services, prior to the mid-1970s the council had consciously avoided the abortion issue by not taking a stand one way or the other.

In this regard, the Population Council's ambivalence toward abortion as a birth control measure reflected the general attitude of the family planning movement. "Family planning" itself was a relatively new term developed in 1942 by the Planned Parenthood Federation of America as a more palatable name for "birth control," and this specifically meant artificial birth control. From the outset of the family planning movement in the postwar period, certain leaders such as Hugh Moore and contraceptive manufacturer Joseph Sunnen wanted to include sterilization and abortion under the larger rubric of "family planning." In the late 1960s these men became involved in supporting state campaigns to reform abortion law. Nonetheless, differences over sterilization and abortion as birth control measures found expression within Planned Parenthood, the Population Council, and the Ford Foundation well into the early 1970s. The expansion of federal family planning programs gradually came to encompass birth control, sterilization, and abortion, but acceptance of abortion within the family planning movement came slowly, and sometimes with much resistance from those who wanted to separate birth control from abortion.

After Bucharest, Rockefeller's active involvement in the Population Council waned. He left the running of the organization to others in order to devote himself increasingly to abortion rights and sex education. His involvement in these issues stemmed from a new awareness concerning the status of women in modern society. As a consequence, he provided major support to activist groups involved in political and legal struggles to defend legalized abortion. At the same time, he funded a number of sex education projects. By 1974 he reached the conclusion that any permanent change in policy rested ultimately on changing peoples' attitudes toward sexuality. This concern with sex education led Rockefeller to support projects involving homosexual rights. As a consequence, Rockefeller shared the perspective of many within the abortion movement that reproductive rights embodied larger issues concerned with gender roles and sexuality. The emergence of the proabortion and antiabortion movements in the late 1960s and early 1970s only intensified cultural and religious divisions concerning these underlying social changes. By the 1980s it appeared that Americans were engaged in what sociologist James Hunter called a "cultural war." Although the concept of a "cultural war" exaggerates the political differences within the American polity, the term captures the nature of the polarized debate over abortion and gender-related issues in contemporary America.

•

Four major themes emerge from this history of federal family planning. First, the influence of elite interests and mass political movements is multidimensional, dynamic, and varied in the political process. The second theme follows from the first: although policy implementation brings unintended consequences, policies often fulfill the expectations of policy makers. For this reason, intended consequences in public policy deserve equal attention. Third, the ability of groups, whether a small collection of powerful individuals or democratically mobilized interests, to affect public policy remains dependent on the larger culture—the social mores and values of the society. Finally, the complexity of the policy process, as revealed in the history of federal family planning, does not lend itself to easily categorizing policy actors into the "good guys" and the "bad guys." By drawing upon rich archival and contemporary sources, this study shows that the proponents and opponents of family planning brought to the policy arena well-intentioned concerns about how to make America a better society and the world a better place. This is not to argue that judgments cannot be made about the value of policies or the efficacy of social programs; instead, it is to maintain the importance of allowing contemporaries to speak for themselves and explain their own motivations.

Those who first placed family planning on the policy agenda came from established business, government, and foundation organizations. These men and women tended to come from the same social backgrounds, belonged to the same social clubs, and had easy access to those in political power. Most were upper-class, Protestant, and white. They shared similar outlooks concerning the world and similar biases. While often disagreeing among themselves over tactics, these men and women remained the primary force in advocating greater government intervention in family planning. They orchestrated a lobbying campaign conducted not only in the halls of Congress and in administrative offices but also at private dinners and other social occasions in their residences and social clubs that brought them together with key public officials.

The emergence of the abortion issue, beginning early with the movements to legalize abortion on the state level, changed the dynamic of policy making. The mobilization of the abortion movement brought into the policy arena activists, especially women, organized on the grassroots level. Concerned about the rights of women, the abortion rights movement extended the policy debate beyond the confines of elite circles to the larger public. The corresponding rise of the antiabortion movement brought new activists into the political arena. In this political environment the policy making shifted from elite interests to well-organized social movements that sought to mobilize their own constituencies in order to set the policy agenda.

Those who advocated federal family planning policy and legalization of abortion achieved much in the process. In this way, many of the consequences of federal planning policy were intended. For example, the proponents of federal family planning sought to reduce the rate of population growth in the world and in the United States, and this did, indeed, happen. Beginning in the late 1960s, the rate of population growth in the world slowed because of economic modernization as well as interventionist family planning programs. In the three decades from 1960 through 1990, Western Europe and North America experienced declines in their overall birthrate to the extent that Europe had a declining rate of population growth. The United States would have declining rates as well, without high immigration. Moreover, many nations in Asia and Latin America showed sharp declines in the rate of population growth.

Widespread use of contraception coincided with declining rates of population growth. Advocates of federal family planning wanted artificial contraception to become widely available. Here again, they achieved a major goal. By 1990 an estimated 50 percent of couples in the world used contraceptives. In the United States, contraceptive practice through artificial contraception and sterilization reached an estimated 80 percent among adults.

Although many within the family planning movement felt at least initially that legalized abortion should not be included as a birth control measure, the movement for liberalized abortion in the United States was achieved through the mobilization of population activists and women's organizations. Beginning on the state level, liberalized abortion laws were enacted by many state legislatures. In issuing the *Roe* decision, the Supreme Court completed this process. Legalized abortion became a right guaranteed under the Constitution of the United States. Abortion activists experienced less success in convincing Congress to fund abortion, but by 1996 few believed that *Roe* would be overturned in the immediate future. As a consequence, policy debate over abortion turned to the regulation of abortion, as democratically mobilized groups struggled in the states and nationally over the extent and legality of abortion restrictions.

Federal family planning was advocated as an instrument for addressing problems related to poverty, welfare dependency, and out-of-wedlock births. While the rate of poverty in the United States fell in the 1960s, the decline came primarily from economic growth and social legislation for the elderly. In the late 1970s and 1980s, however, rates of poverty began to increase. At the same time, out-of-wedlock births continued to climb, rising ominously in the 1980s and 1990s. Federal family planning failed to reduce the number of people living in poverty or the number of out-of-wedlock births. Matters might have been worse without federal family planning, but the policy in itself proved ineffectual as a tool for addressing the complex social problems of poverty, welfare dependency, and out-of-wedlock births.

Policy change in federal family planning occurred within the context of a "sexual revolution," evidenced in changing attitudes toward sexual mores and behavior and sexuality itself. Although this revolution was never as complete or as deep as many claimed—most Americans remained quite traditional in their sexual practices and their views toward marriage—significant cultural changes set the parameters of the debate over family planning and abortion. By the 1970s the great majority of Americans accepted artificial contraception and family planning. Thus, while there was sharp disagreement over legalized abortion and federal support for abortion, the acceptance of family planning meant that government-supported contraception programs remained established policy. Even while fiscal and social conservatives sought to reduce expenditures for family planning in the 1980s, few questioned whether government should be involved in these programs. In short, the culture that accepted artificial contraception protected federal family programs from experiencing the fierce political attack that legalized abortion elicited. Moreover, the importance of culture proved critical in setting the confines of the debate over federal family planning policy as it emerged in the late 1960s and took shape under the Johnson and Nixon administrations, as well as informing the subsequent politics of abortion. As a consequence, this study examines family planning within the larger context of these cultural changes.

Moreover, many of the advocates of federal family planning welcomed the sexual revolution. Although the full ramifications of the sexual revolution were not understood at the time advocates of federal family planning policy began to lobby the White House and Congress to pursue activist intervention policies, the widespread use of contraception by Americans was an intended consequence of much of this activity. Furthermore, men and women such as John D. Rockefeller 3rd and Mary Calderone became actively involved in instituting sex education programs designed explicitly to change American attitudes toward sex and sexuality. An integral part of these programs was an attempt to change American sexual mores and cultural attitudes toward gender roles and homosexuality.

Although there is an extensive literature on the social, political, and legal aspects of birth control and abortion in the United States, the opening of important archival collections has provided the opportunity for a new scholarly perspective into family planning policy in the postwar period. In 1995 I was granted special access to recently opened, unprocessed

Population Council papers and the unprocessed John D. Rockefeller 3rd papers at the Rockefeller Family Archives in Tarrytown, New York. In addition, I undertook extensive research in the Planned Parenthood Federation of America papers at Smith College; the Ford Foundation Archives; the Frederick Osborn papers and American Eugenics Society papers at the American Philosophical Society Library; the recently processed Hugh Moore papers and the still unprocessed Frank Notestein papers at Princeton University; the National Catholic Welfare Conference papers at Catholic University; the Theodore Hesburgh papers at the University of Notre Dame; and the archives of the Federation of Americans for Immigration Reform (FAIR) in Washington, D.C. I also used major presidential collections, including the papers of Harry S. Truman, Dwight D. Eisenhower, Lyndon B. Johnson, and Richard M. Nixon. In addition, I have examined the records of key governmental agencies located in the National Archives.

By relying on these extensive archival collections, as well as a large secondary literature, I hope to provide an objective account of how federal family planning became established policy in the United States. While my primary focus remained domestic family planning, this study touches on international family planning programs as well. In discussing domestic family planning, I sought to represent fairly the perspectives of the proponents and opponents of federal family planning, as well as the views of those involved in the abortion debate. To accomplish this, I quote extensively from individuals and groups in order to convey their perspectives and policy positions as the debate over federally sponsored contraceptive programs emerged after the Second World War and grew in intensity with the legalization of abortion. Because of the sharp rhetoric used by participants in this debate, I avoided such terms as "pro-life" and "pro-choice"; instead, I use "antiabortion" and "proabortion"—terms that seem to me more accurately descriptive of the policies actually pursued by the groups in question. The complexity of the policy process and the positions articulated by participants in this policy debate defy such rhetorical categories as "pro-choice" and "pro-life." Whether I have accomplished my task, I leave to the reader to judge.

Donald T. Critchlow
Hong Kong, May 1998

1

Laying the Foundation
for Federal Family Planning Policy
The Eisenhower-Kennedy Years

In the immediate aftermath of the Second World War, a global war from which the United States emerged as the predominant world power, most Americans felt a heady confidence in their future as a nation.[1] There were those, however, who remained less sanguine about the future. A new enemy threatened humanity: rampant population growth. The fundamental cause of war, these people held, lay in a Malthusian paradox: as civilization advances, population grows at a geometric rate and eventually outdistances food supplies and natural resources. The consequence is famine, war, and death. While the exact population of the world remained unknown in 1945 (demography itself was a much less exact science at the time), it was apparent that many nations, especially in Asia and Africa, suffered from a population crisis. The Second World War proved all too clearly the consequences of what happens when nations experience food and natural resource shortages and the lack of living space to support their populations. That there was a circularity to this reasoning—the last war proved that there was a population crisis, and a population crisis led to world conflict—did little to dissuade these neo-Malthusians from predicting an impending population explosion that would inevitably create the conditions for global political, social, and economic instability. To make the world safe for American democracy, global population needed to be controlled. American know-how and technology were needed to avert another war.

These new Malthusians envisioned planning on a global scale never before undertaken in the history of the world. Only when the world's leaders understood the nature of the impending crisis would humankind be safe. Only when the nations of the world came together to control their populations could there be real social progress and cultural advancement for the peoples of the earth. Only then could another world war be prevented. This vision for a better world lay behind the population movement that emerged in the postwar years. Initially concerned about the international problems of overpopulation, this small group of men and women later shifted their attention in the early 1960s to the social consequences of overpopulation in the United States.

Yet, in 1945, only a few individuals, mostly intellectuals involved in the social and natural sciences, and a few popular writers, focused their attention on the population issue. Although familiar with one another's work, they had not coalesced into a coherent movement. Indeed, their interest in population, while sharing mutual concerns, varied. The efforts of one man, John D. Rockefeller 3rd, gave shape to the population movement as it emerged in the 1950s. Bringing wealth, prestige, and tempered leadership, Rockefeller became a pivotal figure in a movement that transformed American domestic and foreign population policy.[2]

Initially, Rockefeller focused his attention on contraceptive research and the training of demographers and field-workers to develop population programs abroad. As the decade of the fifties drew to a close, however, he joined with experts in the foundation community and population activists to lobby the White House and Congress to fund international family planning efforts through the foreign assistance aid program. In the 1960s the population movement, while continuing its international efforts, turned its attention to domestic family planning programs. In this capacity the population movement played a critical role in shifting public policy toward family planning from neglect to active involvement. While the movement sought to raise public consciousness concerning overpopulation, its primary efforts involved convincing political leaders in the White House and Congress to support federal involvement in family planning as an antipoverty measure.

The Emergence of the Population Movement in the Aftermath of War

As a loosely knit population movement took shape in the 1950s, sharp divisions arose over urgency and strategy. Still, there was a consensus among the experts, as one Rockefeller Foundation officer explained to Rockefeller, that "the world's population [including America's] was growing too fast and in a haphazard way."[3] In this way, a small group of men and women, numbering only a few hundred, set the context of the policy debate, helped formulate regulatory and legislative changes, and served to implement family planning services for federal, state, and local government agencies that lacked an adequate family planning infrastructure.

Others joined Rockefeller to form a loosely knit population movement that brought together diverse groups, including birth control advocates, eugenicists, and proponents of population control. Although they shared similar concerns, these groups brought different perspectives to the movement. Among the most prominent of these groups was the birth control movement that had emerged in the early twentieth century, led by Margaret Sanger and other feminists, which had initiated the call for the legalization of artificial contraception. This group, organized around Planned Parenthood Federation of America (PPFA), established in 1942, imparted a rights focus to the movement. Planned Parenthood saw family planning primarily in terms of individual freedom and the right of families, especially women, to determine the spacing of their children. Leaders of Planned Parenthood voiced concern about overpopulation, but their focus remained the rights of women and families to control reproduction through contraception. The emergence of the civil rights movement and the women's movement in the late 1960s gave impetus to the "rights" aspect of the cause for federal family planning policy.

Although Sanger utilized eugenics arguments to promote birth control, especially in her writings in the 1920s and 1930s, the eugenics movement stood as a distinct group from the birth control advocates.[4] Indeed, in the early twentieth century, many eugenicists had reservations about birth control because they feared that family planning would reduce the birthrate among the upper and middle classes, the very sort of people who should be having more children in order to "improve" the native stock of the race. The eugenics movement emerged in the Progressive Era to demand that the native stock of Americans be strengthened by eliminating "deviant" populations and reducing the social burden of crime, poverty, prostitution, and illegitimacy—social ills often associated with "mental idiocy." By the 1920s eugenicists had developed a program to "improve the race" through birth control, sterilization, and immigration restriction. This eugenics movement paralleled the birth control movement and remained a presence in modern family planning circles, although the emphasis on the "quality of population," with its negative connotations, was replaced in the 1940s with a positive concern to improve the "quality of life" of the population.

These two groups, birth controllers and eugenicists, were joined by proponents of population control, who became the dominant voice for federal involvement in family planning policy in the early 1950s. Population control provided a more neutral context for discussing contraception and family planning. Advocates of population control sought to address problems of social stability, war, poverty, and economic development in the United States and the developing nations through family planning programs, including birth control and sterilization. (Initially, through the 50s and 60s, advocates of population control remained divided on the issue of abortion as a means of limiting population growth.) Those advocating population control sought to solve these larger social problems with a technical solution—family planning—rather than confronting directly problems of social inequality, wealth and income redistribution, racism, and imperialism.

Among the advocates of population control, opinion divided over the urgency of the population problem. At one end of this spectrum stood representatives of the philanthropic foundation community, who prided themselves on their scientific objectivity and cautious approach to policy change. They believed that while the population problem remained serious, the issue should be addressed through private efforts and a gradual change in public policy. The Population Council, an organization founded in 1952 by John D. Rockefeller 3rd, and the Ford Foundation provided the leadership to this approach. These organizations drew upon the expert advice and work of social scientists, who remained wary of cataclysmic warnings to the public about an impending overpopulation crisis. While concerned about the problems of overpopulation in the world, including the United States, these experts viewed policy change as an incremental process that came from careful research and the persuasion of political leaders.

At the other end of the spectrum stood activists such as Hugh Moore, who viewed overpopulation as a national and global emergency that needed to be addressed immediately and with radical, coercive measures if voluntary programs failed. A millionaire who founded the Dixie Cup Corporation, Moore published the widely read pamphlet "The Population Explosion" in 1954. In this pamphlet Moore warned of an immediate social and economic crisis caused by global overpopulation. Written in the immediate aftermath of the Second World War, as tensions between the Soviet Union and the democratic nations of the West erupted into a cold war, "The Population Explosion" called for population control as necessary to prevent the spread of communism in underdeveloped nations. Moore's language of anticommunism was largely rhetorical and was intended to rally American officials to support international family planning. Although he remained fervently anticommunist throughout his career, overpopulation remained his overriding concern. He was obsessed by the overpopulation crisis.

Initially, Moore worked with Planned Parenthood to bring this issue to the public, but by the late 1950s he became convinced that the leaders of the organization placed too much weight on the rights of women for contraception, while not giving enough attention to the primary problem, overpopulation. If the overpopulation crisis was to be remedied, he believed, individual rights might have to be disregarded in the interest of society; voluntary choice in family planning could not necessarily be relied upon to meet a crisis that threatened the entire planet. This led Moore to form the Population Crisis Committee in 1963.

Rockefeller and his associates at the Population Council always felt uncomfortable with what they perceived as Moore's "alarmist" rhetoric and approach to overpopulation. While the Population Council and Planned Parenthood cooperated with Moore in lobbying the federal government to initiate international and domestic family planning programs, tensions among the groups were apparent throughout the period. Still, whatever their differences in approach and strategy, these groups had much in common. Those involved in the movement to activate federal family planning generally came from the same social backgrounds and shared a belief that overpopulation was a major problem that called for the attention of political leaders in the United States. To address the population crisis in the world and the problems of overpopulation in the United States, they believed that the U.S. federal government needed to become actively involved in family planning programs, internationally as well as domestically.

Moreover, in calling for the federal government to take action, they believed that their main opposition came from the hierarchy of the Catholic Church in America. Historically the Catholic Church had opposed artificial contraception, sterilization, and abortion. As such, the church hierarchy in America presented an obstacle to federal family planning policy. Given this opposition by the church, the paramount question became this: How could the federal government be persuaded to enter into family planning policy without arousing political opposition from Catholic voters? As a result, behind many of the tensions within the movement lay differences over how best to address the Catholic question. For his part, Rockefeller wanted to encourage liberals within the Catholic Church to change the official position concerning artificial birth control. In taking this approach, Rockefeller carefully cultivated relations with reformist elements within the church, while at the same time coaxing public officials to move forward gradually in initiating federally funded family planning programs. Moore remained considerably less optimistic about changes within church doctrine. Perhaps church doctrine might change in the future, he said, but in the meantime a population crisis loomed, and the world could not afford to wait for Catholics to come to their senses

about artificial birth control. He wanted government intervention immediately at whatever political cost to the policy makers in Washington.

If the leaders in the population movement approached the Catholic
question differently, they agreed that the primary opposition to federal
family planning came from the church. In part, the differences between
Catholics and the proponents of federal family planning reflected class differences. Largely upper-class Protestants, the leaders of the movement
reflected the bias of their social backgrounds. They tended to favor capi-
talistic economic development, but defense of the capitalist system as such
was not their primary concern. In fact, big business's assumption that
expanding population was equated with economic growth was seen as a
serious obstacle to population control. Overpopulation stood above any
specific attachment to a particular economic system. As a result, family
planning became an ideology in itself. Subsequently, proponents of family
planning, while believing that the issue should remain nonpartisan, proved
surprisingly flexible in their political allegiances. For example, Rockefeller
maintained close familial ties with the Republican party—after all, his
brother Nelson would have a career in the Republican party as governor of
New York and later as vice president in Gerald Ford's administration—but
Rockefeller would support Jimmy Carter in 1976. Similarly, Rockefeller's
counterpart in the population movement, Hugh Moore, began as a
Democrat but increasingly voted Republican, beginning with Dwight D.
Eisenhower in 1952.

Members of the population movement drew intellectual support for
their views on overpopulation from similar sources. Specifically, a neo-
Malthusian argument found expression in a number of books and articles
written in the aftermath of the Second World War.[5] Among the most
influential books of the time was William Vogt's *Road to Survival* (1948). In
this popular book Vogt, then director of the conservation section of the
Pan American Union, framed his argument around environmental conservation. In so doing, he also articulated the neo-Malthusian case for seeing
the Second World War and the emerging cold war as manifestations of a
population crisis. In short, Vogt integrated Malthusianism with environ-
mentalism and international peace. His own interest in conservation
through his hobby of bird-watching, which he pursued after being crippled by polio in adolescence.[6]

Vogt expressed deep antiwar sentiments, common to many in early postwar population circles. He declared that prewar Japan, "unwilling or not
wise enough to seek a sharp limitation of her population, was faced with the
dilemma: starve or fight." Japan chose to fight, instead of addressing its
population problem. In turn, he cast the growing tensions between the
West and the Soviet Union in similar stark terms. To avert another world

war in the future, he called upon individual nations to undertake "vigorous birth control campaigns." He wrote, "If the United States had spent two billion dollars developing ... a contraceptive, instead of the atomic bomb, it would have contributed far more to our national security." At home, he warned that rampant population growth in the United States was depleting the nation's natural resources and undermining social stability. He endorsed H. L. Mencken's 1930s proposal for "sterilization bonuses," especially for the indigent. "From the point of society," he declared, "it would certainly be preferable to pay permanently indigent individuals, many of whom would be physically and psychologically marginal, $50 or $100 rather than support their hordes of offspring that, by both genetic and social inheritance, would tend to perpetuate their fecklessness."[7] Translated into nine languages, *Road to Survival* became an international best-seller.

A well-developed research apparatus supported the work of writers such as Vogt. In 1951 Vogt became national director of PPFA; Robert Cook headed the Population Reference Bureau; and Fairfield Osborn was president of the prestigious New York Zoological Society and the Conservation Foundation.[8] By the 1950s a number of organizations were actively engaged in population research, including the Scripps Institute at Miami University, the Office of Population Research at Princeton University, the International Union for Scientific Study of Population, and the Washington-based Population Reference Bureau. Population research was also supported by organizations with more specific missions, including Planned Parenthood, the American Eugenics Society, and the Conservation Foundation. These organizations enabled researchers to conduct their work and assisted them in sharing their findings with one another in an informal network of policy experts and activists. Still, in the early 1950s they had not yet formed a well-organized lobby or a coherent movement. It fell to Rockefeller to give form to the movement.

John D. Rockefeller 3rd Establishes the Population Council

Rockefeller brought to the population movement a philanthropist's concern to make the world a better place. The eldest son of John D. Rockefeller Jr., he embodied his father's commitment to contribute to society. He was quite different from his four brothers—the domineering and politically minded Nelson; the venture capitalist Laurence; the tragic Winthrop, who fled his family to start a new life in Arkansas; and his brilliant younger brother, David, who became president of Chase-Manhattan Bank. Tall, thin to the point of being gaunt, with the chiseled features of his grandfather and father, Rockefeller graduated from Princeton in 1929 (where the senior class, in an act of whimsy, voted him "Most Likely to

Succeed"). In college he tutored immigrant children, and after college he went on a world tour, participated in a New York study on juvenile delinquency, and became a trustee of the Rockefeller Foundation, the General Education Board, the Rockefeller Institute, the China Medical Board, and thirty-three other boards or committees. With the outbreak of the Second World War, he expanded his philanthropic activities by joining the Child Refugee Committee, the USO, the American Red Cross, and a host of other groups. In late 1942 he joined the navy, where he eventually became a special assistant on Far Eastern affairs to Under Secretary of the Navy Artemus Gates. From his first travels to Japan in 1929 and his involvement in Asia during the war, Rockefeller developed a reputation as an expert on the Far East.[9]

He became increasingly alarmed by the crowded conditions he saw during his travels in Asia and Africa following the war. He called for a dual strategy of increasing the food supply in developing nations through what became known as the green revolution—a program designed to improve agricultural production through high-yield crops—combined with containing population growth through advanced birth control technology and birth control programs in developing nations.[10] Rockefeller believed that population issues needed to be placed on a firm scientific basis that would address both the biomedical issues related to reproduction and the social implications of rampant population growth. This perspective led him to urge the Rockefeller Foundation to undertake a population program. In 1948 the foundation, at his initiative, sent a team of social scientists to survey public health and demography in Asia. Headed by Marshall C. Balfour, regional director in the Far East of the foundation's international health division, the team included Roger F. Evans, assistant director for the social sciences for the foundation, and Frank Notestein and Irene B. Traebner of the Office of Population Research at Princeton University.[11] Following their investigation, the team proposed the formation of a new population division within the foundation. After a prolonged discussion, however, the foundation's board decided against forming a new division that went beyond the medical field. Opposition to the proposal came from many sources within the foundation. Prior to the board meeting, Rockefeller Foundation officers initiated a meeting with the self-assured and powerful Francis Cardinal Spellman of New York to discuss the matter. Although the specifics of the meeting are not known, apparently Spellman indicated that he could not support this activity. Furthermore, staff members in the international health division believed that the field of birth control might antagonize leaders of the many Catholic countries they worked in, especially in Latin America. Moreover, they argued, the Rockefeller Foundation was in the job of saving lives and thereby, in effect, speeding population growth.[12]

The decision reflected the Rockefeller Foundation's predisposition to avoid politically controversial issues. Moreover, many within the foundation remained unconvinced that population control promised any success in the immediate future. Without an effective means of contraception, population control on a grand scale remained impossible, even if political leaders in the developing nations of the world, and American politicians, accepted fertility control. In 1952 this kind of political consensus simply did not exist. Also, many at the Rockefeller Foundation believed that Western technology and the application of American agricultural methods could meet the food requirements of the world's growing population. In short, the Rockefeller Foundation expressed a different sense of faith in American technology. Yet, behind its humanitarian impulse for global change and its belief that American technology meant progress, the Rockefeller Foundation, in deciding not to enter the population field, revealed its conservative temperament.

While deeply disappointed by the foundation's decision, John Rockefeller 3rd held a deeper, even grandiose, vision of reform. This confidence that the world could control its global population growth, if given the proper technical assistance and the technological means of contraception, led to his decision to found his own organization—the Population Council. If the Rockefeller Foundation wanted to avoid the critical issue facing the postwar world, then he would establish his own organization devoted solely to the population problem. Following the foundation's rebuff, Rockefeller assigned his associate Donald McLean to explore with Frank Notestein, a Princeton University demographer, the possibility of creating a program in population research and development. Yet it was in a fortuitous meeting in the men's room just off the main corridor on the fifty-sixth floor of Rockefeller Center that the plans for a separate organization took shape. In this accidental meeting, Rockefeller bumped into Lewis Strauss, a former investment banker and an original member of the Atomic Energy Commission who had recently left the Truman administration to work for the Rockefeller Brothers Fund. Upon hearing Rockefeller's plans for a new population organization, Strauss proposed that the first step in forming a new organization could be calling a meeting of leaders involved in demography and birth control, as well as related fields, under the auspices of the National Academy of Sciences, headed by Detlev Bronk.[13] Strauss told Rockefeller, "It [the new organization] could be put together under the aegis of the National Academy of Sciences. Det Bronk is president, and I'm sure he'll be happy to sponsor it if we give them money to do it."[14]

This proposal to form a separate organization immediately won the endorsement of the Rockefeller family. Legal counsel Donald McLean reported, "My own feeling is that he [Rockefeller 3rd] has the time to do it and that one of the things he most needs is some activity which will occupy his full time five days a week." McLean added, "It seems to me that if he works at this conscientiously for a year or two he might make a consequential dent in the problem which to date is in its infancy and the importance of which is not questioned by anyone."[15]

Founded in November 1952, the Population Council grew out of a carefully orchestrated Conference on Population Problems held in Colonial Williamsburg, Virginia, that summer. Sponsored by the National Academy of Sciences, the conference brought together scientists, demographers, social scientists, and birth control leaders in an intensive two-day meeting.[16] The preliminary planning for the conference began with several dinner meetings earlier that spring between Rockefeller, Bronk, and Strauss. Bronk, as president of the National Academy of Sciences, proved especially important in these meetings. From his experiences in the Japanese and European theaters during the war, Bronk considered the population problem the most important issue facing the postwar world.[17] He played a central role in supporting Rockefeller's proposal to form the Population Council that was subsequently endorsed at the Williamsburg conference.

The small group that gathered at Williamsburg—twenty-six participants—saw themselves as in the vanguard of the population movement. As one participant at the conference observed, private philanthropy through such a council was necessary because the population field was "too hot for either governments or international organizations to face."[18] Conference members, including twenty-four men and two women, came from the world of policy making, foundations, and elite academic institutions. They were consciously aware of their own class biases. Warren Weaver, representing the Rockefeller Foundation, noted that the conference reflected a specific perspective when he declared, "I will be blunt. . . . we are talking about population from the point of Western Protestant philosophy, and what is from the point of view of the planet, a minority point of view." This led another participant to ask whether the proposed council should contain a number of strong Catholics, to which Kingsley Davis, a demographer from the University of California, Berkeley, replied, "If the committee were required to have representation of diametrically opposed points of view, it would be hamstrung. To get this thing really moving, we have to assume the committee will have in mind people with similar points of view."[19]

This sense of mission translated into a concern with both the quantity and the quality of population. Lewis Stadler, a botanist from the University of Missouri, observed that there had been a "steady" deterioration in the quality of the population because of "mutations." If geneticists could eliminate defective genes, he declared, "they will be able to isolate quality genes." Stadler's remarks generated a lengthy discussion on the quality of the current gene pool. One participant supported Stadler's asseveration by agreeing that "modern civilization had reduced the operation of natural selection by saving more 'weak' lives and enabling them to reproduce." Still other participants felt that the rate of this deterioration was critical to understanding the gene pool. Most participants agreed, however, that the focus of the new council should be on how to reduce fertility, not on how to improve the quality of the gene pool. Nevertheless, a strong undercurrent remained within the conference concerning the quality of the population. Indeed, an initial draft charter of the council submitted by Rockefeller called for the promotion of research so that "within every social and economic grouping, parents who are above the average in intelligence, quality of personality and affection, will tend to have larger than average families." This paragraph would be dropped when Thomas Parran, a Catholic and former surgeon general, told Rockefeller, "Frankly, the implications of this, while I know are intended to have a eugenic implication, could readily be misunderstood as a Nazi master race philosophy."[20]

Rockefeller envisioned the Population Council as assuming "leadership in thinking, planning, and action in the broad field of population." The council's activities, he felt, should be confined to those that "cannot be accomplished more effectively elsewhere," including basic and applied research and providing technical assistance in countries where population pressures were most acute. He called for coordinating work in demography, public health, agriculture, the social sciences, and the training of professional personnel in these areas. While the council focused its activities on basic reproductive technical assistance programs abroad, he also believed from the outset that it should develop knowledge of the "optimum population of the United States in relation to its potential material and cultural resources."[21]

The decision to incorporate the Population Council as a separate organization concerned with such a controversial issue worried John's brother Nelson, who was preparing for a career in politics. During a breakfast meeting held at the exclusive Knickerbocker Club, the two brothers met to discuss the implications of the new council for the family.[22] Shortly after the meeting, John recounted the discussion to his counsel, Donald McLean. He recalled that he told Nelson, "You expressed considerable concern not because of any lack of appreciation of the problem, but rather my interest might be used in ways that would reflect on the family. You have particularly in mind problems that might be created for those members of the family interested in politics." Noting that most newspapers had ignored the founding of the Population Council, he persuaded Nelson that the council would present itself to the outside world as a scientific agency concerned with objective research and the academic training of demographers. This concern to distance Rockefeller's public involvement in the Population Council was made more explicit by McLean, who told Rockefeller 3rd that "a responsible board of directors whose integrity and motives could not reasonably be questioned by the outside world could associate you with the results [without the political fallout]. Even though your money is primarily involved, it would not be necessary for you to bear alone the weight of any attack which might be made."[23]

With this in mind, Rockefeller appointed a distinguished board of trustees composed of Frederick Osborn the nephew of the celebrated Henry Fairfield Osborn, who became the council's first administrative head; Princeton University professor Frank Notestein; and Thomas Parran, then serving as dean of the Graduate School of Public Health at the University of Pittsburgh. At its first meeting, the board elected three new trustees, Detlev Bronk; Karl T. Compton, chairman of Massachusetts Institute of Technology; and Lewis Strauss. The following year, the board was enlarged to include Theodore W. Schultz, chair of the Department of Economics at the University of Chicago; Frank G. Boudreau, president of the Milbank Memorial Fund; James B. Conant, president emeritus of Harvard University; and Caryl P. Haskins, president of the Carnegie Institute. With such a distinguished board, Rockefeller and the Population Council was protected from any would-be critics.

The Population Council Begins Work

Rockefeller served as the president of the Population Council, leaving the day-to-day operations to his executive vice president, Frederick Osborn, who brought to the council a distinguished background in population. In 1957 Rockefeller stepped down as president to become chairman of the board, turning the presidency over to Osborn. Osborn's background in business and science made his appointment seem exceptionally appropriate. After having served as a railroad president and banker, the forty-year-old Osborn had retired from business in the late 1920s. Retreating to a small office at the American Museum of Natural History, he undertook an extensive three-year program to study evolution and population. He then became a charter member and president of the Population Association of America and a key figure in the establishment of the Office of Population Research at Princeton University. As a trustee of the Carnegie Corporation and the Milbank Memorial Fund, he supported one of the first major field studies of population and heredity in America, the famous Indianapolis Study of Social and Psychological Factors Affecting Fertility in Families. At the same time, through his involvement as president of the Eugenics Society, he sought to transform eugenics into a scientific discipline concerned with the quality of life.

Under Osborn, the Population Council gained international prominence. With a $600,000 grant from the Ford Foundation in 1954 and an additional $1.2 million gift from Rockefeller 3rd, the council played a principal role in establishing an international network of population experts who shared a set of assumptions about population dynamics and a consensus regarding population intervention. Additional grants were received from the Rockefeller Brothers Fund, members of the Rockefeller family, and Mrs. Alan M. Scaife and Cordelia S. May.[24] The Ford Foundation's involvement in population research bolstered the council's confidence in its mission.

Over the course of the next two decades, the council's staff and field officers became involved in technical assistance programs to implement population programs in developing countries. Intent on establishing itself as the leader in demographic studies, the council established a demographic advisory committee composed of the leading scholars in the field.[25] In its first year of full operation in 1953, the Population Council offered eight fellowships for advanced training for graduate students in demography. The council played a central role in the establishment and development of regional centers for demographic training and research in Bombay, India (1957), Santiago, Chile (1958), and Cairo, Egypt (1963). At the same time, it provided assistance for demographic studies at the nation's leading universities, transforming demography into a policy science and establishing a network of experts in the field who could be called upon for technical assistance in international family planning programs, congressional testimony, and policy innovation.[26]

The building of a global network of population experts laid the intellectual and institutional foundation for the key shift in American population policy that would occur in the next decade. In the process, demography became not just a science but a policy science that viewed intervention in population growth as necessary. Professional demographers, academically trained at leading universities, became members of a profession that shared a core body of knowledge, a consistency in methodology, and a common discourse. Institutionalized through professionalized associations and supported by the philanthropic community, including the Population Council, the Rockefeller Foundation, the Ford Foundation, and the Milbank Memorial Fund, as well as other foundations, population experts accepted intervention in population with an almost evangelical fervor.[27]

Under the leadership of Frederick Osborn, the Population Council cultivated connections within established political and scientific circles and avoided public controversy. The council focused its activities on basic reproductive research and the training of scientific personnel to provide technical assistance in family planning programs, especially in developing countries. Through an extensive fellowship and grant program, the council reshaped the field of demography.[28]

In July 1959 Osborn stepped down from the presidency to hand the reins over to Frank Notestein. Close friends, Osborn and Notestein had cooperated in establishing the Population Council's reputation in the population field. Osborn left the office confident that within the next decade the problem of overpopulation would be addressed. He assured Rockefeller, "My belief is that the next ten years will see a real fall in birth rates and that we will have had a share in bringing it about."[29]

Notestein brought to the organization his experience as one of the leading scientific demographers in the country. After receiving his doctorate at Cornell University in economics, Notestein had worked at the Milbank Memorial Fund before joining the Office of Population Research at Princeton University in 1936.[30] Under Notestein the council made a full commitment to initiating "action programs" to provide technical assistance to population programs abroad. Through these action programs the council provided grants for the purchase of contraceptive materials and programmatic needs, as well as technical personnel for training, research, and administration, depending on the needs of the country. The Population Council had been involved in these activities before Notestein assumed the presidency, but under his leadership the council made a conscious and full commitment to this area.[31]

Shortly after assuming office, Notestein informed the Rockefeller Brothers Fund that this decision to embark on an action program was based on several factors, including the "noticeable progress recently in the development of new methods for controlling fertility and in the broadening knowledge of demographic factors" controlling population growth.[32] Notestein believed that this was a logical and necessary step for the council to undertake. If the Population Council did not undertake direct involvement in family planning, he believed, then some other private agency or foundation would, and the importance of the council would diminish. Furthermore, reduction of birthrates, as one staff member said, was a means, not an end, so that when the birthrate is "under control the council could be in a strategic position to work in other areas, such as population quality." This decision to enter full-scale into technical assistance programs, however, caused other staff members concern. Indeed, one dissenting member of the staff warned that "direct action" might "weaken the usefulness of the Population Council in the scientific area." Instead, action programs should be left to International Planned Parenthood Federation, with its "strong local units serving especially propagandist purposes."[33] Such dissent found little support in Notestein's drive to take the Population Council into action programs. After spending thirty years in population research, Notestein appreciated the value of scientific inquiry, but in 1959 he realized the time for action had arrived.

This move to active intervention in population control was made possible by an extraordinary growth in council funds during the previous decade. By 1959 the council had an income of $1,036,000, which would rise to over $5 million by 1964. From its founding in 1952 through the end of 1964, the council received a total of $28 million in gifts and grants, with $19 million of this amount coming from foundation grants and $9 million from individuals. Support from the Ford Foundation proved especially important. That foundation entered the population field when it sent its first mission to advise on India's developing program for fertility control. This mission supplied technical advisers and research programs, which prepared a greatly enlarged and important program run by the Ford Foundation in India.

Ford's entry into the population field paralleled its commitment to supporting the Population Council's action programs. The Ford Foundation made its first grant to the council in 1954 when it awarded $600,000 for demographic training. This was followed by a one million dollar grant in 1957. In March 1959 the Ford Foundation awarded a $1.4 million grant to the council to support medical, physiological, and biological reproductive research. Other Ford Foundation grants followed.[34] Additional support was received from the Rockefeller Brothers Fund, the Milbank Memorial Fund, the Scaife Foundation and family, the Avalon Foundation, the Carnegie Institute, and, on a more modest level, the Sloan Foundation.[35]

Through these funds the Population Council expanded its fellowship programs in demography and its medical fellowships in the physiology of reproduction from five in 1954 to over fifty by 1964. More important, the council played a key role in developing large-scale population programs throughout the world. With the council's assistance, South Korea started a National Family Planning Program in 1961, with an annual budget of $8.3 million. Pakistan made family planning a part of its second five-year plan and implemented a large-scale action program in 1962. In Malaysia, Ceylon, Barbados, and Hong Kong, family planning organizations were established with local government support, employing council field officers. Experimental and pilot projects were established by the governments of Taiwan, Tunisia, Thailand, and the United Arab Republic with the assistance of council consultants. The council felt that exploratory work in Latin America should begin with the establishment of demographic research programs. The council understood that such programs served as the first missionary step in instituting population control programs. As Frederick Osborn observed, trained experts in these countries "stimulated recognition of the dangers of the too-rapid growth of local population," the first step in influencing native ruling elites.[36] The council remained less optimistic about Africa, which awaited development of effective local departments of health.[37] By the time Notestein left the presidency in 1968, the council had field officers stationed in approximately fifty nations, a staff of over ninety professionals, and a budget of over $11 million.

In these programs the council promoted the use of intrauterine devices (IUDs) as "cheap, convenient and safe, requiring a minimum of both personal and professional attention." Although oral contraception, the pill, was used as well, the council preferred the IUD because it placed less responsibility on the user. In promoting the use of the IUD, the Scaife Foundation and personal donations from Cordelia Scaife May proved especially important.[38] A grant of $500,000 in 1962 was used to launch a general field study program. An additional $3 million donation was used to make more than one hundred grants to institutions in twenty-five countries to test the effectiveness the IUD. At the same time, Scaife funds were used to host two international conferences on intrauterine contraception.

As a consequence of this work, "country after country" began using the IUD in their family planning programs. The increased demand for IUDs created supply problems. To remedy this situation, the Population Council provided grants and technical assistance for the domestic manufacture of the Lippes Loop in Korea, Hong Kong, Taiwan, India, Pakistan, Egypt, and Turkey. The council estimated that nearly 7 million women throughout the world received IUDs. The results of the program were mixed, however. Ford Foundation and Population Council field studies showed that in many countries over half the women who received IUDs stopped using the device after a period of less than twenty-four months. Reasons given included menopause, widowhood, and desire for another child, while 20 to 30 percent of these women complained of physical discomfort. Many of these women reverted to the pill, sterilization, or abortion.[39]

While the Population Council focused primarily on international family planning during these years, interest in family planning in the United States remained a concern. Rockefeller believed that the objective of the council was to build a quality program that would "gain the respect of others in this country and abroad." Still, in 1964 he lamented that not enough was being done with family planning in the United States. He considered Planned Parenthood "basically a propaganda organization," so he urged the council to move faster in promoting family planning in the United States. He also lamented that the federal government was not involved more in addressing the population problem, which he explained was "partly because of the sensitivity of the problem, partly because it is politically hard to handle, and partly, I would say, in some cases, largely, because of the uncertainty as to just what steps can be taken by interested government leaders."[40] Nevertheless, the council continued to express an interest in domestic policy and supported the preparation, publication, and widespread distribution of a short volume, *Does Over Population Mean Poverty?*[41]

This concern to win over public opinion led the council to appoint Bernard Berelson as director of communications in 1962. While the council spoke of the need to make the general public aware of the population problem abroad and at home, its focus always remained influencing leaders. Berelson, who later became Notestein's successor, brought to the council impressive credentials in this field. During the Second World War he served as an analyst for the Foreign Broadcast Intelligence Service. Following the war he became director of the Bureau of Applied Social Research at Columbia University, and then was an associate professor and dean of the Graduate Library School at the University of Chicago from 1947 to 1951. Following this he served six years as director of the Behavioral Sciences Program at the Ford Foundation (1951–1957) and then returned to the University of Chicago (1957–1960) and Columbia University (1960–1962).

Berelson believed that effective communication concerning population was a behavioral science issue. Shortly after assuming his duties at the Population Council, he wrote: "Here is a problem that has everything: a combination of high public policy on one hand and the most delicate personal values on the other; resistance deriving from the most powerful forces—religious and moral scruples, ignorance and superstition, perceived community disapproval, individual sexual behavior. . . . Can the behavioral sciences rise to the occasion?" He believed they could. "We need to focus on voluntary family planning methods, mainly contraception and sterilization. Abstinence and abortion are out on sexual, moral and human grounds." He believed that the task of the behavioral sciences on this issue was to convince individuals to accept birth control as a right to space their children. In turn, the program should be to "persuade a wife or husband to undertake sterilization after the birth of their third of fourth child."[42] Of course, in proposing this program he did not mention that he and his wife had five children.

Hugh Moore in Opposition

Rockefeller saw the Population Council as a way of providing leadership to a movement dominated by "alarmists." Indeed, Rockefeller and his associates criticized what they considered extreme and hysterical proponents of population control. For example, Vogt's *Road to Survival* was perceived as "marred by vituperative passages in which everything from private property to the Pope and communism are rather indiscriminately damned."[43] While giving the appearance of friendly cooperation, the council deliberately dissociated itself from "extremists" such as Vogt, as well as from population control advocates such as Hugh Moore.

Moore, fanatical on the issue of population control, presented a contrast to the reserved, scientific-minded Rockefeller. A millionaire in his own right after having sold Dixie Cup to the American Can Company, Moore devoted his life and wealth to thwarting the "population explosion," a term he coined. Born in Kansas in 1887 and raised in Missouri, Moore interrupted his college career at Harvard University when he dropped out of school at the age of twenty-one to join his brother-in-law in New York City. There he promoted his idea of a paper sanitary drinking cup to replace the common cup that could be found in train stations, hospitals, and other public places. The first day he went out to sell his "Dixie" paper cup, he reminisced, he was asked, "What's this for?" In 1957, when he sold his business to the American Can Company, 40 million people a day were using his Dixie cups.[44] The Dixie cup had earned him a fortune.

Moore entered the population movement through his involvement in peace activities in the 1930s and his support of an Atlantic Union plan to integrate the democracies of Western Europe and North America in the postwar period. Before the outbreak of the Second World War, Moore became active in the National Peace Conference, a peace lobby composed of church leaders and businessmen. Shortly after the Munich crisis in September 1938, Moore joined a delegation of peace activists that met with Franklin Roosevelt. As the most prominent businessman of the delegation, Moore took the lead in trying to persuade Roosevelt to call a world economic and disarmament conference to avert war in Europe. Roosevelt quietly listened to the delegation for over an hour and then politely dismissed their proposal, declaring that he would not negotiate with "thugs" such as Hitler.[45] With the outbreak of war in Europe, Moore became active in the Committee to Defend America by Aiding the Allies. He saw the purpose of the committee as providing support to England in its fight against fascism, but not by lobbying to get America into another European war. Headed by internationalist Clark Eichelberger, the committee published Robert Sherwood's advertisement "Stop Hitler Now," which appeared in newspapers across the country.[46] Moore later used this technique of newspaper advertisements to promote population control.

In 1944 Moore established the Hugh Moore Fund with the specific goal of promoting world peace. In 1945 he joined Wendell Willkie in organizing Americans United for World Peace Organization, a lobbying group to support the ratification of the United Nations charter. Following the ratification of the United Nations treaty by the Senate in July 1945, Moore was ousted as president of the organization, as the committee was transformed into a "one-world" government group. Moore was not a simpleminded believer in one-world government. Instead, Moore turned his attention to the Atlantic Union, a group that called for a common market and federated government of Western Hemisphere nations in Europe, North America, and South America. Supported by key figures in the foreign policy establishment, including Justin Blackwelder, Will Clayton, John McCloy, and Marriner Eccles, many of them who later would join Moore in his population work, the Atlantic Union became a well-funded organization that focused its attention on free trade, the development of a common market in Europe, and cooperative programs that would lay the foundations for an eventual federated government of Western democracies. Already by 1946, Moore revealed strong anticommunist feelings. Following Henry Wallace's speech in 1946 calling for rapprochement with the Soviet Union, Moore wrote a close friend, denouncing Wallace as "a sincere fuzzy-minded, left-winger, who has thrown his lot with the communists."[47] A lifelong Democrat, he increasingly voted Republican in the 1950s and 1960s.

Moore's involvement in population stemmed directly from his internationalist activities. The link between the two came to him in what can best be described as a religious revelation after reading Vogt's *Road to Survival*. He gave Vogt credit "for really waking me up" to the fact that global overpopulation was "the basic cause of future wars" and "the spread of tyranny and communism."[48] Although he was warned by Frank G. Boudreau of the Milbank Memorial Fund that Vogt was not an expert in population (indeed, Boudreau declared, "there is just enough truth in the book [Vogt's] to make it dangerous"), Moore set out to meet Vogt at Planned Parenthood.[49] Taken by Vogt's belief that a population crisis was imminent, he agreed to hire a research assistant for Vogt after learning he did not have one.[50] A man of action, believing there was not a minute to lose in this time of crisis, Moore decided to make population his sole concern. He brought a passion to his work that often offended the more staid Population Council.

Following his conversion to population control, Moore became involved in the PPFA, to which he offered funds and advice. Concerned that PPFA was not involved enough in the international population problem, he joined Mrs. Philip Pillsbury, the scion of the Pillsbury fortune, to help found the International Planned Parenthood Federation (IPPF). He assigned the director of the Moore Fund, Thomas O. Griessemer, a former German refugee who had fled Nazi Germany and a follower of

Clarence Streit's World Federalist movement, to draft the constitution for IPPF.[51] Still, Moore's energy and his belief that immediate action was needed could not be contained in the Planned Parenthood organizations. Convinced that Planned Parenthood remained too focused on what he called the "family aspect" of birth control, as opposed to population control, he decided to form his own organization, the Population Action Committee, in 1953.

Gathering around him a group of wealthy businessmen and public figures, including Marriner Eccles, Will Clayton, Pierre S. Dupont, Ellsworth Bunker, Elmo Roper, and John McCloy, Moore called for immediate mobilization against an impending population crisis. He declared that while Rockefeller had established the Population Council as a research group, "There is a need, and a real opportunity at this time for an action group."[52] Moore believed that overpopulation had become a "belated hot issue," which some people believed was going to come out all right in the end, but he believed people really needed to be scared in order to become aware of the full implications of the problem. Even with the establishment of a separate organization, he continued to support IPPF. In March 1960 he organized the World Population Emergency Campaign to place IPPF on a solid financial base. By the time the emergency campaign merged with PPFA to form Planned Parenthood–World Population in 1961, the campaign had turned over hundreds of thousands of dollars to Planned Parenthood for overseas work. As Dorothy Brush, an early associate of Margaret Sanger and president of the Brush Foundation noted, Moore gave "International Planned Parenthood the wings to get off the ground."[53]

One of Moore's first efforts was the publication in 1954 of a widely circulated pamphlet, "The Population Explosion," which warned that the population crisis was playing right into the hands of the communists. An initial printing of 20,000 was followed by a second and third of 50,000. By 1967 the pamphlet had run through thirteen editions, and over 1.5 million copies had been distributed.[54] Moore wrote to Rockefeller, "We are not primarily interested in the sociological or humanitarian aspects of birth control. We are interested in the use which Communists make of hungry people in their drive to conquer the earth."[55] Although Rockefeller politely thanked Moore for the pamphlet, privately he told close associates that he was offended by its anticommunist rhetoric and its presentation of the population problem.[56] Moreover, the Population Council worried that Moore's strategy might lead to a public backlash. Osborn warned that Moore's approach to the population problem might "set the movement back ten years." The "Madison Avenue technique," he declared, "may be effective as a fund raising gambit in this country, but when applied to overseas population matters it could be dangerous."[57] Whatever doubts

Rockefeller and others at the Population Council had about Moore, there was no doubt, as Elmer Roper, a well-known political pollster and a close friend of Moore's, noted that "Hugh Moore brought a vivid sense of urgency to the [population] movement."[58] It was this sense of urgency that would lead him to organize the Population Crisis Committee in 1965.[59]

The Contraceptive Revolution Comes

Participants in the population movement, even in these early years, understood that government involvement in family planning was necessary if population control was to succeed. Private organizations and philanthropic foundations could play an instrumental role in activating government involvement by establishing model family planning programs, lobbying for changes in federal policy, and supporting those in government who sought to enlarge federal assistance programs. Initially, population activists focused their attention on international family planning through foreign assistance programs, but it was understood from the beginning that domestic programs needed to be developed as well.

While the stage was being set for this policy shift, those in the population movement realized that the key to better family planning lay in the development of better contraceptive methods. Without better contraceptive technology, specifically methods that placed less reliance on the user, family planning remained impossible on a massive scale. Because artificial contraception remained a sensitive subject, pharmaceutical companies before the Second World War shied away from supporting contraception research and development. Here the role of private research was critical in the general absence of research by the federal government or by the reticent pharmaceutical industry. Thus, the responsibility for contraceptive research fell to the philanthropic community, with the Population Council playing a leading role.

Following the model used in developing demographic studies, the council established a medical advisory committee composed of leading figures involved in reproduction research, including George Corner of the Carnegie Institution and two New York physicians, Alan F. Guttmacher of Mount Sinai Hospital and later president of Planned Parenthood, and Howard C. Taylor of Columbia-Presbyterian Hospital. To direct the medical side of the program, the council appointed Warren O. Nelson, a world authority on male reproductive biology. In 1954 the council established a fellowship program in medicine for graduate students, physicians, and scientists involved in basic reproductive research. In 1956 the council obtained a grant from the Rockefeller Brothers Fund to create a biomedical research laboratory at the Rockefeller Institute, the precursor to

Rockefeller University. Headed by Sheldon Seagal, a reproductive endocrinologist, the laboratory was substantially expanded in 1959. Along with conducting and sponsoring basic research, this biomedical laboratory became actively involved in the development, testing, and distribution of an IUD. Because of the controversial nature of contraceptive research, the Population Council in 1957 decided to fund research indirectly through the National Committee on Maternal Health (NCMH), established by Robert Latou Dickinson in the 1920s. Christopher Tietze, a specialist in medical statistics, received a grant from the committee to establish an office at the New York Academy of Medicine to evaluate contraception research.

In the early 1950s most experts believed that the development of a truly effective means of artificial contraception lay at least a decade away. Artificial contraception in the early 1950s meant the use of condoms, the diaphragm, and feminine douches using various jellies, foams, or solutions. Such methods placed heavy reliance on the user and sometimes proved dangerous to women. Moreover, the search for better and cheaper contraceptive methods that had begun in the interwar years appeared to have come to a standstill. As a consequence, the population movement confronted, as the leading historian of the birth control movement later noted, a single disheartening fact: "Contraceptive technology had not advanced since the perfection of the spring-loaded diaphragm in the 1920s."[60]

It was not for want of trying. Indeed, in the 1930s Clarence Gamble, heir to the Proctor and Gamble fortune, devoted himself to the development of a more effective and accessible contraceptive. Until his death in 1966, Gamble was involved in almost every aspect of the birth control movement, from contraceptive research to population control.[61] Born in Cincinnati, Ohio, and raised in a strict Presbyterian family, Gamble received his medical training at Harvard University. After an unsuccessful career as a medical researcher, Gamble discovered the "Great Cause"— birth control—to which he would devote his life. He saw in birth control "the most effective social and eugenic measure of the day."[62] Influenced by Edwin Grant Conklin, a Princeton embryologist who articulated a eugenic millenarianism with a fear of social catastrophe, Gamble brought to the birth control movement a fanatical devotion. His interest in birth control began when he sought an effective contraceptive jelly for his wife. This interest led him to fund the Pennsylvania Committee for Maternal Health Betterment, founded by his Princeton classmate and Harvard fraternity brother Stuart Mudd. In 1933 Gamble was elected president of the Pennsylvania Birth Control Federation. Under Gamble's leadership the federation denounced New Deal public relief efforts and instead proposed that federal funds be reallocated to establish birth control programs. Federal relief offered only to ameliorate the system; birth control went to the heart of the problem—the poor were having too many children, and the better sorts of people were not.

Gamble began to search for contraceptives that could be used to reach the poor without the aid of clinics or physicians. Birth control in the 1930s had become a $250-million-a-year business, with Americans spending about $38 million on condoms and over $200 million on "feminine hygiene" products to prevent conception. Diaphragms that needed to be inserted by trained medical personnel, either physicians or nurses, accounted for only 0.5 percent of the contraceptive market. In 1934 Gamble established a research program through Robert Dickinson's NCMH to test products already on the market and to find better, cheaper, and more readily available contraceptives for the masses.[63] Convinced by Dickinson that the cause of birth control would be advanced through the discovery of a simple birth control method that could be used by women at home, Gamble funded a six-year research program. Collaborating with Dickinson, Gamble called for the use of "household" contraceptives, including homemade spermicidal jellies and wool tampons soaked in vinegar, alum, or citric fruit juices as substitutes for rubber pessaries.

The search for simpler birth control led Gamble to fund, through the NCMH, the hiring of Randolph Cautley, a management consultant, to undertake a study of the contraceptive industry. From this study, new standards would be set for the industry. The *American Journal of Obstetrics and Gynecology* began calling on Cautley for testing all contraceptive products advertised by manufacturers. This demand for new standards created an unexpected opportunity to further the cause of birth control—the involvement of the federal government in regulating the industry. The Venereal Disease Control Act of 1939 initiated a campaign by the U.S. surgeon general to prevent venereal disease. To accomplish this, condoms needed to be safe. In pursuit of this goal, the Food and Drug Administration, after consulting with the NCMH, began regulating the industry through the use of the Federal Trade Commission Act's false advertising clauses. Thus while the Comstock Act (1873) made sending contraceptives or information about them through the mail a federal crime, the federal government imposed regulations on an industry that had restricted access to the public.

While involved in bringing new standards to the contraceptive industry, Gamble pursued his central interest, the mass delivery of contraceptives, by establishing and funding birth control programs in West Virginia, North Carolina, Florida, and Puerto Rico. These efforts in the South established this region as a leader in the state birth control movement. By 1944 Gunnar Myrdal, in his mammoth study of race relations in the United States, was able to declare, "The South now leads other sections of the country in accepting birth control.... it is reasonable to assume that

the large number of undesired Negroes in the rural districts also has something to do with the lack of opposition on the part of the White South."
He added, "Southerners will never publicly admit that they would like to
see the Negro population decrease, but they do point to the poverty that
could be avoided." Nonetheless, he noted that "birth control is taboo as a
subject for public or polite conversation even more in the South than in
the North."[64]

Gamble's efforts in Puerto Rico were especially noteworthy in making
the island into a laboratory for policy innovation, program development,
and the testing of new contraceptive methods.[65] In Puerto Rico the birth
control movement created an environment in which it could not only test
new technologies and programs but also develop political techniques later
used on the mainland. In 1902 Puerto Rico's territorial legislature added
to its criminal code a provision that made the teaching of contraception an
offense punishable by up to five years in prison. All contraceptive devices
and information were included in this ban. In this environment the birth
control movement found it heavy going until José Rolon, a Howard
University–trained physician practicing in the city of Ponce and an avowed
communist, organized the first Birth Control League in 1925. Birth control advocates found support for their cause when a Brookings Institution
study, *Puerto Rico and Its Problems* (1928), linked population growth to the
poor economy. Given respectability by this study, birth control advocates
quietly began to establish clinics under the auspices of private hospitals.[66]

All seemed to be going smoothly until a letter written by Cornelius
Rhoads, a physician working in San Juan's Presbyterian Hospital under a
Rockefeller Foundation grant, became public. This unmailed letter was
picked up by one of Rhoads's laboratory assistants and published in the
January 27, 1932, edition of *El Mundo*, a leading daily newspaper. The con-
tents of the letter proved shocking. Rhoads wrote, "The Puerto Ricans . . .
are beyond doubt the dirtiest, laziest, most degenerate and thievish race of
men ever inhabiting this sphere." Continuing, he said, "What the island
needs is not public health work but a tidal wave or something to totally
exterminate the population."[67] Although the territorial governor, James R.
Beverly, called for a formal investigation of the letter, he worsened matters
when he declared in his inaugural address in early 1932 that "sooner or
later the question of our excessive population must be faced," and the issue
was not only the quantity of the population but also its quality. President
Herbert Hoover demanded that Beverly withdraw his statement, but by
this time Puerto Rican nationalists had interjected birth control into the
political debate by denouncing birth control as an imperialist program.

Franklin Roosevelt's appointment of James Bourne, a former superin-
tendent for Hills Brothers canneries on the island, to the directorship of

the Puerto Rican Federal Emergency Relief Administration (PRFERA) in 1932 created new opportunities to further the cause of birth control in Puerto Rico. Bourne, along with his wife, Dorothy, who had organized the School of Social Work at the University of Puerto Rico, was a strong advocate of birth control. At his instigation, birth control was incorporated into the federal relief program, despite territorial legal constraints. He found a supporter in Rexford Tugwell, a government economist who was sent by Washington on a fact-finding mission. Tugwell reported back to Henry Wallace, secretary of agriculture, "Our control of the tropics seems to me certain to increase immigration from here and the next wave of the lowly . . . succeeding the Irish, Italians and Slavs . . . will be these mulattos Indians, Spanish people from this south of us. They make poor material for social organization, but you are going to have to reckon with them."[68] At Tugwell's urging, the territorial administration of Puerto Rico was removed from the War Department and placed in the newly created Division of Territories and Island Possessions in the Department of the Interior. In 1934 Ernest Gruening was appointed head of the new division. Gruening, a Harvard-trained physician, was an early supporter of Margaret Sanger. In 1921 he and his wife had joined Sanger as delegates to the First American Birth Control Congress. In Gruening the Puerto Rican birth control movement found an able sponsor.

Gruening, as head of the U.S. Division of Territories, supported the birth control program through Puerto Rico's Federal Emergency Relief Administration. Although Gruening received complaints from San Juan's Roman Catholic bishop, Edward V. Byrnes, the PRFERA continued to push birth control. In the summer of 1935, Gladys Gaylord, executive secretary of the Maternal Health Association of Cleveland, arrived in Puerto Rico to help institute an islandwide birth control program that encompassed services, research, and training. When the FERA program was terminated by the Roosevelt administration, however, the birth control program floundered, only to be reactivated by the Puerto Rican Federal Reconstruction Administration under its new presidential appointee, Ernest Gruening.

The rapid growth of federally supported birth control programs led to a showdown with the Roman Catholic Church in Puerto Rico. Fed information by San Juan's Bishop Edward Byrnes, the *Baltimore Catholic Review* carried a front-page story in the summer of 1936 that criticized federal involvement in supporting family planning in Puerto Rico. In a presidential election year, this news proved decisive. Presidential operative James Farley, himself a Catholic, intervened to end the program.

With the closing of federally sponsored family planning programs, Eric Matsner, medical director of the American Birth Control League, contacted Clarence Gamble to fund family planning in Puerto Rico under private auspices. Gamble dispatched his associate Phyllis Page to Washington to meet with Gruening to discuss the problem.[69] Receiving Gruening's tacit approval and backed by Gamble's money, Page traveled to San Juan to organize family planning services through the Maternal and Child Health Association. Page believed that the island provided a "very suitable field for a study and the greatly overcrowded population would justify such a study."[70] After meeting with Page and Gamble, a number of sugar planters opened birth control clinics on their plantations. By late 1937 Page reported there were twelve clinics operating under medical supervision, serving over a thousand women.[71] These clinics dispensed foams and jellies, as well as promoting the use of diaphragms. Page found diaphragms especially useful in Puerto Rico, as she said, "due to the lithe figures of the women, their long fingers, lack of inhibitions in regard to sex, and their teachability."[72]

In 1937 the Maternal and Child Health Association successfully introduced legislation in the territorial legislature to legalize birth control in Puerto Rico. Fearing a potential backlash from nationalists, Gruening advised the American governor of the island, Blanton Winship, to leave the island and appoint Rafael Menendez Ramos, commissioner of agriculture, to serve as acting governor in his absence. On May 1, 1937, Ramos signed the legislation into law. This law was immediately challenged in the courts when six directors of the Maternal and Child Health Association were indicted by local officials despite the new legislation. Gamble came to their defense by engaging the legal services of New York attorney Morris Ernst to defend them. In late 1938 a U.S. district court found the defendants innocent by upholding the validity of the new birth control legislation.

When Tugwell became governor of the island in 1941, additional federal support for family planning proved forthcoming. At the urging of Eleanor Roosevelt, Surgeon General Thomas Parran announced that the U.S. Public Health Service would consider state health department requests for "child spacing" programs. In May 1942 the Public Health Service began to promote contraceptive programs in order that women workers in Puerto Rico would not lose work because of unwanted children.[73] The birth control movement had learned how to conduct a political campaign through sympathetic federal administrators and the courts, while at the same time establishing a "living" laboratory for testing new birth control technologies and programs. Of equal importance, policy activists learned that by linking birth control to health care, family planning could be made politically palatable.

Meanwhile, Gamble was learning additional lessons on the mainland. At the same time he was involved in Puerto Rico, Gamble conducted a campaign to bring family planning to the South in the 1930s. Southern health and social service officials revealed particular anxieties that blacks were having too many children and adding to state health and welfare costs. In North Carolina he supported the efforts of George M. Cooper, the assistant director of the State Board of Health, in establishing sixty-one birth control clinics. Through Gamble's efforts, six other states— South Carolina, Alabama, Florida, Georgia, Mississippi, and Virginia— officially integrated contraception services into their public health programs. When the U.S. Public Health Service announced that federal public health grants could be given to local health services, the major recipients of this program were in those southern states where family planning programs had been established through Gamble's efforts.[74]

During the Second World War, Christopher Tietze, a refugee from Nazi Austria and a medical statistician at the Johns Hopkins School of Public Health, convinced Gamble that the issue facing the family planning movement was global overpopulation, not only a eugenic problem of over-breeding by "inferior" stocks. Immediately following the war, Gamble asked Tietze to collaborate on a study of a new intrauterine contraceptive device.[75] Although Tietze demonstrated the effectiveness of the new coil, the study was poorly received by the medical profession. The disappointed Tietze resigned from the NCMH a short time later to take a position as an intelligence officer in the State Department. With the death of Robert Dickinson in 1950, the committee became a shell of its former self. Only in 1957 would it be revived when Frederick Osborn offered Tietze a position evaluating family planning programs through the NCMH. Shortly afterward, the NCHM was reorganized, leading Gamble to resign and establish the Pathfinder Fund, a new organization for his activities.

Tietze's review of population control programs in the 1940s showed that conventional methods were "getting nowhere fast."[76] Fearing an impending population crisis, Tietze decided to reevaluate IUDs. He learned from Alan Guttmacher, a member of the medical advisory committee of the NCMH, that Lazar C. Margulies, a German-trained colleague in the obstetrics department at Mount Sinai Hospital in New York City, had developed a molded plastic IUD that could be unwound into a thin rod that enabled the device to be slipped easily into the uterus. In tests the plastic IUD proved highly effective. At Tietze's and Guttmacher's urging the Population Council committed itself to the development of an IUD, investing more than $2.5 million in the clinical testing and statistical evaluation of the device. The IUD became the favored birth control method recommended by the Population Council in its technical assistance family planning programs abroad throughout the 1960s.

Meanwhile, other scientists pursued other avenues of research that portended new possibilities for family planning. At the Worcester Foundation for Experimental Biology, Gregory Pincus sought the development of a revolutionary birth control method, the anovulant pill. In the 1920s and the 1930s estrogen, the primary hormone secreted within the ovary, and progesterone, the hormone secreted during pregnancy, had been isolated. Although the therapeutic effects of these hormones quickly became apparent, their cost precluded widespread medical use. To produce only a fraction of a gram of estrogen, the ovaries of eighty thousand sows needed to be processed. In 1939, however, a German chemist, Adolf Butenandt, working with two American chemists, developed synthetic estrogen. A short time later, Russell Marker, an organic chemist at Pennsylvania State University, discovered that a wild Mexican yam provided a cheap supply of synthetic hormones. In the summer of 1943 he established a small laboratory in Mexico City to produce synthetic progesterone. These scientific discoveries made the development of a hormonal contraceptive a real possibility in 1950s, but it took two scientists, Gregory Pincus and John Rock, to achieve the final breakthrough—the oral contraceptive.

In 1937 Gregory Pincus took a research position at Clark University, where his close friend Hudson Hoagland had established a small biology research laboratory. Supported by grants, Pincus pursued his research on mammalian reproductive systems and the role of steroids in the human body. Disenchanted with academia, Hoagland and Pincus established the Worcester Foundation for Experimental Biology in 1944, largely with the support of C. D. Searle and Company. Searle, one of the nation's leading pharmaceutical companies, had entered the race against its competitors Merck and Upjohn to synthesize the steroid cortisone. When Merck chemists won the race to synthesize cortisone, Pincus proposed a new program of directed research to develop a contraceptive hormonal injection or pill. After Searle refused to support this new research, Pincus turned to Planned Parenthood to fund the project. Receiving less than $10,000 from PPFA, Pincus's project remained underfunded, and the prospects of his developing a birth control pill remained dim. At this point Katherine McCormick, an heir to the International Harvester fortune, stepped into the picture.

Distraught over Planned Parenthood's lack of commitment to contraceptive research and its lack of progress on this front, even though she had been contributing funds to PPFA's small research program, McCormick had been convinced by her longtime friend Margaret Sanger that she should specifically target her giving by sponsoring Pincus's research. With Sanger and another friend, she visited Pincus in the early summer of 1953 and offered him $10,000 a year on the spot. Both Sanger and McCormick wanted a contraceptive that allowed women to control reproduction easily and safely. McCormick later enlarged her contribution and gave $150,000 to $180,000 a year for the rest of her life. With her support Pincus asked

John Rock, a gynecologist and a Roman Catholic who had been working on female ovulation, to join him. Pincus gained additional support from Searle to develop contraceptive compounds, while John Rock conducted the scientific tests of these compounds on his patients. When a supply of synthetic progestin was contaminated by a tiny amount of estrogen, Pincus and Rock discovered that when the two hormones were combined, there was a lower incidence of breakthrough bleeding in the ovulation-inhibiting cycle of medication. This discovery led Searle to produce the first oral contraceptive pill, Enovid.[77]

Pincus decided to test the new contraceptive in Puerto Rico, which by this time had become a laboratory for contraception research.[78] Emigration from the island in the immediate postwar years seemed to give added urgency to the island's population problem. One Rockefeller Foundation officer noted that Puerto Ricans were "flooding New York City at a rate of 1500 a week with many of them getting on the relief rolls within a month after they arrive here." He viewed birth control in Puerto Rico as a "technical" and "social" problem.[79]

In late 1955 Pincus announced the scientific breakthrough to a Planned Parenthood Conference on Human Fertility. A contraceptive revolution was to occur in the lives of average men and women. No less important for those policy makers and elites concerned with overpopulation, they now had the technical means to control population growth.[80]

The Draper Report Brings Family Planning to the Policy Table

Rockefeller believed that private philanthropic interests alone could not address the overpopulation problem. Government involvement was needed if the problem was to be solved. He wrote Osborn, "I believe we need to become more aggressive. . . . In suggesting we be more aggressive, I realize full well that the population problem is a sensitive one. The sensitivity is, of course, not confined just to religious factors, but includes also political considerations."[81] Rockefeller and the Population Council still looked at overpopulation as an international problem, an issue that needed to be addressed through family planning programs in developing nations. The U.S. government, Rockefeller felt, should contribute to these efforts by supporting family planning through its foreign assistance aid program. As a consequence, beginning in the late 1950s Rockefeller increasingly lobbied American policy makers to pursue more activist public policies. Joined by population experts in the Population Council and the foundation community, as well as Hugh Moore and other population activists associated with Planned Parenthood, Rockefeller now undertook a quiet public campaign to place population on the political agenda.

The year 1959 proved a turning point in federal family planning policy when a presidential committee charged with investigating American military assistance programs released its final report. Headed by General William H. Draper, a Wall Street financier, the committee called for family planning assistance to military aid programs. With the approach of a presidential election, the Draper report immediately became a political issue that drew opposition from the Catholic bishops, divided Democrats, and elicited support from Planned Parenthood and liberal Protestants.

Surely, Eisenhower had not expected such a furor in 1959 when he appointed Draper to head his Committee to Study the United States Military Assistance Program. Concerned with waste in America's foreign aid programs, yet supporting foreign aid, which had come under attack by the right wing of his party, Eisenhower expected the committee to offer cost-cutting measures, while providing a rationale for an internationalist foreign policy. Draper brought to the committee a distinguished background in finance and the military without any hint of being a radical. After many years in investment banking in New York, where he was a vice president at the prestigious firm of Dillon, Reed and Company, he had joined the army in 1940 to serve on the general staff. After the outbreak of war he commanded the 136th Infantry Regiment in Hawaii until he was recalled to Washington to take charge of terminating and settling war contracts. After the war he was transferred to Europe to become economic adviser to General Lucius Clay, postwar commander in chief of the U.S. forces in Europe. From 1947 to 1949 Draper was under secretary of the army, and in 1952 he was appointed by President Harry S. Truman as U.S. special representative in Europe to coordinate the Mutual Security Program for Europe and to represent the United States in the North Atlantic Treaty Council. In November 1958 Eisenhower appointed him to chair the committee on the military assistance program.[82]

Through his interest in international relations and population, Draper had developed a close friendship with Hugh Moore. Draper's interest in family planning dated to the American occupation of Japan. As under secretary of the army, he worried that the "rapidly growing population in the next few years would bring Japan back to the level of semi-starvation."[83] Moore played a critical role in urging Draper to take on the population issue in his report. Later, Draper recalled how Moore invited him to his New York apartment and "practically forced the so-called Draper Committee to speak its piece on population problems."[84] Shortly after this meeting, Moore again invited Draper to his apartment in order to be briefed on the population issue by Robert Cook, the director of the Population Reference Bureau. (Moore served as chairman of the Population Reference Bureau, whose purpose was to translate demographic facts concerning overpopulation into everyday language that could find its way into columns in newspapers throughout the world.)

Following his meeting with Draper, Cook reported to Frederick Osborn at the Population Council that the meeting lasted all afternoon, until nearly seven in the evening. This meeting was followed up with consultations between Draper's staff, Cook, and members of the Population Council. Cook later complained that these meetings took up four days of his time. Still, his report was well received. In a lengthy memorandum, "The Impact of Population Growth on the Strength of the Free World," he concluded that the reduction in population growth was the only alternative to solving problems in the developing and industrialized nations, but he recommended that direct participation by the U.S. government in this problem was "inadvisable." The principal role in reducing population, he argued, should fall to philanthropic agencies and foundations."[85]

Draper ignored Cook's advice and pushed for direct American involvement in international family planning. Population control, he argued, meant "decreasing opportunities for communist political and economic domination" in developing nations.[86] At the same time, the committee argued, "No realistic discussion of economic development can fail to note that development efforts in many areas of the world are being offset by increasingly rapid population growth." The Draper report argued that the problem of overpopulation had been caused by the decrease in mortality rates, attributable to public health campaigns that have been "phenomenally successful in many countries." While the problems of rapid population growth and adequate economic progress must be faced and solved by individual countries, the report stated that the United States should be prepared "to respond to requests for information and technical assistance in connection with population growth." The committee therefore recommended that the United States should cooperate in formulating plans to deal with the problem of rapid population growth and indeed should increase assistance to local family planning programs related to maternal and child welfare. Such assistance should be integral to the American Mutual Security Program. While it was not feasible to make the implementation of birth control programs in foreign countries a precondition of aid, the Draper committee staff strongly recommended that "the United States should make promotion of birth control techniques an explicit item of the technical assistance program."[87] Eisenhower sent the report to Congress with no recommendations for action, simply asking that it be "carefully considered and, where appropriate, taken into account in formulating next year's program."[88]

Draper's recommendation immediately drew opposition from the American Catholic Church hierarchy. The National Catholic Welfare

Conference (NCWC), the principal organization of the Catholic bishops in America, issued a public statement on November 29, 1959, decrying the use of federal funds to promote artificial birth control at home and abroad. In the statement the bishops denounced the Draper committee as part of a "systematic and concerted" campaign of "propaganda."[89] The volatility of the issue quickly became apparent two days later when presidential hopeful Senator John F. Kennedy (D-Massachusetts), a Roman Catholic, endorsed the bishops' stand in a press release dated November 28 that sought to separate the church-state issue, while opposing American aid for family planning.[90] Although Kennedy claimed to have reached his decision prior to the bishops' statement, his challengers for the Democratic nomination, Senators Hubert Humphrey (D-Minnesota) and Stuart Symington (D-Missouri), and Adlai Stevenson (D-Illinois), saw an opportunity to hurt the growing Kennedy bandwagon by endorsing the Draper report.[91] They were joined by representatives of the Unitarian Fellowship and other liberal Protestant groups, as well as by Planned Parenthood, which criticized the bishops for trying to impose religious values on a pluralistic society. As the issue became increasingly heated, Kennedy found support from California governor Edmund Brown and New York City mayor Robert Wagner. Meanwhile, *New York Times* columnist James Reston rallied to Kennedy's defense.[92]

Anxious to avoid becoming embroiled in this controversy, Eisenhower backed away from supporting Draper's recommendations. Speaking at a morning press conference on December 2, 1959, Eisenhower replied to *Newsweek* correspondent Charles Roberts when asked about American family planning assistance that "I cannot imagine anything more emphatically a subject that is not a proper political or governmental activity or function or responsibility." While noting that he had "no quarrel" with the Catholic bishops (indeed, "they are one of the groups that I admire and respect"), the issue was not a religious one for him but one of the proper role of government. The U.S. government should not "interfere with the internal affairs of any government," he declared, perhaps somewhat disingenuously given American intervention in a number of countries during the Eisenhower years. Nonetheless, if foreign nations wanted assistance, they should go to "professional groups, not to governments. . . . That's not our business."[93] Eisenhower's statement caused a firestorm as leading population control advocates and liberal Protestant theologians denounced his position. Former president Harry Truman called birth control a "false issue," designed by the Republicans to embarrass Kennedy. Episcopal bishop James Pike, a recent appointee to the Civil Rights Commission, criticized Eisenhower's stance, while Alan Guttmacher publicly claimed that Eisenhower was inadequately informed on the issue.[94] Later,

Eisenhower changed his position on federal support to family planning, but in 1959 the first round went to the opposition.[95]

The rejection of the Draper report drew immediate criticism from population control advocates. Moore wrote to Rockefeller that "no time is to be lost. The population bomb is building up to an explosion as dangerous as the H–Bomb and with as much influence on the prospects for progress or disaster, war or peace." He argued that voluntary sterilization needed to be promoted immediately, and he sent Rockefeller a pamphlet, "Voluntary Sterilization: Is It an Answer to the Population Bomb?" At the same time, he felt that philanthropic foundations, large and small, needed to get involved in international assistance programs, since the American government was avoiding its responsibility.[96] Moore's plea for foundation involvement did not directly influence Rockefeller, given the general perception of Moore in Rockefeller Foundation circles, but the Population Council had already reached the same conclusion that federal intervention was needed.

The Population Movement
Lobbies the Kennedy Administration

Federal involvement in family planning remained discreetly modest in the immediate postwar years. Surveying federal involvement in family planning in late 1955, PPFA concluded that federal funds were being secured upon request by state health officers through a regular appropriation from the U.S. Maternal and Child Health Department "without identifying its use." Through this program seven states (Alabama, Mississippi, North Carolina, Virginia, Florida, Georgia, and South Carolina) had established birth control programs available to women for postpartum checkups. In addition, a number of local public health agencies had established birth control clinics in Arkansas, California, Delaware, Illinois, Maryland, Michigan, and Missouri.[97] From cooperative experiences with many of these state health programs, Planned Parenthood recommended that "it is important to de-emphasize publicity in getting programs underway, as it often stymies progress through influence and threats of the Roman Catholic opposition." Instead, PPFA urged its local affiliates to cultivate relations with local welfare and health officials. "It is helpful to Public Health and Welfare people," the national PPFA told its local representatives, "if you can begin to develop local community support through homes for unwed mothers, court officials, the Salvation Army, YMCA, American Red Cross, the Mental Health Association, Kiwanis, Lions, and other social clubs and the Junior Civil League and the League of Women Voters."[98]

With the approach of the 1960 presidential election, the population movement sought to push the issue forward without causing a political backlash. Indeed, Vogt wrote to Moore in the summer of 1960, shortly before the Republican and Democratic national conventions, that after an extensive discussion involving many people about "getting something" into the party platforms, "my conclusion is that if we can get them to *refrain* [italics added] from putting in anything that we don't want it will be about as far as we can go." He noted that Charles Percy, an Illinois Republican, and Chester Bowles, whose wife has been a PPFA worker on and off for years, were "for them," but this was not enough support to tempt a political fight.[99]

Behind this fear of a political backlash lay a fear of arousing Catholic opinion in the country. Mary S. Calderone, medical director of Planned Parenthood, articulated this anxiety most eloquently when she wrote to Cass Canfield, a PPFA activist and New York publisher, on the eve of the 1960 election that pitted Senator John F. Kennedy against the Republican nominee, Richard M. Nixon. Declaring that the federal government needed to get involved, she observed that even those sympathetic to federally sponsored family planning pussyfooted around, afraid to offend any group. She asked rhetorically, "Offend whom? . . . The Catholics obviously. . . . It must be the Catholics in our country that we are afraid of. Why? What can they do to us if we insist on the rights of non-Catholics?" She then made an astute political observation that gradually became accepted among population activists. "It is my personal belief," she said, "that Catholics do want to be on the side of the angels—politically speaking. I think we lose every time we put a Catholic in the position of taking a stand or making a decision, which, of course, must be an adverse decision." Viewing the election as critical, she declared, "If our greatest broad objective is that of changing birth control, then the first thing to do, I think, is the election. I don't think Kennedy's election will deal with it. On the contrary, it may even strengthen opposition," although "he will be anxious to show he is not the Catholic Church." She recommended that after the election, population activists begin to lobby those in power within the federal government.[100] This is exactly what the population movement did following Kennedy's election. Meetings with government officials revealed timidity on both sides, however.

Initial contacts focused primarily on State Department officials but soon extended to officials in domestic programs. By 1961 the U.S. government had become involved in an ancillary way in supporting birth control programs through the training of health educators who included in their work an interest in family planning. Led by Robert Barnett, assistant to Under Secretary of State George Ball, certain key officials in the Kennedy administration sought to extend the government's involvement in international family planning. In early 1962 Barnett requested a meeting with the

Population Council to review its technical assistance programs. At the meeting, Barnett wanted to know specifically what could be done to "influence the mood" in the United States around the population issue. Council staff members told him that "there was a danger of a backfire" because too much was already being done in this direction; they instead recommended that a presidential commission be formed on "human resources." They also suggested that a high-level government meeting be held with representatives from the Population Council and the Roman Catholic Church. George Ball, who was sitting in on the meeting, immediately vetoed this idea.[101]

Furthermore, when Cass Canfield from IPPF learned of the idea of a presidential commission, he opposed it because the commission might be "too timid or might advocate some such thing as immediate legislation that would arouse sleeping dogs." Canfield told Notestein that he agreed with Barnett, who "keeps telling me it's important to keep stirring up the population issue without, of course, going so far as advocating anything that would arouse strong vocal opposition in Congress."[102]

Meanwhile, Moore continued to conduct a campaign to push Kennedy for further action. Moore felt that the Population Council had "deteriorated under the philosophical theorizing of Frank Notestein," and as a consequence, the council was too timid in pushing the administration toward family planning.[103] Moreover, he considered Kennedy's attitude toward population "quite casual." As a consequence, in order to "put Kennedy on the spot," he placed a full-page advertisement, called an "Appeal to President Kennedy," in the *New York Times* (August 27, 1961) and the following day in the *Wall Street Journal* (August 28, 1961). The ad called for the federal government to address the "population explosion."[104] Also, Moore urged Draper to become active in Washington in pressing the population issue.

With Moore's encouragement, although he probably did not need much, Draper initiated a one-man lobbying campaign in Washington. He seemed to be everywhere. In early 1962 Draper joined Canfield in calling upon key administration officials. Canfield brought added influence to these meetings. He was one of the few publishers in the nation who was a Democratic party contributor; he had published John F. Kennedy's *Profiles in Courage*; and his son had married into the Kennedy family. They met with Walter Rostow, head of the policy planning staff, to discuss the population issue. Next they called on George McGhee, assistant secretary of state, whom they considered on "their side," and urged the government to send experts to underdeveloped countries to assist in family planning programs. This meeting was followed by a meeting with Averell Harriman, assistant secretary of state for Far Eastern affairs, to explore the use of the pill in Asia. A week later they met with Kennedy's national security adviser, McGeorge Bundy, and encouraged him to bring the population issue to the president's attention. They also met with the chair of the Senate Committee on Health and Welfare, Senator Abraham Ribicoff (D-Connecticut) to get his backing for a scientific conference for broader research at the National Institutes of Health. Finally, they met again with Robert Barnett to lay out a strategy to move Kennedy to agree to the formation of a high-level committee of population experts to advise the White House on population policy. This proposed committee would include representatives from the Population Council, IPPFA, the Population Reference Bureau, and the medical community.[105]

Barnett encouraged them to support new legislation providing U.S. funds for family planning.[106] Following the meeting, Draper arranged for a statement from Cardinal Richard J. Cushing of Boston praising John Rock's new book, *The Time Has Come*, to be sent to all members of Congress.[107] Moore mused, "I understand that some of our timid friends thought that you may have gone too far—that you are becoming like myself, a bull in a china shop."[108] If nothing else, Moore prided himself on "not being afraid to take chances."[109]

Draper's activities paid mixed dividends. The proposal for a White House advisory committee on population came to naught. On the other hand, President Kennedy approved enlarging NIH activities to include reproductive research. Draper's work with Mary Calderone to get the U.S. military to implement a family planning program for service families also paid off when the navy, army, and air force made contraceptives available to service personnel.[110]

Throughout the early years of the Kennedy administration, the Population Council continued its cautious approach to domestic family planning. The institution's primary attention was directed toward international technical assistance programs and reproductive research, but by the early 1960s the council began to explore the possibility of cooperating with other groups such as Planned Parenthood in establishing experimental demonstration programs in the United States. For example, in early August 1963 Berelson wrote the New York office of PPFA to support their proposal for "An Experiment in Family Planning Services for Depressed Socio-Economic Groups in New York City." "I strongly believe that the proper strategy for moving ahead with implementation of family planning programs throughout the world," he wrote, "is through a number of carefully planned experiments of this kind in order to learn as quickly as possible what is effective for different kinds of populations." Soon afterward, the council passed along to Alan F. Guttmacher, president of PPFA, a proposal from the Southern Christian Leadership Conference (SCLC) entitled "To Make Family Planning Available to the Southern Negro Through Education, Motivation, and Implementation of Available Services." Noting that the council could not provide financial support for the proposal, it hoped that PPFA could. Shortly afterward, PPFA and SCLC formed a cooperative family planning program in Philadelphia, but any extensive involvement in family planning, either by PPFA or the Population Council, awaited a major shift in federal policy.[111]

On the whole, these first steps on the part of the federal government were modest. Yet population activists understood that the size of the steps was less important than the fact that they had been taken. The Draper report, issued in an election season, introduced the population issue to the larger American public and raised the issue of federal support for population programs. Eisenhower backed away from supporting the report's recommendations. Still, the population issue and federal involvement in family planning had been brought to the table.

From such inching forward, larger steps would follow. The Kennedy administration hardly marked a watershed in family planning policy, but family planning advocates found encouragement during those brief years of the Kennedy presidency. Shortly before the president's assassination in November 1963, Frederick Osborn wrote to a friend praising Kennedy, noting that he had confronted the Russians, called their bluff in Cuba, and "mastered the Pentagon." On civil rights, "the most important thing on the home front," he has been attacked by both sides, endangering his political position, but has kept his extraordinary balance. "I think," Osborn declared with unusual hyperbole, "he may go down as one of our great presidents."[112] Osborn and others in the movement realized that, under Kennedy, the stage was set for an important shift in federal population policy. That was to occur in the Johnson administration.

The stage had been set by the formation of a loosely organized population lobby. Its efforts initially targeted international family planning, but within the decade this movement turned to domestic family planning policy. With this new focus, American federal family planning would be changed from general neglect to a critical instrument of domestic policy.

2

Moving Forward Quietly
Family Planning in the Johnson Administration

Following John F. Kennedy's assassination, Lyndon Baines Johnson launched the Great Society to eliminate poverty in the United States. Family planning became integral to his War on Poverty. Because Johnson feared a political backlash from Roman Catholics and African-Americans, his administration quietly pursued a policy of funding family planning programs through existing federal agencies. Congress proved much more willing to press ahead on family planning legislation, even without White House approval. Understanding the political situation, the population lobby worked actively to educate the nation about the threat of overpopulation, while cultivating liberal opinion within the Catholic Church. At the same time, leaders of the population movement undertook an extensive lobbying campaign to expand federal family planning programs as a means of reducing welfare costs and the number of out-of-wedlock births among the poor. In 1967 Congress enacted the first explicit family planning legislation through the Social Security amendments that mandated specific federal expenditures for family planning. This legislation went generally unnoticed, however, when Congress became caught up in an acrimonious debate over welfare reform also embodied in the Social Security legislation. By the time Johnson left office in 1968, a policy revolution in federal family planning had occurred, setting the stage for the further expansion of family planning programs under Richard Nixon.

Johnson Takes the First Steps Toward a New Policy

"We have suffered a loss that cannot be weighed," Lyndon Baines Johnson told the nation on the day of Kennedy's assassination. "I will do my best. That is all I can do." Johnson's modest statement belied his grand ambitions for the nation. Following Kennedy's death, Johnson launched a crusade to bring racial equality and economic opportunity to all Americans. Within the next five years, under his administration Congress enacted more legislation than under any other president—laws affecting civil rights, education, and medical care for the elderly and the poor. Promoting his "Great Society," he called upon Congress to end poverty in America in his lifetime.

A former history teacher, he sought to impart historic meaning to his administration by waging a "war on poverty." At his urging, Congress voted in 1964 to establish the Office of Economic Opportunity (OEO), the centerpiece of his efforts. Headed by Sargent Shriver, Kennedy's brother-in-law and former director of the Peace Corps, the OEO was charged with managing a vast array of programs designed to eliminate poverty in the United States, including a Community Action Program (CAP) that sought to enlist the poor themselves in the fight against poverty. At the same time, other social welfare programs in the Department of Health, Education, and Welfare (HEW) were expanded, first under Secretary Anthony Celebrezze and then under his successor, John Gardner. These Great Society welfare and health programs provided a conduit for family planning policy during these years.

Family planning offered a means of solving a social problem through technique without directly confronting the underlying structural issues of income inequality, race, or the breakdown of traditional values and culture, as evidenced by a growing divorce rate and out-of-wedlock births that began to skyrocket in the mid-1960s. If the federal government could prevail upon the poor to have fewer children, it followed, the rate of poverty could be reduced. The key was to make family planning accessible to the estimated 5.2 million poor women in need of birth control.

Behind much of this drive to eliminate poverty through family planning lay a deep anxiety about the breakdown of the American family, especially among African-Americans. Indeed, early in his administration, Johnson addressed the faculty and students at Howard University, a black institution in Washington, D.C. He observed that a key to understanding the "special nature of Negro poverty" lay in the disruption of the black family under "centuries of oppression" stemming from slavery. Mincing no words he declared, "Perhaps most important—its influence radiating to every part of life—is the breakdown of the Negro family structure. . . . The family is the cornerstone of our society. More than any other force it shapes the attitude, the hopes, the ambitions, and the values of the child. And when the family collapses it is the children that are usually damaged. When it happens on a massive scale the community itself is crippled."[1] Obviously, although Johnson did not say this, family planning offered a means of addressing the welfare problem by preventing unwanted children from further disrupting the African-American family.

Herein lay the hitch: family planning, as advocated by its proponents, could eliminate poverty, but the critical issue was how to make such programs accessible to the poor. To establish family planning on a national scale—without coercion—entailed massive new appropriations by Congress, the acquiescence of potential opponents of federally funded family planning, especially the Catholic Church and the African-American community, and the establishment of an extensive delivery system, made all the more difficult without a national health care system. Furthermore, the poor themselves would need to be persuaded, if they were not already convinced, to undertake family planning as something in their own interest. And this in itself was no mean task.[2] Nationalism within the black community sought to equate family planning with racial genocide. Albeit expressed by a vocal minority, this opinion nonetheless resonated within the larger community and did not make matters any easier for the proponents of family planning in the mid-1960s.

To convince the nation that the federal government should be involved in family planning entailed a shift in public attitudes, consciousness, and policy. Johnson showed he was a visionary in his call to end poverty in his lifetime, but he remained above all else a cautious politician who typically looked ahead to the next election. He perceived family planning as an explosive issue that could split the Democratic party by driving the white Catholic vote to the Republican party. Already concerned about the effects of civil rights legislation on the white ethnic vote in the North and the South, Johnson remained wary of pushing ahead too quickly on the population issue. Therefore, he decided to move gingerly on family planning, first by raising the population issue as an international problem in his State of the Union Message in 1965, then by encouraging quiet action on the domestic side through the existing federal bureaucracy.

These initial years between 1965 to 1967 proved critical in laying the foundations for a major shift in federal domestic family planning policy and legislation. The population movement, led by the Population Council and the Population Crisis Committee, joined by Planned Parenthood Federation of America (PPFA) and the Ford Foundation, played a crucial role in placing family planning on the presidential agenda through their lobbying efforts with key officials in the executive and legislative branches of the government. Nonetheless, as one high-ranking White House official later recalled in explaining the shift in federal family planning in this period, "the single most important thing" was the role of Lyndon Baines Johnson. While the Senate hearings conducted by Senator Ernest Gruening (D-Alaska) from 1963 to 1965 kept the problem before the public, the pivotal person remained the president.[3] Still, it is doubtful that Johnson would have tied family planning to the War on Poverty without the persistent prodding of the population lobby.

Throughout the first years of his administration, Johnson did not support congressional demands to enact new legislation that would have mandated federal family planning. Instead, the Johnson administration encouraged international and domestic agencies to initiate family planning programs without new legislation. Thus, the Agency for International Development extended family planning to its overseas aid program, while various programs within the HEW expanded funding for family planning through its various programs. In 1966 the OEO issued guidelines that allowed funding for family planning on the community level to married women with children. At the same time, family planning became available for families of military service personnel, Native Americans, and other groups under federal jurisdiction. While family planning programs expanded rapidly in these years, although not to the degree demanded by Congress or the population lobby, only in 1967 would specific legislation be enacted that mandated federal family planning on the state level. This legislation, embodied in the Social Security amendments of 1967, passed with little notice by the public or the opponents of federally sponsored family planning because it was carefully hidden in a larger welfare reform bill.

This incrementalist approach prior to 1967, however, had profound consequences in how family planning developed in the United States. Of immediate consequence, no single agency, especially on the domestic side, was designated to take charge of family planning policy. The inevitable outcome was that a number of agencies in the federal government entered into family planning with varying degrees of commitment, depending on agency leadership, availability of funds, and opportunity. The outcome was a mix of family planning programs that extended through HEW, the Interior Department, and the Defense Department. In the process, a variety of delivery programs were developed, often lacking coherence, as well as executive or congressional oversight. Also, the lack of a uniform national health care system meant that family planning programs did not have a ready-made infrastructure for the delivery of services. Moreover, the implementation of family planning programs relied heavily on nonprofit organizations such as the Population Council, the Ford Foundation, and, most important, Planned Parenthood of America for the delivery of services and for program innovation.

Furthermore, Johnson's cautious approach to family planning meant establishing close relations with the hierarchy of the Roman Catholic Church, especially the bishops in the National Catholic Welfare Conference (NCWC). Two Roman Catholics in the administration, presidential aide Joseph Califano and OEO head Sargent Shriver, were assigned to cultivate relations with the church hierarchy.[4] Through the early 1960s until the publication of *Humanae Vitae*, Pope Paul VI's encyclical issued in the summer of 1968, which reconfirmed the immutability of natural law doctrine, policy makers and population activists entertained hopes that the Vatican would change its position against artificial birth control. For this reason, the Johnson administration did not want to antagonize the church.

Indeed, critics of Johnson's cautious approach to family planning feared that the administration kowtowed too easily to the Roman Catholic hierarchy. Writing to Hugh Moore in late 1965, Phyllis Piotrow, executive secretary of the Population Crisis Committee, complained that a White House order to HEW, the Agency for International Development (AID), and OEO to draft future plans for family planning had been dropped. She concluded, "I understand there is a tendency now for the White House to back off a little from straight birth control issues, mainly, I am afraid, because of developing Catholic opposition."[5]

Educating the Public About Overpopulation and Sex

Along with fearing a backlash from Roman Catholic voters, Johnson did not want to get too far ahead of public opinion. He relied on the population movement to raise the public's consciousness about the threat of overpopulation. To accomplish this, the population movement undertook a concerted public relations campaign through a steady stream of books, pamphlets, and magazine and newspaper articles.[6] This campaign was aided by the involvement of key publishers and editors who were actively involved in the movement, including George Hecht, editor of *Parents Magazine*. The drumbeat around the population crisis reached crescendo by the early 1960s. Readers of popular magazines were faced with a barrage of articles warning of an impending population crisis abroad and at home. Women readers were inundated with articles like "Are We Overworking the Stork?" (*Parents Magazine*, 1961); "Why Americans Must Limit Their Families" (*Redbook*, 1963); "Intelligent Woman's Guide to the Population Explosion" (*McCall's* February 1965); "Overpopulation: Threat to Survival" (*Parents Magazine*, 1967); and "Population Increase: A Grave Threat to Every American Family" (*Parents Magazine*, 1969).[7] Men's magazines were less given to talking about the booming population. Indeed, from 1959 to 1974 only one major article on the subject appeared in a prominent men's magazine, in this case *Esquire*, although the warning was apocryphal: "Human Race Has, Maybe, Thirty-Five Years Left."

This anxiety concerning overpopulation also found its way into popular fiction during these years. Perhaps this was most apparent in science fiction of the day. Isaac Asimov, the nation's best-known science fiction author, was one of the first writers to take up the theme of overpopulation in his book *Caves of Steel*, published in 1954. Three years later, Robert Silverberg discussed institutionalized population control in his *Master of Life and Death*. A graphic and grotesque story of mass homicide resulting in a futuristic world of overpopulation appeared in D. G. Compton's *Quality of Mercy* (1965). One of the most horrifying depictions of the consequences of overpopulation came in Harry Harrison's *Make Room! Make Room!*, a novel published in 1967 that described an overcrowded society that encouraged voluntary euthanasia and mass cannibalism. Harrison's novel was the basis for the movie *Soylent Green* (1973), starring Charlton Heston. A novel from India by Lee Tung, *The Wind Obeys Lama Toru* (1967), pursued this theme further, as did *Logan's Run* (1967), the widely read novel by William F. Nolan and George Clayton Johnson about a tightly controlled futuristic society that revolved around hedonism, drugs, sex, and youth, while the population was controlled through spectacular mass executions of everyone at age twenty-five. *Logan's Run* was also made into a film.

In the following decade this theme of coercive population control found expression in Leonard C. Lewin's *Triage* (1972), Peirs Anthony's *Triple Détente* (1974), and Chelsea Quinn Yarbo's *Time of the Fourth Horseman* (1976). Related to this theme of coercive population control were Malthusian anxieties about overpopulation and the environment, found in such novels as John Hersey's *My Petition for More Space* (1974). Larry Niven and Jerry E. Pournelle, an American and English team of science fiction writers, made use of Malthusianism in their clever novel *The Mote in God's Eye* (1974), a tale about the earth's invasion by hostile aliens who have been driven from their tightly structured, feudalistic world by uncontrolled population growth.[8]

The overpopulation issue received its greatest attention with Paul R. Ehrlich's *The Population Bomb*, published in 1968 and distributed by the Sierra Club, an environmental organization based in California. Consciously using the title of Hugh Moore's pamphlet published a decade and a half earlier, Ehrlich's book became a best-seller when it became a Book of the Month Club main selection. Within two years, Ehrlich's jeremiad that the earth faced immediate catastrophe had gone through thirteen printings. Although Ehrlich, a professor of biology at Stanford University, brought high academic credentials to his project, his book was not an academic monograph but a manual designed to awaken and activate

Americans. He warned that unless immediate steps were taken, the 1970s would be a decade of mass starvation, irreparable environmental disaster, and war. Underlying each of these problems, he found, lay global and domestic overpopulation. He believed that the "key to the whole business . . . is held by the United States. . . . So, besides our own serious population problem at home, we are intimately involved in the world crisis." He urged his readers to write letters to the president, Congress, and the pope to take action. He called for people to demand zero population growth at home and abroad, if the planet was to be saved. "Above all," he exhorted, "raise a stink." Although he felt that adding sterilants to water supplies might have to be considered in the future, he recommended "coercive moral legislation" that discouraged American couples from having more than two children, including taxing additional children and high luxury taxes on layettes, cribs, and diaper services. He suggested that couples who delayed marriage, childless couples, and sterilized men should be rewarded through prizes, lotteries, and government grants.[9]

This continued talk of overpopulation had its intended effects, as evidenced in survey data. In 1959 Gallup reported that 75 percent of the public were aware of the population explosion but only 21 percent were worried about it, compared with 79 percent who were not. Even in 1965 those concerned about the problem had risen to only 30 percent. Nonetheless, 72 percent of Americans felt birth control information should be available in the United States; on the other hand, only 54 percent felt that the United Nations should provide birth control information to other nations. Support for providing birth control information in the United States continued to rise throughout the decade, although Americans continued to express reservations about the United Nations providing information. By 1968 Americans had come to accept artificial contraception as a normal part of their lives. In fact, following Pope Paul's statement barring artificial methods of birth control, a striking 65 percent of American Catholics disregarded the message and reported that it was possible to be a good Catholic and use artificial contraceptives. Furthermore, by 1971, just as baby boomers were entering childbearing years in large numbers and despite an actual decline in the rate of births, an extraordinary number of Americans (41 percent) believed that the present population in the United States was a major problem, while another 46 percent believed that it would be by the year 2000.[10]

This change in public attitude occurred in the midst of a social and cultural transformation in America. The 1950s, in hindsight, became a "golden" period for the traditional family, as Americans then married more readily at younger ages and, as a result, produced more children than ever before in modern history. The United States in this decade had one of the highest marriage rates in the world. By 1950 almost 70 percent of males and 67 percent of females over the age of fifteen were married. Furthermore, the divorce rate dropped to only 10 percent in 1950. Because of this marriage boom, more children were born. The rising birthrate reflected economic prosperity—people could afford children, and the middle class wanted more children. Surveys showed that most Americans thought three or four children "ideal."[11]

Behind this apparent stability, however, people's attitudes toward sex were changing, leading to talk by the early 1960s of a "sexual revolution" among American youth, although it still remains unclear how much sexual practices had in fact changed at this point. Alfred Kinsey's *Sexual Behavior in the Human Male*, published in 1948, introduced to the public a broad portrait of American sexual behavior that suggested people were more promiscuous and experimental than previously imagined. Although Kinsey's survey methods and motivations were later disputed, this study, crammed full of charts, tables, and graphs, gave every appearance of being dry and scientific. Nonetheless, his study quickly became a best-seller. Five years later, in 1953, Kinsey followed up his study of the human male with a report on female sexual behavior that reinforced what became a stereotypical image that many Americans led secret sexual lives.[12] Other evidence of changing attitudes toward sex became evident with the publication of Hugh Hefner's *Playboy* magazine, which offered readers revealing photographs of "Bunnies," bare-breasted women posed in stilted, but for the time exciting, positions.[13]

By the time Johnson came into the White House, there was widespread discussion of a sexual revolution that left many Americans feeling quite uncomfortable. Methodist bishop Gerald Kennedy of Los Angeles summed it up: "The atmosphere is wide open. There is more promiscuity and it is taken as a matter of course now by people. In my day they did it, but they knew it was wrong." *Time*, observing this "second sexual revolution" (the first having occurred in the 1920s), noted that the "cult of pop hedonism and phony sexual sophistication grows apace."[14] Others welcomed this revolution with open arms, however. The publication of Helen Gurley Brown's *Sex and the Single Girl* in 1962 suggested that sexual experimentation was prevalent among younger, single women. Brown quoted one unidentified young women as saying, "I have yet to encounter a happy virgin." Brown recommended that young women avoid guilt. "Married love," Brown observed, "can be sunny and sweet and satisfying, but an affair between a single woman and her lover can be unadulterated, cliff-hanging sex."[15]

Similar sentiments were found among others from the avant-garde. In San Francisco, Jefferson Poland, a libertine, formed the Sexual Freedom League to encourage free love. Others joined in renouncing traditional morality. Lawrence Lipton, author of *The Erotic Revolution: An Affirmative View of the New Morality* (1965), declared, "The Old Morality no longer fits the needs of a society that is rapidly outgrowing such traditional categories as urban and rural which once defined their [*sic*] cultural patterns and moral imperatives." To those who asked what should replace the old morality, he replied, "There is nothing that can be put in place of the old except experimenting with the new."[16]

The popular press, social psychologists, and theologians weighed in to comment on this sexual revolution. In the spring of 1964, *Newsweek* ran a six-page feature story entitled "The Morals Revolution on the U.S. Campus." Mostly, what they found was largely talk and the little action, rather mild compared with what was to come later. *Newsweek* quoted one University of Chicago coed as saying, "If two people are in love, there's nothing wrong with their sleeping together, provided no one gets hurt by it." She was reported to have been "in love twice and slept with both boys." Another student was quoted as saying, "Stealing food from the dormitory refrigerator would be more condemned around here than fornicating on the living-room couch." However shocking these words might have been to an older generation, and it is not clear that they were, traditionalists might have felt some reassurance in the fact that *Newsweek* found 75 percent of female students still virgins. Harvard sociologist David Riesman, however, insisted that those who think this sexual revolution is "all talk" should know that "there has been change, a real change, even though you can't prove it statistically."[17]

How widespread this sexual revolution was in general American society remained unclear, but it was evident that "something" was happening, and it left many confused, others excited, and all aware that American society was experiencing a change of some sort. Social scientists reported that "the pill" had removed the fear of pregnancy or guilt feelings among young teenagers and college coeds who increasingly engaged in premarital coitus, even without the prospects of marriage from their partners.[18] Other surveys in the late sixties revealed that the proportion of college females having premarital coitus in a dating relationship increased from 10 to 23 percent in 1968. These studies indicated an increased tolerance toward premarital sexual relations, an increased number of coital partners, and a substantial decline of guilt feelings after the first coital experience.[19] As the decade drew to a close, Howard S. Hoyman, a professor of health at the University of Illinois, was able to conclude: "We are confused about the kind of advice we should give young people regarding sexual conduct. Many people no longer consider premarital sexual intercourse to be a sin. Indeed some religious and ethical leaders—although not advocating sexual promiscuity—would consider premarital sexual intercourse to be a moral not an immoral act, under certain circumstances."[20]

Indicative of this change in cultural attitudes toward sexual relations was the Supreme Court's decision to legalize the sale of contraceptives in *Griswold v. Connecticut* in 1965. The decision overturned an anticontraceptive statute enacted in 1879 under the guidance of Phineas T. Barnum, the circus promoter and temperance advocate, then a state representative. The *Griswold* decision garnered little opposition, from either the Catholic Church or other moralists. This, in itself, was not terribly surprising given the changes occurring within the general culture and the church. Still, the Court's reasoning reflected a new attitude toward the notion of "privacy" that would have profound implications for future legal decisions, as well as for America's dichotomous sense of private-public separation.

In Justice William O. Douglas's first, lackadaisical draft of *Griswold*, he derived the right to use contraceptives from the First Amendment freedom of assembly. Upon reading the draft, Hugo Black objected that "the right of a husband and wife to assemble in bed is a new right of assembly to me." At that point, Paul Posner, a law clerk, suggested that the Connecticut statute violated the right to privacy implied in the Third, Fourth, and Fifth Amendments. In the end, a five-to-four majority supported Douglas's brief.[21] Although later criticized for its expansion of the privacy doctrine, the decision reflected changing public attitudes toward sex.

This legal change reinforced cultural and social changes that were already occurring. This new sense of privacy fit well into the new singles culture that emerged in the 1960s, as single working women became a important feature of economic life. The rapid expansion of the retail and service sector in a booming economy drew single, as well as married, women into the workforce. In the 1960s young, unmarried professionals gained enormous discretionary buying power, representing a $60 billion market for business. With economic affluence came demands for new sexual freedom.

Coinciding with the emergence of this single, professional culture came the youth rebellion of the late 1960s.[22] As college students joined the civil rights and anti-Vietnam War protest movements, they also called for an end to campus regulations governing visiting hours in dorms, while demanding the distribution of oral contraceptives at university health services, coed dorms, and the right to live off campus without being married. Along with antiwar buttons, students wore buttons proclaiming "Take it off" and "I'm willing if you are."

Along with cultural radicalism and political protest, the hippie counterculture in the latter part of the decade further challenged traditional sexual mores. The hippie movement first attracted attention in early 1967 with a "human be-in" in Golden Gate Park in San Francisco. The guru of this movement, Timothy Leary, a Harvard University research psychologist, urged America's youth to abandon middle-class values for a drug-oriented, sexually free, and antimaterialistic lifestyle. In the summer of 1969, hundreds of thousands of youth gathered in Woodstock, New York, for a three-day rock festival at which they indulged in drugs, nudity, and sexual encounters. This defiance of sexual taboos found its way to Broadway, where musicals such as *Hair* and *Oh! Calcutta* displayed nudity and explicit sexual language.

While attitudes toward heterosexual relations were changing, so were attitudes toward homosexuality. The Second World War had brought many homosexuals together for the first time in the armed forces. In the 1940s the first gay bars were established in such diverse places as San Jose, Denver, Kansas City, Buffalo, and Worcester; by the 1950s Boston had more than two dozen gay bars. While homosexuals experienced arrest and police raids in the 1950s, the following decade brought homosexuality out into the open. A riot on June 27, 1969, in New York City, which occurred when the police tried to close a homosexual bar, the Stonewall Inn in Greenwich Village, launched the gay liberation movement. Radical gays, under the slogan "Gay Power," called for the end of repression of homosexuals.

This cultural revolution set the context for a radical shift in federal family planning policy. As more Americans began to use artificial contraception as a means of limiting family size and spacing children, it became easier to persuade them that the poor deserved the same right to control the size of their families. This, along with a genuine desire to address social problems among the poor in the first years of the Great Society, which turned sour in reaction to racial riots in the late 1960s, made federal funding of family planning increasingly acceptable to the majority of Americans.

The Population Movement Courts Potential Opponents

Even in the midst of this sexual revolution, the Johnson administration was hesitant to push federal family planning too quickly. Behind Johnson's hesitancy was the fear of a potential backlash from African-Americans and Roman Catholics. Both groups actively voted Democratic and were thereby critical to the success of the Great Society. Aware of this, leaders in the population movement sought to cultivate leaders in both communities.

Although the Urban League and the Southern Christian Leadership Conference (SCLC) had endorsed federally funded family planning, militant black nationalist radicals and Black Muslims had assailed family planning as a plot against their community, even before Johnson assumed office.[23] To counter this opposition, PPFA cultivated relations with civil rights groups, while establishing a community relations program and appointing blacks to the national board.[24] As early as 1962, PPFA officials had met with Malcolm X, a leader in the Nation of Islam, to discuss the Black Muslim's opposition to family planning. At the meeting Malcolm X stated that family planning was being directed against "colored nations" of the world, but he gave the impression that the rhythm method and coitus interruptus were acceptable because "family planning requires discipline, and we are a disciplined people."[25] These efforts, however, did little to assuage black militants. In early 1966, for example, at a conference on family planning sponsored by the Southern Christian Leadership Conference, members of the Student Nonviolent Coordinating Committee disrupted the meeting, declaring, "Birth control is just a plot just as segregation was a plot to keep blacks down. It is a plot rather than a solution. Instead of working for us and giving us rights—you reduce us in numbers and do not have to give us anything."[26]

Such sentiments found expression among other black leaders on the local level. One of the more interesting organizations that attracted the attention of PPFA leaders in New York was a West Coast group, Endeavor to Raise Our Size (EROS), founded by a local black activist Walter Thompson. Based in Oakland, California, EROS sought to increase the black population to 60 million by 1980. In a widely circulated pamphlet, "EROS," the group warned that family planning programs threatened black numerical growth, political power, and the social and economic integration of blacks into the American mainstream. The cover of the pamphlet depicted a black man being lynched over a caption that read "Then," while underneath was a picture of "the pill" and a caption that read "Now." The pamphlet warned, "Such unfortunate women among our current poor are now besieged with constant local, state, and federal propaganda. Their despair over being left to their own resources makes them easy prey to the 'fun philosophy' of pill pushers."[27] PPFA officials arranged a meeting with Thompson to hear his concerns, only to conclude that Planned Parenthood needed to remain sensitive to this kind of sentiment, however ill conceived from their point of view.[28]

Even more worrisome to Johnson was the potential of placing the Roman Catholic Church into open opposition with his administration over family planning. Johnson's political instincts were supported by his aides, who warned, "Getting involved in an ideological fight might arrest progress."[29] Public attitudes appeared to be changing, but, ever the wary politician, Johnson did not want to get too far ahead of public opinion; moreover, he feared alienating the Roman Catholic hierarchy if he moved too quickly.[30]

In 1965 the Johnson administration believed, as did many in the population lobby, that the Vatican was moving to change its opposition to artificial birth control. Rumors to this effect spun around policy circles, often based on the flimsiest evidence.[31] Believing that any precipitous controversy might align the church and Catholic voters against his administration, Johnson wanted to move quietly on the family planning issue. This strategy entailed the careful cultivation of the American Catholic hierarchy.

At the same time, administration officials and the population lobby established contacts with key church leaders, while encouraging liberal opinion within the church by working with progressive bishops and liberal Catholic academics and intellectuals.[32] As early as 1962, Winfield Best of PPFA established a weekly luncheon group at the prestigious Century Club to "pursue more energetically the dialogue between Catholics and non-Catholics on public policy and population."[33] Especially important in these efforts to encourage liberal opinion within the church were a series of annual meetings on population held at the University of Notre Dame, from 1963 through 1967, sponsored by the Ford Foundation and the Rockefeller Foundation.

Organized by George Shuster, special assistant to Father Theodore Hesburgh, president of the University of Notre Dame, these annual meetings called "Conference on Population Problems" brought concerned liberal Catholics in the church and the academy together with representatives from the foundation community, PPFA activists, and public officials. Shuster had come to Notre Dame in 1960 at the urging of Hesburgh to help transform the university into a premier institution of higher learning. Hesburgh believed that the key to this lay in receiving public and private funding for further research. As former editor of the Catholic magazine *Commonweal*, former president of Hunter College in New York, and former UNESCO official, Shuster brought to his duties a reputation as a liberal in the Catholic Church. When Cass Canfield of PPFA mentioned to population activist Father John A. O'Brien at Notre Dame that he would like to hold a national conference, Shuster jumped on the suggestion and proposed that the conference be hosted by Notre Dame. Canfield readily accepted. Here was the long-sought opportunity that the population movement had dreamed of—cultivating liberal opinion in the Catholic Church.

Although Shuster's biographer described the circumstances of the meeting as "almost" accidental in respect to long term results, both sides knew what they wanted: a liberal forum to create an oppositional voice within the Catholic Church on the issue of family planning.[34] The Population Council proved an initial grant of five thousand dollars, later supplemented with an additional grant of twenty-one thousand dollars from the Ford Foundation for other conferences. Throughout the planning stages, officials from PPFA and the Population Council worked closely with Notre Dame officials in setting the conference agenda and selecting the guest list

for the conference. Attending the first meeting were twenty-four participants, including James Norris of Catholic Relief Services, Richard Fagley
of the Commission of the Churches on International Affairs, Alan
Guttmacher of Planned Parenthood, Frank Notestein of the Population
Council, Leland DeVinney of the Rockefeller Foundation, and Oscar
Harkavy of the Ford Foundation. For obvious reasons, Shuster wanted to
keep publicity for these meetings minimal, but when Notre Dame received
criticism for this association, the university issued a press release declaring,
"It is not correct to say that any bridge is being built between Planned
Parenthood Federation and the Catholic Church." Shuster added, however, that "this doesn't mean we don't associate with competent people who
happen to be associated with Planned Parenthood."[35]

A mutual interest in liberalizing the church's position on family planning brought together progressive Catholics and population activists at
Notre Dame in what a PPFA official later described as "historic."[36] The
birth control movement had long viewed the Catholic Church's opposition to artificial contraception with aversion, which sometimes found
expression in public statements and private correspondence that revealed
deep anti-Catholic prejudice. Cognizant of this unproductive sentiment
within the movement, and astutely aware of the importance of changing
the Catholic Church's position on birth control, John D. Rockefeller 3rd
and others within the foundation community saw the Notre Dame meetings as an opportunity to form an alliance with Catholic intellectuals and
academics who could help change opinion within the hierarchy. In turn,
Father Theodore Hesburgh, while sincere in his desire to explore the
population and family planning issue, realized that association with the
established foundation community could only benefit his university by
imparting a certain respectability that comes from associating with eastern
philanthropic foundations.

Hesburgh had to walk a cautious path in pursuing this relationship,
though. From the outset of these meetings in 1963, participants understood that they were coming together in order to formulate an acceptable
liberal position for the church on family planning. Only liberal Catholic
academics were invited to these conferences, which were designed to introduce them to experts in population. As a consequence, a quasi secrecy prevailed in the meetings from the beginning. A major storm erupted when a
news service correspondent from the *New York Times* reported that thirty-
seven scholars attending the Notre Dame conference in 1965 had signed a
confidential statement that had been sent to the Vatican commission on
birth control urging the pope to reverse the church's opposition to artificial
contraception. The document declared, "There is dependable evidence
that contraception is not intrinsically immoral, and that therefore there are

certain circumstances in which it may be permitted or indeed even recommended. While marriage is ordered to procreation, the individual acts which express and deepen the martial union need not in every instance be so ordered." When the story first broke, Hesburgh instructed George Shuster to "keep a lid on it with so many people involved," but when confronted with direct evidence, university officials were forced to admit that such a statement had been sent to Rome.[37] In the end, the controversy proved to be a tempest in a teapot when church traditionalists did not express concern over the meetings, other than a brief attack in the pages of *National Review* from conservative columnist Russell Kirk, who ridiculed the "sexumenical" ethos manifested at the Notre Dame conferences.[38]

Hesburgh's willingness to engage in intellectual exchange with the population community, and his political skill in handling controversy, won him friends in the foundation community. In 1965 the Ford Foundation awarded Notre Dame a $100,000 grant to host further population conferences. That same year the Rockefeller Foundation awarded a major grant to a Notre Dame social service project in Chile, and AID awarded the university over $550,000 to study family and fertility changes in Latin America. As Hesburgh told Robert West of the Rockefeller Foundation, "I also understand that there is a general belief that Notre Dame is in a good position to exert a liberalizing influence on certain sectors of intellectual life in Latin America."[39]

During these same years, Hesburgh developed a close personal friendship with Rockefeller. In 1966 Hesburgh was appointed to the executive committee of the Rockefeller Foundation with an understanding that he would abstain on voting on issues involving contraception, sterilization, and abortion.[40] Nonetheless, Hesburgh understood that the Rockefeller Foundation was actively funding family planning projects. For example, the foundation sent him a detailed proposal for a postpartum family planning project in Santiago, Chile, submitted by Dr. Benjamin Viel, who had established the national Committee for Protection of the Family, which included members of the National University and Catholic University.[41] Hesburgh's extensive travels led to a genuine concern with the poor peoples of the world and the problem of overpopulation. At one point he proposed inserting IUDs in 200 million "scrub" cattle roaming around India eating food that could be available to people.[42] Shortly after his appointment to this committee, Hesburgh arranged a highly confidential meeting between Rockefeller and Pope Paul VI to discuss the world population issue.[43]

The White House took an active interest in these activities. Shortly before his trip to Rome to meet with the pope, Rockefeller met with McGeorge Bundy to discuss the proposed visit. Bundy said that "if the

Pope did take a more liberal stand on population control that would of course make it easier for the President to take another step forward." Then he grinned, adding that "perhaps the White House wasn't moving as fast as the Catholic Church, but it did not have as far to go." He suggested that pressure needed to be continued in moving the White House forward. He said that Bill Moyers, an ordained Baptist minister, had become a key figure in this area, and that anything that could be done to bring Secretary Celebrezze of HEW along as well would be useful. It was agreed that Celebrezze should be "worked on" in a "low key" way.[44]

A Divided Population Movement
Lobbies the White House and Congress

From the outset of the Johnson administration, the problem lay in how quickly the federal government should become involved in supporting family planning programs, without arousing large elements of the public already uncomfortable with a liberalizing culture. The population movement insisted that federal intervention be accelerated. In 1964 federal involvement in family planning remained minimal. John D. Rockefeller 3rd was gratified, as he told one interviewer, by the way the population issue had attracted the attention of world leaders. On the other hand, he noted, he was discouraged that there had been a lack of action on the issue—"governmental action, private action, any specific and immediate steps to lead to results in terms of meeting the problem." The Planned Parenthood Federation of America, he felt, had "rightly and naturally" focused its emphasis on birth control, but it was basically a "propaganda" organization that attracted criticism. While he felt that PPFA's willingness to take the heat had allowed the Population Council to work without controversy, the population issue needed to be pressed forward in policy circles. Privately, he had already instructed Notestein that the "Population Council must move faster. We must take a greater role, we must assume greater responsibilities."[45]

With an annual budget that had reached over $3 million by 1964, the Population Council remained the premier institution in the population field. The Ford Foundation had proved critical in supporting the council. From 1952 to 1964 Ford contributed $5.7 million to the council's general-purpose budget, or about 25 percent of that category. An additional $3.7 million was provided by Ford for the council's technical assistance programs in Pakistan and Tunisia. Additional Ford Foundation grants were given for the council's demographic programs in Israel and Central America, as well as for the council's basic reproduction research program. Ford Foundation money was supplemented by gifts from Mrs. Cordelia Scaife

May, the Scaife family, the Avalon Foundation, the Carnegie Endowment, Abby Aldrich Rockefeller, Mrs. Jean Mauze, the Rockefeller Brothers Fund, and, of course, John D. Rockefeller 3rd.[46] This endowment imparted a status to the Population Council not enjoyed by others in the field.

Hugh Moore and William Draper agreed that it was of "the utmost importance" to move the federal government to undertake a "crash program in magnitude commensurate with the problem."[47] To accomplish this Moore formed the Population Crisis Committee (PCC), a "citizens" committee based in Washington, to "direct legislative action and influence in favor of more vigorous federal population programs." Most of the supporters of this new committee came from the business and government establishment.[48] Moore invited Rockefeller 3rd to join, but he refused, telling Moore frankly, "I believe my role in the population field can be most effectively carried out if I stick pretty close to the work of the Population Council. I do have real reservations about becoming involved in the propaganda front."[49] Moore, however, envisioned the PCC as more than a propaganda organization. He wanted his new group to influence "vigorously" population legislation in Washington.

Moore invited former Senator Kenneth B. Keating, a close ally of the population lobby in Congress before he lost his New York seat to Robert Kennedy in 1964, to become executive director of the PCC. Keating came highly recommended. Gruening, Stuart Udall, and Frank Church, U.S. senator from Idaho, told Moore that Keating was the "ideal" person for the job. Before accepting the position, Keating had struck a hard bargain with Moore. He received an annual salary of twenty-four thousand dollars, the appointment of his former executive assistant in the U.S. Senate, Phyllis Piotrow, as an office manager, and funding to hire "competent" authors to write magazine articles and reviews under his name.[50]

Establishing an office in Washington, D.C., Keating and the new PCC launched a two-pronged offensive—lobbying and public education. Moore personally took charge of organizing a mass advertising campaign on the population issue in leading newspapers and magazines. In the course of the next half decade Moore organized through the PCC a series of advertisements that focused on the relationship of overpopulation and hunger in the Third World, the environment, urban crime, and other social and economic problems.

Although Moore sought to have the PCC given tax-exempt status, which would have presumably restricted its lobbying activities, from its outset the organization devoted its time to influencing current legislation. In the end the PCC had to register under the Lobbying Act. While interested in forcing the legislative agenda, in the committee's nine months Keating spent most of his time talking to officials in the executive branch and other government offices, while less attention was paid to the legislative side on the Hill.

Moore held high hopes for his new organization. He told his friend Bill Draper that Ken Keating should represent the entire population movement in Washington, including Planned Parenthood Federation, which had recently opened up its own office in Washington. In his typical fashion, Moore suggested that Keating should be given jurisdiction on the selection of Planned Parenthood's Washington representative and supervision of this office, and be kept fully informed on office activities. Moore even went so far as to propose that the Planned Parenthood-World Population (PPWP) move its office close to Keating's so he could have ready access to it.[51]

Moore's imperious attitude toward Planned Parenthood created immediate resentment within the family planning movement. For a while, Keating, an able politician, kept much of this resentment from a public airing. When he unexpectedly resigned from his position after less than a year in office to run successfully for the New York Court of Appeals, tensions between the PCC and PPFA broke into the open.[52] Moore was bitterly disappointed by Keating's resignation, telling a friend that he was disillusioned by the experience; "after all the energy I used to get Senator Keating to head up the Population Crisis Committee, to have him yield to the pressures of Governor Rockefeller to stand for election to New York's highest court" was disheartening.[53] Moore felt let down by Keating and betrayed by Nelson Rockefeller; within a year Moore had broken completely with the latter. As Moore privately told columnist Arthur Krock, a close associate of the Rockefeller family, "for years, Nelson Rockefeller was my fair-haired boy, but the circumstances of his marriage [and prior divorce] convinced me that he was not a man of principle."[54] By 1968 the logic of Moore's politics qualified his support for Richard Nixon, while at the same time he refused to back Nelson Rockefeller's bid for the presidency.

After Keating's resignation, Moore asked his old friend Bill Draper to head the PCC. "Bill," Moore privately confided to a friend, "is by no means the public figure that Keating is, but he is dedicated to the cause and will do a lot more work on the Hill than we were able to get out of the Senator."[55] Although Draper enjoyed good relations with many of the leaders in Planned Parenthood, his appointment did little to persuade Planned Parenthood that the PCC had not been established as a rival organization. Moore did not help matters when he told a number of people that he believed Planned Parenthood was not doing enough in Washington to push for further legislation. These intemperate remarks were difficult to ignore.

As one Planned Parenthood official, Winfield Best, wrote, "Remarks like our loyal friend Hugh Moore's letter to you saying that 'PPFA was not distinguished for its promotion work,' tends to bring out the worst in me." He pointed out that PPFA had been quite active in Washington over the last years, but in his opinion it was clear the PCC was set up as "a counter to PPFA."[56] Some of the difference between the two organizations lay in strategy. PPFA believed in 1966 that the focus should be on working closely with the White House. Best observed that while he was not opposed to working on specific bills, "it is rudimentary good sense in Washington to recognize that often the best way to achieve our objective" is through the executive branch, which "does not require legislation." Best recommended cooperating with the PCC, but others in PPFA believed that a single lobbying organization should be created in Washington.

Even some of Moore's supporters worried about a possible schism in the population lobby.[57] To resolve the conflict, Planned Parenthood proposed the PCC and Planned Parenthood–World Population be merged into a single organization. Moore rejected the proposal outright. In a typically opprobrious manner, he told the PPFA that the suggestion to merge the two organizations and to make "the PCC the financial guts of the population movement is not acceptable. The consecutive management of Planned Parenthood for the last fifteen years have sought control of the movement in America."[58] Draper rejected the proposal as well by trying to cast the best light on the decision when he warned that the two organizations should be kept separate in order to ensure that PPWP did not lose its tax-exempt status as an "educational" organization.[59] As a result, the two organizations agreed to cooperate, but underlying resentments toward Moore and the PCC portended future problems.

Planned Parenthood had a right to be upset with the sudden entrance of the PCC on the scene in 1965. Both PPFA and Population Council officials had initiated an intense lobbying campaign directed at the White House. This strategy of focusing their activities primarily on the president's office had been developed in a series of meetings held in late 1964 between the Population Council and Planned Parenthood at the instigation of John D. Rockefeller 3rd. Under Rockefeller's direction, the Population Council developed a campaign strategy to lobby the White House. After a series of meetings between Population Council and Planned Parenthood officials, it was agreed that two items should be pushed: first, the president should be convinced of the importance of inserting in his forthcoming State of the Union Message before Congress a brief statement calling attention to the problem of overpopulation in the world. Second, they wanted Johnson to establish a presidential commission to investigate population problems at home and abroad. With this strategy in mind, the Population Council and Planned Parenthood undertook a vigorous lobbying campaign in the succeeding months that focused on the contacts in the White House and high-level government officials in the State Department and HEW. The results of the campaign were to be mixed, enjoying more success in influencing Johnson's State of the Union Message than in convincing the president to establish a commission on population.

Meanwhile, Alan Guttmacher traveled to Washington, D.C., to meet officially with key members of the Johnson administration. In a hectic two-day schedule he first met with Dr. Philip Lee, director of Health Services within AID, who told him there had been a "fantastic" change in Washington concerning population problems. Later that day he had lunch with Dr. James Watt from the U.S. Public Health Service, who, in Guttmacher's estimation, was "completely for us." After lunch he went to see Deputy Assistant Secretary of State Richard Gardner, who reported that President Johnson appeared to be "vitally" interested in the population problem but did not want to set a timetable for policy changes. Later in the afternoon, Guttmacher met with officials from the National Institutes of Health to discuss the possibility of getting the armed services to recommend family planning for female military dependents.[60]

This kind of activity was typical of other lobbying efforts conducted by Planned Parenthood and the Population Council throughout the first days of the Johnson administration. Meetings were conducted on a formal and informal basis. A comfortable relationship existed among foundation officers, policy activists, and high-level government officials. At this point the population lobby was not so fully organized, but a loose social relationship existed that came from attending the same schools, belonging to the same clubs, and sharing similar general views of the world and their place in it.[61]

A private dinner hosted in New York City by Cass Canfield of Planned Parenthood for White House assistant Horace Busby in late 1964 suggested the social setting in which population activists operated. Canfield and Busby were close friends and on a nickname basis. Canfield invited to the dinner party Bernard Berelson, Frank Notestein, demographer Ansley Coale, and Donald Strauss. As Canfield privately confided, the sole purpose of the evening was to "educate Horace Busby on the population problem. He has Mr. Johnson's ear." At the dinner, which lasted from 7:30 until late in the evening, Canfield made sure that most of the conversation focused on the population issue. Busby assured the small gathering that the president was "deeply" interested in population and was a strong advocate of birth control, but the White House remained worried that the issue carried "political liabilities." "The facts are," Busby declared, "we are four years ahead of the ideological discussion." Democratic leaders of big cities, he explained, "themselves often Catholics and with a base of Catholic support," have been telling the president that something needs to be done to provide birth control to people on welfare rolls. "In this sense," he said, "the issue has become more of a Negro issue than a Catholic one." He observed that any progress in the area needed to come from Washington, "especially if it is done so there is not any direct confrontation in which people will object." "The President's way on such matters," Busby continued, "is to go ahead and do something quietly and effectively and then manage the objections when and if they occur." This strategy, he concluded to the dismay of his audience, meant that Johnson was opposed to saying anything about population in his upcoming State of the Union Message.[62] The evening ended with Busby telling the group that perhaps a meeting might be arranged with the president, provided Mrs. Albert Lasker was included in the group.[63]

These kinds of private meetings, joined with the formal rounds at government agencies, proved critical in moving the population issue forward in the Johnson administration. After the Canfield dinner, Berelson reported to Rockefeller, "At least we now have another friendly point of contact within the White House."[64]

Shortly after the dinner, Berelson followed up his introduction to Busby by sending him a memorandum written under Rockefeller's name, urging the president to test the population waters. After receiving the Rockefeller memo, Busby told Berelson that he had made good use of it, and it had "inspired all sorts of happenings here at the White House and I am hopeful some beneficial results will emerge."[65]

The Population Council used other avenues to have its voice heard in the White House. Rockefeller wrote to White House adviser McGeorge Bundy to encourage him to link the population problem to the Great Society. "Here at home," he said, "our growing population presents us with problems of urban congestion and sprawl, of relocation of industry and political reapportionment, of mass higher education." To examine these problems he proposed the establishment of a presidential commission on population, preferably announced in the president's State of the Union Message.[66] Meanwhile, Canfield, Berelson, Draper, and others met with other members of the administration, including White House staff and HEW and State Department officials, to move the population question ahead on the policy agenda.[67]

While the administration remained less receptive to a proposed presidential commission on population, the population lobby successfully influenced Johnson's State of the Union Message before Congress in 1965. Pressure for Johnson to include a section on overpopulation was intense. Rockefeller and Draper met individually with Secretary of State Dean Rusk and McGeorge Bundy to pressure the White House to insert a brief statement concerning population into the speech. At the urging of Rusk,

Secretary of Labor Willard Wirtz, and Averell Harriman, a longtime Washington insider, Draper wrote to Bundy suggesting specific wording for the speech that declared the problem of overpopulation was a greater threat than Adolph Hitler had been three decades earlier.[68] In the meantime, the Population Council sent a draft statement on population to be included in the speech to presidential aide Douglass Cater and White House speechwriters Hayes Redmon and Harry McPherson.[69]

This relentless pressure finally resulted in a single sentence that was inserted at the last moment into the final draft. This sentence, written by speechwriter Richard Goodwin, was placed by Bill Moyers into the speech. It read: "I will also seek new ways to use our knowledge to help deal with the explosion in world population and the growing scarcity in world resources."[70] The population lobby was ebullient. This single sentence, unnoticed by many reporters, marked both a turning point in population policy and the first public sign that Johnson planned to link family planning to his Great Society. The population lobby applauded Johnson's speech.[71] The following year Johnson received PPFA's Margaret Sanger Award, although he cautiously designated Secretary of Labor Willard Wirtz to represent him at the Planned Parenthood banquet held in New York City.

Johnson's message encouraged the population lobby and its allies in the administration to call for a presidential commission on population. During the presidential campaign, Draper and Notestein had attempted to place a plank into the 1964 Republican party platform that called for the establishment of a "nonpartisan" presidential commission to investigate the population problem at home and abroad.[72] Although this effort failed, the population lobby remained confident that this proposal could gain bipartisan support. The formation of a presidential commission would bring the policy aspects of the problem to the general public and heighten its place on the policy agenda. Throughout late 1964 Rockefeller and others keep up a steady barrage of memoranda, telephone calls, and letters to administration officials calling for such a commission. He urged Secretary of State Dean Rusk, former president of the Rockefeller Foundation, to encourage the president to establish a presidential commission. Rusk informed Johnson of Rockefeller's proposal but candidly told the president, "I myself feel that a formal commission is not needed, and might indeed stir up unnecessary controversy."[73] At the same time, Rockefeller also pressed McGeorge Bundy to bring his proposal to the president. In late November 1964 his efforts appeared to pay off when Rusk informed him that Johnson had agreed to meet with Rockefeller, Draper, and a small delegation of population activists. Whether Rusk was misinformed about the meeting remains unclear, but the proposed meeting turned into a comedy of errors when the White House refused to meet with Rockefeller and Draper. A flurry of correspondence flew within the White House asking how Rusk got the idea that the president had agreed to such a meeting. Although Draper tried to intervene, Bundy counseled Johnson to "stick with his decision."[74]

Following the election, Rockefeller persisted in his efforts to meet with Johnson. Nevertheless, the White House remained lukewarm toward the idea of meeting with Rockefeller or establishing a presidential commission. In March 1965 Rockefeller wrote to Johnson via McGeorge Bundy, formally requesting a meeting of only "fifteen or twenty minutes." Forwarding the letter, Bundy appended a message to Johnson's special assistant Jack Valenti that the enclosed request to see the president was "one more in a series. The only thing he [the president] needs to know is that Rockefeller has asked about five times for this interview and wants to talk about the population problem." Valenti forwarded Rockefeller's letter to the president, adding, "I recommend that you do not see Rockefeller at this time. The so-called population problem (birth control) is still in my judgment not a matter that the President wants to touch at this time." As a consequence, Bundy told Rockefeller that the president's calendar was too full, but then added disingenuously, "He asked me to assure you of his deep interest and concern regarding the general problem of population, and of his readiness to consider any proposals or suggestions which you put forward in writing or through the staff here."[75] Afterward, Johnson continued to resist the idea of a presidential commission on population, telling his aides, "I think I want to encourage Rockefeller, but that doesn't mean that Rockefeller encourages me."[76] Finally, Rockefeller got the message and told Johnson in late October 1966 that "it would be best from every point of view to defer a final decision [on the presidential commission on population] until after the [midterm] elections."[77]

Johnson Presses Forward

Even under this intense lobbying effort, Johnson insisted that his administration maintain a low profile on family planning. Within the administration, Harry McPherson was designated the "White House birth control specialist," charged with the responsibility of moving family planning efforts ahead on the 1967 budget. As a result, family planning efforts remained uneven. In 1965, for example, the AID provided only technical assistance through the development of health services and population surveys. At home, HEW still had not developed a formal policy on family planning, although a number of southern states had developed family planning programs. The underdeveloped state of family planning became all too evident when Katherine B. Oettinger, director of the U.S. Children's Bureau, contacted Planned Parenthood to ask for its help. She told PPFA that her agency was not pushing family planning with "great vigor," but she hoped that state agencies would request maternal and child health program funds for birth control. To encourage this activity she requested from PPFA a list of affiliates and medical staff to call upon for advice because she was "rather ignorant" about fertility control. Nonetheless, she believed that many teenage pregnancies came about because young girls do not have adequate information about physiological and biological functions, and therefore she felt that communities and schools should offer sex education courses, while unmarried women should make the choice of using federally subsidized birth control.[78]

Further evidence of the poor state of federal family planning appeared in a review of government birth control programs privately prepared by Phyllis Piotrow for the PPC soon after Johnson's State of the Union Message in 1965. Piotrow concluded that the government's involvement was "minor in nature, involved limited sums of money, small-scale projects, and a generally cautious approach. Moreover, the success and vigor of the programs depend entirely on the personnel administering them."[79] International family planning was primarily the responsibility of AID, which in March 1965 announced that it would provide advice, technical assistance, and other appropriate help to foreign nations specifically requesting aid to deal with population problems. Approximately $2.7 million was allocated for population work, nearly half of it targeted at Latin America. Domestically, HEW, under the Maternal and Child Care and Mental Retardation Planning amendments (1963), was authorized to provide funds through the Children's Bureau for state grants-in-aid and project grants for family planning. In fiscal year 1965, grants had been awarded to twenty-four states, totaling only about $1.75 million. The Public Health Service supported community health services through project grants and grants-in-aid to states on a formula basis for use determined by the individual states. Nonetheless, categorical (specific) authorization for family planning grants remained nonexistent, and for this reason the Public Health Service did not know to what extent federal, state, and local health funds were being used for birth control and other kinds of programs. Shortly after Johnson's State of the Union Message, Secretary of the Interior Stuart Udall directed the Public Health Service to make family planning services available to Native Americans. Finally, the Department of Defense allowed dispensaries and infirmaries local control over family planning services.

In these early years, Congress appeared much more ready to push the issue.[80] In 1965 eight family planning bills were introduced, and Senator

Ernest Gruening (D-Alaska), a longtime advocate of family planning, opened hearings to urge that family planning be made available on a universal basis as a right to parents. A bipartisan approach to family planning was privately encouraged by the White House, which maintained close contact with General Draper in his work with Republican congressional leaders. In late 1966 Republican leaders drafted a statement on population that called for a bipartisan approach to the problem. Neither party wanted to go too far out on a limb without the other, lest they find themselves stranded without a way of getting back to the center. Nonetheless, in the mid-1960s bipartisanship prevailed on the population issue.

Tensions remained in the Johnson administration concerning the pace of family planning policy. In the spring of 1965, OEO director Sargent Shriver's proposal to issue a set of regulations concerning OEO family planning grants opened a fierce dispute with HEW secretary Anthony Celebrezze. Celebrezze argued that the publication of any new regulations would "arouse widespread controversy." Instead, he felt that OEO should follow general federal policy of leaving the political problems of implementing family planning to state agencies that received federal welfare grants. Finally, the issue was taken to the White House, where Shriver argued that the OEO could not get away with this "subterfuge" because OEO was making Community Action Program (CAP) grants to private agencies, and unless certain restrictions were placed on these agencies they would "undoubtedly" create programs that would "provoke even more controversy."[81] The White House refused to become involved in the fight, even though presidential aides Douglass Cater and Bill Moyers told the president that "there is every evidence that even the Pope realizes the times are changing."[82] Without White House intervention, Shriver was able to go ahead and issue new OEO regulations that allowed for family planning project grants to be awarded through the CAP projects. These regulations, however, still proved highly restrictive. Community groups were allowed to establish family planning programs provided that client participation remained entirely voluntary and that family planning advice and assistance were given on a variety of birth control methods, including the rhythm method, oral contraceptives, IUDs, and condoms. Program funds were not to be expended for abortions or sterilization, and contraceptives were not to be provided for unmarried women or women not living with their husbands, but only to married women living in a two-parent household.[83]

Even within the OEO, Shriver's regulations, although more liberal than what Celebrezze had wanted, drew criticism. Certain OEO officials criticized the regulations as limiting clinics from informing their patients as to whether one method of birth control was more effective than another.

Also, many felt that "hysterectomies might be a necessary procedure in family planning." More important, the limit of twelve dollars per year per patient for birth control supplies, usually pills, was considered too modest to be effective.[84] At the same time, Hugh Moore and the Association for Voluntary Sterilization denounced Shriver for "foot dragging" on birth control by charging that his opposition to voluntary sterilization through OEO programs was "discriminating against the poor."[85] Columnists Rowland Evans and Robert Novak joined the fray and attacked the exclusion of unmarried women from OEO-funded family planning programs. "Yet the precise heart of the problem," they declared, "is unmarried women and married women not living with their husbands. The American problem of exploding population is centered in illegitimate Negro births in the slums of the great Northern cities."[86]

While the administration took heat from those who felt OEO regulations were too timid, the White House steadily moved forward on family planning. In early August 1965 Johnson established an informal White House task force on family planning composed of representatives from the Bureau of the Budget, HEW, and the State Department. The special task force was directed to investigate whether "a far-reaching program could be developed" in the area of family planning. Specifically, the goal of the task force was to explore whether HEW family planning services could be expanded to unwed mothers within existing legislation. At this point the Johnson administration continued to oppose new family planning legislation, although a prominent, vocal minority led by Senator Gruening called for such legislation.[87]

A short time later, presidential aide Harry McPherson called a highly secret meeting with HEW officials—referred to as the "Never-Never Committee"—to discuss liberalization of family planning policy. The committee proposed that the restrictive policy that prevented single mothers from receiving subsidized contraception should be changed "without fanfare." The committee noted that the CAP had funded six community family planning projects covering ten thousand women in the last year, but this was "barely scratching the surface." Current policy limited family planning assistance to married women with husbands. Concerned with breaking the cycle of poverty, as well as slowing the rising rates of out-of-wedlock births, the committee believed that the key lay in providing single women, especially women under the age of seventeen, with contraception. The committee realized the delicacy of this issue. After a series of meetings, the committee disbanded, having concluded that liberalization of the program would have to be delayed for the next few years until the political groundwork was laid for a policy shift. "With or without fanfare," a confidential memorandum declared, "development [of such a program] would have to be carefully thought out to avoid misunderstanding by civil rights groups, religious, and other groups."[88]

Even as the administration took care to avoid alienating the Roman Catholic hierarchy, it met resistance nonetheless. In January 1966 the newly appointed secretary of HEW, John Gardner, who had replaced Celebrezze the previous July, issued for the first time departmental regulations that made federal funds available through grants to states for family planning. After these regulations were released, a storm broke when the National Catholic Welfare Conference (NCWC) publicly condemned the administration. In a public statement, the bishops denounced the regulations as an infringement on the "privacy" of married couples. The bishops declared, "It is necessary to underscore this freedom because in some current efforts of government—federal and state to reduce poverty—we see welfare programs increasingly proposed which include threats to free choice of spouses."[89]

Stunned at first by the statement, the administration responded immediately to repair its relations with the bishops. Within a matter of weeks the administration felt confident that little damage had been done by the statement, although some population activists such as the irrepressible Hugh Moore were less sanguine about Catholic opposition to family planning. The White House, however, understood that the key to Catholic opinion rested in not deliberately antagonizing the bishops, if it could be avoided. With this in mind, the White House sent Sargent Shriver and Joseph Califano to meet formally with representatives of the conference, while at the same time initiating a series of private meetings with Father Francis Hurley, assistant general of the NCWC, to express the president's "disappointment" that the bishops had gone public with their concerns. In reply, Hurley told them that the statement represented a majority within the conference but then confided to Califano that he believed this represented "the last trumpet of the older American bishops." Califano reassured Johnson that he felt "responsible for not doing more in this area" and promised to "make more frequent contacts" with the bishops in the future.[90]

Within the White House it was agreed that "despite its cantankerous spirit," the statement represented a step forward because the bishops "tacitly accepted family planning services so long as they were not 'coercive.' " General Draper and Rockefeller met with Douglass Cater to inform him that they had met with key Republicans, including Eisenhower, congressional leaders Gerald Ford and Melvin Laird, as well as Senator Everett Dirksen, in order to make sure that the Republican leadership continued to take "a forthright stand on population planning so that it does not become a partisan issue."[91] Furthermore, Wilbur Cohen at HEW told the administration that whatever stance the American bishops took on family planning, they would not "sway a tremendous number of Catholic voters" who were already using artificial contraception. Noting that the bishops in the end had proved to be "quite conciliatory," Cohen told Johnson, "There's a moral in that."[92] Although Johnson continued to worry about "flack" from the "Catholic bloc" in Congress led by Hugh Carey (D-New York) and Clem Zablocki (D-Wisconsin), the administration felt reassured that it could move forward on family planning. Only in the late 1960s, with the emergence of the debate over legalized abortion, would significant and well-organized political opposition to family planning appear.

The appointment of John Gardner to head HEW marked a step forward for federal family policy. In early 1966 Gardner approved new HEW guidelines encouraging states to apply for federal matching grants for family planning programs. The new guidelines upset the Catholic bishops but clearly linked family planning with the general War on Poverty. As a White House aide told Johnson, "Family planning is a social measure. . . . Family planning is a crucial part of community efforts to reduce poverty and dependency. Office of Economic Opportunity researchers have concluded that family planning is probably the most effective anti-poverty program currently available."[93] Alarmed by the growing rate of out-of-wedlock births among poor blacks, which welfare experts saw as contributing to poverty, the administration believed that the new HEW regulations would "embolden state and local agencies to ask for federal funds and technical assistance" to expand family planning programs. In May, four months after the regulations were issued, Gardner created a new post of deputy assistant secretary for science and population, headed by Dr. Milo Leavitt, who was assigned to work closely with Dr. Philip Lee, assistant secretary for health and scientific affairs.

By 1966 over thirty states provided family planning services, but at this point federal appropriations for family planning remained modest. Indeed, federal and state financial assistance helped local family planning programs to varying degrees in only twenty-nine of forty states providing family planning services.[94] OEO had launched fifty-five projects designed to provide family planning information and services to indigent women. Located in housing projects, churches, and local health centers, these services remained restricted only to married women living with their husbands.[95] Moreover, the Children's Bureau had budgeted less than $3 million in formula grants to states for family planning. The Public Health Service provided family planning through its comprehensive health services for Native Americans, Alaskan natives, and dependents of uniformed services personnel. In turn, the Office of Education had funded 645 projects for developing family life and sex education programs. Furthermore, on October 3, 1966, the secretary of defense announced that family planning and services would be available, subject to space and facilities, to any eligible dependent "wife" of military personnel upon request.[96]

The Children's Bureau, along with the OEO, became a key agency in promoting family planning. In 1967 the bureau's family planning budget was increased to $50 million through its maternal and child health program and its maternity and infant care program. By 1967 approximately two hundred thousand women received support through these two programs, but the bureau was hamstrung by restrictions that limited matching grants to state and local agencies. This policy deliberately excluded voluntary agencies such as Planned Parenthood from receiving federal funds administered through state and local agencies. Moreover, although many states had established family planning programs, these efforts were uneven. Because of the historical development of family planning in the 1930s under the guidance of Clarence Gamble and other eugenicists, the South had developed the most extensive programs, while northern states such as Illinois and New York had programs only in their largest cities. South Dakota, Vermont, and Wisconsin provided no family planning services at all.[97]

Even with the entry of the federal government into this area, family planning services remained largely within the private sector. As a consequence, the federal government, lacking its own infrastructure to distribute contraceptives and implement services, was forced to rely on the nonprofit sector in fundamental ways. For example, by 1966 PPFA affiliates in thirty-six states provided family planning to 320,000 women, of whom 35 percent were on welfare. Federal regulations prevented PPFA affiliates from directly receiving federal grants or federal funds through state and local agencies. These funding restrictions handicapped federal efforts to extend family planning services to the states and, in turn, handicapped the nonprofit sector.

Congress Amends the Social Security Act in 1967

The year 1967 marked a critical advance for the family planning movement. The first indications that the administration was ready to press the population issue further came in January when President Johnson boldly declared in his State of the Union Message that "next to the pursuit of peace, the really great challenge of the human family is the race between food supply and population. . . . The time for concerted action is here, and we must get on with the job."[98]

Meanwhile, Congress moved forward with a legislative agenda that allowed a major shift in federal family planning policy. On the international front, Congress enacted the Foreign Assistance Act (1967) and under Title X earmarked $35 million for family planning. The second piece of legislation, the Social Security amendments (1967), provided a breakthrough that the population lobby was looking for on the domestic policy front.

Tucked away in an elaborate piece of legislation to amend the Social Security Act of 1935, federal family planning attracted little attention from the media or opponents of federally funded birth control programs. Instead, the central focus of the legislation became caught up in a heated partisan debate over welfare reform, specifically congressional proposals to implement workfare programs for mothers of dependent children. Passed in the midst of budgetary cutbacks that called for a freeze on Aid to Families with Dependent Children (AFDC) and an explosive environment created by racial riots in the summer of 1967 in Newark, New Jersey, Detroit, Michigan, and elsewhere, this legislation revealed increasing political polarization within America.

While Congress debated "permissive" welfare policies, federal family planning was quietly introduced into the legislation. Specifically, the new legislation required state welfare agencies to develop family planning programs and allowed the federal government for the first time in history to extend grants to voluntary, nonprofit private groups such as Planned Parenthood. This critical piece of legislation created a symbiotic relationship between public funding agencies and the voluntary, nonprofit sector. The fact that this significant piece of family planning legislation passed without great controversy reflected the intensity of the debate over welfare reform embodied in the bill but it also showed the bipartisan support family planning enjoyed at the time. Republicans and Democrats, conservatives and liberals alike, agreed that family planning provided a solution to the perceived welfare problem and social discord created by unwanted, out-of-wedlock births, especially among poor blacks, in the late 1960s.

The family planning section of the bill was promoted by Congressmen George Bush (R-Texas) and Hermann Schneebeli (R-Pennsylvania). Both Bush and Schneebeli had close associations with the family planning movement. Bush's father, Prescott Bush, had promoted birth control as a U.S. senator from Connecticut. Indeed, his advocacy of birth control had helped cost him his seat in Congress in the late 1940s. Schneebeli had been Nelson Rockefeller's college roommate. The legislation designated that at least 6 percent of appropriated HEW funds were to be designated for family planning projects. Under the amendment, states were required to make family planning available to adult welfare recipients by requiring local welfare agencies to develop family planning programs. Tied closely to the welfare portions of the bill, federal family planning was promoted as a means to prevent or reduce the incidence of out-of-wedlock births. Moreover, it was this amendment that allowed federal funds to be awarded to private organizations such as Planned Parenthood.[99]

Yet the family planning aspects of the legislation went unnoticed because Congress became caught up in a debate over a workfare proposal promoted by Wilbur Mills (D-Arkansas), chairman of the House Ways and Means Committee. The House bill, while increasing Social Security benefits, also included mandatory referral of welfare mothers to work-training programs and provided a technical freeze on the number of dependent children that could be aided by federal funds.[100] The measure immediately drew opposition from liberals in the Senate, led by Robert Kennedy, who was already considering a challenge to Johnson for the 1968 Democratic presidential nomination. Supported by an array of groups—including state and local welfare administrators, welfare activists organized by George Wiley into the National Welfare Rights Organization, organized labor, and the NCWC—liberals in the Senate were able to remove the contentious workfare portion of the final bill, while Social Security benefits were raised 13 percent across the board. The omnibus bill also enacted a comprehensive child and maternal health care program that allowed the federal government to expand its family planning programs.

As a consequence, a policy revolution had occurred in federal family planning policy that went generally unnoticed by the public and the critics of family planning. Strongly supported by Rockefeller and others in the population movement, the 1967 amendments brought the federal government gently, but explicitly, into the business of family planning.[101] Nonetheless, the administration still hesitated to make the issue too prominent in its public agenda. This became evident when the administration opposed legislation proposed by Senator Ernest Gruening and Senator Joseph Tydings that explicitly mandated a program of $225 million for categorical grants for family planning and called for a White House-sponsored conference on family planning.[102] As one White House aide said in opposing this legislation, "Our problem is that we don't need any legislation and support of any bill specifically directed at birth control problems may actually set us back if it encounters serious obstacles in Congress." The White House did not want to call attention to the issue of family planning, lest it might "polarize public opinion, particularly at any time prior to the Pope's final decision on birth control."[103]

In the summer of 1967, a review of HEW programs conducted by Frederick Jaffe (Planned Parenthood), Oscar Harkavy (Ford Foundation), and Samuel Wishik (Columbia University) led to the creation of a new position in HEW, deputy assistant secretary for population and family planning, to be headed by Katherine Brownell Oettinger, former director of the Children's Bureau.[104] Nonetheless, the Harkavy report criticized HEW for not placing a priority on family planning programs.

In 1967 the federal government rapidly expanded its family planning programming. The OEO issued new guidelines that gave local CAP agencies the option of establishing their own eligibility criteria for family planning programs that no longer excluded single women or those not living with their husbands. By late 1968 OEO was supporting 160 family planning programs in thirty-six states, Puerto Rico, and the District of Columbia; OEO-funded Comprehensive Neighborhood Health Centers provided additional family planning services.[105]

In order to finance the federally mandated expansion of state welfare family planning services, HEW provided matching grants at 85 percent through 1969. Title IV provided federal funds for demonstration projects related to reducing welfare dependency, mental retardation, and medical indigence, as well as projects targeted at Cuban refugees, Native Americans, Alaskan natives, and migrant agricultural workers and their families.[106] At the same time, HEW appropriations were rapidly expanded through the Children's Bureau's Maternal and Child Health Service grants to states for family planning, which rose from $1.5 million in 1965 to $2.5 million in 1969. In turn, special project grants for maternal and infant care, including family planning grants, grew from a mere $350,000 in 1965 to $21 million by 1969. All in all, these grants provided family planning services to three hundred thousand women.[107]

Rockefeller Worries That Not Enough Is Being Done

Even as HEW officials touted these programs, they continued to worry that not enough was being done to contain, as one departmental staff member put it, a "burgeoning" population that threatened to overwhelm health care and social services. Officials complained that, because of limited fundings, only a small portion of the reputed 5.2 million women in need of family planning were being covered.[108] Although demographers later challenged this figure—which had been arrived at by Planned Parenthood—it was clear that family planning programs were experiencing serious problems in meeting the needs of the poor.[109] Furthermore, not only were services lacking in many areas, surveys showed that in some programs there was a dropout rate of nearly 50 percent among clients.

Especially alarming to family planning advocates was the growing number of out-of-wedlock births. Since 1950, welfare officials reported, there had been an 83 percent increase in reported out-of-wedlock births. By the late 1960s such births took an even more dramatic jump upward. By 1965 the national out-of-wedlock birthrate had risen to 2.9 percent for whites and nearly ten times higher for nonwhites, 23 percent. Especially disconcerting to policy makers was the finding that rates among black teenagers aged fifteen to nineteen were bounding upward with seemingly little impediment, so that some large cities such as Cleveland reported that nearly half of all unwed pregnancies occurred among teenagers.[110] These rates led the Children's Bureau to call for an expeditious expansion of family planning programs that would be specifically targeted at teenage unwed mothers in order to interrupt what was perceived as "the cycle" of failure that increased welfare dependency and the "continued reproduction of illegitimate offspring."[111]

This link between out-of-wedlock births and the need for family planning changed family planning from an international problem into a domestic problem related to welfare dependency and the breakdown of the American family. Representative Paul H. Todd (D-Michigan), an active voice for federal family planning programs in Congress, summarized the general sentiments of those involved in the issue when he wrote to Katherine Oettinger in 1966, "Certainly, from the standpoint of most of us, it would be ideal if the first illegitimate birth could be avoided by avoidance of promiscuity. But if we do not yet have the tools to discourage promiscuity, we should consider using such tools as we have to avoid illegitimacies." Expressing the optimism of the day, he concluded, "Population policy, if wise, can not only alleviate the crisis, and minimize the problem, but can enable us to avoid inhumane and debilitating natural methods of control if we implement policy properly."[112]

Concerned about the inadequacy of family planning programs, Rockefeller renewed his proposal to establish a presidential commission on population. Throughout this period, Rockefeller had remained an active voice in the population movement, working with other foundation leaders and policy experts to publicize the overpopulation problem, meeting with congressmen and high government officials to discuss tactics and strategy to move the issue onto the political agenda, and directing his associates in ways to promote legislation, revise regulations, and ensure implementation of family planning. Always understated, he nonetheless was relentless. In 1967 he gathered signatures from over thirty world heads of state, calling attention to the global population crisis.[113] In collecting these signatures, Rockefeller called on his extensive personal connections with world leaders. The State Department and the White House office kept a watchful eye on Rockefeller's activities. After some hesitation, Johnson finally added his signature to the "World Leaders' Statement on Population," even though the Soviet Union refused to sign it, denouncing the petition as "bourgeois" and "neo-Malthusian."

By late 1967 the Johnson administration felt confident enough about the family planning issue to meet with Rockefeller to discuss his proposal for a presidential commission.[114] Behind the scenes, Johnson aides continued to worry that such a highly visible commission might retard progress that had been made on federal support for family planning.[115]

This tepid response to the proposal for a presidential commission revealed continued worries within the Johnson administration that this issue would become politicized if it became too public. After all, presidential commissions are not often seen as radical agencies for social or political change. Indeed, it is the nature of commissions to deflect criticism and usually avoid tough policy choices. So, what did Johnson fear? Clearly, it was not a backlash from the Catholic hierarchy. By 1968 the bishops had tacitly agreed to support federal family planning, provided it was "noncoercive" and allowed for "natural" family planning. Instead, growing racial tensions and the acrid aftermath of racial riots in 1967 left the Johnson administration sensitive to complaints from the black community that family planning programs were aimed at targeting poor blacks. The racial riots that followed the assassination of Martin Luther King Jr. on April 7, 1968, only heightened these anxieties within the administration as the nation watched police and the National Guard battle looters in Chicago, Washington, D.C., and other cities. By the week's end, forty-six people had died in rioting across the nation.

In tense times, Johnson decided to tack a middle course. Instead of a presidential commission, in the summer of 1968 he appointed an in-house Advisory Committee on Population and Family Planning, headed by Wilbur Cohen, Rockefeller, and high-level government officials involved in family planning at home and abroad. Rockefeller acquiesced in this compromise, privately writing Johnson that "many of the Black Power advocates associated with the Poor People's Campaign now in Washington would greet the announcement of such a commission with hostility."[116]

The Committee on Population came as one of Johnson's last acts to promote federal family planning. Shortly before its formation, Johnson stunned the nation when he announced that he would not seek reelection. Pursuing its charge in the midst of a weakened presidency, the committee reviewed the status of federal family planning efforts under the Johnson administration. Much had been accomplished, but more needed to be done. The final statement, "Report on Family Planning," provided a record of accomplishment for the administration. The report went over familiar territory. In 1963, when Johnson had assumed office, only a few state health departments were providing family planning services, but by 1968 the majority of state health departments were providing such services. In turn, HEW funding for family planning had increased steadily from $8.6 million in 1965 to $28.2 million in 1968, with $56.3 million appropriated for fiscal year 1969.

Of this, formula grants through Maternal and Child Health Services had nearly doubled, from $1.5 million in 1965 to $2.5 million in 1968, while special project grants for maternity and infant care had risen nearly fourteenfold, from $350,000 in 1965 to $6.3 million in 1968.[117] More important, the Social Security amendments of 1967 mandated that not less than 6 percent of the funds appropriated for Maternal and Child Health Services needed to be designated for family planning services under state health plans. Through these programs nearly three hundred thousand women were receiving family planning services. The report also noted that in 1967 HEW had created a deputy assistant for science and population, thereby institutionalizing the department's commitment to family planning. At the same time, the Office of Education had encouraged family life education and sex education through grants and funded projects.[118]

This was an impressive record, but the Cohen committee noted that private agencies continued to serve 500,000 poor women, or 200,000 more than federally funded programs. Even this remained inadequate, however, in meeting the needs of the estimated 5.2 million poor women for family planning. Family planning services, the report concluded, should be radically expanded. As a consequence, the committee renewed the call, long sought by Rockefeller and the population lobby, for the creation of a Center for Population Research and a presidential commission on population.[119]

The election of 1968 brought a Republican, Richard Nixon, into the White House for the first time in eight years. The committee's report was forwarded to President-elect Nixon with the hope that he would continue the policies of the Johnson administration. Nixon's election, however, elicited fears in population circles that family planning might fall off the presidential agenda. In the frenzied decade of the 1960s, much had been accomplished from the perspective of population activists. Federal family planning legislation had been enacted, programs implemented, and a consensus reached among policy makers, activists, and the public that federal family planning was essential to a better society. By linking federal family planning to the War on Poverty, the Johnson administration implicitly accepted a perspective that a technical solution of having fewer children could be found to those deeper social problems of welfare dependency, out-of-wedlock births, and urban decay.

The Johnson administration, of course, did not see family planning as the only tool for addressing social problems in the United States. It was only a modest part of the Great Society, but this was enough for the population lobby. Family planning had been placed on the policy agenda. Now, their only concern was where the new president, Richard Nixon, stood. A close reading of the public record revealed little of Nixon's views on the population question or family planning. Nixon, it proved, was not to disappoint them.

3

Implementing the Policy Revolution
Under Johnson and Nixon

The Johnson administration made family planning integral to the Great Society's War on Poverty. The election of Richard Nixon to the presidency in 1968 cast doubt on the prospects of federally supported family planning services under a Republican administration. But Nixon proved to be even more enthusiastic about family planning, believing that it offered a long-term solution to the perceived welfare problem, rising social expenditures, and the higher incidence of out-of-wedlock births. Working with the population lobby, Congress enacted the Family Planning Services and Population Research Act (1970), which mandated the development of family planning programs on the state level. This legislation occurred within a social context of changing social mores and widespread use of contraceptives by the middle class.

Yet lacking a well-developed infrastructure to provide family planning on the local level, federal and state government turned to private organizations such as PPFA to provide services. The foundation community, led by the Population Council and the Ford Foundation, developed demonstration projects in cooperation with public agencies. This cooperation between the public and nonprofit, voluntary sectors marked the creation of a welfare system that blended public funding with private, nonprofit organizational participation. The symbiotic relationship between government and private agencies characterized a welfare system unique to the United States. Yet a close examination of family planning programs on the community level reveals the difficulties inherent in this arrangement. Financial scandal and political manipulation marred some programs, while bureaucratic entanglements, inefficiency, community apathy, and political opposition proved the more common experience.

Nixon Proves He Is a Friend of Family Planning

In 1968 the population movement expressed high confidence in what had been accomplished in the last decade, especially during the Johnson years, but at the same time activists and many experts worried that "time was running out." Although the rate of population growth in the United States had shown a steady decrease since the late 1950s, reaching a birthrate in 1966 equal to the low level of the economic depression of the 1930s, demographers worried that the post-war "baby boom" population was about to launch a new wave of births. More important, demographers noted that the poor and black populations had considerably higher fertility rates than the rest of the population, a sure sign, it seemed, that all was not well within the American population.[1] On the eve of the presidential election, the Population Council commissioned Dr. Leslie Corsa, director of the Center for Population Planning at the University of Michigan, to review the current status of family planning in the United States.

Corsa's report expressed the belief that not enough was being done in the way of family planning. Written clearly with an eye on the next four years, Corsa's report called for more direct family planning legislation than what had been contained in the Social Security amendments the previous year. Corsa noted that the issue of whether the federal government should be involved in family planning had been "fully resolved." Yet Congress continued to be "reluctant to clarify its own domestic family planning policies" by not appropriating enough funds to meet the needs of poor women for contraceptive services and counseling. Indeed, the report declared that "the United States has problems similar to those of many 'less developed' countries in providing family planning for its 'less developed' population."[2] The report found that most Americans received contraceptive services through private medical care, but maternal health services for the poor were "grossly inadequate and fragmented and uncoordinated in most places." Efforts to improve family planning for the poor through existing public health and welfare programs, including OEO and Children's Bureau projects, as well as Planned Parenthood programs, had led to a "confusing mix of fiscal arrangements and service activities." PPFA affiliates had expanded its services from 125,000 clients in 1960 to 316,400 clients in 1966. Similarly, the number of state health departments providing services had grown from seven in 1960 to thirty-seven in 1967. Direct federal services to such groups as Native Americans, military dependents, and recipients of care at federal public health hospitals had been increased so that by the first nine months following October 1, 1966, when family planning services had been made available to military dependents, over 478,000 patient visits had been made, 98 percent for oral contraceptives. Even with this great expansion of services, federal financial support was woefully "insufficient." Corsa concluded that "perhaps this country can learn from some of the developing nations that it is possible to equalize opportunity for family planning for all citizens." The report set the stage for the president to make the next four years a period of accelerated federal family planning in America.

Other studies suggested the inadequacy of Medicaid programs in providing family planning services as well.[3] A 1967 survey by Planned Parenthood–World Population (PPWP) indicated, for example, that the Medicaid program had failed to provide family planning services for medically indigent women.[4] As a consequence, many experts believed that Title XIX (Medicaid) had failed to provide an alternative to categorical support of family planning through project grant programs. Nonetheless, federal officials believed that Medicaid would by necessity have to play a more substantive role in financing family planning services through third-party providers. This meant, however, that Medicaid assistance, provided by states, which set their own eligibility and benefits standards, would not be uniform nationally. Moreover, only ten of the twenty-five states covering family planning benefits for the categorically needy authorized the financing of family planning services through both private physicians and clinics.[5]

This poor state of affairs led social scientist Sar A. Levitan, a longtime defender of the Great Society, to complain in 1969 that "instead of funding existing family planning organizations directly, OEO chose to funnel all of its family planning funds through community action agencies." Furthermore, he noted that Planned Parenthood affiliates received two of every five projects delegated by Community Action Agencies (CAA). "Planned Parenthood affiliates," he discovered, "were the first and most frequent seekers of family planning funds, and because in many communities they were the only groups able or willing to mount family planning programs, CAA's often delegated the programs to them."[6] In another article, written that same year, Levitan concluded that the "blame for the slow progress in birth control programs for the poor must be placed at the feet of federal officials who have circumvented or prevented the expansion of birth control programs." Warning that the public opinion was being thwarted, he declared that this provided yet "another illustration of the ability of federal agencies not only to disregard public sentiment, but to stymie presidential prodding and congressional intent." He ended his broadside with a simple question: "What will the Nixon Administration do?"[7]

Richard M. Nixon's election in 1968 came at a tumultuous time in

America's history, marked by racial riots that followed Martin Luther King Jr.'s assassination the previous April, Robert Kennedy's death that June, and continued antiwar activity throughout the country. Nixon defeated his Democratic rival, Hubert Humphrey, by less than 1 percentage point with his offer of a "secret plan" to end the war in Vietnam and his promise to restore "law and order" and clean up the "welfare mess." Although liberals continued to despise Nixon, he proved to be in many respects a reformer by offering new policy initiatives in welfare, health care, federal aid to the states, the environment, and executive reform.[8] At the same time, convinced that he could lure white southerners and blue-collar ethnic voters away from the Democrats, Nixon tacked a course of espousing "law and order," appointing perceived conservatives to the federal courts, and opposing busing of children to achieve school integration.

During the presidential campaign of 1968, Nixon had attacked the "welfare mess." He knew that many Americans had grown resentful of the Great Society's welfare measures. Nonetheless, his initiatives for a guaranteed income program (the Family Assistance Plan) and a national health program showed that Nixon, always the politician, wanted to beat the liberals at their own game. His concern with the spiraling rise in welfare costs and high incidence of out-of-wedlock births led him to see family planning as an instrument that could control welfare costs. Family planning was an issue that cut across ideological lines, and early in his administration it enjoyed broad bipartisan support. Although family planning policy became increasingly politicized as the abortion debate entered the public arena, Nixon was able to move family planning forward with the enactment of major federal legislation that for the first time in the nation's history called for a national population policy to control population growth. Thus, during the Nixon years, federal family planning not only was expanded but it also became institutionalized as domestic social policy.

At first, however, the population movement greeted Nixon's election with a wary eye. Great strides in family planning had been made under the Johnson administration, but in 1968 it was by no means certain that family planning would remain on the presidential agenda. Pope Paul VI's long-awaited encyclical on birth control, *Humanae Vitae*, issued on July 29, 1968, disappointed many who believed that the Catholic Church might change its stance on artificial contraception; it also raised concerns that Nixon might back away from actively supporting family planning.[9] Because of the enactment of the Social Security amendments in 1967, family planning had been mandated by Congress. Still, Nixon's commitment to expanding these efforts remained unknown, although the Republican platform had bluntly stated, "The worldwide population explosion in particular with its attendant grave problems looms as a menace to all mankind and will have our priority attention."[10]

As a consequence, population experts and activists kept a close watch on the Nixon administration in its first days to see where the new president stood on family planning. Shortly after Nixon took office, Oscar Harkavy, population officer at the Ford Foundation, sent Robert Finch, secretary of HEW in the new administration, a letter urging him to pursue family planning policy as a means of addressing the problem of poverty in the nation. "We hope," he wrote, "that increasing funds will be made available to enable all the women of our nation who want them to receive effective, dignified family planning services. While birth control is not a cure for poverty, nor a solution for the problems of the cities, significant reduction of the numbers of unwanted children will make these problems easier to confront."[11]

Many within the population movement considered themselves Republicans, so hopes remained high. John D. Rockefeller 3rd, for example, believed that his influence in the administration might increase because of his family's clout in Republican circles and because his brother Nelson represented the "liberal" wing of the party. Soon after the election, Population Council staff had crafted a carefully designed strategy for using this influence in committing the new administration to expanding federally funded family planning through the establishment of a presidential population commission chaired by Rockefeller, a new institute on population research within the National Institutes of Health, and a special assistant in the White House. Critical to this strategy was utilizing existing contacts within the Nixon administration, people such as presidential science and technology adviser Lee DuBridge, as well as developing relations with new members of the administration, specifically Robert Finch, secretary of HEW, presidential domestic affairs adviser Daniel Moynihan, and chair of the Council of Economic Advisers, Arthur Burns. The Population Council felt that support within Congress for family planning remained "enthusiastic." When Ernest Gruening failed to be reelected to his Senate seat in Alaska, Joseph Tydings (D-Maryland) took up the population banner, although council staff noted that he was not a member of the key committees on this issue.[12] Furthermore, the council felt that it had a friend in Representative George Bush (R-Texas), a member of the House Ways and Means Committee and chair of the Republican Task Force on Earth Resources and Scientific Affairs; it noted that Warren Magnusen (D-Washington) had become the new chairman of the Senate appropriations subcommittee for Health and Senator Ralph Yarborough (D-Texas) chaired the authorization subcommittee, while Senator Jacob Javitts (R-New York) sat on both health subcommittees.[13] The key was linking this congressional support with a White House commitment to family planning policy.[14]

Early reports of where the new administration was headed on family planning appeared positive. The appointment of Louis Heller, a physician who had fought for family planning in New York City, to the upgraded position of assistant secretary of health and population pleased the staff at the Population Council. For a brief period they had worried that the new administration might abolish the post previously held by Katherine Oettinger.[15] Further good news came when Robert Finch and Daniel Moynihan reassured Rockefeller that family planning would remain a top priority under Nixon.[16] Nonetheless, to ensure that this remained so, Rockefeller wrote to Moynihan, "In my opinion the present administration has a real and exciting opportunity" to make the transition from "concern to action in family planning."[17] "There is so much," he declared, "that needs to be done and time is running out."[18] Encouraged by the response, Rockefeller sent to Lee DuBridge, science and technology adviser to Nixon, a draft of a presidential speech to Congress on population. He also welcomed DuBridge's suggestion to meet with the president in the near future. "I cannot tell you how much it means having a friend such as yourself in the White House to work with on questions such as this one—population—which is so important in terms of the well-being of mankind."[19] Shortly afterward, Rockefeller met with Moynihan for lunch and passed on two more memoranda to be given to Nixon.[20]

Rockefeller and the population movement found more ready access to the White House under the Nixon administration than they had with Johnson. The time seemed propitious for family planning in America. There was a growing concern about the effects of pollution, the abuse of natural resources, and the relationship of population size to these problems. Between January and July 1969, over thirty bills related to family planning were introduced in Congress. Paul Ehrlich's *The Population Bomb* (1968) had drawn national attention to the population explosion and had led to the founding of a new organization, Zero Population Growth (ZPG), that called for a radical reduction in world and domestic population growth.[21] At the same time a number of writers, including Kingsley Davis, a demographer at the University of California, were suggesting drastic measures to reduce population growth, including ending tax reductions for children or licensing childbearing privileges. Some activists even proposed putting contraceptives into public water supplies in order to control fertility.[22]

While Ehrlich laid the foundations for popular support for population control, political support came from George Bush's Republican Research Committee Task Force in Earth Resources and Population. After extensive hearings held in early 1969, the committee issued a news release that Secretary of HEW Robert Finch planned to strengthen federal family planning efforts.[23] At the same time, Moynihan pressed the president to move forward on the population question.[24] On July 18, 1969, Nixon called for Congress to enact new family planning legislation.[25] In this twelve-page message, Nixon declared that "population growth is among the most important issues we face. . . . And they agree that the time for such planning is growing very short." The main part of his address focused on the population problem in the United States. While food supplies might appear adequate to feed the growing American population, he warned that "social supplies—the capacity to educate youth, to provide privacy and living space, to maintain the processes of open, democratic government—may be grievously strained." Moreover, he cautioned that current indications were that the decline in the fertility rate might be coming to an end. To address these issues he called for an increase in spending for population and family planning, the establishment in HEW of a separate agency devoted to family planning, and closer coordination between HEW and OEO. Furthermore, he proposed the creation by Congress of a Commission on Population Growth and the American Future.[26]

The population movement was ecstatic. The president had committed himself publicly and forcefully to family planning policy. Rockefeller immediately telegrammed Richard Nixon, "I was deeply impressed by your message today," modestly adding that "the Commission on Population is a good idea. If I can help, let me know."[27]

Nixon's proposal brought forth the Family Planning Services and Population Research Act (1970) and the establishment of the Commission on Population Growth and the American Future.[28] Specifically, the Family Planning Act created two new agencies within HEW, the National Center for Population and Family Planning under the direct supervision of the assistant secretary for health and scientific affairs, and the National Center for Family Planning Services. (Secretary Finch had already established the National Center for Population in October 1969, but the new act ensured legislative authorization.) The legislation provided $382 million for services, research, and training, and instituted Title X of the Public Health Services Act, which would become the primary source of federal funding for contraception, other than Medicaid.[29]

The bill reflected the Nixon administration's commitment to family planning, as well as visible criticism from congressional advocates of family planning that more needed to be done. In a budget-cutting mood, the House appropriations subcommittee on HEW had unsuccessfully attempted to reduce 1969 appropriations for family planning specifically authorized by the Social Security amendments of 1967. Furthermore, bureaucratic opposition within HEW had effectively blocked full integration of family planning into public health programs.[30] This opposition led Senator Tydings and Senator Ralph Yarborough, chair of the Senate Labor and Public Welfare Committee, to introduce the Family Planning Services and Population Research Act with the clear intention of creating a distinct bureaucratic base for family planning programs in HEW through the National Center for Population and Family Planning.

From the outset the bill drew widespread support from both parties.[31] Concerned with escalating welfare costs, Republicans and Democrats alike saw family planning as a means of addressing the costly problems of welfare dependency, as well as other social problems related to urbanization, the environment, and pollution. These latter issues, however, were of secondary importance to the welfare problem. Senator Thomas Eagleton (D-Missouri) expressed the general sentiment of Congress when he declared, "The economic and social aspects of family planning services must be taken into account. There is a definite relationship between poverty and family size."[32] Although the legislation enjoyed bipartisan support, Senator Tydings pressed initially for a separate categorical grants program to fund family planning. Arguing that family planning programs in HEW had been "mismanaged" and that opportunities for expanding family planning had been missed by Secretary Finch, Tydings argued that "any realistic campaign to eliminate poverty in America must include programs that make family planning information and services available on a voluntary basis."[33]

Speaking for the administration, Finch opposed the new categorical program called for by Tydings, arguing that existing legislation provided for grants to state and local governments, as well as private organizations.[34] In the end, Tydings dropped his provision for a categorical grant program after he was promised that HEW would strengthen the Office of Population Affairs, even though he worried that the administration might "chisel" on its promise.[35] Unfortunately for the population movement, Tydings's strong voice for family planning would be lost in the Senate when he was defeated for reelection in November 1970, on the eve of legislative triumph.

At the same time, little opposition to the bill emerged during the hearings. While Reverend James T. McHugh, director of the Family Life Division of the NCWC, worried that the "voluntary" nature of federal family planning might not be enforced, he raised little serious criticism of the bill, other than stressing the point that the church remained opposed to any federal efforts to fund abortions. Representatives from local Catholic groups that had begun to coalesce around the abortion debate proved more critical of the bill and urged Congress to support better health care, early childhood education, and vocational programs. Still, these community groups did not present a well-organized opposition to the bill, so their influence on the final legislation was minimal.[36] In the end, the Family Planning Services and Population Research Act passed the Senate unanimously and the House by a 293 to 32 vote. On December 24 Nixon signed the first explicit family planning and population legislation ever passed by the U.S. Congress.[37]

Throughout the process of enacting this new legislation, Rockefeller, Hugh Moore, and William Draper actively lobbied Congress. Their involvement in the process proved critical; indeed, Moore later claimed that Congress enacted the legislation because of his behind-the-scenes involvement. Moore, typically, was given to hyperbole, but there remains little doubt that the population movement was important in shaping the final legislation and securing its final enactment. Rockefeller worked closely with Moynihan in tracking the legislation as it worked its way through Congress. Acting on Moynihan's advice, Rockefeller met with key members of Congress involved in the legislation, including John Moss (D-Connecticut), William Dawson (D-Illinois), and John Blatnick (D-Minnesota), who chaired various hearings on different aspects of the legislation.[38] Rockefeller was pleased to report that Representative George Bush "facilitated" handling of the bill by arranging its transfer to the Committee on Government Operations.[39]

Hugh Moore's involvement in the legislative process proved even more critical to the Family Planning Services and Population Research Act. The PCC took out full-page newspaper ads to bolster support for the bill. After the bill's passage in the Senate, however, prospects in the House appeared dim. Speaker of the House John McCormack (D-Massachusetts) was an active Catholic from a heavily Catholic state, and his commitment to the new legislation was not at all certain as the session was drawing to a close. At this point, as Moore told the story, the newly appointed president of the PCC, General Arthur O'Meara, a Catholic who had discussed his appointment with Cardinal Cooke before accepting the post, went to McCormack and convinced him to take up the legislation in the House. Moore claimed that this was decisive in passage of the bill.[40]

The population movement celebrated the victory. Appointed to chair the commission authorized under the new legislation, John D. Rockefeller 3rd immediately set to work selecting members for the new Commission on Population and the American Future. Working closely with Moynihan and key members of Congress, Rockefeller put together a commission that reflected, as he put it, "the pluralistic society." The commission consisted of twenty-four members, including four members of Congress, demographers, social scientists, and representatives from business, labor, and the medical profession. To ensure its broad representation, Congress approved the appointment of young people, women, and ethnic minorities.[41] The commission would meet for the next two years before its final report was issued.[42]

In 1970 the population movement was jubilant. Initial doubts about Nixon had been dispelled by the new legislation. Further good news came when the new secretary of HEW, Elliot L. Richardson, announced at a congressional luncheon, attended by representatives from the Population

Council, Planned Parenthood, and other groups celebrating the passage of the Family Planning Act, that the administration would seek an additional $6 million in family planning grants in fiscal year 1971. This was in addition to the increased authorization of $573 million under the Family Planning Services and Population Research Act.[43] The largest increase came for project grants to enable local public agencies and, significantly, private nonprofit organizations to initiate or expand existing programs. The new budget also reflected the administration's intent to transfer OEO family planning services to HEW by 1972.

In order to expand family planning programs, the Nixon administration allocated increased funding to state and local welfare and health programs, while providing more funds to private organizations such as Planned Parenthood for family planning services.[44] The Social Security amendments of 1967 mandated the establishment of family planning programs by state welfare programs receiving federal welfare funds. Title IV of the amendments provided federal matching funds at 85 percent through 1969 and 75 percent subsequently. In turn, the act provided funds for demonstration projects related to the prevention and reduction of dependency through family planning programs and contraceptive services for the mentally challenged, medically indigent, Cuban refugees, Native Americans, Alaskan natives, and migrant workers and their families.

Creating the Second Welfare State

The great expansion of the welfare state under the Nixon administration, and the coincident growth of federally funded family planning programs that followed the enactment of the Family Planning Services and Population Research Act of 1970, created a new paradox that remains apparent in the contemporary liberal state: at the same time that federal social policy became increasingly active and centralized, there occurred a greater involvement of the nonprofit, voluntary sector in implementing social policy. This parallel development of the centralized welfare state and the voluntary sector was no coincidence. The growth of federal social programs mobilized the nonprofit sector, while, in turn, the nonprofit sector, through policy innovation and program implementation, helped legitimize the modern welfare state.

As the traditional federal system eroded in the 1960s when the federal government, through the Great Society, extended its powers at the expense of state power, the nonprofit sector was called upon to help design, implement, and administer social programs mandated by federal legislation.[45] As a consequence, the voluntary sector expanded in the 1960s at the very time the federal government enlarged its social welfare programs. As one leading student of the voluntary sector noted, "The voluntary sector, rather than constituting an alternative to the welfare state, was largely its creation."[46]

During the Johnson and Nixon administrations, the American social welfare state underwent a significant transformation. During these years the welfare state was expanded to include a new national health insurance plan for the elderly and the poor (Medicare and Medicaid), employment and training programs for the unemployed, social service and housing aid for the disadvantaged, and family planning for the poor. From 1965 through 1980 government spending on social welfare grew by 263 percent in inflation-adjusted dollars. Federal spending expanded from 11.5 percent of the gross domestic product in 1965 to 19.5 percent in 1976, before falling slightly to 18.5 percent in 1980. From 1965 through 1975 the enormous growth of these expenditures came from the creation of new programs. Furthermore, beginning in 1967, federal spending on social welfare surpassed state and local government expenditures for the first time, reaching over 60 percent by 1980.[47]

The expansion of the welfare state in the 1960s and 1970s promoted the emergence of a government-nonprofit partnership. As the welfare state expanded, the federal government, lacking an extensive delivery infrastructure, was forced to rely on the nonprofit sector as a service provider. The federal government generated the funds, set regulations, and oversaw the programs, but it turned the actual delivery of services over to other public agencies, operating on the local and state levels, and to private organizations. This new welfare system—the second welfare state, if you will—blended public and private action. This "mixed" welfare state that emerged in the late 1960s and 1970s marked a creation unique to the United States, reflecting a deep-seated American tradition of associative enterprise that combined self-reliance and private voluntarism with communitarianism and government activity.[48] The new relationship became especially prominent in family planning programs in these years. The Nixon administration took the first major step in rationalizing federal family planning through the enactment of the Family Planning Services and Population Research Act (1970), which established the National Center for Family Planning Services in HEW, as well as mandating the development of family planning programs on the state level. Lacking a well-developed infrastructure to implement the expansion of federally funded programs, however, the federal government relied on private organizations such as PPFA to provide services. Also, the Population Council expanded its domestic service program by contracting with the OEO to provide contraceptive counseling and services through a cooperative arrangement of medical schools and hospitals. The Ford Foundation entered into domestic family planning by funding demonstration programs in a number of major cities.

However important the role of these nonprofit organizations was in developing a national family planning program, the record of their involvement in these years revealed the limitations inherent in this second welfare state. In the end, both the Population Council and the Ford Foundation withdrew from active participation in family planning programs in the United States when they discovered cooperation with the federal government was severely hampered by bureaucratic infighting, squabbling between federal, state, and local agencies, and intrusive government oversight into their programs. As a consequence, family planning policy during these years suggested that the emergence of the new welfare state created a symbiosis between the public and private sectors, but this relationship remained painfully uneasy, with neither party feeling fully comfortable with the other.

Family planning policy under the Nixon administration, therefore, provided continuity with the Johnson administration. Even before the landmark legislation in 1970, HEW Maternal and Child Health Services grants to states had risen to $2.5 million in 1969. Special project grants for maternal and infant care, including family planning grants had increased to $21 million in 1969, up from $350,000 in 1965. Similarly, the OEO was supporting 160 family planning programs in thirty-six states, Puerto Rico, and the District of Columbia. Additional services were provided through OEO-funded Comprehensive Health Centers. Furthermore, new OEO family planning guidelines issued in 1968 gave local CAP agencies the option of establishing their own eligibility criteria for family planning programs that no longer frowned on providing services to single women or women not living with their husbands.[49]

Implementing Family Planning Services: The Ford Foundation Experience

The critical question remained how best to deliver these services.[50] Under Title X of the Family Planning Act, HEW was authorized to make grants to private health and family planning clinics, as well as public health agencies. The Family Planning Services and Population Research Act funded private, nonprofit family planning clinics in America, although it should be noted that in fiscal year 1968 nearly 40 percent of OEO grants for family planning had gone to Planned Parenthood. An equal number of family planning grants went to CAPs, with the balance made to health organizations. Planned Parenthood affiliates were often the first and most frequent seekers of family planning grants, and because many communities lacked family planning facilities or agencies to implement programs, PPFA local organizations proved critical in developing a national family planning program. PPFA tended to use funds to open new clinics in poor neighborhoods, while public health departments usually used OEO funds to expand existing clinics.

At the same time, where no facilities existed, OEO simply paid physicians for services rendered in their own offices or entered into loosely cooperative arrangements with local health department personnel. The OEO gathered little information on how these private "nondelegated" programs operated. Moreover, there was little cooperation among local agencies concerning family planning, other than the notable exception of the Los Angeles Regional Family Planning Council, which received OEO funding in 1968 to establish a single, coordinated program. By the time Nixon came to office in 1969, OEO had funded from the time of its establishment 159 family planning grants, 63 to Planned Parenthood, 25 to health departments, 2 to hospitals, 8 to others, and 61 to CAPs.[51] Another 32 grants were awarded to comprehensive health center programs that provided family planning.

Family planning projects confronted continued problems in reaching targeted populations and then keeping clients once they had been found. High dropout rates continued to plague family planning programs at every level. A family planning program in West Virginia, sponsored by the Population Council and the Children's Bureau, failed to "get off the ground" because of "inadequate time to prepare the groundwork for this new service, lack of sufficient professional personnel, ... relatively poor transportation facilities within the counties and a population that had not been prepared for the program."[52] Similarly, a study of 159 family planning clinics in Georgia discovered many patients found the clinic locations and clinic hours inconvenient, and interviews overwhelming, repetitive, and long.[53] Eager to find better ways to implement family planning programs, federal administrators sought innovative approaches. Here the nonprofit, philanthropic sector, led by the Population Council, the Ford Foundation, and Planned Parenthood, played a critical role in exploring better ways to deliver contraceptive services. The experience of these programs illustrated, however, the difficulties of contracting with the federal government.

In the late 1960s both the Ford Foundation and the Population Council became directly involved in government service programs. This shift away from policy research to policy implementation would have significant implications for both organizations, later leading to recriminations from within as well as political attacks launched by outside critics who accused them, especially the Ford Foundation, of having become political tools of the Democratic party. The Population Council drew less criticism for its

involvement in community service programs, primarily because it remained less visible to public scrutiny. Nonetheless, the Population Council's own experience in federally funded service programs proved equally
disappointing.

Criticism of the foundation's population program provided the cap-
stone to criticism that had been growing since 1965 when the Treasury
Department issued a devastating report on tax abuses by philanthropic
foundations. Congressional critics led by Wright Patman (D-Texas) were
incensed by the report.[54] Furthermore, conservatives had become agitated
by the Ford Foundation's support for voter registration drives in the South
and school redistricting in Manhattan.[55] Further controversy came when it
was discovered that in 1967 the Ford Foundation had awarded grants to
eight members of the staff of the late Senator Robert F. Kennedy (D-New
York), with the personal approval of the foundation's new president,
McGeorge Bundy. His arrogant defense of these grants in early 1969
before the House Ways and Means Committee, then considering an
omnibus tax reform bill, did little to assuage conservative critics. John D.
Rockefeller 3rd was able to thwart the most punitive parts of the House
bill by issuing a separate report through the Rockefeller-financed Commission on Foundations and Private Philanthropy, chaired by Peter G.
Peterson. Responding to the report, Congress enacted the Tax Reform Act
of 1969, which corrected many of the worst abuses of charitable organizations. These attacks revealed the Ford Foundation's vulnerability to accusations that it was not simply a nonpartisan, philanthropic institution
interested in objective research.

From 1952 through 1977, when it reevaluated its activity in this area,
the Ford Foundation committed $222 million to population work, the
largest share (56 percent) going to reproductive sciences and contraceptive
work.[56] While most of the Ford Foundation's activity involved international family planning and support for basic reproductive research, Ford
became increasingly involved in domestic family planning programs. As
early as 1962, the foundation's trustees affirmed their intention "to maintain strong efforts in the United States" in order to "achieve a breakthrough on the problems of demography, the motivational factors in
family planning, and the political and social consequences of population
control."[57] Even after it became evident that the Johnson administration
was committed to family planning as a critical component of the War on
Poverty, the foundation worried that family planning services would not
become "available to the extent implied by existing policy statements."[58]

This concern led the foundation to begin making small grants to support demonstration programs intended to improve the delivery of contraceptives and to catalyze major federal support for family planning. By

initiating these demonstration programs, officers believed, as one foundation report said in 1968, "as we prescribe for Delhi, so must we take account of Detroit."[59] Beginning in 1966, the foundation made its first domestic grants, totaling about $2 million.

The purpose of these grants was to support experimental programs intended to improve delivery services, not to underwrite ongoing programs. Ford's most dramatic involvement in family planning came in Louisiana, where the Ford Foundation supported the work of Dr. Joseph Beasley that led to the development of a statewide family planning program. Beasley's program was then touted as a model for family planning programs throughout the country and even internationally.[60] With this first flush of success, Ford Foundation officers congratulated themselves on the role private philanthropy could play in supporting public programs. When charges of political corruption and misappropriation of funds began to circulate, the foundation distanced itself from the program. The Louisiana experiment provides an illustration of how anxious family planners were to implement programs, often throwing caution to the wind.

In 1965 more than half of Louisiana's black population, which constituted 30 percent of the state's general population, was poor. More than a fourth of the state's black families received public assistance.[61] Until 1965 the state of Louisiana did not have a single family planning clinic, nor did Planned Parenthood have a single chapter in the state. That year Beasley, a physician at Tulane Medical School, established the Tulane Center for Population and Family Studies for the sole purpose of conducting a state survey on contraceptive practices among the indigent population. He focused his efforts on Lincoln Parish, a rural county where 43 percent of the women were in the lowest income group and accounted for 94 percent of the illegitimate births. His studies showed that for every dollar spent for family planning, the state would save over thirteen dollars on welfare costs. He realized that an argument linking reduced welfare costs to providing family planning services to poor black women would appeal to policy makers.

Armed with his findings, Beasley convinced the state attorney general to reinterpret the criminal code against birth control in order to allow family planning services to be provided through county public health care agencies. Meanwhile, he curried favor with the Catholic Church hierarchy to win support for his program. After a series of meetings—critics later maintained that were held in some of New Orleans's finest restaurants over bottles of old wine—the church officials took the position "We will not endorse, but we will not oppose." Beasley's first grant to establish a family planning program in Lincoln Parish came in 1965 from the HEW through the Children's Bureau. In 1967 the Ford Foundation awarded an additional three hundred thousand dollars to Beasley to assist his family planning program. This small demonstration program quickly proved a success when family planning services were provided to 75 percent of all the poor women in the parish. Within two years, he claimed, births to indigent women declined 44 percent, compared with the decline of 25 percent in the four surrounding parishes. At the same time there was a corresponding decrease in the total number out-of-wedlock births and fewer births to teenagers. (Later critics from the state medical establishment charged that these figures were misleading because decreased fertility and out-of-wedlock births were evident throughout the state.)

In July 1967 Beasley successfully extended his work to metropolitan New Orleans. Within the year HEW approved a $1.75 million grant to develop a statewide program. Operating with continued support from the Ford grant, specifically awarded for this purpose, Beasley soon was managing eighty-eight clinics in sixty-three parishes, reaching over forty thousand women. The Ford Foundation provided funds for research, development, and evaluation, but suspicions began to arise regarding the accuracy of Beasley's figures.[62] Nonetheless, in 1970 his program received another matching grant of $1.2 million from HEW for family planning. When the grant was held up by the HEW bureaucracy, Ford provided emergency funds to continue the "demonstration" aspects of the program. That the Ford Foundation had to supplement Louisiana's state programs in 1970, while federal funds were tied up in the HEW bureaucracy, only indicated some of the difficulties of a federal system of social programming. The Ford Foundation was forced to intervene because, in the words of a foundation officer, "this large-scale federal funding is both inflexible and unpredictable from one year to the next."

By 1972 Beasley had opened 148 clinics. During these years his program administered fifty-five grants from diverse public and private sources. Federal funds amounted to about $14 million. The organization employed 533 people, many of them black community outreach workers, and met an average monthly payroll of $260,000. Beasley moved to incorporate his operation into the Family Health Foundation, which expanded its focus to comprehensive community health programs, early childhood education, and national and international family planning, supported by AID and Ford Foundation grants. The Louisiana program was replicated in Illinois and other states. One Ford Foundation officer concluded that Beasley had proved "beyond a doubt that the combination of strong leadership, sophisticated management techniques, high-quality services, and adequate funding ensure a high degree of family acceptance in urban and rural areas. It is a useful model not only for other parts of the United States, but to some extent for other countries as well."[63] Pilot projects were proposed for Brazil, Colombia, Mexico, and Venezuela. The Family Health Foundation produced its own movie, *To Hunt with a Cat*, to promote its project. Beasley became a national spokesperson for family planning. He was elected chairman of the board of directors of Planned Parenthood, appointed to a visiting endowed chair of population and public health at Harvard Medical School (funded by Hugh Moore), and served as a consultant to the World Health Organization, the State Department, AID and the World Bank. There was even talk of a Nobel Prize.[64]

Yet as the Louisiana program expanded there developed a constant need for funds to keep the programs running. The liberalization of federal funds on a new nine-to-one match to state funds, and the liberalization of eligibility to include teenagers, allowed Beasley to further expand his client base. Growing numbers of out-of-wedlock births among teenagers became a concern of the Family Foundation, as studies revealed that women under twenty-one years of age were four and one-half times as likely to incur an accidental pregnancy, while illegitimate births in the public hospital skyrocketed 40 percent from 1967 to 1970.[65] This insatiable demand for funds to keep the machine operating opened the foundation to political manipulation.

In 1971 black militants began charging that the program was a racist program aimed at genocide in the African-American community. At the same time outreach workers in project areas reported intermittent harassment from Black Muslims. One outreach worker reported that a community meeting was disrupted when Muslims broke into the clinic and accused her of being a "pill-pusher" and "a traitor to her race."[66] Neighborhood black political grassroots organizations such as the Southern Organization for United Leadership (SOUL) and Community Organization for Urban Politics (COUP), funded by OEO, demanded patronage. In response, Beasley promoted his critics into top management and hired other nationalist critics and their relatives in other positions. A system of kickbacks to black contractors and relatives of Governor Edwin Edwards was put into place.

Finally, in December 1972, the Louisiana State Medical Society presented preliminary evidence that the Family Health Foundation had double billed the government for the same services. Four months later, in April 1973, a federal grand jury requested by the medical society was convened. United States Attorney General Gerald Gallinghouse indicted Beasley on charges of attempting to defraud the government, mail fraud, and obstruction of justice. Launching what Gallinghouse called "the most extensive investigation in the history of the state," the inquiry widened to include Beasley, Family Health Foundation officials, the governor's brother, top administrators of Tulane Medical School, and grant officers at the

Rockefeller Foundation. Surprisingly, the Ford Foundation's involvement passed unnoticed, although neither the Rockefeller Foundation nor Ford was accused of direct involvement in what became known in the state as "Our Own Little Watergate."

Federal and state investigations revealed that state politicians and relatives had taken trips on a foundation plane to Latin America and other places. The foundation had rented office space in Washington, D.C., as a base for lobbying the thirty-eight agencies that supported it and in doing so it had spent federal money for entertainment, foreign travel, liquor, flowers, and apartments. Questions were raised about the misuse of private donations from the Rockefeller Foundation and the Ford Foundation for federal matching grants. One audit revealed that political contributions had been made to two governors, two state senators, and a state supreme court justice. In the midst of this investigation, the Family Health Foundation placed Senator Joseph Tydings on retainer for $40,000 a year and Harry Dent, former counsel to President Nixon, for $20,000 a year. Beasley tried to fight back by buying television time to appeal for community support. It did little good. In the end the federal government found that $6.2 million had been improperly used. After three separate trials involving a variety of charges, Beasley was sentenced to two years in prison. Released after he had served seventeen months in prison, he had his medical license to practice in Louisiana revoked. Beasley took a position in health and nutrition at Bard College in New York, where Ford Foundation grants permitted him to work on prenatal nutrition. To many in Louisiana, he remained a Robin Hood who had tried to help the poor, only to become ensnared in the Byzantine tangles of southern politics.

The Louisiana experiment in family planning proved to be the most dramatic example of the political shoals that awaited the family planner on the state level. Bureaucratic entanglement was common and could frustrate the most conscientious of administrators. This was all too apparent in the Ford Foundation's experience in supporting Planned Parenthood programs in New York City, which represented the more typical experience for family planners in these years.

In New York, local and state public health agencies relied heavily on Planned Parenthood to develop and deliver family planning services. By 1968 the number of low-income women in the city receiving family planning services through government facilities had tripled in a three-year period, from 15,000 to over 45,000. The city's Health Department, which had opened its first family planning clinic in 1964, was operating twenty such clinics, with the expectation of doubling this number if additional federal funds became available. Indicative of its commitment to family planning, the Health Department had organized an interagency council for family planning services. Similarly, the city had established sixteen community-based family planning programs, fifteen of them since 1968. This rapid expansion of city family planning programs, however, created financial and organizational problems. Observing this situation, the Ford Foundation noted, "Understandably, such rapid movement into a field considered off limits until so recently has caused operational problems for the agencies involved."[67] Community organizations involved with welfare agencies had little experience or expertise in administering family planning clinics, while the Health Department and hospitals had more experience in clinic operation but little in outreach programs. As a result the Health Department and Human Resources Agency turned to Planned Parenthood for help in recruiting and training community workers and family planning personnel.

Active since 1916, Planned Parenthood of New York City (PPNYC), under different names, remained the largest single provider of family planning, serving approximately thirty thousand lower-income women in eleven clinics located throughout the city. More important, PPNYC already had played a key role in developing publicly supported family planning programs in cooperation with city and public health agencies. For example, in central Harlem the PPNYC brought together local municipal hospitals and local antipoverty agencies into a family planning program and helped write a successful proposal to the state Human Resources Administration for funding. In Long Island, PPNYC worked with local hospitals and five public agencies to establish the first permanent family planning clinic. Similarly, in Brooklyn, a local CAP contracted with PPNYC to provide assistance in setting up a family planning clinic.

Acting at the request of the city health and welfare agencies to assist them in expanding their programs, PPNYC turned to the Ford Foundation as a source of support. The PPNYC proposal declared, "The time is right—now—for a massive expansion of family planning services in New York City." The proposal noted that economically the programs appeared on a sound footing, with Medicaid providing birth control supplies and reimbursements to hospitals for the cost of services provided. Still needed, however, were personnel to administer the programs. Specifically, PPNYC sought a two-year grant that would provide funding for the hiring and training of family planning administrators and other personnel, as well as equipping clinics, installing patient record systems, and establishing clinic procedures.[68]

Awarded the grant, Planned Parenthood moved aggressively to ensure that New York City would become the "first major urban center that will have family planning services adequate to meet its need."[69] By 1970 PPNYC, in cooperation with the Department of Health and the Human

Resources Administration, had established ninety-one clinics and family planning programs, trained people in thirty-nine different public and private agencies, and offered orientation programs to 641 health and welfare workers.[70]

Bringing coherence to the various state, local, and private programs involved in family planning proved to be difficult. Furthermore, the national headquarters of Planned Parenthood resented PPNYC's fund-raising activities, which drew funds away from the national office. This dependence on raising private funds, while competing with their national organization and procuring government funds, created financial snares for a local agency such as PPNYC. For example, in 1968 PPNYC ran into "severe" financial problems when its fund-raising campaign proved "disastrous" and its Medicaid funds were held up because of a battle between the New York State Department of Social Services and the state Department of Health. This dispute between the two state departments was so "acrimonious," reported PPFA in requesting emergency funds from the Ford Foundation, that the two state agencies refused to talk to one another. As a result, Medicaid reimbursements for family planning services performed by PPNYC were delayed. The situation worsened when PPNYC got into a dispute with the national PPFA over fund-raising. Ford provided a grant to allow PPNYC to continue its operations until the dispute was finally resolved, but this kind of situation proved typical of general problems private providers encountered in working through state and federal funding agencies.[71]

While the Ford Foundation's involvement in Louisiana and New York City established the importance of philanthropic activity in supporting programs, this track record clearly was uneven. The foundation's involvement in a local Baltimore teenage pregnancy prevention program in 1971 illustrates the kinds of tribulations family planners confronted. A Ford Foundation study had revealed that in 1970 there were fifteen thousand out-of-wedlock births in Baltimore, even though the overall birthrate for the city was declining. Most of these births occurred among poor, black women, many of them teenagers. An estimated 5 percent of Baltimore's nonwhite girls aged sixteen and younger gave birth to an out-of-wedlock child. Moreover, 20 percent of this group already had one or more children born out of wedlock. The Ford Foundation found that many of these young women lacked information and held "vague" ideas about how one became pregnant. Moreover, the Ford Foundation reported, "Sexual activity is high and there are few social and family pressures that serve as inhibiting influences."[72]

To address this situation, the Ford Foundation awarded a $250,000 grant to the Baltimore Planned Parenthood affiliate in cooperation with the Baltimore Urban League and Johns Hopkins School of Hygiene and

Public Health to develop an educational and contraceptive service targeted at Baltimore's inner-city black teenage female population. Foundation officers felt that private, voluntary efforts were needed because "the prevention of premarital teenage pregnancy has been identified as a major concern by Washington officials responsible for family planning but the government is not yet ready to finance demonstration programs." The foundation hoped that this demonstration program might "pave the way for large-scale government funding in the future." If successful, the program hoped to receive funding from OEO and HEW.[73]

Designed by Dr. Thomas Saski of the Department of Population and Family Health of Johns Hopkins University, the program focused on the racially mixed area of west Baltimore. The program called for the hiring of community field-workers who were to make contact with families of teenagers and direct them to a sex education course to be given in several neighborhood locations. The course was to provide "comprehensive" instruction that integrated sex attitudes, hygiene, marriage problems, and the complexities of boy-girl relations at an early age. All minors were to have written permission of parents or guardians. Aware that a similar course developed at Cordozo High School in Washington, D.C., the previous year had failed, the organizers of the Baltimore demonstration program believed that the key to a successful program rested on keeping "indigenous" field-workers in the community who would target two thousand unmarried girls between the ages of twelve and eighteen.

The program got off to a quick start. A field-worker contacted 1,189 families and subsequently enrolled close to a thousand teenagers. Difficulties soon arose, however, when most of the white teenagers dropped out for unexplained reasons, leaving a little more than 680 black teenagers. Attendance at the classes averaged about 25 girls, but most only appeared once and then dropped out. Field-workers attributed the failure to lack of adequate education techniques and audiovisual materials, but the problems appear to have been deeper. Only 123 girls who remained in the program received contraceptive services. Of these, three-quarters were aged fifteen or younger. More than a third of these 123 girls were not sexually active, so the program failed in its primary goal of reaching those most likely to have out-of-wedlock births—sexually active teenagers. Subsequent interviews with sexually active girls who did not enroll in the program revealed that they felt "they could take care of themselves." At the end of three years, field-workers found, "Programs of sex education and family life values in twelve to eighteen-year-olds in hard core poverty areas have been strikingly unsuccessful as out-of-wedlock births continued to rise." In the end, the program never gained community support, nor did it receive federal support. The program was deemed a failure, but in the meantime the foundation awarded the New York City Board of Education a $174,525 grant for sex education, leading a foundation officer to declare, "It is of course unfortunate that lessons learned in the Baltimore project were not more fully available at the time the staff work was being done on the grant for the program in New York."[74]

The Baltimore experiment revealed the inherent difficulty in delivering family planning to the poor: even when family planning services were available, participation often remained low, dropout rates high, and complaints about the side effects of contraception—whether oral or mechanical—persistent. The net effect was that out-of-wedlock births continued to climb, while family planning appeared to have little effect in addressing deeper social problems underlying domestic poverty. Surveys showed that in some programs there was a dropout rate of over 50 percent among clients. Similarly, a detailed study of federally financed family planning programs in the St. Louis region showed that dropout rates on average were 38 percent. The rate coincided with the average rate of women in the general population who discontinued use of contraceptives. For example, a Princeton National Fertility Study estimated that approximately 6.4 million women had used oral contraceptives since 1960, but of these, one-third had discontinued use, largely because of unpleasant side effects. In a study of Minnesota women, close to half reported discontinued use of the pill.[75]

Implementing Family Planning Services: The Population Council's Experience

One of the most innovative programs designed to address the problems of greater numbers of out-of-wedlock births came from a Population Council "postpartum" demonstration program. This program marked the Population Council's move into domestic service programs under its president, Bernard Berelson. Funded by OEO, the program utilized major metropolitan and university hospitals to provide inner-city poor with contraceptive services. The idea that after delivery women might be especially open to contraceptive services including sterilization had been explored by the Population Council in its international family planning programs developed in the mid-1960s. Furthermore, OEO officials were convinced that providing hospital services to women after birth was economical and efficient.[76]

Although the postpartum program was funded by OEO, the Population Council had first developed it two years earlier through an international program. The project began in 1966 with a few hospitals in developing countries and quickly expanded to include twenty-six hospitals in fifteen countries. The effectiveness of this program suggested that a similar program might be developed in the United States. In the early spring of 1968, a series of meetings were initiated by John D. Rockefeller 3rd with representatives of nineteen leading medical schools, the Ford Foundation, the Urban League, Planned Parenthood, and OEO and HEW officials to develop a demonstration postpartum program in the United States. At these meetings OEO officials expressed an opinion that a national family planning program was "unrealistic and unworkable" given the current delivery system. Representing HEW, Assistant Secretary of Health Philip Lee noted that direct federal funding of these programs had proved more effective than working through various local and state departments of health.[77]

By November 1968 the Population Council had prepared a detailed proposal for setting up the program with leading medical schools across the country. Included in the program were Case Western University, the University of Chicago, Columbia University, Emory University, Johns Hopkins University, the University of Florida, Albert Einstein Hospital, Harlem Hospital, New York Medical College, the University of Pennsylvania, the University of Pittsburgh, Temple University, Wayne State University, West Virginia University, and Yale University.[78] The program called for these fifteen hospitals to extend family planning services for the poor in their respective communities by contacting women who had recently delivered a child or undergone an abortion. The proposal stated as its explicit goal to reduce the number of teenage pregnancies and illegal abortions. "The medical school center, with its broad base of knowledge and medical manpower," the proposal declared, "has the greatest capability of all health care providers to direct a truly comprehensive family planning program."[79]

The administration of the program presented an odd arrangement in which the OEO provided funds and oversight; the Population Council administered the project; and the hospitals provided local services. The program expected to reach approximately seventy-eight thousand women in its first year. The OEO insisted that the Population Council disburse funds, administer the general program, and regulate the activities of the individual hospitals. This created immediate tensions between the OEO and the Population Council, which saw its role as one of coordination, not enforcement of OEO regulations.

The Population Council wanted to ensure administrative flexibility by having each school and hospital structure its own program within the general guidelines of the proposal. For example, medical schools at Case Western University, Emory University, Johns Hopkins University, the University of Florida, and West Virginia University worked closely with county health and local family planning clinics. In turn, Albert Einstein Hospital, New York Medical College, Temple University, and Wayne

State University coordinated their work with local departments of health and welfare, as well as local OEO programs. Many of the hospitals established sex education programs through local boards of education or local Neighborhood Youth Corps agencies. Each project, however, was expected to involve community neighborhood associations and to have community representatives on the board, as dictated by OEO policy.

The project was innovative, designed to incorporate a variety of approaches fitted to local situations. If successful, this demonstration—it was believed—could be expanded to hospitals and medical facilities across the country. Moreover, the program offered a solution to the lack of infrastructure that federal officials in HEW and OEO saw as detrimental to the implementation of a national family planning program. Through federal and nonprofit sector cooperation, it provided a means of addressing growing social problems related to poverty, teenage births, illegal abortions, and inadequate sex education.

Nonetheless, for all its promise the program got off to a rocky start, even before the grant was awarded. HEW officials had encouraged the Population Council to submit a proposal and had suggested that funds would be easily attainable, but HEW backed out of its promise when funds became tight. Instead funding was picked up by the OEO. When he heard that HEW had backed away from its commitment, Berelson angrily wrote Philip Lee at HEW that he was "disappointed and personally distressed" by the outcome. What angered him most, he said, was that HEW could have told him a year earlier that funding was not going to be forthcoming: "Yet what we were told yesterday we could have been told months ago, before we undertook all the risks, costs, and potential embarrassment to ourselves and the medical schools attendant upon the development of the overall proposal."[80]

Although the OEO picked up the proposal, expressing great enthusiasm for its potential, funding was further delayed by what the Population Council saw as bureaucratic incompetence on the part of the OEO. After one in a series of meetings, a Population Council representative reported in a confidential memorandum, "All in all, a worthless meeting, hastily arranged by HEW (even though considerable lead time was given) and without adequate preparation on their part." Upset by these bureaucratic delays, Berelson wrote Philip Lee at HEW, "I feel bound to report to you how disappointed and personally distressed I am at the outcome. In view of the department's statements about the high priority given to population and family planning matters, I had hoped that such difficulties by now would be overcome."[81] Berelson felt that the medical school group was being "used" by Katherine Oettinger, head of HEW family planning, to protect her budget from congressional cutbacks."[82] Finally, after nearly two years of planning and bureaucratic wrangling, the project was launched in June 1969 with a $1.9 million grant from the OEO under the new Nixon administration. A change in administrations did not improve relations between the Population Council and the OEO, however.

The guidelines set down by the OEO in awarding the grant proved to be tremendously burdensome for both the council and the hospitals involved in the project. Immediately problems arose between the council and the OEO when contract letters failed to go out to the medical schools from the OEO. While OEO officials assured the Population Council that it was understood that the council would be integral to all "policy deliberations," the lines between "policy" and "administration" quickly became blurred. The OEO criticized the council for inefficiency for not providing five copies of quarterly reports to be submitted by the individual hospital projects. For their part, the medical schools complained about having to issue monthly reports that were administratively costly and "useless." Moreover, once the programs got started, reimbursements from OEO were often delayed, so that the Population Council and the medical schools were placed in the position of having to cover $913,000 in reimbursements to the projects in the first year.[83] The OEO did not soothe feelings when it complained that medical schools were not including representatives from the local communities that were being served. As a consequence, the Population Council felt that it was caught in the middle between an overly demanding and inexplicably hostile federal bureaucracy that did not understand the projects and medical schools that felt they were not being supported. As one council officer wrote, we are getting it in "the neck from both sides. We get the chores of doing OEO's budget cutting dirty work and their administration."[84]

Meanwhile, the medical school programs were running into myriad problems in administering family planning projects in poor communities. Upset by the progress of the programs, the OEO commissioned a review of the project by the Westinghouse Learning Corporation. Issued in early 1970, the report was scathing in its criticism. Westinghouse reported that medical school officials particularly resented OEO restrictions on sterilization and abortion and that many of the projects had circumvented these restrictions. At the same time, many of the projects had met with "active resistance by racial and religious elements" in the community.[85]

For example, the report found that the Harlem Hospital and Columbia Presbyterian Hospital had come under attack by militant blacks for running a "genocidal program." In a pamphlet published by a community group calling itself the United Black Front, these hospitals were accused of not informing young blacks of the "dangerous after-effects of birth control pills or abortions." The pamphlet played on anti-Semitic prejudices by declaring that the hospitals were pursuing a policy set forth by the "'City Elders of Protocol" [*sic*] who feared a growing black population." The inflammatory pamphlet declared, "Under the supervision of Donald P. Swartz (a Zionist sympathizer) abortions are now being performed on our—you—black women of Harlem on a massive basis. . . . Dr. Swartz has successfully murdered more than 800 unborn Black babies in less than two months' time." Furthermore, the pamphlet declared, "Either we get off our rear ends, on our own, and fight for our survival as a people, or else just lay down."[86]

The report noted that other medical schools were experiencing similar problems in the black community. The University of Chicago Medical school project drew heavy criticism from community black leaders who raised similar charges of genocide. The Westinghouse report used these kinds of attacks as examples of how the medical schools had not fulfilled their obligation to foster support within their communities. The Population Council tended to minimize such criticisms. In a report to the OEO written shortly before the Westinghouse report was issued, the council observed that "Black Power" resistance to family planning was only "episodic, but nonetheless family planning needs to change its 'sales image' by broadening community representation."[87] Moreover, Westinghouse found that abortion and sterilization operations were being performed at a number of medical schools, clearly in opposition to federal guidelines that explicitly outlawed the use of federal funds for these kinds of operations. Typical of this resistance to OEO guidelines was the Johns Hopkins Medical School project headed by Hugh Davis, the inventor of the Dalkon Shield IUD. Under Davis, the project pursued an active policy of performing sterilizations and abortions. Davis noted that 16 percent of the women clients at his east Baltimore clinic had selected surgical sterilization. "Sterilization in the female," he declared, "has been made simple, economical and exceedingly convenient, and the acceptance in our patients is a testimonial to the ready availability and effectiveness of the procedure. We hope that improved methods of sterilization, abortion, and birth control will become more widely available."[88] Support for postpartum sterilization also found favor as a means of birth control at other project sites, including the Wayne State University family planning project in Detroit and the Emory University project in Atlanta.

These violations only exacerbated tensions between the OEO and the Population Council. OEO officials demanded that funds not be used for abortion and sterilization. In addition, OEO officials criticized projects for not including community representatives on their boards and for implementing projects that served income populations other than the poor. For example, the Emory University program provided family planning services for its college students using OEO funds. When the OEO tried to impose further conditions for renewing the grant in early 1970, the Population Council decided to terminate its contract with the OEO. Berelson informed the OEO that the council had "reluctantly" decided to withdraw from the program because of the "unacceptable conditions proposed by your staff."[89] Internally, the council decided that its role as middleman between the OEO and the hospitals had left the council in an untenable position. "Perhaps most serious of all," one staff member observed, "it siphons too much of our energy, talent, expertise, and attention onto domestic problems . . . [while] our real mission is overseas. There's already lots of domestic talent. If one were to hazard a guess from political trends it seems reasonable to expect the American overseas involvement will be increasingly questioned, while more money is focused on domestic problems. . . . If our overseas role is even questioned by foreigners in view of lack of effort in the U.S., we can defend ourselves (as well as it is possible to defend against a charge) by pointing to other agencies which are active in the United States."[90] Without the Population Council's support, the project was doomed and lasted for only another year.

By the mid-1970s both the Population Council and the Ford Foundation had withdrawn from direct involvement in domestic family planning programs. The painful history of working with federal administrators left a lingering bitterness. Within both organizations, officers concluded that active involvement in providing family planning services had detracted from their principal missions to provide basic medical and social science research. Their role was that of policy innovators, not program administrators. The expansion of public state and local family planning programs no longer necessitated the active involvement of the Population Council and the Ford Foundation. Moreover, foundation and council officers concluded that the time and money spent in developing these programs, and the energy given to squabbling with hostile federal bureaucrats, had been wasted.

Although the experiment in family planning programs conducted in the United States by the Ford Foundation and the Population Council proved to be short-lived, the federal government, nonetheless, continued to rely heavily on nonprofit organizations such as Planned Parenthood and private providers to maintain family planning services. This created a symbiotic relationship between the public and the voluntary sectors in American family planning policy. This arrangement meant, however, that federal restrictions would entail placing restraints on program development and flexibility. The emergence of an acrimonious debate over legalized abortion politicized the issue when Congress imposed restrictions on federal family planning funding. The politics of abortion created a maelstrom that affected both the Nixon administration and the population movement.

4

The Backlash
Roman Catholics, Contraceptives, Abortion, and Sterilization

In 1968, the year Richard M. Nixon won the presidency, opposition to federal family planning came mostly from those groups sympathetic to the Great Society. This is to say that the Roman Catholic Church hierarchy supported Johnson's War on Poverty, and for this reason it remained hesitant to condemn outright federal support of family planning programs. Thus, the bishops took a position that insisted that federal family programs should be "noncoercive" by informing clients about various contraceptive methods, including the rhythm method. Similarly, the African-American community, particularly nationalists and Black Muslims, accused federal family planning programs of being "genocidal" but generally accepted, albeit critically, federal social programs. Finally, a growing number of feminists, while demanding the right of women to control their bodies through contraception and abortion, criticized federal family programs as population control programs that targeted poor women and minorities without attacking the underlying social causes of poverty.

To understand the politics of family planning policy in 1970, specifically the abortion issue and international family planning (federal support for contraception never became a hot political issue domestically), this chapter examines Catholic opposition to artificial birth control and the constraints felt by the Catholic bishops about mounting direct opposition to federal family planning programs. More vociferous opposition to family planning came from black nationalists and radicals. The emergence of the abortion issue in the late 1960s, as reformers sought to liberalize abortion laws on the state level, mobilized opposition from the Catholic Church. The politics of abortion transformed the politics of population and family planning policy.

While the abortion issue tended to divide groups along ideological lines of liberal and conservative, it is worth noting that many gray areas remained in this ideological polarization. For example, many feminists spearheaded the campaign against federally funded involuntary sterilization of poor women, and many of these feminists, along with many blacks leaders, remained leery of the population control aspects of American international and domestic family planning programs.[1] No doubt, the abortion issue politicized federal family planning policy and broke bipartisan support for such programs. Ideological and party divisions, however, were never absolute. For example, many antiabortion Catholics remained progressive on social issues concerning welfare, health care, and civil rights.

The Roots of Catholic Opposition to Artificial Contraception and Abortion

Historically, the Roman Catholic Church opposed artificial contraception and abortion. It is one of the great ironies that a Roman Catholic, John Rock, played a central role in developing an oral contraceptive, "the pill," that allowed women to control reproduction effectively. The introduction of the pill in the 1960s transformed sexual relations between males and females, gender relations, and sexual consciousness in America. And, with oral contraception, sexual activity became separated from reproduction. This separation imparted a new independence to both women and men, married and single alike. Through oral contraception, single individuals engaged in sexual acts without the absolute fear of further entanglements brought about by the prospects of pregnancy.

Confronted by this contraceptive revolution, the American Catholic Church divided on its proper response. Many within the church welcomed the development of the pill as a technological advance that would enable couples to develop deeper personal relationships that would strengthen the bonds of marriage. Following on the heels of Vatican II, those who believed that the church should accept the pill thought it was a natural sequence to reforms within the church that gave greater emphasis to individual freedom, lay authority, and social responsibility for practicing Catholics. At the same time, the pill provided a means to address the worldwide population problem that most Catholics, including the authorities in the Vatican, accepted as a serious issue confronting the world. For those Catholics who insisted that Vatican II meant further reform within the church—theologically, liturgically, and socially—the pill offered an opportunity for the church to confront and embrace modernity. Because the church sanctioned natural family planning through the rhythm method, Roman Catholic doctrine appeared to accept at least the concept of family planning. Reformers within the church argued that oral contraception should be seen as a technical advance that guaranteed better results than natural family planning, the rhythm method. Furthermore, Catholic supporters of oral contraception were quick to point out that "traditionalists" often came from the celibate male clergy.

Others, however, worried about the theological consequences of any change in the historical position of the church concerning artificial contraception. For a church that based its doctrines on tradition and faith, any repudiation of a long-standing position when suddenly confronted with a new technology meant the subversion of the traditional church teaching. Theologically, the church opposed artificial contraception based on the principle that God had given to humanity the gift of life in divine likeness. This perception of the gift of life, embodying divine attributes, remained the basis of the church's opposition to contraception and abortion. To accept the pill meant the eventual acceptance of abortion, a tenet most Catholics found repulsive.

Besides theological considerations, traditionalists were less sanguine about the social consequences of the pill on promiscuous behavior, the degradation of women, and the breakdown of the family. Artificial contraception, they argued, meant the erosion of traditional values, the exploitation of women for sexual pleasure, the separation of individual freedom from social responsibility, and the splintering of corporate community.

In the early 1960s the lines between these two positions in the church were not sharply drawn. Sides had not hardened, so discussion remained open. Furthermore, most Catholics accepted the proposition that there was a world population crisis. Indeed, in 1965 the editors of the conservative magazine *National Review* ran a series of articles addressing the population explosion in which they took quite seriously the issue of the world's burgeoning population. The conservative editor of the magazine, William Buckley Jr., went so far as to declare that birth control was "not exclusively a moral issue."[2] For many, the question remained whether overpopulation should be addressed through economic development or through reduced population by means of birth control. Moreover, there was general agreement, as one leading Jesuit theologian observed in response to a Vatican inquiry about the status of birth control within the American church, that "a great many Catholics, both priests and laity, are thoroughly confused about the Church's teaching and their own obligations."[3] As a consequence, the American church hierarchy appeared unwilling to reject categorically the federal government's increasing involvement in family planning programs. Torn by their own doubts, able to understand the strengths and weaknesses of their own positions and those of their opponents, the American church looked to the Vatican to resolve the issue.

Many hoped that the Vatican might change its position on artificial contraception. Historically, Catholic moral teaching was explicitly hostile to the obstruction of the free passage of sperm to the egg and therefore condemned the use of condoms and diaphragms. The development of the pill raised the possibility, however, that "natural law" would not be infringed upon because oral contraception did not interfere with the free movement of sperm. This was exactly the point John Rock made in his widely reviewed *The Time Has Come: A Catholic Doctor's Proposal to End the Battle over Birth Control* (1963), in which he argued that the use of the pill by married Catholics did not violate church teaching because the pill created a regulatory "safe period" that did not interfere with the natural process of the sexual act.[4] In this way, Rock made the case for seeing the pill as a variant of the rhythm method, which the Vatican had approved as an acceptable means of birth control in 1951. Although Rock's position was disavowed by the hierarchy, Buckley observed, "he has not been exactly anathematized—precisely because the problem is undergoing a most intensive examination."[5]

The morality of contraception was not a new question for church authorities. The ancients believed that certain drinks and potions could be taken orally to prevent conception. Papyric evidence shows that upperclass Egyptian women of the Twelfth Dynasty (1850 B.C.E.) used crocodile's dung as a pessary, irrigated the vagina with honey and natron, and inserted a gumlike substance in the vagina. Contraceptives included lint tampons moistened with the juice from fermented tips of acacia shrubs, as well as drinking certain magical herbs for successive mornings. Many ancient Greek and Roman writers spoke of controlling population, including Aristotle, Plato, Hesiod, and Lucretius. Pliny the Elder (23–79 C.E.) recommended taking the small worms out of the body of a certain spider and attaching them with a piece of deerskin to a women's body before sunrise. Soranos of Ephesus (98–138 C.E.) recommended using pessaries impregnated with honey, or douching with certain fruit juices such as pomegranate and fig. Aetios of Amida (fl. 527–565) recommended that a women should wear a cat's testicles in a tube across her navel. Others claimed that spitting three times into a frog's mouth would prevent conception for a year, while still others thought that tossing a jasper pebble during coitus would prevent conception. Saint Albert the Great (1193–1280) recommended eating bees.[6] Whatever the efficacy of these practices, several of the church fathers, including Augustine, Hippolytus, Chrysostom, and Jerome, explicitly condemned such methods as immoral.

In the nineteenth century the Catholic Church continued to express opposition to contraception, but in France priests took the position that parishioners need not be corrected for practicing artificial contraception, if reform of their behavior seemed unlikely. The growth of Malthusian Leagues in the late nineteenth century, in which birth control was advocated as a panacea for major social ills and as a goal in itself, led the church to take a more hostile position toward contraception. This coincided with the European and American revival of Thomistic philosophy, based on the natural-law doctrines of Saint Thomas Aquinas. As a consequence, church officials began a vigorous campaign against contraception, instructing priests to warn against the sin of "onanism." Belgium's Cardinal Mercier, in a pastoral letter on the duties of married life, instructed confessors to declare onanism a sin. In 1913 the German church hierarchy condemned artificial contraception; this was followed by condemnation by the French hierarchy in 1919 and the U.S. hierarchy. This hostile movement against contraception found Vatican expression when Pope Pius XI promulgated *Casti Connubii* (1930), condemning birth control and sterilization.

In these same years, the church undertook a broad discussion of the theology of marriage and the family, although the concern with the breakdown of the family in America was not new. As early as 1879, Bishop John Ireland of St. Paul, Minnesota, had warned that "a moral chaos is threatening and the foundation of all social life, and the family is breaking up under violent passion." The rising divorce rate following the First World War elicited similar concerns, leading the archbishop of New Orleans to declare in 1930, "Unless the torrent of unbridled lust is stemmed, ... moral gangrene will set in sooner or later and destroy the Republic as it formerly destroyed powerful kingdoms and empires." Catholic spokesmen denounced individualism, socialism, feminism, materialism, and other "false philosophies" in the "neopagan" milieu of the modern world.

The perception that the survival of the family as an institution could no longer be taken for granted led the National Catholic Welfare Conference (NCWC) to organize a Family Life Bureau under its jurisdiction in 1930. While concerned with promoting Catholic family values through conferences, pamphlets, and education, as well as supporting reform legislation and social reform measures that promoted a "family living wage," the Family Life Bureau also opposed efforts by private or public groups to promote birth control.[7]

Nonetheless, by the end of the Second World War, Catholic attitudes toward methods of contraception were undergoing reevaluation. Although still opposed to artificial contraception, the church tempered its views of contraception in general. Indeed, in 1951 Pope Pius XII announced that the church accepted the systematic use of the sterile period (the rhythm method) for couples with a "serious economic, medical or social reason" for avoiding children. This acceptance of the rhythm method suggested an accommodation to contemporary married life and a recognition of the costs of raising a family, the growth in world population, and the longer time required to raise and educate children in a technically advanced society. This new position on birth control through the rhythm method, church theologians argued, did not constitute a deviation from moral tradition and the integrity of the moral act. In what many opponents saw as a fine splitting of hairs, the church maintained that couples could restrict intercourse to those periods that are considered most favorable for either the avoidance or promotion of pregnancy, in contrast to contraception, which constituted a deliberate attempt to inhibit or impede the normal physiological process. Under church doctrine, marriage did not oblige couples to engage in conjugal relations, and while marriage obligated couples to provide for the conservation of the human race, under certain conditions of a medical, eugenical, economic, or social nature, consenting couples were not obligated to have sexual intercourse, and thereby could forgo having children either for a time or throughout marriage.[8]

This change in church doctrine toward contraception—with its use of modern medical knowledge and its talk of "sterile periods"—proved to be a Pandora's box of theological and social problems that would be pried open by the introduction of the pill in the early 1960s. If sterile periods were acceptable as a means of preventing contraception, then was not the pill simply a means of prolonging this period for the benefit of couples who desired to space their children or prevent birth for medical, eugenic, economic, or social reasons? Was not the population crisis a just enough social cause to limit the number of children brought into this world? Would not the use of the pill enhance and strengthen Christian marriage, as the Anglican church had declared in 1960? Was the church's position that couples could not consciously inhibit life through contraception acceptable in a modern world?

These were the questions that confronted the church in the 1960s. The American church continued to maintain its position opposing contraception, but deep ambivalence was evident among the bishops, theologians, and the laity. Federal support for family planning presented another set of problems. While the Vatican initiated a review of its position on birth control in 1963, church officials in America felt restrained in publicly condemning federal family planning outright, even though they voiced their concerns to high government officials about increasing involvement and support of these programs. As a result, the American bishops through the NCWC tempered their opposition by insisting that government-sponsored family planning programs be noncoercive and provide information concerning the rhythm method.

American Catholic Bishops Cannot Decide
on Federal Family Planning Policy

This unwillingness to oppose outright or to mobilize against federal involvement in family planning stemmed from a variety of sources unique to the American Catholic experience. Of primary importance was the place of Roman Catholicism in a pluralistic democracy. Anti-Catholic sentiment had manifested itself throughout American history since the founding of the colonies, finding expression in the nativist movements during the antebellum and postbellum periods in the nineteenth century. The election of 1928, in which Al Smith, a Catholic, received the Democratic party nomination, invigorated anti-Catholic feelings, evident in Ku Klux Klan anti-Smith rallies at the time. Reaction to this vitriolic anti-Catholic crusade, however, led to improved interfaith relations, and during Franklin Roosevelt's administration more Catholics were appointed to office than ever before. This close association with the Democratic party, in which Catholic social justice philosophy was translated into New Deal liberal philosophy, would have important consequences for the American Catholic Church as it basked in its new acceptance in democratic society.

Nonetheless, Father Charles E. Coughlin's anti-New Deal movement, his willingness to associate communism with the New Deal, and his open anti-Semitism after 1938 reawakened hostility to Catholicism. Furthermore, the church's support of the pro-Franco nationalists in the Spanish civil war only led to greater alarm among liberals. Harold Ickes, Lewis Mumford, and Van Wyck Brooks individually expressed dismay about the specter of "political Catholicism." Indeed, Brooks told Mumford that he was losing sleep over Catholic influence in the nation: "For the Catholic Church is growing so bold in this country. It defeats every measure for decent living."[9] Similarly, journalist George Seldes equated Catholicism and fascism in Spain and Germany in his *Catholic Crisis* (1939).[10]

Anxious to show that Catholics accepted democratic culture in a pluralistic society, the bishops worried about a perception that the Roman Catholic Church was trying to impose its theological views on artificial conception on the electorate.[11] Most bishops did not want to be perceived as reactionary; indeed, more positively, they wanted the American Catholic Church to be seen as making a progressive contribution to society. Furthermore, Catholic social justice teaching, articulated by figures such as Father John A. Ryan, an enthusiastic New Dealer, and others, had been widely accepted in the American church.[12] Finally, the Catholic charities benefited from Great Society programs as recipients of major educational and community grants. Catholic bishops prefaced any criticism of federal family planning programs with strong affirmations that they supported Johnson's War on Poverty and the Democratic party's liberal social agenda, including civil rights, equal opportunity, and social programs. Surely this support was genuine, but the bishops also worried that if they criticized family planning programs on religious grounds, opponents would raise the issue of the Catholic Church receiving federal funds as a religious body.

At the same time, church officials had become increasingly aware of the lobbying campaign by the population movement to involve the federal government in family planning. At each step of the way, the bishops raised concerns about this trend, although any barricade they attempted to erect to prevent this onslaught was easily surmounted. As early as 1959, largely in response to the Draper report, an internal memorandum had circulated in the NCWC, the official organization of the bishops, warning of a "systematic concerted effort to convince the United States public opinion, legislators, and policy makers that the United States national agencies, as well as international bodies, should provide public funds, support, and assistance in promoting artificial birth prevention." The memorandum reiterated the church's opposition to birth control on the principles of natural law but stressed that "economic development and progress are best promoted by creating conditions favorable to development." It urged the church to support immigration and food production as a counterstrategy and not to "ignore or minimize the problem of population pressure."[13] At the same time, a number of articles began to appear in the Catholic press discussing the Catholic position on world population.[14]

In early 1961, aware of a lobbying effort in the United Nations for greater international involvement in family planning assistance programs, the apostolic delegate representing the Vatican in the United States wrote to the Reverend Paul Tanner at the NCWC to "propagandize by every legitimate means the Catholic view on this matter." Tanner subsequently arranged a meeting with Richard Gardner, assistant secretary of state for international organizations, to discuss the church's position on family planning in the United Nations. Gardner assured him that UN involvement in family planning programs was being pushed by the Scandinavians, and "in all frankness, the United States will oppose any such measures."[15]

The emergence of other family planning proposals in the Kennedy administration, including a National Institutes of Health (NIH) report in 1962 that called for more research on the physiology and control of human reproduction and the proposed Fulbright amendment in 1963 that would have allowed the use of federal funds for international population control programs, brought growing alarm to the church hierarchy.[16] These actions within an administration headed by a practicing Roman Catholic, John F. Kennedy, led the bishops to appraise their strength for what they saw as an impending battle over the issue. In a confidential report to the bishops, NCWC staff member William Consedine provided a candid assessment of the situation. He began his report by observing that the only barrier to the acceptance of federal support for birth control programs domestically was the "wide recognition of the implacable opposition of the Church to such programs." He noted, however, that "if the position of the Church was reversed there is little reason to doubt that affirmative federal support of birth control measures would be enacted reasonably promptly." Nonetheless, he warned that "Catholics are still a minority, but an increasingly effective and articulate one."

This minority status, he continued, necessarily produces only minority representation in Congress, including ninety Catholics in both major parties in the House and twelve Catholics in the Senate. Nevertheless, he noted that Catholic opposition had only forced the NIH to revise its report calling for greater research into reproduction and population, and that the Fulbright amendment had been enacted, with some modification, over the protest of the church. Furthermore, the District of Columbia was about to open its first birth control center using federal funds. Consedine drew what he considered an inevitable conclusion: "These federal developments in the birth control picture show a progressive theme of increasing acceptance of pertinent programs by responsible officials of our government despite the doctrine of the Church. But absent that restraint it takes no imagination to visualize the probability of future activity."[17] The report suggested that already the issue was a losing one, although the church was prepared to resist as best it could.

Signs of change on the contraception issue became increasingly visible with the advent of the Johnson administration. In the spring of 1965 the U.S. Supreme Court ruling in *Griswold v. Connecticut* reversed Connecticut's anticontraception law of 1879.[18] In 1967 further challenges to the distribution of contraceptives by nonphysicians came when activist and Sunnen pharmaceutical salesperson William R. Baird was arrested in Massachusetts after handing a package of Emko vaginal foam to a young, unmarried women following a lecture at Boston University. The Supreme Court overturned his conviction in 1971. Catholic church authorities accepted these decisions without protest after making a conscious decision that Catholic doctrine should not be imposed on the general public through legislation.[19] Little did Catholics realize in 1965 that the *Griswold* decision, with its privacy doctrine, would become the basis for legalizing abortion in the country.

Catholic bishops also realized that many mainline Protestant churches accepted birth control.[20] Thus, the church wanted to tack a careful course of not pressing the issue of contraception too publicly, while at the same time putting up some resistance to federal support of family planning. The question remained just how much resistance to give.

Johnson's State of the Union Message in 1965, the continuation of the Gruening hearings begun in 1963, and the issuance of new family planning guidelines by the Office of Economic Opportunity (OEO) led the Catholic bishops to clarify their stance on federally supported contraception programs. Johnson's call in his State of the Union Message for greater awareness of the population problem caught the bishops by surprise, but they took it as a clear sign that the administration planned to move ahead on family planning if there was not a "hue and cry" from the Catholic community. Monsignor Francis T. Hurley wrote to Monsignor Paul Tanner that a visit from "someone high in the government" (the name was not revealed) reported that Johnson's reference to population in his address was a "trial balloon." Hurley urged the bishops to respond to the address, but it turned out that they were divided on exactly how to respond. When Monsignor John C. Knott called the cataclysmic projections on future population growth "pure speculation," he was roundly criticized by Catholic social scientists for lacking "sophistication" and embarrassing the church.[21]

The Gruening hearings presented other problems for the church when the committee announced that John Rock had been called to testify. The opinion of the NCWC was that Gruening wanted to create controversy by having a Catholic testify at his hearings and would "welcome an attack from some churchmen. This would give him an opportunity to respond during the public hearings." Privately, Speaker of the House John McCormack had assured the bishops that there was little chance of any legislation coming out of these hearings. The bishops' conference recommended that "any discussion of public policy should be avoided to prevent showing division in public."[22] When William B. Ball, general counsel of the Pennsylvania Catholic Welfare Committee, was called before the Gruening committee, the situation changed immediately.

Although Ball supported Great Society social programs, he was a hardliner who recommended that the bishops take a strong stand on the issue of federal family planning. Not everyone among the bishops or the NCWC staff agreed with him, as would become increasingly apparent. When Ball finally testified in late August 1965, his testimony upset many within the hierarchy and its staff. Speaking on behalf of the Pennsylvania Catholic Welfare Committee, Ball made an unusual case *against* federally supported family planning on the basis of individual civil liberties and *choice*. He declared that while he supported the right of the federal government to fund population research, he opposed federally supported family planning because it posed "serious dangers to civil liberty, while offering no genuine prospect of relieving the problems of poverty, crowding, and disease."

He maintained that any government involvement in family planning would be naturally coercive, declaring that "if the power and prestige of government is placed behind programs in providing birth control service to the poor, coercion necessarily results and violations of human privacy become inevitable." What heightened the potential for inquiry into the personal affairs of the individual, he continued, is the necessity of collecting data respecting sexual life or marital relationships. He warned, "It is easy indeed to be mesmerized by concepts of social planning just as it is natural to want the least and shortest steps to solve the worst and most complex of our problems. But we must remember that the planning of families is a thing radically different from the planning of highways, and the government control of birth may come close to being government control of life. We think that this is no place for government." Of course, underlying his and the church's concern with the coercive aspects of family planning was the abortion issue. He declared that "racial eugenicism . . . is inescapable in the proposal. . . . As sterilization and abortion increase in a society, respect for life decreases."[23]

Ball's statement was a powerful enunciation of the church's traditional opposition to federal family planning. Immediately after Ball's testimony, however, a visible backlash within the hierarchy became apparent. A few minutes before his appearance before the committee, Gruening later reported, Ball informed the senator that he was speaking on behalf of the NCWC. This was not Gruening's understanding, and he informed the NCWC that he hoped Father Dexter Hanley's testimony, which had preceded Draper's, would be afforded similar treatment by Catholic news services because it was more moderate (and sympathetic) in its approach to federal family planning efforts. Gruening emphasized, however, that "the last thing" he wanted was to "create controversy with the church."[24]

Controversy was not to be avoided, however. Many within the bishops' conference felt that Ball had been too adamant in his opposition to federal family planning. Indeed, the day following Ball's testimony, Monsignor Tanner, later bishop of St. Augustine, Florida, was quoted in the *Philadelphia Evening Bulletin* as describing Ball's statement as "good," but one that did not represent the view of the NCWC. "We, as Catholics," he told the press, "have no right to impose our views on these people. This is quite a new issue that we will have to resolve carefully." Later, when criticized for appearing to dissociate the NCWC from Ball, Monsignor Tanner claimed that the press had distorted what he had said, but meanwhile other Catholic legal scholars took issue with Ball's position. Robert B. Fleming from the State University of New York, Buffalo, School of Law, wrote Ball that it seemed ludicrous that because of the danger of coercion it was necessary to bar all public programs. This seemed to him a position that largely sacrifices the poor their freedom to "untrammeled moral choice."[25]

Further divisions within the church became evident as the bishops intervened to restrict OEO guidelines allowing for community action family planning programs. In meeting with OEO officials, the bishops appeared to present a unanimous position on the issue, but behind the scenes the bishops were having problems preparing a public statement. Furthermore, NCWC staff members offering legal advice grew increasingly wary of Ball's involvement on this issue.

Ball voiced within the church a call for complete, unrestrained opposition to federally supported family planning. A few months after his testimony, he wrote a lengthy memorandum to the bishops outlining three possible courses of action, including an "ecumenical" approach that offered civil peace and did not jeopardize antipoverty programs by accepting federally supported family planning unconditionally; a "limited opposition" approach that accepted family planning programs provided they banned coercion, protected privacy, limited programs to the married, and excluded sterilization and abortion; and a "full opposition" approach that categorically refused to endorse any federal involvement in family planning. He recommended the latter position. Although he supported the War on Poverty, he urged a campaign of full opposition. He warned that any compromise on this issue meant the proliferation of family planning programs that would inevitably include sterilization and abortion.[26] Nonetheless, a growing sentiment within the NCWC favored the "limited opposition" approach that accepted federally funded family planning programs, provided they remained "noncoercive." Differences restrained the bishops within the conference in their relations with the administration and their involvement with the OEO.

As 1965 drew to a close, William Ball and William Consedine met with Sargent Shriver to discuss the OEO's proposed regulations concerning federally funded family planning. Both Ball and Consedine assured Shriver that the bishops "strongly supported" the administration's antipoverty program and were "anxious" to help in any way possible to ensure its success. Nonetheless, they told Shriver that the bishops held deep reservations about OEO support for family planning. Ball proved to be even more emphatic when he raised questions concerning the OEO's statutory right to fund birth control through the agency. Shriver replied that he was "under pressure" from Alan Guttmacher and Planned Parenthood to finance abortion and sterilization projects, and so he was "adamant" to push ahead with OEO funding of family planning that specifically excluded abortion and sterilization. Ball and Consedine left the meeting with Shriver's assurances that he would keep in contact with the bishops.[27]

Ball was convinced that an argument could be made that the OEO was prevented under its founding statute from funding any family planning program. Moreover, he agreed with conservative scholar Russell Kirk that family planning programs were racist. Kirk had privately written Ball, exclaiming that "los liberales" were "afflicted by a subconscious death-urge, which makes them smile on all diminution of life." Although liberals professed a love of the blacks, Kirk wrote, they are "distressed by the colored man's mere existence, because he's different. . . . These things cannot be confessed to one's own liberal self, of course."[28]

Among the bishops, however, there was a growing confusion over what course to take. The bishops had begun working on a public statement on family planning, but deep divisions quickly manifested themselves within the bishops' conference. At an informal meeting to discuss the OEO's involvement in family planning, Monsignor Francis Hurley, then on the NCWC staff and later to become archbishop of Anchorage, raised a series of rhetorical questions that revealed that many bishops did not want to go too far out on a limb on this matter. He rhetorically asked, "Is not the situation similar to what we said thirty or forty years ago about education not being the federal government's concern? Is there something intrinsically dangerous in government's involvement in family planning? Are we in a position to say that Planned Parenthood has not a right to be in involvement in the poverty program?" NCWC staff members concurred by noting that the bishops should not issue a statement until the pope issued his statement on family planning. In turn, the NCWC staff recommended that Catholics needed to get involved on the local level and that "each bishop will have to handle the issue as he sees fit in his own diocese."[29]

Moreover, Patrick O'Boyle, archbishop of Washington, D.C., and head of the NCWC, received legal advice that Ball's position was untenable. In a careful analysis of the Economic Opportunity Act of 1964, attorney Paul Connolly noted that it was "one of the broadest delegations of authority to a federal administration imaginable." Yet for this "very reason," he argued, this statute offers "bountiful opportunities" to Catholic welfare agencies to receive federal funding. Connolly recommended, "Rather than to attack the use of public funds for birth control, it would seem to me advisable to participate with all proper agencies in the community seeking a solution to the problem of parental irresponsibility, short of advocating the generalized use of contraceptives. I think the general sense of the community is to take positive action to limit childbearing, especially among those who cannot care for their offspring and whose children become public charges." He concluded that "prudence would dictate that the church not appear intransigent" and "cooperate as far as it can within its principles toward alleviating this obvious social evil."[30]

While the bishops attempted to work out their position on birth control, they came under severe attack from the press in late 1965 when Monsignor Knott, representing the NCWC Family Life Bureau, publicly criticized a White House Conference on Health held in early November for being "controlled by advocates of contraception, sterilization and abortion." Columnists Rowland Evans and Robert Novak reported that Knott's attack was a "last-ditch effort against federal birth control programs by conservative elements in the Catholic Church (which opposes all birth control devices)." Evans and Novak reported that not only were officials in "high government places" upset, but "dominant liberal forces in the NCWC itself were unhappy."[31] Taken aback by the criticism, a delegation from the NCWC met with Joseph Califano and Douglass Cater in an attempt to smooth things over.[32]

In this heated context, the bishops felt impelled to issue a public statement concerning their views on birth control, but here was the problem: Exactly what should they say? An NCWC draft statement, "Family Planning and Public Policy," which the conference had been working on since early 1965, did not meet with universal agreement either from the bishops or the NCWC staff, even though the statement took a moderate position. Declaring that family planning was "commendable," particularly when "motivated by considerations of health and welfare of mothers and children," and granting that most Americans "generally agree that family planning is morally justifiable," the statement reiterated the church's position that Catholics endorsed continence which takes advantage of infertile periods. The bishops urged that poverty should be alleviated through "education, training and opportunity for gainful work at good wages." The statement nonetheless accepted that "where a consensus exists as to the need for public assistance in family planning, the government may respond to the request of its citizens for such assistance." The only stipulation of church support for these programs was that family planning not be "advocated" by the government and that funding should not include abortions or sterilization.[33]

This position was markedly different from what William Ball was pressing for in his meeting with OEO officials. Yet even this moderate position in the draft that circulated among the conference proved unsatisfactory to many liberal bishops and church theologians. For example, in a meeting in late 1965, Father Dexter Hanley, Georgetown University theologian, openly declared that the issue of privacy espoused by Ball was "not honest." Furthermore, he told the bishops that the American church needed to acknowledge that "the population is at this moment too heavily concentrated for the economy to support. We also need to acknowledge that, at this moment, some families have more children than their means or physical health will allow them to raise and educate properly." This is a matter of the "common good," which the church simply could not ignore. Ball attempted to rebut Hanley's argument by maintaining that "coercion is virtually implicit in government birth control programs; choice is illusionary especially for the largely illiterate poor and Negroes."[34]

The tide was running against Ball and his supporters, however. As 1965 drew to a close, James Francis Cardinal McIntyre, archbishop of Los Angeles, wrote to Archbishop O'Boyle to recommend that Ball be replaced. He remarked, "In fact, on the question of birth control, I feel that there are others of comparable ability."[35]

Further discussion of the draft statement "Family Planning and Public Policy" by Catholic theologians and other bishops revealed more dissension. As theologians looked at the issue, it became increasingly difficult to make a case for a position that declared contraception immoral but allowed the church to accept and even participate in public programs that involved family planning. For example, John Courtney Murray, S.J., the leading Catholic authority on church-state relations, argued that "contraception today has become an issue of private, not public, morality." It was an issue that went beyond what Saint Thomas had faced, so the church needed to "reconsider our premises."[36]

His views expressed the majority opinion of theologians who confronted the philosophical labyrinth of the church-state relations. For Catholic theologians, of whatever stripe, the issue was painful for a church that had striven for acceptance in modern America. Could the church oppose contraception privately, and then condone federal programs supporting it? If the church's stance derived from moral principles applied to society in general, why was it wrong for the church to impose those standards through legislation? The proponents of federal family planning did not hesitate in imposing their morality on the public, but was the church to be prevented from entering into a public discussion only because its views were deemed religious and theological? Finally, and most fundamentally, what should the relationship be between the church and state be in a democratic society? These were not simple questions, even for the most learned of theologians.

Few bishops or theologians came out squarely in favor of the church's supporting federal family planning. Most recommended either a clearer formulation of the church's position or that the statement be dropped altogether. And, of these two alternatives, most recommended that it be dropped.[37] Led by Laurence Cardinal Shehan of Baltimore and Joseph Cardinal Ritter of St. Louis, the bishops' conference decided not to issue a public statement.[38] As Francis Hurley reported to the Catholic Relief Services, "The bishops were opposed to any public statement and not at all in favor of raising the question of public policy aspects of birth control." He noted that the conservatives wanted a stronger statement, but they could not get it.[39]

Instead, in late August 1965, a summer that had seen the worst racial riots in the nation's history, O'Boyle delivered on his own a widely circulated homily on the Second Epistle of Saint Paul to Timothy 4:3–4, "The time will come when men will not listen to sound teaching, but with ears itching, will pile up for themselves teachers who suit their pleasures. They will turn their ears away from truth to fable." He began by declaring that Americans lived in "extraordinary times," witnessing the "long, hot summer" of tragic riots and bitter recriminations and an escalating war in Southeast Asia. Yet he noted that "the fresh winds of aggioramento"— Vatican II—had swept through the church, and "a remarkable Congress, working in close harmony with the Chief Executive, has courageously attacked such previously insoluble issues as civil rights (including voting rights), aid to education, and the paradox of poverty." Yet he warned that while the church supported the War on Poverty, it could not support linking the population problem and birth control to social welfare programs. Declaring that the church accepted the recent Supreme Court decision overturning the Connecticut birth control law, he said that the logical consequence was that "if the government was enjoined by this decision from forbidding this practice, it logically follows that it likewise should be forbidden to promote it." He urged that the government remain neutral on the issue.[40]

Without a public statement, individual bishops were on their own to tackle the birth control issue, as O'Boyle had done. The NCWC, although not willing to issue a public statement at this point, urged action on the local level. As Hurley recommended to John E. Molan, head of Catholic Charities in New Hampshire, "I think if you take a very firm approach at the start you will stand the best chance of stopping the question from even coming up. In some communities that have approved birth control programs, part of the reason has been that Catholic spokesmen were too quiet."[41] Most decided to ignore the issue. A few intervened, however.

For example, Archbishop William E. Cousins supported Dr. John J. Brennan, an active member of the Milwaukee Catholic Physicians Guild, in opposing the participation of Planned Parenthood in a community action program.[42] In Philadelphia, Archbishop John Krol tacitly supported Cecil B. Moore, head of the local chapter of the National Association for the Advancement of Colored People (NAACP), in attacking a PPFA proposal for a birth control program as "racial suicide."[43] In Trenton, New Jersey, the local antipoverty program rejected a PPFA proposal to seek sixty thousand dollars in federal funds for a family planning project following vigorous opposition from the Catholic Welfare Bureau.[44]

These isolated community efforts gave the appearance of a united opposition by the Catholic Church to federal family planning, but behind the scenes there were even doubts about this strategy. Indeed, a clear shift had become apparent among the bishops in 1966. Ball continued to urge that the bishops make a public issue of HEW/OEO funding guidelines. He believed the administration might be less intransigent in a midterm election year. His recommendations, however, met quiet resistance within the NCWC.[45] Walter W. Curtis, the bishop of Bridgeport, Connecticut, noted that "not everyone in the NCWC department agrees with Mr. Ball." Instead, he suggested that Father Hanley's more liberal position be privately circulated to provide an alternative to Ball.[46] Moreover, in a lengthy staff meeting at the NCWC, both bishops and staff voiced concerns with Ball's confrontational approach. Monsignor Knott found that Catholic couples were resisting marital advice from priests because there was "popular confusion over the Church's stand on birth control." He noted further that "many a confessor said that they have almost given up" on the birth control issue. Furthermore, he maintained that the federal government was not promoting birth control but only giving permission to use funds if the local area concurred.

Others agreed. Monsignor George Higgins noted that if constitutional or legal issues were raised, this might force Congress to enact clear authorizing legislation for OEO policy. NCWC counsel Consedine raised the question of how the church could be most effective in the policy arena: "By condoning what is happening? Or, by a fight of total opposition?" He answered that personally he felt that "we could be more effective by conditioning what is happening."[47] Clearly, there was uncertainty within the American Catholic bishops. In effect, the buck was being passed up to Rome, where a select commission had been meeting since 1963. When they received Rome's answer in 1968, many of the bishops did not like what they heard.

Humanae Vitae *Creates a Furor*

Several months before his death, Pope John XXIII convened a small commission of theologians, social scientists, and physicians in October 1963 to prepare a Vatican statement on the "population question." At its first meeting, the commission agreed that it should move beyond the demographic question and address the church's message on marriage and artificial birth control. After lengthy preparation, a new commission was formed in March 1964 to include thirty-four laypersons, nine members of the clergy, and twelve members of religious orders. Headed by Alfredo Cardinal Ottaviani, a seventy-five-year-old, conservative Italian prelate, the commission included several American delegates: André Helegers, a physician at Johns Hopkins University; John Cavanagh, an American physician living in Rome; and Patrick and Patricia Crowley, founders of the Christian Family Movement, a lay social activist organization based in Chicago.[48]

The commission opened a year later in Rome on March 24, 1965, with legal scholar John T. Noonan, a thirty-two-year-old bachelor, providing a lecture on the history of the church's position on contraception. Looking over his large, horn-rimmed glasses, Noonan spoke for two hours before concluding, "The matter is open enough to deserve the attentive study of the church in light of new scientific, social and historical understanding."[49] His audience understood the underlying message immediately: the church's position on contraception had changed over time. Perhaps the commission should reconsider the official doctrine in light of recent history.

Over the course of the next two years, the commission debated the issue of artificial contraception. Reams of documentation were produced, with clear sides being drawn. Conservatives presented a strong case for maintaining the church's traditional opposition against artificial contraception. Father John Ford, a leading American Jesuit theologian, summarized the traditionalist position when he declared: "Contraception (that is *contra*-ception) involves a will which is turned against new life. . . . It is against this life, in advance, that is, against its coming to being. Your conception is your very origin, your link to the community of living persons before you, the first of all gifts received from your parents, your first relationship with God as he stretched out his finger to touch you. To attack it is to attack fundamental human good, to intrude on God's domain."[50] Others argued for a new relationship between married couples, viewing sexual relations free from the burden of conception as strengthening Christian marriage and fostering the care of children brought into the world. In the end, the reformers carried the day. In the spring of 1967 the commission brought out its final report recommending acceptance of artificial contraception.

Now a debate began in earnest as both sides of the contraception issue lobbied the Vatican to have their positions accepted. Controversy came when a Dutch priest leaked the Vatican commission's majority report to the press. Picked up by an American journalist, Gary MacEoin, the report was reprinted in the Catholic weekly *National Catholic Reporter* on April 15, after the French daily *Le Monde* refused to publish it. The report quickly made headline news in America and Europe, causing a furor on both sides of the Atlantic.[51]

In the midst of this furor, on April 17, 1967, two days after the *National Catholic Reporter* released the commission's report, Charles Curran, a leading Catholic theologian and advocate for artificial contraception, was fired by the board of trustees at Catholic University of America, thereby nullifying the theology faculty's unanimous recommendation that he receive tenure. The ensuing controversy revealed the intense passions within the church over artificial birth control. Little did the trustees foresee the ferocity of protest that their decision would have when two thousand students, joined by the faculty, went out on strike. After intense media attention and a week of student protests, the administration backed down. Archbishop O'Boyle announced, "The board of trustees has voted to abrogate its decision."[52]

After over a year of fervent debate in the Vatican, on July 29, 1968, Pope Paul VI issued *Humanae Vitae*, which reaffirmed the church's opposition to artificial contraception. The encyclical letter noted that great changes had occurred in worldwide rapid population growth, increased exigencies both in the economic field and in education that make the proper education of "an elevated number of children difficult today," the place of women in society, and, above all, the "stupendous progress in the domination and rational organization of the forces of nature." These very changes, the encyclical stated, give rise to profoundly new questions concerning conjugal relations with "respect to the harmony between husband and wife and to their mutual fidelity."

"The problem of birth, like every other problem regarding human life," the encyclical continued, "is to be considered, beyond partial perspectives—whether of the biological or psychological, demographic or sociological orders—in the light of an integral vision" of humankind. In upholding this "total" vision, the encyclical maintained that "conjugal love reveals its true nature and nobility when it is considered in its supreme origin, God, who is love." Conjugal love required "responsible parenthood" and implied a "more profound relationship to the objective moral order established by God." Responsible parenthood meant that "husband and wife recognize fully their own duties toward God, toward themselves, toward the family, and toward society. . . . In the task of transmitting life, therefore, they are not free to proceed completely at will, as if they could determine in a wholly autonomous way the honest path to follow; but they must conform their activity to the creative intention of God, expressed in the very nature of marriage and of its acts, and manifested by the constant teaching of the Church." In conformity with this vision, the encyclical reiterated the traditional church position that "direct interruption of the generative process already begun," through abortion, even for therapeutic reasons, was "absolutely excluded." Equally excluded was direct sterilization, whether permanent or temporary.

Most important, the encyclical opposed artificial contraception because it deliberately induced infecundity. In an argument that later critics viewed as overly scholastic, the encyclical distinguished artificial contraception from "natural" family planning. Artificial contraception deliberately prevented conception, while the method of "natural" family planning was only abstinence. The difference between natural family planning and artificial contraception was this: "In the former, the married couple makes legitimate use of a natural disposition; in the latter, they impede the development of natural processes."

The encyclical ended by calling for the creation of "an atmosphere favorable to education in chastity, that is to the triumph of healthy liberty over license by means of respect for moral order." The encyclical declared—and here lay the heart of its social concern—that "everything in the modern media of social communications which leads to sense excitation and unbridled customs, as well as every form of pornography and licentious performances, must arouse the frank and unanimous reaction of all those who are solicitous for the progress of civilization and the defense of the common good of the human spirit."[53]

The American reaction in to the encyclical was severe. *U.S. News and World Report* described the pope's pronouncement as creating a "crisis of authority" within the church.[54] Hugh Moore found the encyclical "incredible" and "disastrous."[55] Father John O'Brien at the University of Notre Dame wrote Moore that "the vast bulk of Catholics in the United States supported population control" and encouraged him to undertake a campaign to "send millions of counter-letters to the Pope." Working with O'Brien, Moore organized a massive counterattack. A petition signed by twenty-six hundred scientists criticizing *Humanae Vitae* was published in the *New York Times*, the *Wall Street Journal*, and the liberal Catholic journal *Commonweal*. O'Brien arranged to have the statement translated into German, Spanish, and French, and it was sent to every American bishop as well as to key bishops throughout the world.[56]

Truth be told, American Catholics did not need much encouragement. The Los Angeles Association of Laymen openly declared its opposition to the encyclical, proclaiming, "We will not leave the church. We will not be thrown out." John Noonan and six other Americans on the Vatican commission called a news conference to announce that the encyclical was not infallible and that Catholics should follow their own consciences.[57] At Catholic University, professors in the Department of Theology, joined by sixty local parish priests, signed an open letter protesting the decision, leading Cardinal O'Boyle to suspend twenty professors and the priests.[58] Although the suspension of the professors was overturned by the bishops' conference on grounds of academic freedom, the parish priests were not given the same due process. Within six months the majority of them left the priesthood. The auxiliary bishop of St. Paul-Minneapolis resigned in protest, although many claimed he left the priesthood because he wanted to marry and used birth control as an excuse to do so. In Baltimore the crisis was handled differently when Lawrence Cardinal Shehan carried on private conversations with fifty-five dissenting parish priests, convincing them to uphold *Humanae Vitae* in the pulpit, the confessional, and the classroom. (Or so he said. In fact, he turned a blind eye. Nevertheless, his actions won universal praise.[59])

The euphoria that had flourished after Vatican II in many American Catholic circles had been shattered. Parish numbers fell as many Catholics left the church. Furthermore, there was open rebellion concerning the encyclical among Catholic women. In 1955 only 30 percent of Catholic women used some form of artificial birth control; by 1965 the rate had increased to about 51 percent, and by 1970 the level had reached 68 percent. Catholic sociologist Andrew Greeley found that same year that only 15 percent of priests demanded conformity of their penitents concerning church doctrine of contraception.[60] This trend toward secularization was further revealed when Charles Westoff, a Princeton University demographer, reported shortly afterward that only 9.5 percent of white, married Catholic women, aged eighteen to thirty-nine, conformed with church teaching on birth control by never using any form of contraception or by using the rhythm method only. Westoff concluded that except for sterilization, Catholic and non-Catholic contraceptive practices were "quite similar," and "the wide gulf between official Catholic doctrine and the birth control behavior of Catholics can only deepen in the next few years."[61]

The end result of these controversies was that a practical victory for academic freedom in Catholic higher education had been won at Catholic University. Furthermore, within the church the right of married couples to exercise individual conscience on birth control became a de facto policy. Nonetheless, the theological critique of natural-law reasoning severely undermined a fundamental principle of Catholic social thought and a key element of the church as a shared moral community.[62] This was to have profound implications for the church when it confronted the issues of sterilization and abortion.

Abortion Divides the Nation

Even before the Supreme Court legalized abortion in the *Roe v. Wade* decision on January 22, 1973, a movement to reform abortion laws had emerged in the mid-1960s.[63] Although not well organized, this movement formed a loose coalition of women's groups, population movement activists and organizations, and single-issue abortion advocates.[64] Nonetheless, prior to *Roe* a grassroots movement, focused primarily on state-level legislation, had emerged.

A primary impetus to this campaign came from stricter enforcement of nineteenth-century abortion laws by local officials beginning in the 1940s. Under abortion laws enacted in the late nineteenth century, all states allowed exceptions for therapeutic abortions performed in order to save a woman's life. Nonetheless, physicians disagreed on the conditions that mandated a therapeutic abortion and on methods. Furthermore, current scholarship indicates that abortion was more widespread and accepted than previously thought. Unaware of widespread abortion practices in hospitals and medical clinics, church officials largely ignored the issue of therapeutic abortions in hospitals.[65] Nonetheless, in the first half of the twentieth century medical therapeutic abortions appeared to be a relatively common operation.

Recently scholars have discovered surveys that reveal a surprisingly large number of women having undergone abortion operations. For example, the birth control clinic operated by Margaret Sanger in New York found in a survey of ten thousand working-class clients in the late 1920s that 20 percent of all pregnancies had been intentionally aborted. Similarly, a comprehensive survey of women in a Bronx birth control clinic in 1931 and 1932 found that 35 percent of its clients had had at least one abortion. Frederick J. Taussig, the leading expert on abortion in this period, estimated that there were at least 681,000 abortions per year in the United States.[66] In fact, in the depression years of the 1930s, as historian Leslie Reagan has found, "women had abortions on a massive scale," usually performed by doctors in clinical conditions. A high percentage of these abortions occurred among more affluent women, but poorer and working-class women had a large number as well.[67] The Kinsey Institute found that upper- and middle-class women aborted 24.3 percent of their pregnancies in 1930 and 18.3 percent in 1935. This evidence suggests that the medical profession accepted a de facto expansion of therapeutic abortions.

In the 1940s, however, local prosecutors and the police cracked down on therapeutic abortions, while at the same time hospitals began enforcing rigorous guidelines for what was considered therapeutic. The repercussions of these changes quickly became evident: those who received safe, legal, therapeutic abortions in hospitals were mostly white women with private health insurance; illegal abortions appear to have increased, creating a new level of secrecy. This repressive climate occurred at the very time that growing numbers of women entered college and the workplace, leading them to postpone childbearing.[68] This crackdown on therapeutic abortion in the two decades preceding the 1960s set the context for the movement to repeal abortion laws.

In the 1940s and 1950s abortion advocates pursued a deliberately conservative approach by appealing to doctors and lawyers. Supported by Planned Parenthood, the American Law Institute drafted a model abortion law in 1959 that became the basis for a number of limited reforms of abortion laws enacted by state legislatures in the 1960s.[69] Media attention and public support for therapeutic abortions grew following the much-publicized case of Sherri Finkbine, a middle-class mother of four and host of a local *Romper Room* television program in Arizona, who attempted to get a legal abortion after learning that a drug she had taken, thalidomide, caused fetal deformity. Following her abortion in Sweden, the Vatican issued a statement denouncing the abortion as murder.[70] An epidemic of rubella measles, a disease that often caused fetal deformity when contracted by a pregnant woman, further fueled the abortion reform movement.

In 1964 Alan Guttmacher organized the Association for the Study of Abortion, primarily a New York–based educational organization that advocated reform of abortion law. This led the medical community in many states to call for limited abortion reform measures. By the late 1960s a number of professional organizations endorsed either reform or repeal of abortion laws, including the American Civil Liberties Union (1967), the American Medical Association (1967), the American Public Health Association (1968), and Planned Parenthood (1969).[71] Between 1967 and 1969 fourteen states passed legislation based on the American Legal Institute's recommendations for therapeutic abortions under special circumstances, including rape, fetal deformity, incest, or maternal health.[72]

While this reform movement initiated changes in existing state legislation to allow for therapeutic abortions, more militant voices called for repeal of all abortion laws to allow women the right to abortion in consultation with their physicians. Much of the repeal movement took place within state and local organizations. Typical of these state activist groups were the Illinois Citizens for Medical Control of Abortion, founded in 1966 by population activist, anesthesiologist, and mother of five Caroline Rulon "Lonny" Myers, and an Episcopalian priest employed by Planned Parenthood, Don Shaw; and the more militant California-based group, Society for Humane Abortion, founded in 1961 by Patricia Maginnis, who with her colleague Lana Clarke Phelan denounced restrictive abortion laws as sexual discrimination that imposed "slavery in the cruelest sense" upon women.[73] In early 1966 the California abortion repeal movement got a boost when St. Louis contraceptive manufacturer Joseph Sunnen decided to finance the California Committee for Therapeutic Abortion. Sunnen quickly enlisted UCLA public health professor Ruth Roemer and Episcopalian clergyman Lester Kinsolving. This group supported reform legislation in the state as the first step in repeal of abortion laws.[74]

In 1968 Lawrence Lader, a longtime associate of Hugh Moore, suggested to Lonny Myers in Chicago that a national organization be formed to give focus to state organizations that wanted to move beyond reform to repeal of abortion laws.[75] Both agreed to enlist population activist and University of California at Santa Barbara biology professor Garrett Hardin in forming this new national organization, the National Association for the Repeal of Abortion Laws (NARAL). They were joined by politicians such as Richard Lamm, a Colorado state legislator who called for restricted population growth. The abortion reform movement found additional support from the newly organized Zero Population Growth (ZPG), in which Lader served on the board, which formally endorsed abortion law repeal a year after its founding in 1969. In some areas ZPG activists were the only organized representatives of the nascent abortion movement.[76]

Further mobilization on the national level came when the Socialist Workers party, a Trotskyite Marxist sect, established the Women's National Abortion Action Coalition (WONAAC). Although many feminists boycotted this organization, WONAAC organized nationwide demonstrations in 1971 and the Abortion Action Week into a series of nationwide demonstrations.

The emergence of the women's movement provided further momentum to the abortion repeal movement. The mobilization of the feminist movement profoundly affected the nature of the policy debate by emphasizing the importance of women's right to abortion, captured in the slogan "My Body Belongs to Me," worn on buttons by many women at the time. In the first half of the century, early feminists such as Margaret Sanger, Mary Ware Dennett, and Hannah Stone, among other women, had played a prominent role in organizing Planned Parenthood and other organizations in the struggle to gain legalized birth control through artificial contraception. Many of these women, including Sanger, were opposed to legalized abortion. A second generation of feminists, especially within Planned Parenthood, critically linked the legal right to contraception to feminist concerns by framing their struggle as a woman's right.[77] Women such as Harriet F. Pilpel, legal counsel to Planned Parenthood, and Sarah Weddington, the lawyer who brought *Roe* before the Supreme Court, joined other women in the struggle to legalize abortion. Also, individual women played an important role in promoting family planning as members of Planned Parenthood, the Population Council, or the PCC, as well as in federal agencies. Katherine Oettinger emerged as a key figure in developing family planning policy within the federal government, and Phyllis Piotrow at the PCC lobbied for federal intervention in family planning programs. In the struggle for legalized abortion, however, women assumed a more important voice within the policy debate. The introduction of the women's movement into the abortion issue emphasized the importance of women's rights as a critical component in the struggle, shifting the debate from just a population issue into a rights issue.

Founded in 1966, the National Organization for Women (NOW) endorsed abortion law repeal at its second national convention in 1967 when NOW founder and author Betty Friedan was joined by younger activists in pushing through a repeal plank. This led a number of delegates from NOW to resign their membership in the organization, but even then many NOW chapters were not willing to tackle the issue because of lack of resources and because these chapters were preoccupied with economic issues in the late 1960s and early 1970s. While many NOW members remained divided over the abortion issue as a focus of the organization's attention, more militant feminist groups on the local level made abortion central to their struggle for women's liberation.[78] For example, the Chicago Women's Liberation Union (CWLU), an activist group composed of younger women with backgrounds in the New Left and the antiwar movement, viewed the right to abortion as part of a broader social agenda. In 1970 CWLU activists initiated the Total Repeal of Illinois Abortion Laws that organized mass rallies and demonstrations, although for ideological reasons they assiduously avoided direct legislative lobbying. In New York the militant feminist group Redstockings held "counterhearings" to protest state legislative hearings, which they thought favored antiabortion proponents. In 1970 feminist activists in Detroit held a "funeral march" protesting the deaths of women killed by illegal abortions. By 1971 feminists were staging "speak-outs," street theater, and other demonstrations in favor of abortion. Because militant feminists called for abortion on demand as an absolute right, NARAL officials tended to worry that these demonstrations alienated more people than they won over. Nonetheless, feminists provided a groundswell for the repeal movement.[79]

NARAL proved highly effective in its campaign. In just two years after its founding in 1968, major victories were achieved in four states, with Hawaii becoming the first state to repeal its law, thereby permitting hospital abortions of "nonviable" fetuses.[80] New York followed with legislation that removed all restrictions on abortions performed in the first twenty-four weeks of pregnancy. Legislation to liberalize New York's abortion laws had been introduced in 1966, but it was not until two years later, when Governor Nelson Rockefeller appointed a commission to study the question, that the effort gained serious momentum. The commission, led by Christopher Tietze and Alan Guttmacher, issued a report that called for liberalized abortion. Subsequent abortion legislation was defeated in 1968 and 1969, but the bill finally passed the state senate and then barely passed the state assembly when George M. Michaels, representative of Auburn, switched his vote. Signed into law by Governor Rockefeller on July 1, 1970, this measure enabled New York to have one of the most liberal abortion laws in the nation. Within nine months after the law went into effect, the number of legal abortions in the state surpassed one hundred thousand.[81] State legislatures in Alaska and Washington enacted similar laws. Thirteen other states allowed abortion to preserve the life of the woman or to protect her physical or mental health, qualifications that were often loosely interpreted by physicians. Another twenty-nine states made abortion unlawful except when it was necessary to save the life of the woman.[82]

By the mid-1960s the antiabortion movement appeared on the state level to counter the growing strength of the abortion repeal forces.[83] During the fight over legalized abortion in California in 1967, James Francis Cardinal McIntyre of Los Angeles was instrumental in establishing a Right to Life League and a group of Catholic women who called themselves MOMI (Mothers Outraged at the Murder of Innocents). The Los Angeles diocese hired a public relations firm, Spencer-Roberts Associates, to lobby against a reform bill introduced in the California legislature by State Senator Anthony C. Beilenson. Although Cardinal McIntyre personally phoned Governor Ronald Reagan to oppose the measure, the bill passed the state legislature and Reagan, claiming he had no choice, signed it into law in 1967. Similarly, the bishops in New York issued a joint pastoral letter urging Catholics to oppose an abortion reform bill before that state's legislature.[84]

Although the institutionalized Catholic Church supported the antiabortion movement as it grew in the mid-1960s, groups emerged on the local level, often without official endorsement by the church hierarchy. Still, some local priests joined local residents in forming some of the grassroots groups. For example, Father Paul Marx, an antiabortion activist and a proponent of natural family planning, established the Human Life Center at St. John's University in Collegeville, Minnesota, with the financial support of Harry G. John, the reclusive Catholic heir to the Miller Beer fortune. Standing only five feet in height, with snow-white hair, Marx earned a national reputation for his opposition to abortion and became a kind of folk hero among many early antiabortion activists, although later critics within the movement accused him of self-promotion and extremism.[85]

In general, however, the antiabortion movement often mirrored the peculiar character of local activists. Typical in this regard, Patricia Driscoll in Oakland, California, formed the Family Life Center in 1975 with modest support from the local bishop. Working with a half dozen volunteers, she distributed thousands of pamphlets attacking legalized abortion and promoting sexual abstinence. Similarly, Edward Golden in Troy, New York, organized a small "pro-life" group in 1967 in an attempt to thwart liberalization of the abortion law in his state. By 1970 there were between fifty and seventy local antiabortion groups in the state. Also in 1967 the first permanent state antiabortion group was organized in Virginia. The Illinois Right to Life Committee was formed in 1968, and the Minnesota Citizens Concerned for Life, which attracted a membership of ten thousand by 1973, became a model for other state groups. Other state organizations were founded in Minnesota, California, Florida, Colorado, Michigan, Illinois, and Pennsylvania. These groups covered the political spectrum from right to left. In Milwaukee, Wisconsin, Pam Cira, a counselor for sexual assault victims in the local district attorney's office, formed Feminists for Life. Another feminist antiabortion advocate, Juli Loesch, organized Prolifers for Survival in 1971, a group that preached nuclear disarmament and antiabortion.[86]

While the majority of antiabortionists were Roman Catholic, a number of the most prominent early leaders were Protestants, including Mildred Jefferson, an African-American, Harvard University-trained physician in Massachusetts; Carolyn Gerster in Arizona; Judy Fink in Pennsylvania; and Marjory Mecklenburg in Minnesota. Many of these Protestant leaders accepted family planning and sought to disassociate the birth control issue from the abortion issue. Indeed, Fred Mecklenberg, the husband of Marjory Mecklenburg, remained a strong supporter of Planned Parenthood and urged the antiabortion movement not to object to family planning or the work of activists such as Dr. Beasley in Louisiana.[87]

As early as 1966, the National Conference of Catholic Bishops, the successor to the NCWC, instructed Monsignor James McHugh, director of its Family Life Bureau, to monitor abortion law reform. To do so, he organized the National Right to Life Committee (NRLC), an advisory committee intended to create links with the antiabortion groups springing up across the country. The following year, the National Conference of Catholic Bishops budgeted fifty thousand dollars to fight abortion reform efforts.[88] In mid-1971 the NRLC was established as a national coordinating organization to provide material and information to the various local and state organizations. The NRLC included vocal "progressive" forces from the outset, including Prolifers for Survival and Feminists for Life. By mid-1972, as the presidential election approached, there were 250 local and state groups loosely affiliated with the NRLC. In these early years the NRLC cooperated with the Family Life Division of the United States Catholic Conference until the national organization was restructured in 1973. The bishops conference initiated "Respect Life" programs to activate Catholics on the parish level.[89]

Still, within the movement, critics charged that the NRLC was too closely linked to the Catholic Church. Clearly, the church hierarchy played a critical role in establishing NRLC. Moreover, the majority of NRLC's membership (70 percent) was Roman Catholic. In many ways the composition of the NRLC membership mirrored the composition of NARAL's membership, although with important differences. Both organizations drew from largely white, suburban, middle-aged, college-educated women. The majority of both organizations, NARAL and NRLC, were women (78 percent and 63 percent respectively); most were married (55 percent of NARAL's members, compared with 87 percent of NRLC's members); and most were college educated (with 46 percent of NARAL's members having an advanced postgraduate degree, compared with 32 percent of NRLC's members). The distinguishing difference lay in religion. Approximately 70 percent of NRLC's members were Roman Catholic—two and one-half times the proportion in the general population—compared with only 4 percent of NARAL's members. Almost none of NRLC's members were Jewish, compared with 17 percent of the membership of NARAL—about eight times the proportion in the general population. Neither organization attracted many African-Americans.[90]

Throughout the seventies antiabortion remained primarily a Catholic issue. In 1967 the Association of Reform Rabbis and the United Synagogue of America in New York criticized the bishops for their opposition to abortion reform as "hard and unbending." Shortly afterward, twenty-one rabbis and ministers formed the Clergy Consultation Service on Abortion to aid women seeking abortions. Similarly, that same year, the American Baptist Convention endorsed abortion in cases of rape, incest, or mental incompetence, or when the woman's health was endangered by a pregnancy. Within the next two years, southern Presbyterians and the United Presbyterians took favorable stands on legalized abortion. The United Church of Christ voted to support the removal of abortion from penal law altogether. Most remarkable, given its subsequent reversal in the mid-1980s, the Southern Baptist Convention affirmed a position close to that of the American Baptists.[91] While Mormons opposed abortion on religious grounds, the Catholic Church remained in the forefront of the antiabortion movement.[92]

Nevertheless, conservative Catholics felt that the National Conference of Catholic Bishops was too theologically liberal and too wedded to a social justice agenda that encouraged Catholics to vote for pro-choice Democrats. These ideological divisions led to a number of splits within the movement. In 1974, following *Roe v. Wade*, the NRLC disassociated itself from the Catholic bishops, who in turn created a new organization under their influence, the National Committee for a Human Life Amendment (NCHLA). Meanwhile, another split occurred in the movement that same year when the American Right to Life Association (ARTLA) was chartered as an alternative to NRLC. Although much smaller, ARTLA accepted abortion in the cases of rape, incest, statutory rape, and fetal deformity. The ecumenical organization elected George Williams, a Protestant, as chairman, and made Catholic actress Loretta Young the honorary chair. Serving on the board were Arthur Dyck from Harvard

Divinity School and Jewish law professor Victor Rosenblum. ARTLA pursued a strategy of reducing abortion by emphasizing programs that aided pregnant women and protected women in the workplace. Within the year, more militant Catholics, including Charles Rice and Brent Bozell, brother-in-law of William F. Buckley Jr., resigned from the organization in protest because of its "liberal" stance.[93]

These divisions in the antiabortion movement reflected ideological tensions, even ideological inconsistencies, within the ranks of antiabortion activists. If abortion was considered murder of a human being, then the inevitable question arose whether a democratic society could in fact legalize abortion. Would the mass murder committed under the German Nazi regime have been any more acceptable if it had been voted on by the majority of Germans or if it had been upheld as constitutional by the German courts? On the other hand, could a willful religious minority, maintaining a distinct theological position, impose its views on a democratic, constitutionally organized polity with a strong tradition of individual rights? These issues were not easily resolved, and inevitable analogies with the antislavery issue in antebellum America and prohibition in the 1920s came to mind. Furthermore, these issues posed especially difficult problems for Roman Catholics, who after experiencing past prejudice and discrimination had gained acceptance, social status, and economic advancement in postwar America.

Catholic conservatives, in fact, were divided over acceptable forms of protest against abortion. These differences became evident early in the antiabortion movement when Brent and Patricia Bozell organized the militant Catholic group Sons of Thunder to undertake civil disobedience against abortion clinics. In March 1970 University of Dallas philosophy professor Frederick Wilhelmsen, a member of the group, led a small group of students, faculty, and local activists that broke into a Planned Parenthood clinic in Dallas. Brandishing placards that read "Stop Fascist Genocide" and "Viva il Papa," they prayed the rosary until they were arrested by the Dallas city police.

A more dramatic protest occurred two months later in early June, when the Sons of Thunder marched on George Washington University Hospital in Washington, D.C. After holding a Mass at Stephen Martyr Church, celebrated by four priests—including an African-American, a Chinese, and a Hispanic—the Sons of Thunder, wearing khaki clothing, red berets, and rosaries draped around their necks, marched to the university hospital. There the three hundred demonstrators heard speakers, including one who declared, "America, . . . you are daggering to death your unborn of tomorrow. The very cleanliness of your sterilized murder factories gives off the stench of death." When the police arrived, seven demonstrators were arrested, all later found guilty and given suspended prison sentences.[94] These demonstrations dismayed "law-and-order" conservatives, already upset with antiwar and student demonstrations on the left. William Buckley denounced the demonstrators in the pages of his *National Review*, declaring that "the Sons of Thunder have moved precious few of the unconvinced over to their side."[95]

Antiabortion activists found themselves in a changing climate as state legislatures enacted abortion reform laws. Public opinion surveys revealed that the majority of Americans accepted these changes. Nonetheless, Americans remained deeply divided on the issue of unrestricted abortion. As early as 1965, a Gallup poll revealed that 77 percent of Americans felt that abortion should be legal when a women's life was in danger, while a mere 16 percent opposed abortion under these circumstances. Support for abortion dwindled, however, to 54 percent (32 percent opposed) when the child might be deformed, and fell to only 18 percent (72 percent opposed) when abortion was desired because the family could not support additional children. Moreover, a slight plurality of Catholics (46 percent) favored legal abortions in cases of health being endangered or in cases of mental and physical deformity of the fetus.[96]

These polls revealed deep ambivalence toward abortion and continued vacillation among the American public. In 1969 another Gallup survey revealed that when Americans were asked if they favored a law that would permit an abortion at any time during the first three months of pregnancy, only 40 percent favored abortion in these circumstances, while 50 percent were opposed. Yet three years later another Gallup poll showed that 64 percent of Americans supported liberalized state abortion laws, while only 31 percent opposed these changes in state law. Another poll conducted by Gallup later in 1972 revealed the country to be evenly divided on whether abortions should be performed at any time during the first three months of pregnancy, with 46 percent in favor and 45 percent opposed.[97]

Perhaps these differences showed that Americans favored legalized abortion, depending on how the question was asked. Although Gallup polls broke the respondents down only by religion, and occasionally by education and income levels, other surveys revealed that African-Americans throughout the 1970s and most of the 1980s were far less supportive of legalized abortion than whites. Indeed, in all but one of the surveys between 1972 and 1991, blacks took a consistent antiabortion position. Social scientists differed over why blacks remained less supportive of abortion than whites. While a few social scientists argued that black opposition to abortion came only from a nationalist minority, others noted that black Americans showed greater religiosity and doctrinal orthodoxy, and this provided a major source of antiabortion attitudes among African-

Americans. In general blacks were more likely than whites to pray daily (70 percent of blacks compared with 53 percent of whites), to attend church regularly (54 percent to 42 percent), to believe the Bible is inerrant (57 percent to 32 percent), to attend evangelical churches (69 percent to 29 percent), and to report intense personal religious experiences (30 percent to 18 percent).[98]

A number of African-American religious leaders, most notably Jesse Jackson, emerged as militant opponents of abortion. In the 1970s, as head of People United to Save Humanity (PUSH), a Chicago-based civil rights group, Jackson acknowledged that he personally abhorred abortion because he felt that only the intercession of his grandmother had prevented his mother from aborting him. He brought a pronounced religious opposition to abortion, telling a group of students, "I'm contending that unless we put human life second only to God in our lives, we're becoming a Sodom and Gomorrah . . . [W]e have an obligation to take sex and life as a far more sacred event than we do now."[99] He modified this position later in his presidential campaigns.

Still, many black leaders and organizations, including the Congress for Racial Equality (CORE) and the NAACP, had endorsed family planning. Indeed, in 1966 Martin Luther King Jr. received the Margaret Sanger Award for Human Rights. Nonetheless, militant spokesmen from black nationalist groups and the Black Muslims denounced family planning and abortion as "black genocide."[100] Leaders, including Julius Lester, Dick Gregory, Daniel H. Watts, and H. Rap Brown, called upon blacks to continue to reproduce in order to avoid race suicide.[101] While most middle-class blacks had accepted birth control, *Ebony* magazine reported in March 1968 that opposition to family planning among poor blacks had grown because of a "very prevalent idea that birth control actually means 'black genocide.'"[102]

By equating birth control and abortion with genocide, nationalists from the Black Muslims and other separatist political groups sought to establish, in effect, a distinct morality from the dominant white culture that had come to accept birth control and legalized abortion. In their fervor to separate from what they perceived as the hegemonic white culture, black nationalists articulated a radical vision of a "shared moral community" within the African-American population.

For example, the Black Muslim newspaper, *Muhammad Speaks*, kept up a steady attack on federal family planning programs as a white plot against the black community. Elijah Muhammad, the leader of the religious sect, had explained the origins of the white race as an insidious consequence of selective breeding through birth control. He claimed that in ancient times a renegade black scientist named Yacub, working with Satan, made use of a rigid birth control law to kill off many black babies, leaving only pale-skinned, blue-eyed, blonde-haired things, later called "white men," but who were actually "devils."[103]

Opposition to family planning, however, extended beyond the Muslim movement. In Pittsburgh, Dr. Charles Greenlee, a black physician, and William Haden, a community activist, forced the closing of a Planned Parenthood clinic in the Homewood-Brushton district, and then warned that firebombings and riots would occur if any attempt was made to reopen the clinic.[104] Such threats were taken seriously. That same year a family planning clinic in a black neighborhood in Cleveland was fire-bombed. In 1969 five family planning facilities were denied funding because of Haden's activities.[105]

Other nationalists also denounced family planning, abortion, and sterilization. In 1971 a black nationalist speaking at Indiana University denounced abortions by noting that aspirin cost more money than did an abortion for a poor black women because the government paid for "birth control" but not for health care. He drew the conclusion that the government did not care whether blacks lived or died, as long as they did not have children. The Black Panthers, a revolutionary political group, joined in these attacks, often pointing out that Jewish doctors were involved in family planning programs. When New York State liberalized its abortion law, a Black Panther wrote, "Black people know that part of our revolutionary strength lies in the fact that we outnumber the pigs—And the pigs realize this. This is why they are trying to eliminate as many people as possible before they reach their inevitable doom." This view found frequent expression in the Black Panther newspaper, the *Black Panther*. Writing in the March 9, 1969, issue of the newspaper, Van Keys, a member of the East Oakland branch of the party, declared, "The racist tells you to take birth control pills to kill, to murder life that might have existed if you had not." The racist, he continued, encourages black women to take the pill for sexual freedom or to limit families, but these reasons bear examining. "Why do you feel the need for sexual freedom, escalation, and protection? Why are you drowning in bills? . . . I'll tell you why, because of the ways of racism. They are planning mass extermination of people they consider dispensable."[106] A steady barrage of anti-family planning and antiabortion articles appeared in the revolutionary newspaper, denouncing birth control and upholding "having babies" as a revolutionary act. The titles suggest the intensity of feeling brought to the issue: "The Anatomy of Extermination" (March 9, 1969); "And Pharaoh Said" (April 20, 1969); "A Word for Panther Parents" (December 11, 1969); "Birth Control" (February 9, 1969); "Towards a Revolutionary Morality" (March 15, 1971); and "Concerning Birth Control: Potential Revolutionaries" (May 31, 1970).

Black Panther female members supported the party line against family planning and abortion. Writing in the *Black Panther* in 1970, Brenda Hyson warned that New York State's recently enacted abortion law would be used by "the oppressive ruling class" to kill off blacks and other oppressed people before they were born. Although abortion was voluntary, she said that it would lead to involuntary abortion and compulsory sterilization. Black women, she proclaimed, would reject abortion just as they had "rejected the attempt to force family planning in the guise of pills and coils."[107]

Other black women picked up this radical critique of family planning as an instrument of social control, but they nonetheless demanded the rights of women to "control their bodies" through contraception and abortion. Black activist Toni Cade, editor of an anthology of black feminist writers, pointedly wrote that she was aware of the "national call to the Sisters to abandon birth controls, to not cooperate with an enemy determined to solve his problems with the bomb, the gun, and the pill; to instruct the welfare mamas to resist the sterilization plan that has become ruthless policy for many state agencies; to picket family planning centers and abortion-referral groups, and to raise revolutionaries." She knew that "it's not for nothing, certainly not love, that birth control clinics have mushroomed in our communities." Nevertheless, black women, she extolled, needed to look at "the oppressive nature of pregnancy and the tyranny of childbirth." The liberation of black women from welfare, poverty, and oppression begins, she declared, with women seizing control of their bodies through contraception and legalized abortion.[108] These feminists condemned the nationalist call for black women to have more children as a "revolutionary act," and instead viewed contraception and abortion as a means of liberation, reverberated in the writings and speeches of black feminists in these years.[109]

The charge that federal family planning targeted the African-American community appeared to find shocking verification, however, when it was revealed that two young sisters, Minnie Lee Relf, aged twelve, and Mary Alice Relf, aged fourteen, had been sterilized by an HEW-funded Montgomery, Alabama, CAP in 1973. The incident caused a national firestorm that led to congressional investigations of federally funded sterilization programs among black poor women. The episode began when two representatives of the federally financed county Community Action Agency called on Minnie Relf, an illiterate welfare mother of four, to instruct her that two of her daughters needed shots. Trusting that the agency had the best interests of her children in mind, Mrs. Relf put her "X" on a paper without realizing that she was allowing a sterilization operation for her daughters, Minnie Lee and Mary Alice. The sterilization of the Relf sisters became national news when Joseph Levin, a lawyer, filed suit against the federal government. Subsequent investigations found that eleven other women (ten of them African-American) had undergone sterilization operations funded by the Montgomery Community Action Agency. Matters worsened when American Civil Liberties Union lawyers revealed that other black women in North Carolina and South Carolina had been sterilized by federally funded programs without their consent.[110]

Revelations of this sterilization program came to light following the presidential election of 1972, but congressional hearings conducted by Senator Ted Kennedy (D-Massachusetts) exposed the politics within the Nixon administration concerning HEW sterilization policy that preceded the election. Congressional investigations revealed that on May 18, 1971, the OEO, under Deputy Director Wesley Hjornevik, instituted a new policy that permitted funding for voluntary sterilization services. In developing the guidelines to implement this new policy, the Family Planning Division of the agency received assistance from the American Public Health Association, Hugh Moore's Association for Voluntary Sterilization, and Planned Parenthood. On two occasions in 1971, while the guidelines were being developed, the Family Planning Division sent letters to all community action agencies requesting that they withhold funding for voluntary sterilization services until the guidelines could be issued. On January 10, 1971, the guidelines were officially approved by Deputy Director Hjornevik; a month later, twenty-five thousand copies of the guidelines had been printed and were ready for distribution. At this point the Family Planning Division was informed that issuance of the guidelines needed to be approved by the White House before they were distributed.

Warren Hern, head of the OEO Family Planning Division, was flabbergasted by the news. Community action agencies throughout the country and members of Congress had been requesting the guidelines for months. Hern felt that the delay had created "a dangerous and urgent situation." In particular, he worried that sterilization surgeries would be undertaken without patients being given adequate counseling and without their informed consent. Nonetheless, he was assured that the delay was not "political," but that the White House wanted to get a legal reading of the guidelines. When Hern contacted the White House legal counsel's office, headed by John Dean, to see where the guidelines stood, he received a reprimand. Finally, after four months of being stonewalled, Hern resigned in protest.[111]

By the time he resigned, Hern realized that sterilization had become a political issue in the White House. Behind the scenes, Paul O'Neill, an official in the Office of Management and Budget, and James Cavanaugh, a White House staff member, had intervened when they first heard about the sterilization guidelines. The guidelines had been brought to their attention by Leon Cooper, an ambitious black physician, a Democrat, who had become director of health affairs at the OEO. The National Medical Association, the black equivalent of the American Medical Association, had come out strongly against family planning programs and instead proposed a comprehensive health care program with birth control as only part of the package. Anxious to acquire status with his peers, and concerned that wholesale sterilization would occur in the South by white doctors targeting poor blacks, Cooper opposed the guidelines. He was joined in his opposition by archconservative Howard Philips, an assistant to the director of the OEO. Through their efforts, Cooper and Philips were able to enlist White House aide Charles Colson, who had been assigned the task of developing a "Catholic strategy" to win the white ethnic vote for Nixon in the upcoming election. The result was that the guidelines were buried. Meanwhile, sterilization operations occurred under OEO funding in Tennessee, Alabama, and South Carolina, dramatically revealed in the case of the Relf sisters. A detailed study of national sterilization policy revealed that of 22,175 female patients sterilized in 1972, over 40 percent were black and 30 percent received public assistance.[112] Sterilization had become intertwined with presidential politics.[113]

While the OEO and the White House were debating OEO sterilization policy, the abortion debate was heating up on the state level as antiabortion groups mobilized to repeal recently enacted abortion reform legislation. In New York, antiabortion activists, mostly Catholics, pressured the state legislature to repeal abortion legislation passed in 1970. In Michigan, abortion activists led by physician Jack Stack had placed a referendum on the November state ballot that would allow a woman and her physician to choose abortion at any time during the first twenty weeks of pregnancy. A similar abortion repeal measure had been placed on the North Dakota ballot, although activists felt there was little chance of its passage. In Michigan it was a different story. There abortion activists received almost fifty thousand dollars, most of it from the United Methodist Church, which was used for massive media advertising in the final four weeks of the campaign. Abortion activists felt momentum was on their side, especially when they learned that the Supreme Court had decided to review state abortion laws in Texas and Georgia.[114]

In Michigan, Jack Stack predicted on the eve of the election that the abortion reform would pass by a 61 percent majority based on his polling. The final tallying of votes on November 7 shocked abortion activists. A decided majority, ironically 61 percent—the same number that Stack had said would support repeal—voted against the measure. In North Dakota the repeal measure went down by an overwhelming 77 percent to 23 percent.[115] In New York only the veto of Governor Nelson Rockefeller prevented the overturning of abortion legislation. The only hopeful sign was that Sarah Weddington, the attorney who had brought *Roe* before the Supreme Court, won election to the Texas state legislature by a margin of almost fifty thousand votes. Nonetheless, Larry Lader at NARAL admitted that the "abortion movement has been increasingly pushed to the defensive in recent months." He advised repeal proponents to forgo media appearances with antiabortionists: "We must refuse to give equal time in debate to a minority point of view whenever such a tactic is possible."[116] Alarmed, Lader wrote to Hugh Moore, "We have learned in the last year we cannot beat the Roman Catholic Church with the pennies we've lived on."[117]

These events left the proabortion movement reeling. The backlash caught them by surprise. Perhaps the one person who saw most astutely this backlash coming was someone neither the abortion repeal movement nor the Catholic Church had occasion to consult—a lonely figure in Washington, D.C., Richard M. Nixon.

5

Richard Nixon and the Politicization
of Family Planning Policy

Nixon's enthusiasm for family planning as an instrument of social change and a remedy for correcting what he and others in his administration perceived as the "welfare mess" found expression in his support for forming the Commission on Population Growth and the American Future, headed by John D. Rockefeller 3rd. The establishment of the commission in 1969 fulfilled Rockefeller's decade-long dream. Rockefeller hoped that this commission might further awaken the public and policy makers to the problems of overpopulation in America. Rockefeller's high hopes for the commission crashed, however, in a political environment increasingly polarized over civil rights, war in Vietnam, and abortion. Support for the commission's work was hindered by divisions within the population movement itself over the efficacy of voluntary family planning programs. Critical of voluntarism, more radical activists such as Paul Ehrlich and Garrett Hardin suggested that coercive family planning measures to protect the general interest of society needed to be explored. Furthermore, internal divisions within the commission itself played havoc as meetings turned into acrimonious debates over immigration, abortion, and the very purpose of the commission. The continuing decline in the American birthrate belied the urgency of the commission. By the time its final report was issued in 1972, the political climate had changed significantly.

The debate over legalized abortion ensured opposition to the report's recommendations. The controversy over legalized abortion began on the state level and then quickly moved to the national level. Then, on January 22, 1973, the Supreme Court announced in *Roe v. Wade* and *Doe v. Bolton* that abortion was a constitutional right. The majority of the court, in a 7 to 2 vote, found abortion laws in Texas and Georgia unconstitutional. For family planning advocates it was a day of celebration, the culmination of a long struggle. Their lobbying efforts with Congress and the White House paled in comparison with what the highest court in the land had accomplished in a single stroke. Lyndon Baines Johnson's death that very day drew public attention away from this momentous decision, but to family planning advocates it seemed a fitting tribute to the president who had put family planning in place. To antiabortionists, the *Roe* decision was a day of mourning.

Yet, contrary to those who see *Roe* as the beginnings of a polarized electorate, the decision only crystallized divisions that had already become evident in the struggle over abortion on the state level.[1] Decided within days of Richard Nixon's second inauguration, the *Roe* decision drew no public comment from the president. Nonetheless, as early as 1971 Nixon had publicly stated that his "firm personal and religious beliefs" led him to "consider abortion an unacceptable form of population control."[2] Furthermore, a month earlier he had ordered Secretary of Defense Melvin Laird to follow state laws regarding abortion for military personnel rather than set a uniform federal policy.[3] He had intervened personally in an attempt to convince Governor Nelson A. Rockefeller of New York to veto the recently enacted liberal abortion law in that state.

The clearest evidence that the issue had become politicized, however, came in the midst of the presidential reelection campaign in May 1972 when Nixon rejected the report of the Commission on Population Growth and the American Future that called for liberalizing abortion laws and federally supported family planning services for adolescents. Looking toward the upcoming presidential election and the possibility of breaking the Democratic stronghold on the blue-collar Catholic vote, Richard Nixon took a firm stand against the report, which had been bitterly condemned by the Roman Catholic bishops in a fierce letter-writing campaign. One of the great ironies of the success of abortion reform was that it shattered bipartisan support for federal family planning policy and helped take population control off the presidential agenda.

Following Nixon's successful reelection to a second term, federal family planning programs continued to expand through new legislation. Nonetheless, the emergence of the abortion issue changed the tenor of the policy debate. As antiabortion and proabortion groups mobilized, policy shifted from the confines of elite foundations and organizations to include democratic, grassroots groups. In the process, issues concerning overpopulation became less important in the public debate than did abortion.

By 1974 John D. Rockefeller 3rd began to reconsider his position on traditional family planning programs. While he lamented the politicization of the issue, he, too, had begun to have doubts about the efficacy of birth control as the sole means of addressing the population problem. This became apparent when Rockefeller stunned delegates at the United Nations World Population Conference in Bucharest, Romania, in August 1974 in a speech criticizing the use of family planning programs to address social and economic problems. Rockefeller's speech had immediate reverberations in population circles in the United States. Rockefeller's transition from a strong proponent of family planning to his open criticism of population control in 1974 reflected a dramatic shift in his own thinking and illustrates the politicization of family planning policy that was already apparent in the immediate years preceding *Roe v. Wade*, only to intensify after the decision.

The Rate of Population Growth Declines, Divisions Grow

Beginning in 1968, a sharp decline in the rate of population growth in the United States, as well as in many developed nations, set an unfavorable climate for population policies proposed by the Rockefeller report. In 1968 population growth had fallen to a postwar low of 17.5 births per thousand. For the first time in the postwar period, the national birthrate fell below what demographers called the "replacement rate" of the native population. This meant that, excluding growth due to immigration, by 1968 America was experiencing zero population growth. This declining rate of population growth called into question the scare tactics of Hugh Moore, Paul Ehrlich, and others who had warned of an impending population crisis. Neo-Malthusian predictions of coming disaster, world famine, and social crisis appeared wrong, suggesting that the doomsayers, much like the Reverend Thomas Malthus in the early nineteenth century, were "Chicken-Littles," exaggerating every sound in the forest into a catastrophe.

Differences within the population lobby became apparent within this demographic context. Moderates within the foundations and Planned Parenthood sought to distance themselves from Moore's Population Crisis Committee (PCC) and others who called for "scare" tactics and more coercive family planning measures. For example, Planned Parenthood believed that Moore was hurting the movement by his continued jeremiads conducted through a barrage of newspaper advertisements that linked population problems to environmental disaster, urban crime, and social instability. Planned Parenthood appreciated Moore's support for abortion reform on the state level, including his financial support of abortion reform campaigns in Nevada, New York, Michigan, and other states prior to *Roe*.[4] Moreover, Moore provided major financial support to a former

PCC employee, Lawrence Lader, in his efforts to organize the National Association for the Repeal of Abortion Laws (NARAL), a coalition of seventy-five national and state organizations working to liberalize state abortion laws.[5] Nevertheless, Planned Parenthood and the Population Council differed with Moore over strategy and viewed with alarm his talk of an impending cataclysm unless more radical measures were undertaken.

These differences proved critical in further dividing the population movement. For his part, Moore remained convinced that the Population Council and Planned Parenthood were too timid in their approach to overpopulation. Rockefeller "knows the answers," he said, "but like Frank Notestein, is inclined to think that maybe things will come out all right."[6] Moore believed firmly that people needed to be scared before they would act on the population problem. In 1968 he launched a massive advertising campaign to scare the American people into action. For his so-called Manhattan Project, Moore hired a New York advertising firm to develop ads that linked the population problem in America to problems of urban decay, crime, and pollution. The purpose of the campaign was to make the population problem "real." Our primary audience, he wrote, is "the President, the cabinet, a hundred people within the executive department, and 600-odd congressman, but our secondary audience is the population movement and 5000 influential citizens, particularly in the Northeast." Moore invested over $1.2 million of his own funds in the effort.[7]

Problems arose when one of these advertisements—"Have You Been Mugged Today?"—appeared at a time of heightened racial sensitivity following racial riots and the growth of black nationalism in the civil rights movement.[8] Depicting what many perceived as a young black man mugging a victim, the advertisement was publicly denounced by the leadership of Planned Parenthood as "racist." George N. Lindsay, chairman of Planned Parenthood, quickly dissociated his organization from the ad by calling it "disturbing" in its "false" implication that "the poor were responsible for the 'population explosion,' and were responsible for the increase in violent crime, but also for air and water pollution and the deterioration of our quality of life." He warned that the ad "feeds the suspicion being promulgated by nationalist groups that birth control is a 'genocidal plot' against Negroes." He worried that rumors of other ads linking the population explosion to rape, pollution, the costs of welfare, and the intransigence of the Catholic Church could only lead to a backlash.[9] He was joined by Donald Strauss, another leading PPWP official, who declared that the ad had "set back the cause of Planned Parenthood a good long way."[10] Angered by the Moore's ad and wanting to quickly distance themselves from Moore, the executive committee voted within days to go on record as "drastically opposed to the spirit and content of the advertisement."[11] The PCC was flooded with mail from leaders of Planned Parenthood condemning the ad. Even William Draper privately withdrew from the advertising campaign and protested to Moore about the content of the advertisement.[12]

Moore and the PCC responded aggressively to Planned Parenthood's attacks. Writing to John Rock, one of the few activists who had risen to PCC's defense, Moore declared, "The fact of the matter, of course, is that Planned Parenthood arrogates to itself the right to control policy in the entire population movement—which is of course ridiculous."[13] Harold Bostrom, a Wisconsin businessman and close associate of Moore's, was even more pointed in his reply to Planned Parenthood: "Let us be pariahs. . . . If you fear reprisal from whatever quarter, let us go it alone. I think this is as it should be. We can be an effective agency if we can provoke concern, if we can raise the dead, if we can instill the dread of crimes, whether they be in the United States or in Vietnam. There is only one hope for the world, and that is to get those in power running scared."[14]

A year later the International Planned Parenthood Foundation attempted a "reconciliation" by proposing a merger of IPPF and the PCC. Moore rejected the offer out of hand, replying, "I would not water down the character of our organization to suit the conservatives in Planned Parenthood." He joined Bostrom in resigning from the governing board of IPPF and withdrawing his financial support. As Bostrom told Planned Parenthood, he felt that attacks on Moore were "unwarranted," adding that Planned Parenthood seemed more interested in "caressing all members of our society."[15]

Moore believed that one of the reasons the overpopulation crisis had taken a backseat to such issues as the war in Vietnam and civil rights was because Planned Parenthood and other groups did not want to push the links between overpopulation, war, and social protest. The environmental movement in the late 1960s gave him hope that the full ramifications of overpopulation in relation to other issues might be seen by the larger public, especially college students.

Shortly after Nixon entered the White House in 1969, Moore observed, "It seems that many students are getting tired of their Vietnam campaign and are swinging to this new cause [environmentalism]—our cause. . . . These newly converted youngsters will be interested in the techniques and tools which have been used up to now."[16] A short time later he supported Harold Bostrom in organizing a national meeting, the First Congress on Population and the Environment, held at the University of Wisconsin. This meeting brought together representatives of the Conservation Foundation, student environmental groups, and leaders of the population movement to hear an array of speakers, including Philip Hauser,

Garrett Hardin, and Paul Ehrlich. Bostrom excitedly reported to Moore, "I think the big breakthrough is coming. We will bring together the conservationists, the birth controllers, the anti-pollutionists, those against crime, war, poverty, insurrection and social decay—all societies under one roof. We will create a confederation of people working under one roof. We will create a confederation of people working to survive on this planet. The politicians will listen, and eventually, we will have the Pentagon and the Red Army listening."[17]

Moore believed that the new environmental movement would energize the population movement by introducing a new generation to the problems of overpopulation. Concerned that the environmental movement still had not linked overpopulation to the environmental problem, Moore actively sought to tie the population issue to a nationwide environmental teach-in, planned for April 22, 1970. To do so, he arranged for a new pictorial edition of *The Population Bomb* to be produced and distributed throughout university campuses across the country. In addition, a taped radio program featuring Paul Ehrlich and David Brower was distributed free of charge to over three hundred college radio stations. Shortly before the environmental teach-in, Moore used his private resources to finance a new advertising campaign that featured an appealing picture of a newborn infant over a personal letter signed by Moore addressed to President Nixon. The letter began, "We can't lick the environment problem without considering this little fellow."[18]

In linking the two issues, population and the environment, Moore continued to use radical rhetoric by now warning of environmental cataclysm, even though the message was formulated more benignly than his earlier ads. Yet once again, his rhetoric alienated many in the population movement, including John D. Rockefeller 3rd and the staff at the Population Council. Shortly before his death in late 1972, Moore and his friends lamented that "John D. considers our environmental posture too radical."[19] Nonetheless, Moore died believing that the population issue had found new life in the environmental movement. Indeed it had, but by 1972 the population movement had become seriously divided.

Much of the division within the ranks of the population movement expressed differing assessments of the effectiveness of family planning programs at home and abroad in addressing world overpopulation. Underlying these differences lay a more fundamental difference over whether the population problem should be seen as a bomb about to explode, bringing disaster to all, or a serious issue that would continue to have critical social, economic, and cultural ramifications unless it was addressed in the near future. On one side stood Hugh Moore, Paul Ehrlich, and Kingsley Davis; on the other side were John D. Rockefeller 3rd, Frank Notestein, and

Bernard Berelson—the radicals and the moderates. By the late 1960s, however, a third voice began to emerge, radical feminism, one no less critical of the effectiveness of family planning programs than were Moore and company. Unlike those suggesting more coercive measures, however, many feminists accused policy makers of ignoring social inequality and the status of women in the traditional family.

The moderate wing continued to be led by the officers at the Population Council, who often seemed to view the population problem from the Olympian heights of social prestige and detached expertise. The moderates urged patience: "Give family planning programs a chance to work. They are new. Already the birth rate is declining, not enough for us to be content, but it's a start." Fearing a population meltdown unless the issue was addressed immediately, the radicals dismissed voluntary family programs as ineffectual. Not enough poor women enrolled in the programs, and those who did tended to drop out too easily. Moderation in the face of social crisis was foolish, softhearted, and irresponsible. Suggestions for more coercive measures began to be heard in radical circles.

Complaints about the voluntary nature of family planning appeared early in the population movement but became increasingly apparent as federal family planning programs failed to stem increased numbers of out-of-wedlock births and a perceived growing underclass. Kingsley Davis, a well-known demographer at the University of California, Berkeley, vented these complaints about the efficacy of voluntarism in family planning in his widely read article "Population Policy: Will Current Programs Succeed?" that appeared in *Science* in 1967.[20] Davis's article caused immediate reverberations in population circles because he had been a leading voice for population control for over twenty years. He began his essay by noting, "Most observers are surprised by the swiftness with which concern over the population problem has turned from intellectual analysis and debate to policy and action." Nonetheless, he declared that there were clear "limitations" inherent in the voluntary aspects of these present programs: "By sanctifying the doctrine that each woman should have the number of children she wants, and by assuming that if she has only that number this will automatically curb population growth to the necessary degree, the leaders of current policies escape the necessity of asking why women desire so many children and how this desire can be influenced." Policy makers seem to believe that "something they vaguely call population control can be achieved by making better contraceptives available" and by relying on couples to undertake "family planning." Such assumptions, he declared, are false. Instead, he said, only community-enforced fertility control could remedy the crisis of overpopulation. Promulgating community fertility control as an alternative to individual choice reflected

Davis's belief that more coercive measures were needed if "zero population" growth was to be attained, as it should be. As a first step he proposed the use of indirect coercion measures such as tax incentives to single individuals who postponed marriage, inducements for women to continue their education and develop professional careers (thereby delaying marriage and childbearing), and redefining sex roles (so women would not define themselves in terms of motherhood). He believed that these measures alone would not correct the problem, however. More drastic, coercive approaches needed to be considered.

This call for zero population growth, Davis realized, might offend many policy makers. He declared, "The measures that would be required to implement such a goal, though not so revolutionary as a Brave New World or a Communist Utopia, nevertheless, tend to offend most people reared in existing societies." But achieving zero population growth meant that parents would have to relinquish the right to have the number of children they wanted. He realized, however, that a list of coercive measures necessary to lower the birth rate read like "a catalogue of horrors," and therefore government leaders would find coercive policies "unacceptable" until a social crisis had occurred. He concluded that current family planning programs needed to be kept in place ("contraception is a valuable technological instrument"), but the "unthinking identification of family planning with population control is an ostrich-like approach in that it permits people to hide from themselves the enormity and unconventionality of the task."[21] Davis left it to his readers and future researchers to decide what kind of coercive measures might be necessary, but he left no doubt that he believed current voluntary family planning programs had failed.

Davis's article appeared on the eve of a revolution in family planning. In the following years Congress enacted new legislation that rapidly expanded federally funded family planning programs, the Social Security amendments (1967) and the Family Planning Services and Population Research Act (1970). Davis's pessimistic assessment of family planning programs before federal family planning had been fully implemented appears premature or prophetic, depending on one's perspective. Nonetheless, such sentiments became increasingly apparent in the following years in radical population circles, even as the rate of population growth continued to fall.

Strangely enough, it seemed that the decline in the rate of population growth fostered hysteria. Dismissing the decline as an aberration that blinded people to the impending disaster, radicals called for even more drastic measures to constrain population growth. For example, Melvin M. Ketchel, a professor of physiology at Tufts Medical School, argued that if pills, loops, and other voluntary means of contraception did not defuse the population explosion—and he did not have any confidence that they would—then a "safe fertility control drug" needed to be developed to be added to the water supply. This agent, he believed, should "lend itself to being easily and unobtrusively taken by the entire population. In large cities, such an agent might be added to the water supply, but other methods would be required in less developed areas." Furthermore, he maintained, this agent needed to be distributed by the government. Just as the government had become involved in addressing the problems of pollution, so should it be involved in overpopulation. "I maintain," he wrote, "that unchecked population growth is at least as serious a hazard as waste products from automobiles and factories."[22]

Ketchel's argument found support among other radicals. Writing in the *Ohio State Law Journal* in 1971, Ronald M. Baker made a well-publicized legal case for placing antifertility agents in the water supply.[23] Warning that family planning was "futile" and that Americans were caught in a slumber in the face of "the plague of overpopulation predicted by Malthus almost two hundred years ago," Baker asserted that such measures were constitutional and necessary under the equal protection clause. He warned in an aside that "the use of anti-fertility agents can be subject to dangerous abuse and should only be employed under the strictest of regulatory supervision."[24] Nonetheless, he believed that such coercive measures were needed.

This belief that more drastic action was needed to reduce rampant population growth manifested itself in the formation of Zero Population Growth (ZPG), an organization created by population "hawks"—a term used at the Population Council to refer to hard-liners who believed voluntarism and traditional family planning had failed.[25] Formed in 1969, ZPG broke with PPFA by declaring, as one founding member, Richard Bowers, put it, "Voluntarism is a farce. The private sector effort has failed." He asserted that legalized abortion in all fifty states, even abortion on demand, would not stop rampant population growth. Even the expenditure of "billions of dollars will not limit growth." Instead, coercive measures were needed to enforce population control. Many in the movement entertained notions of licensing parents to conceive, sterilizing welfare dependents, and enacting new "criminal laws to limit population, if the earth is to survive."[26] Underlying these measures lay an implicit repudiation by ZPG members of the ability of market forces and economic development to constrain population growth. Even if economic development led modern families to have fewer children, as demographic evidence showed, ZPG believed overpopulation would remain a persistent and critical problem.

Key figures in ZPG were mostly academics, many of them from fast-growing California, including Paul Ehrlich, elected first president of the organization; University of California biologist Garrett Hardin; Berkeley demographer Kingsley Davis; Stanford University professors John H. Thomas and Peter H. Ravan; and California State University sociologist Larry Barrett. Financial backing came from former PPFA donors John Tanton, a Michigan doctor, and Carol Fessenden, a longtime PPFA activist from Connecticut. Later, Cordelia Scaife May provided substantial sums through her Pittsburgh foundation. The attitude of the ZPG founders was that the population movement had failed. Although they sought "cooperation," instead of confrontation, with the established population movement, it was evident at the outset that the new organization carried a chip on its shoulder toward PPFA, the Population Council, and the Ford Foundation.[27] As a result, John D. Rockefeller 3rd politely refused to meet with representatives of the group or to join the new organization.

Much of the argument for instituting more coercive measures assumed not only that voluntary family planning had failed but also that the public interest subsumed individual rights. The juxtaposition between the public interest and individual rights, although not noted at the time, was contradictory to the general claim made by ZPG leaders that the right to family planning and abortion was a "private" choice, not one that should be dictated by the general public interest, however defined. Hardin and company attempted to dispose of this contradiction by strained (and sometimes specious) arguments. Social-biologist Marston Bates defended population control as natural to the preservation of a species in his *A Jungle House* (1970). In a series of influential articles, biologist Garrett Hardin found in individual rights the potential for community disaster. Support for societal interest over individual rights found popular expression in Edgar Chasteen's "The Case for Compulsory Birth Control," which appeared in early 1970 in *Mademoiselle* magazine.[28] Chasteen told his largely female audience, "Complete freedom is anarchy.... The more people there are, the less freedom there is." To those who worried that compulsory population control would erode freedom, he replied, "Some will object to compulsory birth control, contending that it smacks of Big Brother or *1984*. On the contrary, it would seem that such Orwellian conditions are inevitable without a policy of compulsory control." If only, he implored his readers, "we can rid ourselves of outmoded values concerning laissez-faire parenthood ... we shall eliminate a host of problems not otherwise soluble, and we shall expand the freedom 'to be' which, after all, makes us human."[29]

These splits in the population movement came at the very time when Rockefeller had achieved his goal in establishing a national commission on population growth. Within the Population Council, staff members rejected ZPG's purpose and strategy. Nonetheless, in an attempt to avoid further fission within the movement, Berelson traveled to Berkeley in the summer of 1970 to meet with Kingsley Davis to discuss their differences. He reported that he came away with "a somewhat better appreciation of Kingsley's point of view" and that he had "renewed a dialogue with him that I hope will not end with this quick visit." Nonetheless, Berelson remained "confirmed in the view that he does not have any realistic suggestions as to what we should be doing to solve the population problem in the near run." Furthermore, he had been put off by Davis's accusation that "I had been brainwashed by conservative demographers who still could not understand the magnitude, character, or urgency of the task.... Mollycoddling won't do." Davis also told Berelson that it had been a mistake turning programs over to health people. "That was a disastrous mistake," he asserted, "because what is needed is not a health program but a population program."[30]

Frank Notestein proved even more critical of Davis and the ZPG movement. He dismissed Davis's call for compulsory control as "tendentious nonsense."[31] Writing to Donald A. Collins at Planned Parenthood, he declared that "zero rate is a suitable population goal, but it does not mean that we should try to achieve it in ten years. The ZPG campaign does not make sense politically or demographically." He worried about the political effects of an advertising campaign that sought to generate support for penalties for high reproduction and rewards for restraint. Such a strategy, he felt, could lead to a political backlash against family planning programs. Furthermore, those "controllers" such as Ehrlich who sought to link population to the environment "often seemed to prefer animals to people," and "in this climate there is a tendency to suggest the problems of pollution arise from population growth rather than from outrageous abuse of the environment. There is a risk that we shall be using population as an alibi for failure to undertake effective management."

Notestein's concern with the demographic side of the argument was even more pointed. He specifically took issue with the proposition that "the proportion of unwanted pregnancies rises [inevitably] as one goes down the educational and income scales, or moves from white to black or from North to South." Unwanted pregnancy, he said, is not "natural" to lower-income groups; greater access to family planning by such groups would decrease unwanted pregnancies. He concluded, "Let's not sell family planning short before we have given it a reasonable chance."[32] These private sentiments found public expression in 1970 when Notestein publicly attacked the ZPG position in his article "Zero Population Growth: What Is It?"[33]

Dissatisfaction with family planning as a means of controlling population growth came just not from the ZPG, however, but also from established demographers. As early as 1967, Donald J. Bogue, a leading demographer at the University of Chicago, caused a stir when he wrote in the *Public Interest* that it was reasonable to assume that "the world population crisis is a phenomenon of the 20th century, and will be largely if not entirely a matter of history when humanity moves into the 21st century." Bogue's argument would be used by critics of population control in organized labor, as well as by popular columnists such as Ben Wattenberg, a former Johnson aide, who left the White House to become a syndicated columnist.[34]

The most radical critique of federally financed family planning came from University of California demographer Judith Blake, who in fact accepted the need to control overpopulation in the United States. Writing from a feminist perspective in a controversial article that appeared in *Science* in late 1969, Blake challenged the very premises of federally supported contraceptive efforts. She began by asking, "By what logic have the proponents of control moved from a concern with population growth to a recommendation favoring highest priority for poverty-oriented birth control programs?" She answered her rhetorical question by observing that proponents of the new policy have "seized" on the poor and the uneducated as the "target" group for birth control action because the rest of the population was "handling its family planning pretty well on its own." Why were the poor reluctant to accept family planning? She found that the population activists assumed either that the poor and uneducated were "irresponsible" or that the poor had not been "educated" in family planning or did not have access to contraceptives. Because it was politically impossible to label the poor as "irresponsible," family planners concluded that the poor had been deprived of their "right" to have "access" to family planning services.

In a close analysis of polling material dating from 1937 through 1969, Blake showed that Americans had consistently supported (ranging from 66 percent to 89 percent) the belief that birth control information should made available by the government to individuals who desired it. Therefore, the assumption that a "generalized and pervasive attitude of prudery on the part of the American public" had prevented birth control information from reaching the poor was false. Instead, she argued that the poor and the uneducated had not accepted artificial birth control (as her statistics revealed they had not) simply because they wanted larger families for cultural and religious reasons. Moreover, surveys showed that the poor and the uneducated especially distrusted government-supported programs. She found from her reading of survey data that the overall level of approval for federally funded family planning fell within lower-income groups.[35] Moreover, she observed that proposals for distribution of contraceptive pills to teenage girls met with significant disapproval among the poor, receiving as low as 15 percent support among poor and uneducated women, and only 13 percent support from their male counterparts.

Blake's argument cut to the quick of the argument for federal family planning. The poor simply did not avail themselves of contraception, even though it was readily available to them, because they wanted larger families than did higher-income and more highly educated groups. She drew the obvious policy conclusion: "In sum, the argument supporting a 'need' for nationwide publicly sustained birth control does not stand up under empirical scrutiny. . . . It seems clear that the suggested policy of poverty-oriented birth-control programs does not make sense as a welfare measure." Furthermore, she worried about the political implications of focusing on the poor, especially blacks, who might perceive themselves as targets of a government program designed to reduce their numbers. At the same time, she warned that the proposal to distribute contraceptive pills to teenage girls runs "a collision course with norms about premarital relations for young girls."

Blake remained concerned with the overpopulation problem. If federally funded family planning would not work—and clearly her arguments precluded more coercive measures targeted at the poor—what did she recommend? Here she made a proposal that appeared commonsensical from the perspective of population control. She argued that if American society wanted to reduce the rate of population growth, the best way to do so was to change the social and occupational roles of women in society. Instead of adhering to cultural "norms" that viewed women as wives and mothers, women should be allowed and encouraged to enter the workforce in occupational careers that often delayed marriage. She found signs that the emergence of feminism presented a counter to this cultural structure that encouraged women to be seen only as child bearers. Furthermore, she found that encouraging signs of "antinatalist" behavior already "exist among us as part of our covert and deviant culture, on one hand, and our elite and artistic culture, on the other." In speaking of "covert and deviant" culture, it was not clear whether she was referring to feminism, youth culture, or homosexuality (homosexuality assumed a reduced propagation of births as well), but it was evident that Blake proposed fundamental social and cultural changes as the best means of reducing population growth.

Blake's argument drew immediate and heavy criticism from the proponents of federally funded family planning.[36] Her desertion from the ranks indicated the deep dissension within the population movement by the time the Rockefeller commission issued its report in 1972. Her article slowly reverberated throughout the movement and the foundation world, eventually even changing the mind of John D. Rockefeller 3rd and his associates at the Population Council.

The Rockefeller Commission on Population Turns into a Fiasco

In 1970 John D. Rockefeller 3rd began his work on the Commission on Population Growth and the American Future without seeming to recognize the changing political climate concerning family planning policy. Or, if he was aware of these political problems, he failed to grasp their full implications. From the first, Rockefeller believed that the population issue and family planning should be kept out of politics. For him the problem was self-evident. Rampant population growth, here and abroad, threatened social, economic, and political stability. The problems seemed so obvious, the consequences of overpopulation so catastrophic, that Rockefeller believed easy agreement could be reached on the issue (with the possible exception of the Catholic Church, but even here he remained optimistic). He firmly believed that the population issue, by its nature, extended beyond politics. It was an issue that all right-minded people could agree was a problem—a problem to be addressed by philanthropists such as himself and nonpartisan medical and social scientists. He discovered, quickly enough, that politics in his own commission belied his optimism.

Working with Daniel Moynihan at the White House, Rockefeller carefully selected the twenty-four members of the commission to represent what he described as the "pluralistic society." Under pressure from the population lobby, Congress had included two controversial issues in the commission's mandate: to assess the implication of population growth for natural resources and the quality of the environment, and to assess various means to achieve a population level properly suited to the nation's environment and resources, and appropriate to the ethical values and principles of American society. Not everyone agreed with these two mandates. Many within the Population Council believed that the environmental issue was being pushed too hard by Paul Ehrlich and his friends, and that a decline in population growth would not necessarily improve the environment. Rockefeller and Charles F. Westoff, director of research for the commission, doubted whether the ethical issue should be considered by the commission. It had been placed on the agenda by proponents of sterilization and abortion through William Draper's efforts. Rockefeller was confident, however, that the Olympian objectivity of the experts appointed to the research staff would ensure a tempered outcome to the commission's work.

Every attempt was made to ensure balance and nonpartisanship. Often this pursuit of objectivity appeared too simple, as if having a representative from labor matched with a representative from business, a white with a minority, a Republican with a Democrat would ensure objectivity and reasoned conclusions. Over half of the White House nominees to the commission were rejected by Congress for being "too partisan."[37] Simply getting the commission selected took three months, but the final result appeared to be a good mix. Joining a staff of twenty population experts— social scientists and demographers—were four congressmen, two students, five women, four ethnic minority members (one Hispanic and three African-Americans), and representatives from business, labor, and the medical profession.[38] Democrats and Republicans were evenly balanced and included Senator Robert Packwood (R-Oregon) with Senator Joseph Tydings (D-Maryland), who after his defeat in the 1970 election was replaced by Senator Alan Cranston (D-California). John Erlenborn (R-Illinois) was to be replaced later with John Blatnick (D-Minnesota). In the second year, James Scheuer (R-New York) joined the commission.

Disagreement cropped up early. While most members of the research staff believed that the rate of population growth should be reduced, this goal was rejected at the first meeting of the commission. Instead, the commission accepted a compromise position that the population should be "stabilized" but not necessarily reduced. Moreover, a number of panels called for an investigation into the overall problems of economic and population growth, that is, the consequences of growth, not how to prevent it. Specifically, Howard D. Samuel, vice president of Amalgamated Clothing Workers of America, Paul Bertau Cornely, a Howard University professor, and Grace Olivarez, a Hispanic lawyer from Phoenix, pushed the commission to take up problems related to unemployment, poverty, and income distribution. David Lelewer, Rockefeller's personal associate, felt that the differences apparent in the commission came down to differing "attitudes toward the crises facing our society." The majority holds that "stabilizing the population will free up the resources and the time to resolve some of these problems." On the other hand, he noted that "our young and minority group commissioners" offer "a more serious indictment of the failure of our political system to deliver the 'American dream' to all of our citizens."[39] In short, from the commission's first meeting, members remained divided on the very purpose of the commission.

Further difficulties emerged concerning the composition of the research staff headed by Princeton University demographer Charles Westoff. Minority representatives criticized the staff as "lily white." Howard University professor Paul B. Cornely, an African-American, complained that "no scholarly presentation was made by minority persons, and no minority firms or consultants were used." He felt that "this paucity in minority input" was due to "the resistance and adamant attitude of the Executive Director."[40] Other meetings turned into acrimonious debates over immigration, racial relations, housing, and poverty. Upset with the continued disputes, one disgruntled committee member concluded that the commission became "a microcosm of the new power electorate—a coalition of minorities who have nothing in common except their minority status."[41]

Understandably enough, no one looked forward to commission meetings. As the commission struggled to draft a preliminary report, three identifiable factions emerged. First, a small "ecological" faction included five members who coalesced around the view that population growth was just one manifestation of humankind's insensitivity to the natural environment. This perspective was coupled with an antiurban, antitechnological, and anti-economic growth bias. The ecological faction was actively supported by Paul Ehrlich, who pressured the commission through a letter-writing campaign designed to link population growth to ecological disaster.[42] The environmental perspective, while carrying some weight in the commission, did not have the numbers to transform the commission into an environmental-population commission that recommended zero population growth.

The next two factions showed the sharpest fissures in the commission because of their size and because they took diametrically opposed, irreconcilable positions. A majority faction believed population growth remained the major issue confronting the nation. Less radical than its ecological counterpart, this group called for sex education, family planning information, and expanded federally subsidized contraceptive programs. The third faction, concerned with social justice, voiced the most discontent. Population policy, this group held, was no substitute for redistribution of wealth, job creation, equal opportunity, and civil rights.

Often the debates came down to the issue that the nation was not doing enough for its own people. Meetings turned into freewheeling discussions about social inequality in America. Finally, an exasperated Berelson wrote his fellow commissioners, imploring them to bury their differences and pursue the same goal. "My reminder," he wrote bluntly, "is that we are a population commission, not a commission on health, or government organization or capacity, or race, or minority ethnic status, or women, or children."[43] These issues are important, he added, but they are not ours. Berelson sought to cajole the commission to take a moderate position on population stabilization that emphasized the importance of "individual decisions" in the general society. He wanted the panel to recommend controlled and moderate population growth—thereby repudiating a zero population growth position. In arguing for this position, he maintained that he rejected a "Chamber of Commerce" position that population growth is always good and the ZPG position that population growth is always catastrophic. He urged the commission to recommend in favor of stable population growth without setting a specific target. Furthermore, he wanted the commission to emphasize the importance of individual citizens in creating stable population growth. The panel, he wrote, should seek to "optimize individual decisions." Behind this technical jargon, Berelson believed that people should have the right to sex education and the right to fertility control through "contraception, abortion, sterilization, and advanced technology." Finally, he called for the liberation of women from the "exclusive childbearing role" in American society, and immigration control for "humanitarian, cultural, and political considerations." When brought to the commission in early 1971, Berelson's position to focus the interim report narrowly on "unwanted fertility" won a narrow 8 to 5 vote.[44] This victory proved short-lived, and in fact probably fueled further dissension.

Ideological differences made consensus difficult and revealed unexpected fault lines. The debate over immigration restriction typified just how divided the commission could be. The immigration issue proved especially heated because the Ninety-second Congress had introduced sixty-five separate immigration bills in 1971.[45] On the commission, the proposal to restrict immigration to the United States drew qualified support from some representatives of organized labor and the African-American leaders.[46] On the other hand, business representatives tended to oppose restriction, even though Rockefeller estimated that immigration accounted for about 20 percent of America's population growth and should be restricted accordingly.[47] Breaking ranks with other labor representatives, Howard D. Samuel opposed immigration quotas because immigration has "enriched our country and reflects our humanitarian concern with peoples of the world."[48] Grace Olivarez, a Hispanic woman usually aligned with the minority supporting the social justice faction, joined business representatives in opposing restrictions on immigration.

Surprisingly, Charles Westoff, research director of the commission, urged Rockefeller not to recommend changes in immigration policy. He quoted Senator Samuel Ervin (D-North Carolina): "No legislative subject that I know of can stir up more emotion than the revision of immigration laws." Moreover, Westoff thought the United States could achieve "near-replacement fertility" (2.1 children) by eliminating "unwanted fertility." Most important, he thought American fertility might dip below replacement in "a decade or so," provoking a "whole new set of concerns.... And it may be useful to think of immigration as a valve that we could open if necessary to supply labor or population generally if this possibility eventuates."[49]

Although a compromise was finally reached in the commission that proposed the rate of immigration should be reduced roughly 10 percent over the next five years, Rockefeller's motion to limit immigration by forty thousand per year during this five-year period failed by a 7 to 10 vote.[50]

The most heated argument arose over abortion. Rockefeller believed that the abortion issue had to be discussed in the final report but should not be included in the interim report because it would become "all-encompassing." Most of the commissioners agreed with him. The very idea that abortion would be dealt with led Grace Olivarez to explode, declaring that she had no intention of attending any meeting if the commissioners were bringing with them a preconceived notion that abortion was going to be discussed.[51] Thus, it was agreed to postpone discussion of the abortion issue until preparation for the final draft in 1971. The postponement saved the commission from breaking up in 1970, but it only delayed the inevitable confrontation.

Rockefeller approached the delicate issue of abortion with calculated moderation.[52] When the time came for writing the final report, however, abortion could not be avoided, and the issue resulted in intractable differences. In the end, the final report revealed the depth of division among the panelists, leading to the inclusion of a minority report. The majority position stated that "in no sense should it [abortion] be considered a primary means of fertility control, but only a back up measure in cases of contraceptive failure." Yet, the majority noted, "We are impressed that induced abortion has a demographic effect wherever legalized. . . . Finally, to the moral poignancy involved in its use must be balanced the moral poignancy of a woman giving birth to an unwanted child and even more, the moral poignancy of the child's prospective life."

Most important, the majority report called for liberalized abortion laws that would allow a woman the right to have an abortion at any time throughout her pregnancy, if she so desired. This recommendation for "abortion on demand" created a firestorm among ethnic minority representatives on the commission. Specifically, Paul B. Cornely and Grace Olivarez vociferously opposed the majority recommendation. Cornely denounced legalized abortion as promoting "permissiveness." "Abortion-on-demand," he declared, "will provide our society with an easy way to eliminate the black and the poor and the disadvantaged and does not address itself to the solution of the major problems such as unemployment, inadequate housing, hunger and poverty which in part cause the suffering and tragedies in our society." He warned that American society had become "impersonal and calloused" toward human life, so to make abortion on demand a national policy would "nurture and feed this attitude in our society. Reverence for human life needs to become an integral part of the societal matrix."[53]

Grace Olivarez, the first Hispanic woman to graduate from law school at the University of Notre Dame, joined Cornely in protesting the proabortion stance of the commission. She argued that abortion was just not a religious issue. She felt that with new contraceptive technology, women could "gain control of our own bodies," but abortion was a surgical procedure that took human life and revealed that women did not, in fact, have control of their bodies. Returning to the social justice theme, she declared, "The poor cry out for justice and equality and we respond by giving them legalized abortion."[54]

Similarly, both Cornely and Olivarez opposed the majority recommendation to provide contraceptive information and services to minors, including voluntary sterilization. When society accepts, he wrote, giving contraceptive advice and services to minors, "then we are striking at the foundation and the roots of family life, which are already weakened by misuse of affluence and technology." Without addressing society's responsibility to support family life, education, neighborhoods, recreational facilities, and creative outlets that make it possible for minors to grow and develop, the "contraceptive approach to minors is the cheapest and most irresponsible way for our society to solve this problem [teenage pregnancy]."[55] Cornely's argument drew little support on the commission. The majority concluded that access to contraceptive services for minors would not necessarily lead to sexual irresponsibility. The recommendation on abortion and contraceptive services to minors easily won a 12 to 2 vote, with Cornely and Olivarez dissenting. The majority agreed that they could issue a minority report stating their differences on abortion and adolescent contraceptive services.[56]

Seeking Reelection, Nixon Rejects the Commission's Report

By the spring of 1972, the commission was ready to release its final report, *Population Growth and the American Future*. The report was in fact two reports, one representing the majority, the other the minority view. The commission's decision to issue the report in three sections over a period of several weeks was intended to gain publicity and to avoid having its recommendations for sex education, the distribution of contraceptives to minors, and legalized abortion dominate the discussion.[57] With hindsight, it might have been better to have avoided publicity altogether.

Instead, the commission sought to garner as much publicity as it could for its recommendations. Newspaper editors and columnists were encouraged to write favorably on the report. Furthermore, Rockefeller hoped that the publication of the report in the spring of 1972 would influence the national committees of the Democratic and Republican parties that were to meet later that summer to draft their party platforms in a presidential year.[58] This public relations campaign backfired, however. The day before the second report, containing the abortion section, was to come out, the Catholic bishops went on the attack and preempted any favorable publicity the report might have attracted in the national press. Having remained generally passive on the contraception issue, the church hierarchy simply could not ignore the commission's proabortion position.

On March 15, 1972, the National Catholic Welfare Conference (NCWC) called a press conference to condemn the commission for having "entered into an 'Ideological Valley of Death.'"[59] Monsignor James T. McHugh, director of the Family Life Division, denounced legalized abortion as a "eugenic" instrument with profound implications for American society. "If the child," he asked, "can be killed in his [*sic*] mother's womb any time she decides he is not wanted, what prevents us from killing the aged, the sick, the mentally or physically disadvantaged, or members of objectionable minority groups when their lives become a burden to others?" He pointed out what he perceived as a contradiction of American society struggling to protect the rights of minority groups while denying "the right to life of the unborn child."[60]

Rockefeller and his fellow commission members had expected criticism from the Catholic Church, but the severity of the attack clearly left Rockefeller reeling. Earlier in the month, he had contacted his good friend Theodore Hesburgh at Notre Dame to see whether there was a way to finesse the issue. "Because I believe so keenly that our Commission Report is positive and constructive," he wrote, " . . . I am wondering if there is some positive step I could take in relation to the report of Church leaders." Hesburgh responded within days, telling Rockefeller that "Catholics generally do not favor widespread use of abortion as a birth control mechanism, although there is an increasing openness in the Church to widespread discussion of population problems and effective means of birth control. I believe most Catholics today would be in agreement on the fact that there is a population problem." Expressing his own "strong feeling against abortion as a means of birth control," he suggested that the only way to get into a direct dialogue with the U.S. Catholic hierarchy would be through Bishop Joseph Bernardin, director of the U.S. Catholic Conference.

Shortly after the release of the bishops' statement, Rockefeller reported to Hesburgh that he had arranged to meet with Bishop Bernardin, but had been "disappointed" that Bernardin had insisted on bringing to the meeting Monsignor McHugh, whom Rockefeller described as the leading critic for the church in terms of the commission's report. At the meeting, Rockefeller felt that Bernardin "deferred" to McHugh. While the meeting was "friendly" and "worthwhile" in that it at least established contact, he could not help thinking "how gratifying it must be to feel so certain of the righteousness of one's cause." The Roman Catholic Church, he wrote, is one of "the great institutions in the world today," but "to support so strongly peace and at the same time to come out against efforts which are basic to peace such as a stabilized world population is hard to understand."

Hesburgh could only reply that he was glad Rockefeller had a chance to talk with Bernardin, but, "Like yourself, I regret that it wasn't with him alone since I am sure that would have been a better conversation." In his correspondence with Bernardin, however, Rockefeller was more pointed, telling the bishop, "What to me is most disturbing is the seeming attempt of a relatively small and highly organized group to impose its viewpoint on society." He concluded his letter by telling Bernardin that he did not expect a reply to his letter because "it [this letter] is my final thoughts" on the subject, not amenable to discussion.[61] Clearly, after the release of the Catholic conference's statement denouncing the commission, Rockefeller was not interested in engaging in a dialogue with the Catholic Church on the issue. The sides had been drawn into a debate that appeared to allow no opportunity for compromise.

Following the bishops' statement, the commission was flooded with letters from Roman Catholics denouncing the final report's recommendation for legalized abortion. The *New York Times* reported that within the first month over five hundred letters and telegrams were received denouncing the commission's stance on abortion.[62] Although the *Times* reported that much of this mail was running five to one against the commission, it described this as a well-organized campaign that suggested widespread and deep anger. For example, one woman from rural New Jersey warned Rockefeller that "God will not be mocked. He will strike not only the little people, but the big people (like you) as well, who consider the environment more important than human life. You talk about the dignity of quality existence, but are willing to commit murder, motivated by situation ethics."[63]

Rockefeller launched a counteroffensive in the national media to dampen what appeared to be growing negative opinion about the commission's report. At this juncture Rockefeller had one primary concern: to win the president to his side—or, at the very least, to make sure he did not come out against the report. He called upon his contacts at the *New York Times* and the *Washington Post*, encouraging them to write positive editorials. When they did, Rockefeller wrote to Katherine Graham, publisher of the *Post*, and John B. Oakes, editorial page editor of the *Times*, thanking them for their "very strong and positive" statements. "It was a most helpful offset," he told them, "to the concerted efforts of a small, well-organized group to discredit the report. It is amazing the impact that such an approach can have in political circles."[64]

At the same time, Rockefeller worked closely with Cynthia Wedel, president of the National Council of Churches, to mobilize Protestant opinion favorable to the commission's report. When the National Council of Churches endorsed the report, Rockefeller felt a small but important victory had been gained. He encouraged Wedel to arrange a meeting with

President Nixon to urge him to back the report against what he felt was a small, well-organized minority trying to impose its antiquated moral views on the majority. "It is interesting indeed," he told her, "how a highly organized effort by a small group directed at the White House and Congress can be hurtful to a report such as ours."[65] Wedel attempted to reassure him by reporting that she was "trying to work behind the scenes with some Roman Catholic leaders to see if we can get them at least to let people *study* the report."[66]

Of course, Rockefeller's accusations against the Catholic bishops' lobbying campaign mirrored the population movement's own activities throughout the decade. More specifically, the presidential commission that produced the report had been created through Rockefeller's well-orchestrated efforts in lobbying the Congress and the White House. Furthermore, it is debatable whether the commission represented, as Rockefeller claimed, a "pluralistic" society. Contrary to early suggestions, Catholics were not represented on the commission as Catholics per se. Still, in many ways, it was beside the point whether the population movement or the Catholic Church represented minority or majority interests, or whether they lobbied, fairly or unfairly, Congress and the White House. Perhaps it was hypocritical of Rockefeller to cry "foul" when the bishops undertook their own campaign against the commission's report. The real point, however, was that the report revealed, for all to see, that the population issue had become politicized because of abortion. And, as such, both sides would lobby political leaders and undertake to mobilize the electorate around the question.

Meanwhile, Rockefeller was worried about Nixon's failure to respond to the report. Although Moynihan had left the White House by 1972, Rockefeller sought his advice. At Moynihan's urging, he wrote Nixon to express his concern at the president's "seeming hesitancy in commenting on the report." He told Nixon he realized that the report "does raise some questions for you. At the same time I am terribly appreciative of our administration's demonstrated desire to act boldly in relation to issues important to our national well-being." He stressed that the commission's report placed an emphasis on "individual freedom of choice and the quality of life."[67] Rockefeller's letter was designed to appeal to Nixon's ego, his sense of historic mission, and his willingness to stand above politics in order to cut new paths in public policy.

Nixon in 1972 did not suffer from any illusion that the abortion issue could be—or, more important, should be—taken out of politics. For Nixon most issues were political, and if they were not political, he was not much interested in them. In any case, he saw the political implications of opposing the commission's recommendations. Here was a chance to gain

Catholic support for his reelection. In the spring of 1972 he was singularly focused on his reelection, and the prospects of realigning the northern, white vote to the Republican party excited him. In fact, he already had Charles Colson working on "a Catholic strategy."[68]

George Wallace's presidential campaign in 1968 showed that the northern ethnic Catholic vote—the backbone of the Democratic party in cities—was vulnerable. Nixon had become increasingly convinced that the Catholic vote was critical to his reelection. "They live," Nixon said, as later recalled by Colson, "in rings around the cities, they're the new middle class."[69] Although the Democrats maintained control of Congress in 1970, the election of James Buckley, the brother of pundit William Buckley, to the U.S. Senate from supposedly liberal New York persuaded Nixon that he was on the right track. Buckley had won the election on a third-party ticket, the Conservative party, against two liberals, Richard Ottinger (Democrat) and Charles Goodell (Republican), by sharpening cultural and law-and-order issues. Moreover, Nixon saw in New York a generally conservative trend as the Conservative party had grown from 141,877 statewide votes in New York in its first race in 1962 to Buckley's victory of 2.1 million in the fall of 1970.

At Colson's urging, Nixon took on two issues that were felt to be of overriding concern to Catholic voters—parochial schools and abortion. On April 6, 1972, Nixon traveled to Philadelphia to tell the annual convention of the National Catholic Education Association that he believed that nonpublic schools must be preserved.[70] A month later, Nixon entered into the abortion debate.

Within his staff, which was overwhelmingly Protestant, only Patrick Buchanan (a Catholic) and Charles Colson (a Protestant) believed that Nixon should take sides on the abortion issue. Most advised cautious silence. Nonetheless, by May presidential candidate George McGovern had gained momentum when he defeated his rival Hubert Humphrey in the Ohio Democratic primary. Humphrey had begun attacking McGovern for being soft on amnesty for those who avoided the draft, marijuana, and abortion, and although he failed to defeat McGovern, these attacks bolstered his campaign. Nixon saw an opportunity to reinforce Humphrey's characterization of McGovern as a wild liberal, while at the same time staking his claim to the Catholic vote by opposing abortion.

On Friday, May 5, 1972, Nixon issued a public statement distancing the administration from the commission's recommendation on legalized abortion and extending contraceptive services to minors. He told the press that he would not comment extensively on the report, but he added: "I want to reaffirm and reemphasize that I do not support unrestricted abortion policies. . . . I consider abortion an unacceptable form of population control.

In my judgment, unrestricted abortion policies would demean human life." He continued: "I also want to make it clear that I do not support the unrestricted distribution of family planning services and devices to minors. Such a measure would do nothing to preserve and strengthen close family relationships."[71]

Two days later, the following Sunday, Nixon released a letter he had sent to Terence Cardinal Cooke of New York supporting his campaign to repeal the recently passed New York abortion law. Nixon told the cardinal that while abortion was not a federal matter (it soon would not be with *Roe*, however), "I would personally like to associate myself with the convictions you deeply feel and eloquently express."[72] Nixon had brought the issue of abortion into the political arena.

Rockefeller was irate. The letter to Cardinal Cooke added insult to injury. On Monday morning he phoned the White House to complain. Reaching presidential aide John Ehrlichman, Rockefeller expressed his anger. Ehrlichman tried to calm Rockefeller down by telling him that the Cooke letter was primarily political. "We don't want to screw up in New York," he told Rockefeller, "especially with the Conservative party." He added that Nixon had not made the abortion issue a federal problem. "We have always tried to pass the abortion issue on to the states," he said, "and we intend on continuing this policy."[73]

Nixon's strategy paid off in the general election. His Democratic rival, George McGovern, a liberal, antiwar U.S. senator from South Dakota, proved an easy target for Nixon. McGovern's call for defense cuts, immediate withdrawal from Vietnam, amnesty for draft evaders who had fled to Canada, and income redistribution allowed Nixon to attack him as an inept radical who wanted "abortion, acid (LSD), and amnesty." In the end, Nixon won the popular vote, polling over 60 percent, and the electoral college, 520 to 17, with McGovern winning only Massachusetts and the District of Columbia. Nixon took 66 percent of the independent vote and 42 percent of the Democratic vote, an especially impressive number given that Eisenhower in 1952 had attracted only 28 percent of the votes cast by Democrats.[74] More important, Nixon captured 60 percent of the Catholic vote, 59 percent of the working-class vote, and 57 percent of the union-household vote. Critical in gaining this vote was a growing ideological polarization within the electorate. Within this context, social issues having to do with urban problems, crime, student unrest, and welfare were critical to Nixon.

The abortion issue proved less potent in the electorate than did the war in Vietnam or the view that McGovern was too liberal to be president. Although abortion did not play a significant role in determining the outcome of the election, voters were gradually changing their views on abortion, shifting toward a more proabortion position.[75] The importance of Nixon's stance on abortion lay not in its specific translation in the polls but in his ability to characterize McGovern as an out-of-touch liberal elitist seeking to impose his values on an electorate that had become increasingly wary of the liberal agenda, including legalized abortion.

Even after the election, Rockefeller clung tenaciously to the work of the commission. He attempted to rally public opinion around the report by forming a new organization, the Citizens' Committee on Population and the American Future. This committee was intended to "keep the report before the public, defend it against its critics, and persuade public officials to act positively on its recommendations." Headed by Carol Foreman and Stephen L. Salyer, a twenty-one-year-old commission member, the committee called for population stabilization, extending reproductive services and sex education to teenagers.[76] The committee accomplished little on the national level, although it produced a film on population that was shown on New York public television shortly after the election.[77] Within a year the citizens' committee had been disbanded, admitting that the population issue per se was off the presidential agenda.

A postmortem of Rockefeller's failure to influence public policy through the presidential commission was offered in a final report written by Carol Foreman, executive director of the Citizens' Committee on Population and the American Future, in late 1973. She concluded—surprisingly given the complete failure of the commission and the citizens' committee—that the commission's report might have won approval in a slightly different climate. She noted that the nation's population growth had declined significantly from the time the commission was formed in 1969 until it issued its report. In July 1969 the fertility rate was 85.5, and by June 1973 it had fallen to 69.0. With such a decline, the report noted that "it would have been difficult to speak of a trauma and a crisis of numbers." The result seemed inevitable in this context. "The American public and certainly the American institutions of government are not usually moved to commit great resources to the solution of a problem until the problem becomes a crisis."[78]

She felt that the abortion issue had only heated up when New York State enacted its abortion law in July 1970 and allowed abortion in the twenty-sixth week of pregnancy. Several months later Hawaii and Washington enacted liberal abortion laws. At each step, the report found, organized opposition developed. "There was never any doubt," the report declared, "that the committee would endorse legalized abortion." Still, "the commission did not anticipate the ultimate extent of the backlash that arose over the issue." Nonetheless, even after accurately describing the fierce backlash over abortion, the report concluded that the final, and significant, "factor" in the failure of the commission, was the change in personnel in the White House, specifically Moynihan's resignation to take a position as American ambassador to the United Nations. Had he stayed on, "maybe the whole reception of the report would have been different."[79] The end result has been that the commission's work has not provided any "dramatic" or new policies or legislation.[80]

Shortly before disbanding the Commission on Population Growth and the American Future, its research director, Charles Westoff, offered a final summary by noting that "Mr. Nixon's reaction no doubt disappointed (to put it mildly) most, if not all of us, but most progress in this field has consistently come from Congress rather than the White House."[81] Westoff's point was debatable—President Johnson and President Nixon had been critical in developing federal family planning programs—but his observation suggested that the focus of population activities now lay in Congress. Here, population activists found further disappointment, although not total defeat. Indeed, family planning initiatives in Congress and the White House were mixed.

Congress Expands Family Planning Funding: Mixed Policies in the Nixon Administration

Congress adopted the Social Security amendments of 1972 (H.R. 1), which further expanded federal support for family planning programs. Under this legislation, states were required to provide reimbursement for family planning services under Medicaid. Previously this had been only an option for states. At the same time, this federal mandate provided 90 percent reimbursement for state family planning services. This legislation specifically sought to ensure that all current, past, and potential welfare recipients who desired contraceptive services would receive them.

Moreover, the legislation required states receiving federal funds to provide family planning services to minors who were sexually active and to other unmarried persons. If states did not comply with this mandate by January 1, 1974, a 1 percent penalty on the federal share of Aid to Families with Dependent Children was imposed. Concerned, however, with rising welfare costs, Congress also imposed a ceiling on welfare reimbursements through the 1970 Family Planning Services Act, while at the same time increasing family planning service funds through Medicaid.[82]

That same year, 1972, Congress authorized special grants for maternal and child health programs under Social Security. These special grants enabled states to finance family planning programs, if they so wished.[83] Although Congress overwhelmingly endorsed this funding mechanism, many worried that these special grants gave too much power to HEW and the states in deciding how these grants might be used. Maternal and child health were broad categories, and funds might not be used specifically for family planning services. These formula grants were often used to finance family planning programs.[84]

The following year, Senator Alan Cranston (D-California), a former member of the commission on Population Growth and the American Future, attempted to address this problem when he introduced amendments to the Family Planning Services and Population Research Act (S.R.1708). Cranston proposed that special grants be turned into specifically targeted categorical grants and that the Public Health Service become the primary agency for family planning. Cranston's proposal ran into immediate opposition from the Nixon White House, which had called for shifting power back to the states under what the administration called New Federalism. Under New Federalism, Nixon called for federal block grants that allowed states and local communities to use these funds as they saw fit. Explicit in New Federalism was a belief that targeted "categorical" program grants should be reduced in order to give state and local governments more program and spending discretion. Opposed to the categorical grant mechanism found in Cranston's bill, the administration threw its support to another bill, (S.R.1632), proposed by Senator Jacob Javitts (D-New York). This bill envisioned the Medicaid system as the central source of federal family planning. With the administration's backing, Cranston's bill was defeated and Javitts's bill was enacted.

In opposing categorical family planning grants, the administration pointed to the great success of family planning in the United States. Medicaid provided the bulk of this funding for family planning programs. In the judgment of the Nixon administration, federal family planning worked well under Medicaid funding and HEW special grants. The system did not need to be changed, and figures proved the case. Family planning had been made available in 2,379 of the 3,099 counties in the United States. Voluntary and other agencies served 41 percent of reported patients, health departments 36 percent, and hospitals 23 percent. As Henry E. Simmons, deputy assistant for health and scientific affairs at HEW, observed, categorical grants had been useful in the past, but "now that the programs are firmly established financing should shift from project grants to Medicaid programs in which states assume the major role in determining program needs in their area."[85]

The Nixon administration remained intent on showing that it fully supported federal family planning when it approved $118 million for family planning and population research. Congress added to the funding legislation a "right of conscience provision" that protected the rights of medical personnel or institutions that did not want to perform sterilizations or abortions because of religious or moral beliefs.[86] Still, the administration won its key point in opposing mandated and specified categorical grants for family planning. Clearly, by 1973, the Medicaid system was the primary source of funding for federal family planning for lower-income groups in the United States.[87]

Still, in 1972 many critics doubted Nixon's full commitment to family planning. Prior to the election, Nixon reversed an earlier decision to allow OEO funding for sterilizations. Following the election, Nixon ordered that no further increases in family planning grants be given; then, in an attempt to control the federal budget, he impounded remaining funds. Moreover, he ordered the disbanding of a separate Center for Family Planning Services in HEW. Nonetheless, these were minor setbacks given the general progress family planning programs had made during the ten years from 1965 to 1975.[88] Although contemporary and later critics complained that federal funding remained inadequate and that services remained underdeveloped, relying too heavily on Medicaid reimbursements to private providers, the critical point remained this: family planning programs had become institutionalized on the federal level. Whatever defeats the population movement experienced under Nixon, family planning programs remained an integral part of federal social policy.

In this regard, the population movement had succeeded in its primary goal. Federal appropriations for family planning had risen dramatically under the Nixon administration. By 1973, the year before Nixon resigned from the presidency as a result of the Watergate entanglements, an estimated 2.6 million women—three-quarters of them low-income—were receiving family planning services in all public and private programs. Furthermore, Frederick Jaffe, president of the Alan Guttmacher Institute and vice president of PPFA, estimated that between 1969 and 1975, U.S. family planning programs averted 1.1 million unwanted births. These averted births, he claimed, resulted in short-term savings to the federal government for health and social welfare services of $1.1 billion, compared with a total federal investment in family planning in these years of $584 million just for clinic programs. Federal appropriations for the family planning clinic program had risen from $32.8 million in 1970 to $159.7 million by 1975.[89]

Rockefeller Reconsiders Family Planning Programs

During the squabbles in Nixon's second term over federal family planning expenditures, a marked shift had occurred in the policy debate. Abortion became the dominant issue. As a consequence, the issue of whether the federal government should be involved in funding contraceptive services became far less important than its involvement in abortion. Federal family planning remained contentious, especially over American participation in international programs, but abortion became the center of a debate that polarized the general public, policy makers, and religious groups in a way that family planning never did.

Rockefeller's involvement in the abortion movement reflected this change in the policy debate. Following the fiasco of the commission, Rockefeller committed himself to defending legalized abortion. This commitment was not new, but it became a central focus of much of his activity in his later years. Rockefeller's involvement in the abortion movement, which will be explored more fully in the next chapter, set the context for his rethinking of family planning programs in the early 1970s. Through his involvement with the abortion movement, he gained a new appreciation for the importance of women in economic development and family planning strategy.

His first active involvement in the abortion movement came in 1972 during a New York State campaign to repeal the state's liberal abortion law. In 1972 the Catholic Church, under the leadership of Terence Cardinal Cooke, had organized a successful grassroots movement to repeal legislation enacted in 1970 liberalizing New York State's abortion law. Acting through his assistant Joan Dunlop, Rockefeller contributed heavily to financing proabortion forces, although to little avail. Only Governor Nelson Rockefeller's veto prevented the legislation from being overturned.[90] Following the New York campaign, Rockefeller continued to support PPFA's congressional lobbying efforts. He kept in close touch with PPFA activists such as Harriet Pilpel and Joan Robbins.[91]

Eliminating or restricting publicly funded abortions became a major goal of congressional opponents of abortion. Following the Supreme Court's 1973 decision in *Roe v. Wade*, the number of federally funded abortions increased dramatically. In 1973 the federal government funded 270,000 abortions at a cost of approximately $50 million. Intent on removing federal support for abortion, in 1973 Representative Angelo D. Roncallo (R-New York) proposed an amendment to an HEW appropriations funding bill that would have eliminated federal involvement in abortion. The Roncallo bill, after a bitter all-night floor debate, was finally defeated by a 247 to 123 vote. Two months later Dewey F. Bartlett (R-Oklahoma) offered a similar amendment, with a qualification that restricted federally funded abortions to those cases necessary "to save the life of the mother." This amendment passed by a 50 to 34 vote but would be defeated in conference.[92] Throughout these debates, he helped fund proabortion lobbying.[93] At the same time, Rockefeller funded the creation of a data bank of antiabortion activists for use by Planned Parenthood.

Even though Rockefeller supported legalized abortion, the Population Council had not taken a stand on the issue as late as 1975. In 1971 the council appointed Daniel Callahan, a philosopher, to a permanent position after he had successfully developed a staff seminar on the ethics of population control a few years earlier.[94] A liberal Catholic, Callahan became a key voice for accepting a proabortion position within the Population Council, although this came after a good deal of debate.

For example, former Population Council president Frank Notestein expressed the general ambivalence felt by many, especially the older leaders, on the abortion issue. Responding to a request to the council by the Indian government to provide equipment for abortions in 1971, Notestein declared in a lengthy memorandum that argued that abortion should be seen as a "personal and social failure. Moreover, its widespread proliferation would, I suspect, detract from the value put on the protection and nurturing of individual life."[95] As the debate heated up in the council, Notestein urged caution. In 1973 he wrote Berelson that while he accepted abortion as the moral right of "every couple, and maybe of every woman, in the first three months of gestation," he consider it "a great tragedy." He added, however, that abortion should be a personal choice, but he was not persuaded to support it as an instrument of population policy. "Facing the general aversion to abortion, we risk, when we make it an instrument of population policy, corrupting the basic idealism of our whole effort at demographic transition." He noted that he had voted for the abortion position in Planned Parenthood because it was an organization concerned "first and foremost with helping individuals deal with personal problems." Nonetheless, he urged the Population Council not to take a proabortion stance, warning, "If we do not watch out we shall justify the assertion of our enemies to the effect that we are basically against life. . . . The world needs some respected group that moves carefully where humanitarian considerations are involved. We can do all that if we constantly and firmly take the anti-abortion stance and use every occasion to point out that the need for abortions is the proof of program failure in the field of family planning and public health education."[96]

The problems raised by the abortion issue only indicated deeper problems within the Population Council concerning its mission and focus of activities. Indeed, Berelson reported in 1971 that the "Population Council faces serious questions about its size and priorities." As Berelson pointed out, the council's pioneering role in family planning had been replaced by new agencies working in the field, including federal programs, as well as the United Nations' Fund for Population, the World Bank, and the World Health Organization.[97] Furthermore, the Population Council had become increasingly aware of a backlash against family planning, especially in

Third World countries. Meeting with major donors, including the Ford Foundation, and AID, the following year, Berelson found that a theme running through the population community was that there were serious difficulties ahead for the population field, "partly because the programs to date have not been successful," largely because of low continuation rates of recipients receiving birth control at home and abroad, and "partly, even mainly, because of political opposition developing in the Third World to this imposition from the outside."[98]

These problems were manifested further the following year when Berelson attended an IPPF conference in Brighton, England, coming away from it with a "heightened sense of the difficulties facing the population movement these days." He discovered that there was a lack of consensus around family planning programs, the importance of population growth, and clear signs of a "backlash." Even the ever-optimistic Ray Ravenholt, head of population at AID, reported in a private conversation with Berelson that "the one thing these people don't seem to want to do is family planning."[99] A short time later, Robert McNamara, who after leaving the Johnson administration as secretary of defense to become president of the World Bank, told Berelson that he was disheartened by the state of family planning. Many of our friends, he confided, see family planning as being "too simple, too narrow, and too coercive."[100]

These anxieties about the future of family planning and the mission of the Population Council manifested themselves at the World Population Conference meeting at Bucharest, Romania, on August 19-30, 1974, in which John D. Rockefeller 3rd was to play a prominent role by delivering a keynote address to the delegates. Rockefeller's disappointment with the presidential commission two years earlier, his involvement in the abortion movement, and growing criticism of population control increasingly informed his perceptions of family planning.

With Nixon's resignation from the presidency following the Watergate break-in scandal, Rockefeller hoped that the Commission on Population Growth and the American Future might receive a more favorable reception from Gerald Ford, who had assumed the presidency on August 9, 1974. He considered bringing the report again to the White House, but on the recommendation of his advisers, he decided that the approaching world conference in Bucharest would provide a more favorable forum for his views.[101] At this point Rockefeller was anxious about the direction of the international family planning program, but he had not formulated a clear alternative to current family planning programs. The appointment of Joan Dunlop as his associate in 1973 proved critical in reshaping his thought. Bringing a feminist perspective to population issues, Dunlop played an important role in helping Rockefeller reformulate his position.

Dunlop came to Rockefeller with unusual credentials. She had worked as an executive secretary to Paul Ylvisaker, director of public affairs at the Ford Foundation, from 1960 through 1967. Ylvisaker had been critical in the development of the "gray areas program for the cities," a multi-million-dollar program that became a model for Johnson's antipoverty urban program. From the Ford Foundation, Dunlop went to work as an assistant to Kenneth B. Clark at the Metropolitan Applied Research Center, which was heavily involved in civil rights. After a year she became special assistant to Frederick O. R. Hayes, the budget director for New York City, under Mayor John V. Lindsay. In 1970 Dunlop became assistant director of the Fund for the City of New York, an independent grant-making agency, originally established as a Ford Foundation project. Thus she joined Rockefeller's staff with an extensive background in urban affairs, having cultivated political connections with the New York foundation and liberal political communities. Perceiving herself as a feminist, although she had not been involved directly in the movement, she encouraged Rockefeller's growing disaffection with family planning as a cure-all for social problems.[102]

In 1974, as Rockefeller began preparing for his Bucharest speech, he already had concluded that more attention to the social needs of women in family planning programs had to be considered. Joan Dunlop supported this shift in thinking. In early May 1974 she wrote Rockefeller that she was quite unenthusiastic about continuing population work "unless the leadership in the United States is removed or makes some very clear policy changes. Draper and Ravenholt [AID] et al are hurting the United States in profound and long-term ways." She added, lest Rockefeller missed her point, "They have hurt your reputation by including you implicitly and explicitly in their articulation of the problem."[103] She began sending him reading material from critics of population control, including the Marxist anthropologist Pierre Pradervand, who argued that "Western and especially American pressure for population control in Africa has been heavy-handed, tactless, and remarkably inefficient." Pradervand maintained that peasant societies tended to be strongly pronatalist, with women having children for economic and social reasons. He observed, for example, that in certain West African tribes, women who had not borne children were often buried apart from the rest of the group. "What we need," Pradervand declared, "is investments in employment, education, basic health, and a better distribution of income and social services. We need new global development."[104]

Working closely with a speechwriting team she assembled, Dunlop helped prepare Rockefeller's Bucharest speech. Dunlop reassured Rockefeller that she had recently had a conversation with David Hopper, a leading Canadian population expert, in which he told her that the speech would mark "a major shift away from family planning" as we know it. She added that the "decision to go the family planning route was the right decision at the time [1950s and 1960s]. Now is the opportunity to increase the experience we have had and to learn from some the sense of disappointment and to build from what we have learned about family planning."[105] In preparing the speech she wanted Rockefeller to emphasize the role of women in economic development. When he appeared to back away from taking a strong enough stand on women in the early drafts, she criticized the speech as too tempered and "too much like knee-jerk liberal stuff."[106]

In taking this new course, Dunlop and her team warned Rockefeller that he should be prepared for "nasty questions" at Bucharest. Her team of speechwriters emphasized, however, that "it is important to keep in mind—and to stress repeatedly—that you are attempting to provide a middle ground between those who say that population problems are everything and those who say they are nothing. You are not turning your back on family planning," but you see development as important.[107]

The old guard at the Population Council saw the speech differently. After reading the final version, an upset Berelson declared that Rockefeller had rejected entirely past statements on population policies, both personally and institutionally. The speech, he declared, "knocked" donor agencies, the IPPF, and the Population Council "way too hard."[108] When Berelson felt his views were not getting through, he opened a personal attack on Dunlop, denouncing her as a "neo-Marxist." An angry Berelson sent Rockefeller a memorandum entitled "Marxist Perspectives on Population" in hopes that Rockefeller would see the light. Dunlop was outraged by the accusation. She crafted a harsh reply to Berelson but in the end decided not to send it, telling Rockefeller, "I found my sense of humor under my pillow overnight; however, this is the letter I was planning to send to Barney: 'I want to take exception in the strongest possible terms with your characterization of this Bucharest speech as having 'neo-Marxist' or a 'New Left ring' to it. Until the 'population establishment' takes arguments of this nature seriously and debates them openly as a search for solutions, you will continue to exacerbate the polarization.'"[109] How much of a sense of humor she had gained "overnight" might have been questioned.

Some of the hostility toward Dunlop came because she was a woman challenging the basic premises that had dominated the council, in regard to its mission but also to the place of women within the organization. This attitude toward women was expressed by Notestein in a memorandum written to Berelson that summarized the history of women within the population movement. Notestein observed that Margaret Sanger and the first generation of female birth controllers had little sense of the importance of statistics, noting: "Maybe she [Sanger] was more willing to be thus misled.

As second-generation suffragists they were not at all disposed to allow the brutish male to be in charge of contraception. Women must have their own methods!" He had even less regard for more recent feminists: "Today's Liberals complain violently that the men are trying to saddle the women with all the contraceptive work. You can't please them if you do, and can't please them if you don't."[110]

Rockefeller was sympathetic to Dunlop's position. Furthermore, his liberal sensibilities allowed him to be open to the concerns being expressed by critics of population control in the developing nations. In the end Rockefeller stayed his course and went to Bucharest to deliver his speech.

By all accounts, Bucharest turned into a debacle. The conference quickly became a debate between the wealthy developed nations and the poor developing nations. Led by the delegation of the United States, headed by Secretary of HEW Caspar Weinberger, the Western nations supported the United Nations' resolution "The World Population Plan of Action," which called for a mandatory and exact 1.2 percent rate of population growth.[111] In response, the Third World nations offered a counterresolution, "Declaration on a New International Economic Order," which called for a radical redistribution of the world's wealth, while describing the "population dilemma" as a "manifestation of economic inequality between nations."[112]

Rockefeller's speech at a plenary session confused most foreign delegates and stunned the American participants. In a calm, reassuring voice, Rockefeller declared, "Clearly, the [family planning] programs that have been undertaken have proved inadequate when compared to the magnitude of the problems facing us. With this background very much in mind, I come to Bucharest with an urgent call for a deep and probing reappraisal of all that has been done in the population field." Having said this, he turned to the central point of his address: "Population planning must be placed within the context of economic and social development." Family planning programs in themselves could not address economic and social problems; family planning was not a panacea but needed to be placed within the larger framework of social reform. Moreover, he declared family planning programs needed to give "new and urgent attention to the role of women . . . [in] any modern development program."

He concluded by repeating the underlying theme of his speech: "Therefore, we of the industrialized nations should be extremely cautious in advising others how to proceed. . . . At the same time, I strongly believe that the developed nations must strive to understand the new and different characteristics of modern development, become more sensitive to the fact that each nation must solve its development and fertility problems in its own way, and stand ready to assist substantially in those processes."[113]

Rockefeller did not recommend any specific programs, but the implications of his talk were clear to the Western delegates. International family planning had failed by not promoting economic and social development. Rockefeller did not reject family planning per se but instead saw population control in larger terms of social change. With economic development, families would have fewer children; education programs created opportunities for economic advancement; health and social welfare programs meant that families would remain less dependent on children to provide care and support of ill and elderly parents; and the promotion of women into better jobs allowed for economic independence and delayed marriages. In articulating this new position, Rockefeller broke ranks with those who saw family planning as a single curative to the world's problems. This placed him on the side of those who demanded social and economic reform.

Ironically, many of the representatives of the developing nations reacted with hostility to Rockefeller's speech. They came expecting to hear a spokesman for imperialism, so they heard what they wanted to hear. In turn, the representatives from the Western industrialized nations understood exactly what had been said. They felt betrayed.

Rockefeller's speech marked only a prelude to the bitter exchange that characterized the conference. The one delegation that proved to be the most opposed to the United States was from the People's Republic of China. Early in the conference, the Chinese delegation dropped the first bombshell when it demanded that all references to China's population problems be deleted from the conference documents. Concerned that the conference would break up even before it began, United Nations spokesmen requested that delegates disregard any references to China's population in conference documents. On the third day, the Chinese dropped their next bombshell when Huang Shu-tse, the vice minister of health, denounced the conference as designed "to carry on and develop the militant spirit of imperialism and hegemonism of the superpowers," rather than finding a means to reduce the world's population. He called for "breaking down the unequal international economic relations, winning and safeguarding national independence, and developing the national economy and culture independently and self-reliantly in the light of each country's specific conditions and differing circumstances."[114] This set the tone for the rest of the conference. Led by representatives of China, Algeria, and Argentina, joined by delegations from Latin America, Africa, the socialist bloc, and the Holy See, the conference rejected the United Nations' plan. Instead it voted to approve a highly amended resolution that called for the redistribution of wealth, social and economic development, and national autonomy in a "new economic order." The resolution marked a major defeat for the United States, and, as one Algerian delegate described it, Bucharest marked "the end of the IPPF generation."[115]

The outcome of Bucharest and Rockefeller's speech shook the population movement in the United States. Nixon's rejection of the Rockefeller commission, debate over abortion, with its corresponding emergence of proabortion and antiabortion grassroots activists, and now Bucharest revealed all too well that population and family planning had become politicized. In this highly charged environment, the philanthropic community, beginning with the Population Council and quickly followed by the Ford Foundation, reevaluated its population activities. In the process, the population movement fragmented into interest groups concerned with abortion, zero and negative population growth, the environment, and immigration. At the same time, the politics of population, family planning, and abortion became polarized, transforming American politics on the presidential and legislative levels. And, in this new political atmosphere, policy formation shifted from elite interests to well-organized social movements intent on mobilizing their own constituencies to influence policy. The abortion debate in America revealed this profound shift of power in a sharply divided world.

6

Contesting the Policy Terrain
After Roe:
From Reagan to Clinton

Following the Bucharest conference, Rockefeller returned to the United States with a new vision regarding the meaning of family planning policy. In pursuing this new outlook, he sought to broaden the meaning of population control to include economic development and bettering the condition of women in developing and developed nations of the world. Under Rockefeller, the Population Council underwent dramatic changes in personnel and set a new agenda in international family planning. This involved withdrawing from active involvement in family planning policy within the United States.

At the same time, concerned with the status of women in the United States, Rockefeller devoted the remaining years of his life to the cause of legalized abortion and sex education in America. Working closely with his associate Joan Dunlop, Rockefeller emerged as a key person in the proabortion movement, providing financial support and direction to a number of groups, including Planned Parenthood, Catholics for a Free Choice, and Catholic Alternatives. Concerned with the mobilization of antiabortion forces in Congress, Rockefeller actively became involved in the politics of abortion. By the time he died in 1978 in an automobile accident, abortion had become a political battle that consumed the White House and Congress.

The fight over legalized abortion mobilized antiabortion groups to overturn *Roe v. Wade* and to restrict federal funding for abortion. In response, supporters of legalized abortion organized to protect the rights of women guaranteed under the Supreme Court decision. With the general electorate divided on the abortion issue, political resolution of this controversy became impossible and the debate intractable. Moreover, the mobilization of grassroots groups meant that power shifted from elite interests, which had played a critical role in the shaping of family planning policy in the first three decades following the Second World War, to social movements organized on the community level. In this shift, overpopulation became less prominent than "rights" issues, as feminists fought to maintain the right of women to have legal abortions and antiabortionists proclaimed the rights of the fetus.

The Population Council Enters a New Era

Rockefeller's Bucharest speech, in effect, repudiated family planning as it had been pursued since the Population Council's inception in 1952. By declaring that family planning in itself was not sufficient to stabilize world population growth, Rockefeller proclaimed a new course of action that called for radical social change that encompassed health, education, the status of women, and social inequality in the less developed nations. This new agenda did not reject traditional family planning per se—birth control, sterilization, and abortion remained necessary components in addressing the problem of overpopulation—but social change and economic development provided a better means of limiting population growth. Nonetheless, Rockefeller's speech sent shock waves through the population establishment in America.[1]

Frank Notestein returned from Bucharest to report that "every action group got its comeuppance. The ZPG and the Negative Population Growth people found out that they were talking to themselves and the world was not at all prepared to listen to them." Similarly, the same was true of the "more strident women's rights advocates. If they had ears (which is to be doubted) they found out that their message was not put into forms that interested Asiatic, African, or Latin American women." In turn, "Planned Parenthood enthusiasts, like me, found out quickly—if they had not already known it—that their pet programs were not high on the agenda of action that interested governments." Referring to Rockefeller's speech, he noted, "On the other hand, social and economic change enthusiasts (like our boss) somehow haven't understood that the ... development processes which are not adequately supported in their own right ... are not likely to be supported." He concluded, "It was a humbling experience for everyone. I've seldom been as blue."[2]

Notestein spoke for many in the population movement who had devoted their professional lives to reducing population growth. Many of these old-timers in the movement saw this new emphasis on social development as a cure to the population problem as utopian. Bernard Berelson, having gone on record describing Rockefeller's speech as "neo-Marxist," continued to express his discontent with the Bucharest conference. In early 1973, following a mild stroke, he had announced his intention to resign as president of the Population Council. Offended by the apparent dismissal of his lifelong work, he left the presidency in a bitter exchange with Rockefeller. Until his death a few years later, Berelson continued to feel that his nemesis, Joan Dunlop, had destroyed the Population Council.[3]

Berelson was not alone in feeling betrayed. Shortly after Bucharest, he attended a meeting held at the Ford Foundation for a select group of twenty key people to discuss the implications of the conference for the population "establishment." At this three-hour meeting, Berelson joined in the general lamentation that the Bucharest meeting had been a farce. Fred Jaffe from Planned Parenthood expressed the general sentiment of the group when he declared that he regretted that "the conference so readily accepted the 'myth' that family planning had failed." Jaffe observed that these programs had "failed in the same way that efforts to overcome poverty in the United States have failed; it is not the programs that are at fault so much as the inadequacy of the effort in relation to the magnitude of need."[4]

These views were shared by others within government. For example, the Agency for International Development's population program under Raymond Ravenholt continued to pursue its policy of controlling population growth through traditional family planning programs. Critical of those who sought to link economic development and social reform to population issues, Ravenholt denounced this "new breed" of social scientists. One official at the Ford Foundation quoted Ravenholt, declaring that "the biggest threat to mass population programs stems from 'revisionist tendencies' promulgated by those unduly concerned with 'irrelevant' issues of social policy or even general health care." Younger social scientists found Ravenholt an "unregenerate conservative" whose single focus on mass distribution of the pill was myopic and his personal style unnecessarily bellicose. They took particular offense at Ravenholt's practice of handing out business cards printed on condoms.[5]

Those who argued against linking population programs to social reform did not necessarily want to maintain the status quo. Indeed, they raised a different set of criticisms that questioned the *voluntary* nature of the programs. Even Ravenholt, perhaps the greatest defender of traditional family planning, raised questions about whether more coercive measures might be necessary in the future. These differing perspectives sharpened divisions within the population movement between those who called for more coercive policies to constrain population growth and those who emphasized individual rights to contraception and abortion. This division became apparent when Cordelia Scaife May, a major donor to the Population Council, resigned from the board of trustees in 1974. Writing personally to Rockefeller to express dismay over his Bucharest speech, she declared that while her "dedication to population control is undiminished," she disagreed that the solution to the population crisis lay in "a redistribution of the world's wealth." Foreseeing changes in the council's future work in the field, she said, "I have found myself more and more often in disagreement with the policy and programs of the Population Council and have felt for some time that I should resign."[6] In a follow-up letter she was even blunter in her assessment that voluntary family planning would not work. "The increase in our population," she declared, "is not being caused by the unwanted children of the poorest women in the United States or by the opposition of the Roman Catholic Church. It is caused by 40 million middle-upper class women who have all the children they wanted." Quoting Kingsley Davis, she concluded, "If having too many children were considered a crime . . . we would have no qualms about taking freedom away."[7]

Those calling for a traditional approach to family planning policy, however, soon found themselves on the losing side of the argument. Rockefeller's speech reflected growing criticism among young social scientists about the efficacy of current programs. This critical assessment of family planning policy led the Ford Foundation to reevaluate its involvement in this field. In late 1973 the foundation reduced its funding of population programs in order to emphasize what one foundation officer called the "nexus" between population growth, income distribution, and economic development.[8] More radical cuts came the following year at the recommendation of Oscar Harkavy, head of the population program at Ford. Writing to his superiors, Harkavy argued that the Bucharest conference revealed that greater attention must be given to such problems as age at marriage, status and roles of women, infant mortality, divorce, community structure, education, and literacy. As a consequence, he recommended a systematic scaling back of foundation support for reproductive research and family planning projects and a redirection of these funds to research and social projects "designed to illuminate the complex series of issues related to cultural change, economic development and population."[9] As part of these cutbacks, the Ford Foundation announced that it was reducing its support of the Population Council. In late 1973 the foundation had called for the council to "rethink its functions in the light of the changed donor situation, the altered socio-political climate within many of the target countries, and the whole disappointing record of attainment to date."[10]

The foundation's announcement that it was reducing its support for Population Council programs left the staff angry and demoralized, feelings that were intensified after the Bucharest speech. Many stated openly that Rockefeller had betrayed them. Word of this talk reached Rockefeller, and it disturbed him. Joan Dunlop sought to reassure him that his speech in fact was seen by most people as a success. She dismissed those critics who referred to the conference as "the babel of Bucharest." Yet she noted that there were clear signs that the leadership of the major donor agencies, especially the Ford Foundation, was "showing signs of retrenching emotionally as well as intellectually. There is now a siege mentality in the population movement."[11]

Whatever Dunlop's assurances, Rockefeller's Bucharest speech left many within the council feeling "let down." Finally, in late September 1974, Rockefeller called a staff meeting to address this discontent. In a question-and-answer session, he sought to reassure the staff about its future work. When one disgruntled staff member pointedly asked Rockefeller to clarify his conception of family planning versus economic development—a dichotomy denied by the staff member—Rockefeller conceded that the terms "development" and "family planning" had not been clearly defined in his speech. He went on to defend his position, however, by arguing that the purpose of his talk was to address the increasing hostility between the developed and developing nations and the "urgent need for an acknowledgment on the part of the Establishment of the viewpoints of the Third World." He recommended that a review committee be established to oversee changes in the council's future program and its leadership in a "transition" period in which he hoped the council would meet with "courage and sensitivity."[12]

A month after this meeting, David Hopper, a member of the Population Council board and president of the International Development Research Center of Canada, was selected to head a review committee. Behind the scenes, Dunlop conducted a campaign to broaden the Population Council's social mission concerning population. As Rockefeller's assistant, her opinions carried additional weight for the obvious reason that her voice often appeared indistinguishable from her boss's. With the backing of Rockefeller, she insisted that more women needed to be appointed to the board and to staff positions. She envisioned establishing a "valuable international network of women concerned with abortion and demanding accessibility to services, not only abortion but also contraception." She saw this as a way of countering the "cries of 'genocide,' 'development as a contraceptive,' and criticism of narrow family planning programs."[13] The appointment of a president sympathetic to these goals was critical to the transformation of the council.

The search for the new president took place in a climate in which the Population Council's future remained in doubt. Staff morale continued to deteriorate as rumors circulated that key divisions were going to be closed. An internal review of staff morale found the situation alarming.[14] With the council's existence in doubt, the search for a new president became protracted. For over a year the search committee grappled with finding the right candidate. David Hopper was offered the position but turned it down. He suggested either Paul Demeny or Charles Westoff, both well-known social scientists in the field, but Joan Dunlop vetoed both, arguing that fresh leadership was needed.[15]

With this in mind, she began promoting an unusual candidate for the presidency: George Zeidenstein, a forty-seven-year-old Ford Foundation field officer, with whom she had become acquainted in the 1960s. Although Zeidenstein had a law degree from Harvard University, he was an unusual choice because he lacked the academic credentials of former council presidents, Osborn, Notestein, and Berelson. Dismissing this question of credentials, Dunlop told the search committee that "he is the only candidate who has taken the women's question seriously." His strength lay, she argued, in his involvement in social change. She noted that in the 1960s Zeidenstein had worked in a downtown Brooklyn development effort. During this time, she said, he went through the "greening of America, in the sense his children dropped out of high school, that his wife began to show signs of independence, and that he grew his hair long, etc., etc., etc." But after having gone through this experience, his family was "now very much back together." Zeidenstein went on to put together one of the best country teams the Ford Foundation had in Bangladesh. Projecting from her own experience, Dunlop concluded that he has "learned that it isn't easy to be anti-establishment, that it isn't easy to work directly with the poor in developing countries, that one needs to use the elite despite one's reservations about their values."[16]

In late October 1975, after a fifteen-month search, the Population Council announced the appointment of Zeidenstein as its new president. The press release of his appointment noted that the Population Council would continue its work in demography, family planning, biomedical research, and contraception but would now emphasize the "interaction between population issues and broader development concerns such as the inclusion of women in the development process."[17]

Under Zeidenstein the council reshaped its mission. Speaking to the board of trustees shortly after his appointment to the presidency, Zeidenstein acknowledged the council's past achievements in "raising to global attention the issue of population growth" by identifying "family planning as a central policy response that governments could make to excessive fertility." Yet, he noted, "high fertility is a problem mainly in relation to the disposition and consumption of resources, inequities in the distribution of capital, income and social and economic opportunities, and inadequate realization of the full potentials of women and men." No longer, Zeidenstein said, should population be seen narrowly as a problem of just global overpopulation. This remained the critical issue facing the world, but the problem needed to be placed in a larger social and cultural context. In pointing to new directions he wanted to take the council, he declared, "We now need to include in population growth related concerns of economic, social, and cultural factors such as resources, income and capital, consumption, productivity, the roles and status of women, health, education, housing, employment, social security and institutional structures; and we should pay greater attention to issues related to migration, urbanization, and morality."

Zeidenstein made it clear that the Population Council would no longer be conceived as an agency that believed the problem of world overpopulation could be solved through a quick "technological fix" through the distribution of condoms, pills, and IUDs. His rejection of technological solutions reflected a radical break with those early pioneers of family planning whom he felt had overestimated the development of better contraceptive devices as a panacea to global overpopulation (while underestimating the social and cultural problems inherent in implementing family planning programs in developing and developed nations). In pursuing this new social agenda, Zeidenstein concluded, the council should build on fundamental research of others and develop "an integrated program of applied research and mission-oriented basic research on human reproduction, fertility regulation technology, sterilization, and abortion."[18]

When he met with the council staff for the first time, he impressed upon them that the council had entered a new era. Describing himself as a "development" person, not a "population" man, he believed that contraception technology would continue to be important, but the meaning of contraception should be broadened. He announced that "abortion will be seen by the council as one form of contraception."[19] The formal endorsement of abortion as a means of contraception marked another important shift within the council.

Zeidenstein's declaration that the Population Council viewed abortion as another method for family planning led to an immediate shake-up in the board of trustees, forcing the resignation of John Noonan. Noonan, a prominent liberal Catholic, had gained national recognition for his learned opposition to *Humanae Vitae*. The emergence of the abortion movement, however, led him into active opposition against *Roe v. Wade*. Noonan told Rockefeller that he was tendering his resignation from the board in the belief that his continued participation would "only embarrass you [Rockefeller], our other colleagues, and myself."[20]

Following Noonan's resignation, Zeidenstein moved to diversify the board by consciously appointing women and representatives from developing nations. To accomplish this goal, from June 1976 to June 1978 the board was expanded from fourteen to sixteen members. In the next two years, the number of women on the board grew from two to six.[21] At Dunlop's urging, Sarah Weddington, the attorney who had brought *Roe* before the Supreme Court and chief counsel to the Department of Agriculture in the Carter administration, was appointed in late 1977.[22] She brought to the board strong credentials in family planning as a member of the board of Zero Population Growth and the Alan Guttmacher Institute. Also joining the board was Mary I. Bunting, former president of Radcliffe College; Margaret Dulany, codirector of the employment program for the Arlington Public Schools in Arlington, Massachusetts; and Helen M. Ranney, professor of medicine at the University of California, San Diego. In addition, six of the board members in 1978 came from developing countries.[23]

As major philanthropic donors cut their funding of the Population Council, program budgets were scaled back to a little over $12 million in 1978. Under financial constraints, programs refocused their research to local studies with particular attention to contraceptive implementation programs and small economic development projects. Through the newly established Policy Center within the council, studies were initiated on the village level to analyze variations in fertility, reproductive cycles, family structure, employment, social mobility, migration, and the status of women. The Center for Biomedical Research remained intact but pursued a program of applied research and development of "new methods for contraception, sterilization, and abortion." Studies were initiated in Chile to collect data on the effectiveness of subdermal implants such as Depo-Provera, which the council believed held "definite potential for use in developing countries."[24]

The international program was reorganized to provide a sharper focus to the demographic impact on economic development and the importance of women to this development. Abortion as a means of birth control received particular attention as a health care issue. In Thailand three major grants were given to evaluate abortion practices in order to provide information to the Ministry of Health for consideration in reviewing proposed abortion legislation in that country. A major project was launched to document the influence on women's roles and status in development programs. To further the council's social agenda at home, grants were given to the Tuskegee Institute, Mount Sinai School of Medicine, New York University, Columbia University, Pennsylvania State University, and the Meharry Medical College to fund summer employment of minority youths in biomedical laboratories.[25]

Rockefeller Promotes Sex Education
and Defends Abortion Rights

When John D. Rockefeller 3rd stepped down as chair of the board of trustees in June 1978, a month before his tragic death, the Population Council had undertaken the agenda he had called for four years earlier in his Bucharest speech. In doing so, the Population Council returned to its international focus. Yet even before his death, Rockefeller had withdrawn from active involvement in the council, assured that his mandate was being fulfilled by Zeidenstein. While Rockefeller kept a watchful eye on the Population Council, his interest turned increasingly to domestic issues concerning the politics of abortion and sex education in the United States. These subjects drew him to greater involvement in domestic politics than had characterized his earlier work.

This change in focus stemmed from two sources. In his work on the Commission on Population Growth and the American Future, he gained new insights into an array of domestic issues confronting America in the 1970s, including abortion, immigration, and sex education. Public reaction to the report revealed to Rockefeller the importance of changing American opinion on these critical issues. At the same time, the younger generation of Rockefellers, especially his own daughters Hope and Alida, exerted a profound influence on him. Both daughters were feminists who actively supported legalized abortion. Furthermore, their cousin Abby, the oldest daughter of David Rockefeller, had become radicalized by the antiwar and feminist movements in the 1960s. After her involvement in the draft resistance movement and her introduction to Marxism through the Trotskyite Socialist Workers party, she helped found with Roxanne Dunbar the Boston feminist group Cell 16, which published the *Journal of Female Liberation*. Influenced by this younger generation, as well as by the logic of his own position, John D. Rockefeller threw his support to the proabortion movement.[26] Writing in *Newsweek* in 1976, he declared, "We must uphold freedom of choice. Moreover, we must work to make free choice a reality by extending safe abortion services throughout the United States." Although he continued to maintain that unwanted pregnancy should be avoided by making contraceptive methods "better, safer, and more readily available to everyone," he stressed that "freedom of choice is crucial."[27]

Rockefeller's language—its emphasis on rights—reflected a subtle change in his own thinking. While he remained concerned with the population issue, he did not frame his argument for abortion in terms of population control. Instead he viewed legalized abortion as a woman's right. Affected by the feminism of his daughters and niece, as well as that of his assistant Joan Dunlop, Rockefeller viewed the abortion debate as a civil rights issue for women and American society. His commitment to legalized abortion as a right reflected the changed character of the abortion debate in the late 1970s. While much of the impetus (although not all) for federal family planning had come from those concerned with overpopulation, the contest over abortion policy became one of individual rights.

Sixty-seven years old in 1973, Rockefeller threw his heart and soul into the abortion issue and sex education. For the remaining years of his life, he enthusiastically supported activist organizations and groups mobilized to defend legalized abortion. In the 1950s and 1960s Rockefeller's correspondence had been filled with letters from world leaders, United Nations officials, presidents, and the elite movers and shakers in the population movement; in the 1970s Rockefeller corresponded, through his associates, with leading activists in the proabortion movement. Where once Rockefeller had refused to speak at a State Department conference on population because he felt it was beneath his dignity, he now became actively engaged in democratic politics on a local level.

He was not alone. The men and women at the Ford Foundation, for example, also manifested a new spirit of activist democracy. Elitism, at least in form and style, had become quite unfashionable in the egalitarian decade of the 1970s. Style changed as power was to be shared—still not equally, perhaps—with ethnic minorities and women. By the 1970s the philanthropic foundation elite had not lost its sense of confidence, but it was willing to join, if only ostensibly, "the people."

The Ford Foundation joined Rockefeller in supporting abortion-related activity. In 1972 the Ford Foundation decided to undertake work "designed to increase the well-being and economic opportunity of poor women." This meant, as a foundation report declared, that "we assumed that women needed to be free to make their own choices about child bearing." As a consequence, foundation grants were provided for legal challenges to abortion and litigation to "eliminate discrimination against poor women in availability of abortion services." In order "to lessen the divisive impact of the abortion debate in the United States," the foundation funded grants to support proabortion religious groups, including Catholics for a Free Choice and the Religious Coalition for Abortion Rights. In addition, grants were provided for objective, investigative projects, including a study by University of Michigan historian Maris Vinovskis on the politics of abortion in Congress and a historical analysis of abortion by scholar James Mohr. The foundation perceived itself as a "neutral" organization in the abortion controversy. "We are seeking to provide grants," it declared, "for reasoned debate while other funders will prefer to support one side or another."[28]

In his own work, Rockefeller kept close track of the Ford Foundation's activities, often coordinating his philanthropic giving with the foundation's support to protect the right to legalized abortion. Other philan-

thropic organizations joined this work, including the Rockefeller Brothers
Fund, the Scaife Fund, the Packard Foundation, the Mott Foundation, the
Kellogg Foundation, and the United Methodist Board of Church and
Society, as well as many other groups and individuals who supported the
proabortion cause.[29] Underlying this commitment to defend abortion
rights, Rockefeller believed ignorance and myth about sexuality were
widespread in American society. Acting upon this premise, Rockefeller
supported sex education programs and homosexual rights.

Along with the Ford Foundation, he became a major supporter of the
Sex Information and Education Council of the United States (SIECUS),
headed by Dr. Mary Calderone, a longtime family planning and abortion
advocate who began her work as a staff member at Planned Parenthood. In
addition, he provided fifty thousand dollars for a sex education program
for teenagers in New York City conducted by the local affiliate of Planned
Parenthood.[30] Similarly, Rockefeller established the Project on Human
Sexual Development in 1974. This project pursued the recommendations
of the Commission on Population Growth and the American Future that
called for widespread and extensive sex education in America. The purpose
of the project was succinctly stated by its executive director, Elizabeth J.
Roberts, who declared in a speech before educators that "despite our
nation's preoccupation with 'sex,' millions of Americans of all ages need
help in understanding their sexuality." She felt that Americans needed to
be educated to see "our sexuality" as "part of our basic identity," expressed
through "our life styles, in our social roles, in the way we express affection,
as well as our erotic behaviors." Influenced by the work of Kinsey, Roberts
believed that early child genital play was critical to the development of
sexual identity, gender roles, and body image. Self-exploration, masturba-
tion, the and the desire "to explore the genitals of other children" was the
most common form of learned experience, and the "anger, anxiety or
moral concern" of adults distorted this "natural activity" and reinforced
the message that sexual activity for females is for reproduction and not for
sexual pleasure.[31]

Although the project was ostensibly established as a research organization, its founders believed that "research alone seldom motivates action."
Therefore, the project was to combine "some original research, some
reanalysis of existing data, and some demonstration projects."[32] Placing on
its advisory board leading social scientists from throughout the country, as
well as executives from the communication industry and philanthropic
foundations, the organization undertook a number projects to produce
children's television programs on sexuality. Roberts worked closely with
the Harvard School of Education and WCVB, the ABC television affiliate
in Boston, to produce a sex education special for young people. She also

encouraged efforts to produce a new television miniseries for children entitled "Love Rock." At the same time, a demonstration sex education program was established in Cleveland, Ohio.[33]

Rockefeller's interest in sex education led him to support homosexual rights. In 1977 he became actively involved in raising money to support a film for educational television directed by pioneer homosexual film producer Peter Adair. Entitled *Who Are We?* the film began as a project to "provide positive role models for young gay people and to dispel stereotypical misconceptions held by gays and nongay people alike." The film depicted eight homosexuals from various walks of life, including a seventy-two-year-old lesbian, a factory worker, a lawyer, and an actress. Encouraged by anthropologist Margaret Mead, who had reviewed Adair's first film, *The Ghost People*, Rockefeller personally became involved in raising funds to produce an hour-long documentary film for WNET on New York public television. To raise this money he hosted private showings of the film for civic and religious leaders in the community in his office in Rockefeller Center.[34]

Rockefeller viewed homosexuality and sex education as changing the cultural context for family planning and abortion policy in modern America. He believed the Rockefeller Commission on Population Growth and the American Future had failed not just because of the political turpitude of the Nixon administration but because of the failure to rally an intransigent and unenlightened public. Changing public attitudes toward sexuality presented a long-range problem; in the meantime, abortion rights needed to be protected immediately through public education and a concerted political campaign.[35]

From 1973 through 1978 Rockefeller contributed close to half a million dollars from his personal funds to the abortion movement. He became a major donor to NARAL, Planned Parenthood, the American Civil Liberties Union Reproductive Freedom Project, the Center for Constitutional Rights, the Association for the Study of Abortion, the Alan Guttmacher Institute, Zero Population Growth, and an array of other activist groups and institutions. The primary purpose of his giving was to ensure that the Supreme Court's decision in *Roe* was not eroded and the right to abortion exercised.[36] In the process, he became actively engaged in supporting political efforts, including support for a retreat of the feminist caucus of the Minnesota Democratic party and Jimmy Carter's presidential campaign in 1976.[37] Convinced that "most public officials who support legalized abortion do so from *conviction* . . . [and] that most public officials who oppose legalized abortion do so from *fear*," he sought to provide an organizational countermovement to the "small, well organized, well financed groups" that engendered this political fear.[38]

Joan Dunlop provided him with a steady stream of reports from various groups. Typical in this regard was Rockefeller's involvement in reviving NARAL, which began to experience organizational and financial problems in the mid-1970s. In 1974 Dunlop reported to Rockefeller that NARAL had lost its momentum after the important role it had played in the abortion repeal movement on the state level. A detailed report of its activities revealed that the group was having "difficulty in finding leadership" on the state level. Although NARAL operated with an annual budget of $185,000 and listed forty-five state affiliates, in many of these states the organizational apparatus was more symbolic than real. In Florida, Kentucky, Louisiana, North and South Carolina, Texas, and Virginia, state membership included only one or two leaders.[39] Concerned about the weakness of NARAL, Rockefeller intervened to boost the organization's annual budget and to fund a Washington office under Karen Mulhauser. Through Mulhauser, NARAL developed a close working relationship with the National Women's Political Caucus and the Women's Campaign Fund.

Mulhauser feared that abortion rights were being eroded by political apathy among "liberal moderates" in the Republican and Democratic parties. This concern led her to undertake an extensive lobbying campaign consciously designed to ensure, as Dunlop put it, that there was "no middle ground" on the abortion issue.[40] Rockefeller's efforts to revive NARAL and Mulhauser's lobbying efforts paid off. By 1977 Dunlop reported that NARAL had experienced "a spirited spurt." Rockefeller's support of NARAL encouraged funding from the Mott Foundation, the United Methodist Church Board of Homeland Ministries, Maryanne Mott Mynet, Robert Wallace, and DeWitt Wallace. Dunlop worried, however, that NARAL still did not provide the "kind of leadership for legislative strategy needed in Washington to fight the numerous inroads on legal abortion."[41]

In order to fill this leadership vacuum, Rockefeller extended support to other legal and political proabortion rights groups such as the ACLU Reproductive Freedom Project. The ACLU project focused its activity on litigation at the local and state levels. Although the Ford Foundation provided major support for the project with an annual grant of $150,000 a year, Rockefeller made annual donations of $20,000, supplemented with additional contributions ranging as high as $40,000. The project also received support from the Rockefeller Family Fund, the Rockefeller Foundation, and the Playboy Foundation, as well as smaller donations from other foundations and individuals.[42]

Rockefeller believed that religious groups remained key to the political battle over abortion. In part this strategy involved, as one activist told Dunlop, separating antiabortion intellectuals from "the rabble-rousing leadership of the anti-abortion forces."[43] Accordingly, Rockefeller funded the mobilization of proabortion religious organizations such as Catholics for a Free Choice, Catholic Alternatives, and the Religious Coalition for Abortion Rights (RCAR). He viewed these groups as necessary to counter the growing influence of the antiabortion movement within the Roman Catholic Church. By the early 1970s he concluded with other abortion activists that the Catholic Church had become a major threat to legalized abortion in America. His associate Carol Foreman reported to him in 1973 that "right to life groups were springing up all over the country. It is quite dedicated and mostly Roman Catholic." She warned that Catholic influence on federal legislation had already become apparent in proposed constitutional "right-to-life" amendments that had been introduced in Congress. While Foreman judged the threat of a constitutional amendment as "moderately serious," the threat of excluding federal support for abortions should be considered "quite serious." She estimated that right-to-life amendments had garnered the support of thirty-eight members of the House (mostly from "young, conservative Republican Catholics") and nine members of the Senate.[44]

Rockefeller found the RCAR a particularly effective organization in mobilizing public support in defense of abortion rights. Organized by the United Methodist Church, the RCAR sought to build a religious coalition to defend abortion rights on the state and national levels. In Washington the RCAR lobbyist, Betsy Stengel, had "the presence to get in the door [of congressional offices] and the intellectual strength to command their attention." Moreover, Rockefeller welcomed her efforts to win over the press. Through Stengel's long conversations with the press, he was told, many journalists had developed an "increased understanding of the abortion debate," as reflected in press reports of antiabortion demonstrations. Between 1973 and 1978 Rockefeller contributed $115,000 to support the RCAR's work.[45]

In order to confront the growing influence of the antiabortion movement in Congress, Rockefeller turned to a tactic that had served him well in the population debate—the deliberate courting of liberal Catholics. He had been a longtime supporter of Daniel Callahan and had helped seed his Institute for Society, Ethics and Life Sciences.[46] During this period Rockefeller remained close friends with Theodore Hesburgh at Notre Dame, even though Hesburgh affirmed his support for the church's antiabortion position. The abortion issue proved to be a much more delicate issue than either population or family planning, however.

Indeed, relations between Hesburgh and Rockefeller became strained in 1976 when Father James Burtchaell—perceived by many to be the heir apparent to Hesburgh—publicly criticized Rockefeller for his article in *Newsweek* defending legalized abortion. Following an exchange of letters in the magazine between Burtchaell and Rockefeller, Hesburgh, in order to relieve tensions, arranged for Burtchaell to fly to New York to meet with Rockefeller and discuss their differences. In a tense meeting that on the surface remained congenial, Burtchaell continued to take exception to Rockefeller's statement that opponents of abortion were "mostly Catholics bent on forcing their peculiar religious beliefs undemocratically upon the nation" by arguing that the antiabortion movement was not only Catholic. Nonetheless, Burtchaell told Rockefeller that he was critical of *Humanae Vitae* and that he had dissociated himself from the right-to-life movement, having been "picketed by them many times and their emotionalism in regard to abortion prevented rational discussion and a reasonable solution." Adding that the church "no longer spoke with one voice on many matters," he accepted abortion in cases of ectopic pregnancy, cancerous uterus, and to save the life of the mother. He proposed that Rockefeller fund the convening of a small group under the auspices of Notre Dame and the Rockefeller Foundation to discuss the abortion problem. While Rockefeller told him that he was no longer on the foundation's board, he encouraged him to apply to the foundation. He warned, however, "I hope you won't have occasion to write any more letters like your first one to me. Both of us, I believe, really want to find a way out and people like us must not take a hard and fast position that will be hurtful to the bigger cause [social justice] in which we both believe."[47]

Rockefeller's efforts to mobilize liberal Catholics on the abortion issue extended beyond cultivating liberals at Notre Dame. For example, he provided a sizable grant to start Catholics for a Free Choice (CFFC), a proabortion lobby group that sought to influence Congress and Catholic opinion by targeting "teenagers in religious schools, the Puerto Rican community, and older women."[48] Dunlop was especially impressed with the leadership of CFFC, noting that its president, Jan Gleason, was well acquainted with people in Congress, and that the organization's secretary, Glenn Brooks, used to work full-time for the national office of the National Organization for Women. Dunlop was even more enthusiastic about the formation of Catholic Alternatives, the service and educational arm of CFFC, which established an abortion counseling service in New York in 1975 after receiving start-up money from the Sunnen Foundation. The clinic was intended to provide "an alternative to the normally guilt-ridden process of the confessional" and "a pronouncement to the hierarchy that lay Catholic women are taking the situation into their own hands."[49] From the outset, CFFC intended the clinic as "an opportunity for a media event." Joan Harriman emphatically declared that "there are 600 Birthright [an anti-abortion counseling organization] clinics across the country who are brainwashing women into having children by making them feel guilty if women want to use contraceptives or terminate a pregnancy." This center was to provide a real service to teenagers and minority women in New York City by targeting teenagers in religious schools through "Sexual Rap" sessions.[50] Along with this benevolent purpose, Catholic Alternatives understood that such a clinic, sponsored by Catholic women, would attract media attention, and thereby provide prochoice groups with "ammunition to bring to Congress in their lobbying efforts."[51] For all of its success, however, Catholic Alternatives found it difficult to expand its base of support and had limited influence on the abortion debate.[52]

As the abortion issue controversy heated up, Rockefeller intensified his political involvement. During the early days of the population movement, he had consciously avoided overt involvement in domestic American politics. The abortion issue, however, drew him increasingly into actively supporting political organizations and politicians deemed important for the abortion cause. This political involvement found conscious expression in his consideration of support in 1972 for the Southern Election Fund. Formed by civil rights activist Julian Bond following Nixon's election in 1968, the fund sought to mobilize African-American voters in the South. Although ostensibly nonpartisan, the Southern Election Fund was seen as a way of liberalizing the South by drawing black voters into the electorate, but Dunlop recommended that funding be provided, although she noted that philanthropic deductible funds could *not* be used for direct election activity. But, she told Rockefeller, "this is where the Southern Election Fund comes in." If the fund could be adequately funded on a year-round basis, it could mount "a day in and day out fund-raising and technical assistance operation which could not only sustain the local Southern poor white and minority electoral activity, but also advance it to congressional, state and regional levels with some realistic hope of success." The purpose in supporting this organization was apparent. She felt that "the eventual defeat and breakup of the Southern congressional bloc represents one of its paramount objectives. This will take time, no doubt; but the Southern Election Fund can certainly hasten the day."[53] While the record is not clear on whether Rockefeller donated money to the Southern Election Fund, it is evident that he was willing to become directly involved in politics.

He donated money, for example, to the National Women's Political Caucus (NWPC) on the recommendation of Dunlop, who told him that through her involvement with the abortion issue she had met the leadership of what she described as the "activist arm of the women's movement." She praised the leadership of the NWPC, including Sarah Weddington, Carol Bellamy, Jane McMichael, and the "charismatic" Ruth Abram. Acting on this high recommendation, Rockefeller donated money to this caucus as a way of showing his support for the women's movement and its importance in mobilizing women to support unrestricted legalized abortion.[54] He understood the importance of supporting political groups and the organized women's movement as essential elements in a war that had been unleashed in American politics following *Roe*.

The Abortion Debate Unleashed in the States and in Washington, D.C.

The abortion issue transformed American politics, as proabortion and antiabortion groups carried their fight to state legislatures and the federal courts. These battles on the state level and subsequent court rulings provided the backdrop for federal abortion policy in Congress and the presidency. So poignant was the abortion issue that it affected every facet of American political life. The struggle occurred on two fronts: nationally, opponents of abortion in Congress sought to repeal *Roe* through enactment of constitutional amendments and to prevent federal funding of abortion. On the state level, antiabortion groups undertook efforts to limit legalized abortion through restrictive abortion regulations. Any understanding of abortion policy in these years must begin with an examination of the war on the state level and subsequent court rulings concerning this state legislation.

The decentralized structure of American federalism, with its fifty state jurisdictions, openly invited political conflict from antiabortion and proabortion groups, both of which developed well-organized and well-funded lobbying efforts on local and state levels. Within two years after *Roe*, approximately 449 abortion-related bills were introduced in state legislatures, and 58 of these bills were enacted. The open resistance to abortion led many public and private hospitals to refuse to perform nontherapeutic abortions. In 1977, four years after *Roe*, Planned Parenthood reported that 80 percent of all public hospitals and 70 percent of private hospitals still refused to allow abortion.[55] As a consequence, only a few providers performed abortions on a regular basis. A decade after *Roe*, the majority of women in West Virginia and Wyoming had to travel outside their home states to have an abortion, while in North and South Dakota only a few clinics performed abortions at all. In ten states— Arizona, Indiana, Iowa, Kentucky, Maryland, Mississippi, Missouri, New Mexico, Oklahoma, and South Dakota—approximately 20 to 36 percent of the women who wanted abortions traveled to other states to have them.[56]

Fights on the state level proved especially contentious. By 1990 thirty-eight states had adopted a labyrinth of regulations restricting abortion. These regulations fell into five broad categories: (1) health regulations requiring physicians and clinics performing abortions to be licensed and to report to public authorities the numbers of abortions performed; (2) bans on advertising and other activities promoting abortion services; (3) viability and postviability regulations; (4) informed consent or spousal consent, and parental notification or consent for minors; and (5) denial of public funding and the use of public hospitals for abortions. These measures erected a complex system of regulations often designed to restrict abortion. As a result, access to abortion varied greatly on the state level. These laws erected a dizzying array of rules and regulations that appeared to subvert any uniformity to the meaning of legalized abortion.[57]

Each state became a battleground between proabortion and antiabortion activists for the hearts and minds of the electorate and the state legislators. Often, the antiabortionists won in the political arena by drawing support from rural districts and suburbs with heavily Catholic populations. Victory within the political arena, however, only threw the battle into the courts.[58] As a consequence, the courts became centers of political struggle. When court rulings went against them, antiabortionists accused federal district justices and justices on the Supreme Court who overturned state antiabortion legislation of being "activists" who willingly subverted the intent of founding legal principles. Similarly, as the composition of the Supreme Court began to change in the late 1980s and 1990s following appointments by Ronald Reagan and George Bush, proabortionists charged that the constitutional right to abortion was being threatened. Court rulings left neither side totally satisfied, and each ruling seemed to aggravate each side equally.

In the two decades that followed *Roe*, the Supreme Court issued twenty major decisions concerning abortion legislation. In general, the Court in these decisions upheld the core of *Roe* but tended to defer to state legislation areas involving procedures and general regulatory guidelines.[59] The balance between the right of privacy of women to abortion and the state's compelling interest to regulate and restrict abortion procedures opened a Pandora's box as many states rewrote their abortion laws. Ostensibly the state laws were written to conform with the Constitution, but quite often state laws regulating and restricting abortion were openly and clearly hostile to *Roe* and *Doe*. The entangling web of litigation on both the state and federal levels during the next two decades placed the Supreme Court in the role of a regulator, minutely determining which state laws were acceptable or unacceptable. These decisions set the context for federal policy making from the Ford administration through the Clinton administration.

After Richard Nixon resigned from office following the Watergate scandal, Gerald R. Ford assumed the presidency on August 9, 1974, a year after *Roe*. Ford entered the White House as the first president to have reached the highest office in the land without having been elected either president or vice president, selected for the office after the elected vice president Spiro Agnew resigned in October 1973. While he remained popular among Republicans in Congress, his stature as president was weakened by the way he attained the office. Nonetheless, he brought to his presidency a calm, reassuring manner and a deep faith in traditional values. He hoped to heal a divided nation that had lost confidence in the political system. His presidential pardon of Richard Nixon for any crimes committed in relation to the Watergate break-in undermined Ford's efforts, but even without this he faced growing acrimony over the abortion issue.

Immediately after *Roe*, the National Conference of Catholic Bishops formed the National Committee for the Human Life Amendment with the intention of enacting a constitutional amendment banning abortion and placing the issue back with the states. By early 1976 more than fifty different constitutional amendments to ban or limit abortions had been introduced in Congress.[60] These separate amendments sought to extend due process protections to the fetus "from the moment of conception," to return to the states the power to regulate abortion, and to define "person," as used in the Fourteenth Amendment, to include the fetus.

At the same time, antiabortion congressional leaders sought to withdraw federal funding for abortions under the Medicaid program unless these operations were deemed "medically necessary." In 1976 the House of Representatives, led by Representative Henry J. Hyde (R-Illinois), successfully placed a rider to an appropriations bill banning federal funding for abortions for any reason. The Senate passed a similar measure with a critical qualifier that federal funds for abortions could be used to save a woman's life. Finally, after a series of intense conference meetings between the two legislative bodies, an agreement was reached to reconcile the House and Senate versions of the bill that accepted less restrictive language. In the House, Hyde denounced the agreement as a "sellout" and continued to press his case in subsequent Congresses. When the appropriations bill reached Ford's desk, he vetoed the measure "based purely and simply on the issue of fiscal integrity." Intent on upholding the appropriations measure, Congress overturned Ford's veto, thereby restricting federal funding for abortions.[61]

Many within Congress believed Ford could not be trusted on the abortion issue. His wife, Betty, publicly announced her support of legalized abortion, and his vice president, Nelson Rockefeller, had made clear his proabortion stance when he had been governor of New York.[62] Nonetheless, congressional opposition to abortion led Ford to support a constitutional amendment to allow individual states to regulate abortion policy. Moreover, when the Hyde amendment was challenged in the courts, Ford instructed his solicitor general, Robert H. Bork, to file an amicus curiae brief in support of the amendment to the Supreme Court.

Ford won Republican nomination for president in 1976 after a bitter challenge in the primaries from the former governor of California, Ronald Reagan, who attacked Ford from the right. As a consequence, Ford steered a middle course, hoping to maintain support within the moderate wing of the party. When Democrats met at their convention, they nominated a political outsider, Jimmy Carter, former governor of Georgia and a wealthy peanut farmer. Proclaiming opposition to "politics as usual," Carter promised to restore virtue and trust to government. Both Ford and Carter wanted to treat the abortion issue gingerly.

The Republican party platform declared, "The question of abortion is one of the most difficult and controversial of our time. . . . There are those in our party who favor complete support for the Supreme Court decision which permits abortion on demand. There are those who share sincere convictions that the Supreme Court's decision be changed by a constitutional amendment prohibiting all abortions." The platform went on to say that the Republican party urges "a continuance of the public dialogue on abortion and supports the efforts of those who seek enactment of a constitutional amendment to restore protection of the right to life for unborn children."

Among the Democrats, the abortion issue proved even more divisive. Carter had launched his bid for the nomination after first winning the primary in Iowa, where he mobilized evangelical voters by his proclamation that he was a "born-again" Christian opposed to abortion. After the Iowa primary, he clarified his antiabortion stance by declaring that he was against abortion but was opposed to a constitutional amendment overturning *Roe*. At the convention Carter clashed with feminists over the abortion plank. After much controversy a compromise was reached in which the platform declared the party's opposition to any attempt to overturn legalized abortion.[63] This mild endorsement of *Roe v. Wade*, however, came only after a major lobbying effort by the NWPC. Nevertheless, Carter specifically disavowed the platform by categorically declaring that "abortion is wrong."[64] During the campaign, Carter downplayed his stance on abortion by stressing economic issues and the "loss of confidence" issue— areas where Ford was most vulnerable.

While the two major party candidates avoided the abortion issue, Ellen McCormack, a New York housewife running on the Right to Life party ticket, interjected it into the 1976 election. McCormack's candidacy hurled single-issue antiabortion activists into the political arena. McCormack, a political unknown, attracted considerable media attention and elevated the importance of the abortion issue in the election. Qualifying for federal matching funds, the Right to Life party waged a graphic television campaign that included spot ads showing a fetus being aborted.[65]

McCormick's campaign drew support from antiabortion activists concerned with Ford and Carter, who had staked out moderate antiabortion positions that alienated activists on both sides. While Ford declared that the law of the land concerning abortion must be upheld, he told a meeting of the National Conference of Catholic Bishops that he believed government had "a responsibility to protect life." Carter disavowed support of any constitutional amendment banning abortion, but his weak antiabortion stance left the women's movement unhappy. Indeed, Rockefeller privately urged Carter to endorse a proabortion position. Although he failed to convince Carter on this issue, he contributed money to the campaign through the Democratic National Committee.[66]

Carter narrowly won the election, with 49.9 percent of the popular vote to Ford's 47.9 percent. The Georgian swept the South, drawing evangelical Christians to the Democratic party. The emergence of an evangelical bloc of Christian voters marked the beginnings of an important change in the electorate and would have profound consequences for both political parties that were not fully apparent at the time. Carter believed that Betty Ford's strong proabortion views and Gerald Ford's ambivalence on abortion had hurt the Republicans and had helped the Democrats win the White House for the first time since 1969.

Once in office, Carter continued to steer a middle course on the abortion issue. Although he continued to oppose a constitutional amendment to restrict abortion, he appointed a Catholic, Joseph Califano, as secretary of HEW. On the other hand, Carter appointed Midge Constanza, a proabortion feminist, to his White House staff. This led to divisions within his administration on the abortion issue following the Supreme Court's ruling in three separate cases on June 20, 1977, that congressional restrictions on funding for abortion through Medicaid did not violate a woman's constitutional right to secure an abortion.[67] In the aftermath of the decisions, Carter declared in a press conference on July 12, "I don't believe that the federal government should take action to try to make these opportunities exactly equal, particularly when there is a moral factor involved." Carter's blunt endorsement of the Court's decision outraged feminists within the administration.

Midge Constanza, an outspoken proponent of federal funding of abortion, organized a meeting at the White House on July 15 among women in the administration to urge Carter to change his position. Joined by HEW Assistant Secretary for Human Development Services Arabella Martinez and Assistant Secretary of Education Mary Berry, the meeting attracted considerable media attention and gave the appearance that Carter did not have control over his own team. When Carter expressed his tempered anger at a subsequent cabinet meeting that a member of the White House staff would organize such a meeting, he was surprised to learn that Secretary of Commerce Juanita Kreps and Secretary of HUD Patricia

Harris did not support the administration's position against federal funding of abortion.[68] As division within the administration became public, Carter drew the ire of the proabortion movement. An agitated Dunlop wrote Rockefeller that Carter had now "gone on record as being in direct opposition to some of the most courageous public statements you have made." Warning of potential divisiveness in the abortion movement, she stated, "There is no middle ground on abortion." The battle for the heart and soul of America was at stake.[69]

The burden of defending the administration's position fell to Secretary of HEW Joseph Califano, who quickly discovered in the congressional debate over the Hyde amendment that it was difficult to appease either side. The Supreme Court's ruling in favor of the Hyde amendment placed the issue back into the hands of Congress. On August 4, 1977, Brooklyn federal judge John Dooling lifted his order blocking enforcement of the Hyde amendment. The removal of the ban fueled the flames of a heated debate that was then waging in Congress over federal funding of abortion. On June 17, shortly before the Supreme Court's ruling, Henry Hyde's unqualified ban on all funding of abortion passed the House in a 201 to 155 vote. Within the Senate, a less restrictive measure that provided exceptions when the life of the mother was endangered and in cases of rape or incest won majority approval by a narrow 56 to 42 vote. This victory in the Senate revealed a clear movement to the antiabortion position as eighteen senators—three Republicans and fifteen Democrats—switched their 1976 positions to support of bans on abortion funding.[70]

The Senate's compromise measure failed to placate antiabortionists in the House who viewed the measure as allowing loopholes that would permit federal funding of abortion when interpreted by the bureaucrats in HEW. Daniel Flood, the Pennsylvania Democrat who chaired the HEW appropriations subcommittee, scathingly voiced these sentiments when he declared, "You could get an abortion with an ingrown toenail with the Senate language."[71] Proabortion activist Karen Mulhauser announced that she was organizing a campaign to mail coat hangers, a symbol of back-alley abortions before *Roe*, to Flood. When the House-Senate conference met, Senator Edward Brooke (R-Massachusetts), who had joined Senators Robert Packwood (R-Oregon) Warren Magnuson (D-Washington) in their fight to fund abortions under Medicaid, insisted on maintaining the Senate's language. Unable to compromise, both sides became inflamed, accusing one another of intransigence. Finally, after nearly five months of heated controversy and acrid charges of bad faith, the Senate and the House agreed to accept language that banned HEW funds for abortions except when the life of the mother was endangered or in cases of rape and incest. On December 9, 1977, Carter signed the measure into law.

The compromise language of 1977, however, left many in the House unhappy, setting the stage for a repetition on of the fight when Congress assembled the following year. The intensity of the debate was only heightened by the approach of midterm elections, when many in Congress would be asked to account for their positions on abortion. At the outset of the session, majority leader Jim Wright (D-Texas) implored the House to accept the compromise language from the previous year. "Last year," he told his fellow members, "there were 28 separate votes on this single subject [abortion]. . . . Heaven knows we heard enough oratory last year on those 11 separate occasions when we debated rules, debated amendments, and debated conference reports."[72] Wright's hopes to avoid another battle were soon dashed, however.

Debate in the House was limited to one hour, leaving just enough time for speakers to declare their positions and express their strong feelings. Edward J. Derwinski (R-Illinois) told the House that last year's "so-called compromise" was "a last-minute adjustment that caught many members unaware and it has not been properly administered by HEW." He was joined by John Rousselot (R-California), who added, "Many members of the House did not really know the full impact of what they were voting for in the conference report," noting that sixty members were not present for the final vote of 181 to 167 that had carried the compromise measure.[73] Once again Henry Hyde, the Republican congressman from Illinois, led the fight against compromise. Under his leadership, Wright's resolution maintaining the previous year's compromise language was defeated in a narrow 212 to 198 vote that split along party lines. In the Senate, majority leader Robert C. Byrd (D-West Virginia) failed to get a unanimous-consent agreement on the Labor-HEW appropriations bill. Through parliamentary maneuvering, Byrd successfully limited debate on further amendments to the HEW appropriations bill, including funding bans on forced busing, restrictions on prayer in public schools, and abortion. When the Senate upheld the compromise language, the Labor-HEW appropriations bill again headed to conference. Once again, abortion proved to be the sticking point. This time, however, budget concerns changed the tenor of the debate. The Labor-HEW appropriations bill cut funding close to $60 billion, forcing Congress to choose "fiscal" responsibility over strident restrictive language. In the end, the House accepted the 1977 compromise language. Nonetheless, abortion opponents were able to add new restrictions on federal funding of abortions in the Peace Corps and Department of Defense budgets.[74]

The effects of these restrictions on the rate of abortion remained hotly contested. Abortion activists claimed that restrictions meant that those in need of abortion services, especially among poor, rural, and teenage women, were excluded. Clearly, these changes disproportionately affected poor, black women. In 1976, prior to Hyde, an estimated 1.1 million abortions were performed in the United States. Of these, 260,000 to 275,000 were paid for through Medicaid or Title X programs. Comparing women who had undergone abortion operations in 1972 and 1975, there had been a sharp increase among single black women during these years.[75]

Still, it is worth noting that family planning funds continued to increase under Carter. In part this increase was in response to activists upset over restrictions, but it also reflected Carter's belief that abortions could be reduced through better family planning. In fiscal 1977 Title X funds rose by $13 million, and in fiscal 1978 funds were increased by $21 million. As a result, nearly forty-three hundred of the nation's five thousand family planning clinics received some Title X funds.[76]

Furthermore, acting on the belief that the way to reduce abortion was through family planning, in 1978 Congress enacted teenage pregnancy legislation, the Adolescent Health Services and Pregnancy Prevention and Care Act, sponsored by Edward Kennedy (D-Massachusetts). The legislation targeted HEW family planning funding at teenagers. First proposed by Eunice Shriver (a longtime abortion opponent, the wife of Sargent Shriver, and Kennedy's sister), the measure was designed to prevent abortion among teenagers. Largely through her efforts on the Hill, this legislation specifically banned abortion services under the program.[77] Nonetheless, many questioned the effectiveness of these programs. One study showed that in 1975 only two out of five women at risk for unwanted pregnancy were estimated to have received family planning assistance. Yet even when such services were made available, they were not often used by those who would have benefited most. A review of such studies led one researcher to conclude, "Even the best comprehensive programs for teen-age parents have had a limited long-term effect in the area of family planning."[78]

By 1978 the proabortion movement appeared to be on the defensive. The mobilization of women against the proposed Equal Rights Amendment shocked feminists throughout the country. In state conventions held under the auspices of International Women's Year as well as other public forums, opposition to state ratification and opposition to abortion on demand surfaced on the grassroots level.[79] Especially disconcerting to many proabortion activists, polls revealed that while a clear majority supported the 1973 Supreme Court decision, a *New York Times/CBS News* survey showed that 55 percent of those interviewed opposed federal funding of abortion.[80] Moreover, antiabortionists had organized an estimated three thousand chapters with 11 million voters, and antiabortion activists presented a clear threat in the congressional elections of 1978.

As both sides laid their battle plans for the approaching election, a further blow to the movement came in July 1978 when John D. Rockefeller 3rd died suddenly in an automobile accident in Tarrytown, New York, on his way to work. His death caught his associates and his family and the abortion movement by surprise. Up to his death, Rockefeller had continued to work six days a week in his New York office. Like his grandfather, he carried a lean, spare physique. A temperate man, with moderate habits, he was in excellent health, except for an arthritic ankle. His financial support and leadership in the proabortion movement came at a critical juncture, just when the supporters of abortion felt embattled.[81] Writing shortly after Rockefeller's death, Roger Williams captured this contentiousness when he noted in the *Saturday Review*, "Opposition to abortion has become the most implacable, and perhaps the nastiest, public-issue campaign in a least a half century."[82]

In the Midst of a Cultural War, Republican Presidents Proclaim Themselves Antiabortion

The emergence of the New Right and evangelical Christian organizations in the late 1970s reflected this growing cultural divide and reinforced polarization between the two major parties. In the process, American politics was transformed as evangelical Protestants and Catholics deserted the Democratic party, thereby setting the stage for the 1980 election.[83]

Although surveys revealed strong opposition to abortion among white and black evangelical Christians, the abortion issue had remained primarily a Catholic issue. The mobilization of evangelical Christian voters strengthened the political salience of the abortion issue.[84] Nonetheless, the alliance between evangelical Protestants and Roman Catholics remained tenuous. Historically, evangelical Protestants had held deep anti-Catholic prejudices that ostensibly presented obstacles to any long-term alliance between the two groups. Moreover, Catholic antiabortion voters and Catholic conservative activists tended to be less concerned with other social issues that concerned evangelical Protestant Christians. While conservative Catholics and evangelical Protestants agreed on their opposition to abortion, conservative Catholics remained less concerned with issues such as school prayer, the role of women in society, homosexuality, welfare, gun control, military defense, and capital punishment. Indeed, surveys consistently revealed Catholics took liberal positions on these issues. These divisions reflected class differences (Catholics tended to be more upper-middle-class and affluent, while evangelical Protestants were less affluent, blue-collar, or newly arrived members of the middle class). At the same time, the more liberal positions taken by Catholics voters, even those of a conservative political bent, reflected social justice teachings of the church.[85] Furthermore,

Roman Catholics tended to vote Democratic, thereby offering a swing vote in presidential elections. At the same time, evangelical Christians confronted doctrinal divisions within Protestantism, especially between Pentecostal Protestants and fundamentalist Christians. The Christian Right, as it emerged, remained based primarily in the Pentecostal movement, which set it apart from fundamentalist Christians.

Conservative Republican party activists, anxious to attract evangelical Christians to a GOP in disarray following Richard Nixon's resignation from the White House and Jimmy Carter's election, began to court the evangelical vote in the late 1970s. By 1976 Republican party affiliation fell to an anemic 20 percent of the voters. Conservative activists believed that the key to winning traditional Democratic voters lay in tying social issues such as school choice and abortion to long-standing Republican causes— free market economics and hard-line defense and foreign policy. In this regard, Richard Nixon had pointed the way in winning the 1972 election.[86]

Conservative activists Richard Viguerie, Paul Weyerich, Howard Phillips, and Terry Dolan proved critical in shaping the New Right political agenda. Viguerie brought to the group his skills as a pioneer in computerized direct mailing; Weyerich, a founder of the Heritage Foundation and the Committee for the Survival of a Free Congress, provided political strategy; Howard Phillips, a former Nixon administration official, understood grassroots organizing; and Terry Dolan electrified the right wing with his fund-raising skills and his relentless "negative" attacks on liberals. Viguerie, Weyerich, and Dolan came from Roman Catholic backgrounds, while Phillips was Jewish. All hated liberalism and disliked establishment Republicans such as Nelson Rockefeller. These conservative activists believed that the antiabortion vote could be captured by the New Right.

These conservative operatives brought their political skills into the congressional elections of 1978 by employing the abortion issue as a wedge that separated liberal economic Democratic congressional representatives from their more socially conservative constituents. By focusing on the abortion issue, antiabortionists delivered staggering blows that left the Democrats wobbling. Once seemingly unbeatable, Dick Clark in Iowa and Don Fraser in Minnesota lost their seats in the U.S. Senate. Liberal Republicans who had waffled on the abortion issue joined the list of the defeated, including Senators Edward Brook in Massachusetts, Charles Percy in Illinois, and Clifford Case in New Jersey. Most surprising in all this, the antiabortion movement won by organizing its members and spending trifling sums of money. Proabortion activists tried to downplay these defeats by pointing out that Governor William Milliken of Michigan had been reelected despite having angered opponents of abortion by twice vetoing legislation that would have eliminated abortion funding; and although Senator Floyd Haskell lost in Colorado as a result of the antiabortion vote, the strongly proabortion governor, Richard Lamm, won handily. Still, few denied that the antiabortion movement had proved its wallop at the ballot box.[87]

The umbrella organization of the antiabortion movement, the National Right to Life Committee, operated on a $1.3 million budget that maintained five full-time and four part-time employees.[88] Fueled by local and state organizational activity and the emergence of energized evangelical voters, the antiabortion movement appeared to be gaining strength on the grassroots level. A demoralized Karen Mulhauser, director of NARAL, admitted, "Had we made more gains through the legislative and referendum processes, and taken a little longer at it, the public would have moved with us." Another political observer noted that the proabortion movement had moved quickly, like an armored column that had outstripped its supply lines.[89]

The emergence of the Moral Majority, formed by fundamentalist Baptist preacher Jerry Falwell in 1979, introduced an overtly Protestant component to this emerging New Right. While Falwell drew national media attention, his Moral Majority never extended much beyond Baptist churches in the South. Furthermore, Falwell's doctrinal opposition to Pentecostalism, with its emphasis on faith healing and "speaking in tongues" (Falwell declared that those who "spoke in tongues" had had too much pizza the night before), alienated a large constituency of evangelical Christians. As a consequence, Falwell's Moral Majority failed to develop an extensive grassroots organization. Later denounced by his opponents as "America's Ayatollah" (an allusion to religious anti-American fanaticism in Iran), Falwell became an important symbol and national spokesman of the emerging Christian Right.[90] Later studies showed that the new Christian Right tapped into deep concerns among many Americans about what they viewed as the breakdown of traditional morality in contemporary America, symbolized especially by the abortion issue and to a lesser degree by the Equal Rights Amendment.[91] Television evangelist Pat Robertson gave organizational coherence to this reaction when he formed the Christian Coalition in the mid-1980s.[92]

Antiabortion Sentiment Ascends in the Reagan and Bush Years

The emergence of the New Right and the new Christian Right set the stage for the 1980 election. By 1979 the Carter administration was in deep political trouble. Unable to control runaway inflation that had reached 13 percent per year, injured by political ineffectiveness on a number of issues including welfare, energy, and health care, and proclaiming that Americans were experiencing a "crisis in confidence," Carter was already politically vulnerable when America's longtime ally, Reza Pahlavi, the shah of Iran, was overthrown by the militant Islamic leader Ayatollah Ruholla Khomeini, who orchestrated the capture of fifty American hostages when the U.S. embassy in Tehran was seized. Although he won the Democratic nomination in 1980 after a bitter primary fight with Senator Edward Kennedy, Carter was easily defeated in the general election by his Republican challenger, Ronald Reagan—former Hollywood actor and governor of California.

During the Republican primaries, Reagan successfully played on the economic failures and foreign policy debacles of the Carter administration. At the same time, Reagan reassured his right-wing base in the Republican party that he was one of them on social issues. On cultural issues, Reagan attacked the "cultural elite" for its betrayal of traditional spiritual values, including prayer in schools and abortion. Once in office, however, Reagan placed these cultural issues on the back burner in order to pursue budget reduction, deregulation, and tax cuts. He continued to use strong antiabortion rhetoric that encouraged abortion opponents.[93]

With antiabortion sentiment seemingly in the ascendancy, Senator Jesse Helms (R-North Carolina) proposed a constitutional amendment that stated that human life begins at conception and that fetuses are legal "persons," protected by the Fourteenth Amendment.[94] Hearings on Helms's proposed amendment opened on April 22, 1981. On the first day, a packed hearing room was disrupted when three women from the Women's Liberation Zap Action Brigade jumped on their chairs and began shouting, "A woman's life is a human life. Stop the hearings!"[95] The protest proved futile. In the end, the Judiciary Subcommittee on Separation of Powers, chaired by John P. East (R-North Carolina), voted to support Helms's bill.

A number of constitutional experts, including many abortion opponents, questioned the legality of the bill, however. This led Senator Orrin Hatch (R-Utah) to draft another constitutional amendment that proposed returning the abortion issue to the state legislatures.[96] The Hatch amendment, however, divided the antiabortion movement. While the National Conference of Catholic Bishops, the National Right to Life Committee, and the National Pro-Life Political Action Committee supported the amendment, other groups, including the March for Life and the Life Amendment Political Action Committee, declared it "a sellout of the principles that have motivated the pro-life movement from its beginning."[97] After extensive hearings that drew some of its sharpest criticism from antiabortionists, the Judiciary Committee split on a 10 to 7 vote to endorse the Hatch amendment. Immediately, proabortion activist Faye

Wattleton denounced the measure "as part of a broader agenda of repression by extremists, by those who are attempting to define morality and enact laws that reflect their narrow interpretations of morality."[98]

The Helms and Hatch amendments played havoc in the Senate. When both Jesse Helms and Orrin Hatch attached their amendments to a debt-ceiling bill, Robert Packwood (R-Oregon) began a filibuster by reading James C. Mohr's *Abortion in America*. Outside the Senate, antiabortion and proabortion groups mobilized their supporters. On September 8 President Reagan stepped into the fray by writing an open letter to the National Right to Life Committee declaring, "One can tiptoe around principles only so long."[99] At the same time he wrote to nine Republican senators, urging them to support cloture. Even Reagan's intervention could not break the deadlock. Finally, on September 15, Hatch made a surprise announcement that he was withdrawing his constitutional amendment. Shortly afterward, the Senate voted 47 to 46 to table Helms's proposal. This ended the movement to amend the constitution to overturn *Roe*.[100]

Antiabortionists found victory in smaller measures.[101] In 1981 the Adolescent Health Services and Pregnancy Prevention and Care Act was refunded as the Adolescent Family Life Act. This reconstructed program required active involvement of religious groups in family planning; prohibited federal funds to any organization (such as Planned Parenthood) involved in abortion or counseling services; mandated that providers emphasize adoption over abortion; and instructed family planning providers to encourage premarital abstinence.[102] By 1985 this program was spending nearly $15 million on fifty-nine demonstration projects to discourage teenagers from engaging in sexual activity.

In the first year of his administration, Reagan cut Title X funds by nearly 25 percent. At the same time, the Department of Health and Human Services issued regulations that prohibited family planning clinics supported by Title X funding from providing any information about abortion—even neutral information.[103] Although Congress subsequently increased funding for Title X programs in 1983 and 1984, this action restored funding only to 1981 levels.[104] Supporters of abortion pointed out the apparent contradiction of the administration's position of not supporting family planning programs that might have prevented unwanted pregnancies in the first place.[105]

Moreover, Reagan staffed his administration with antiabortion activists.[106] His most significant antiabortion appointment came when Richard Schweiker—one of the first supporters of a pro-life amendment—was named to head the Department of Health and Human Services. Schweiker immediately launched an investigation of Planned Parenthood for several violations of federal law. Although the lengthy investigation found no violations, it placed Planned Parenthood on the defensive. When Schweiker resigned in 1983, Reagan appointed Margaret Heckler, a longtime abortion opponent, to the position. When she left HEW in 1985, Reagan appointed a former governor of Indiana, Otis R. Bowen, to the post.

Bowen actively pursued a policy of limiting access to abortion and contraceptives. By the mid-1980s the Department of Health and Human Services received about $145 million in appropriations for Title X for family planning services. Among the ninety grants each year that went to private organizations, Planned Parenthood remained one of the largest recipients, allowing it to serve about 4.2 million women at thirty-nine hundred clinics throughout the country. Pursuing the attack on Planned Parenthood, Bowen attempted to convince Congress to revise the Public Health Services Act to limit abortion services and counseling at clinics receiving federal funds. When this failed, he announced a new interpretation of the Public Health Service Act that banned funding to organizations that performed or counseled abortion. This administrative fiat became known as the "gag rule."[107]

Reagan's most enduring legacy in regard to abortion came with his appointments to the federal bench and the Supreme Court.[108] Reagan remained adamant in his belief that the courts had gone awry. As one Reagan official observed, "The federal courts have become political engines of the left-liberal agenda. *Roe* was just a dramatic example of a system of judging that had run badly off the rails."[109] During his two terms in the White House, Reagan appointed over three hundred judges to the federal bench. In making these selections, the Reagan administration was accused by critics of imposing an "ideological litmus test" on candidates to the court, although this was denied by Justice Department officials.

When Reagan nominated Sandra Day O'Connor, a judge on the Arizona Court of Appeals, antiabortion groups opposed her appointment because of her earlier support of a family planning bill in Arizona that would have repealed existing state law banning abortions. Furthermore, in the early 1970s, along with with population activist Richard Lamm, then a Colorado state legislator before he became governor, she had signed a statement that called for population control in the United States. In her nomination hearings, however, O'Connor refused to answer any questions on the issue. She easily won appointment to the Court as its first female justice in a 99 to 0 vote in the U.S. Senate.

In her first major abortion case on the Court, Justice O'Connor joined dissenters in *Akron v. Akron Center for Reproductive Health, Inc.* (1983). In a 6 to 3 decision the Court struck down as unconstitutional most of the restrictions on abortion that had been legislated by the Akron City Council, including a ban on performing second-trimester abortions in outpatient clinics and a twenty-four-hour waiting period. In her dissent O'Connor noted that *Roe* was "on a collision course with itself" because the trimester approach was "unworkable" in light of changing medical technology that increased viability. Moreover, she echoed U.S. Solicitor General Rex E. Lee's amicus brief, which asserted that the test for state regulation of abortion should rest in the principle of "undue burden." This principle of whether state regulations placed an "undue burden" on women for obtaining an abortion marked the beginning of an important shift in the Court's thinking on the subject and would have a profound effect on subsequent decisions.[110]

In 1985 the Reagan administration made a direct effort to overturn *Roe* shortly after Charles Fried, a Harvard University professor of law, became solicitor general. The occasion came when the Supreme Court decided to hear *Thornburgh v. American College of Gynecologists and Obstetricians* (1986). In making the case to overturn *Roe*, Fried presented a subtle argument that maintained that the privacy doctrine as embodied in *Griswold* should be upheld, but that abortion should be decided by the legislatures. He told the Court, "We are not asking the Court to unravel the fabric of . . . privacy rights which this Court has woven. . . . Rather, we are asking the Court to pull this one thread."[111] This argument allowed the acceptance of privacy claims concerning contraception but challenged the enlargement of the right to include abortion. As Fried said, "Abortion is different. It involves the purposeful termination . . . of potential life. And . . . in the minds of many legislators who pass abortion regulation, it is not merely potential but actual life." Therefore, both sides were divided on the issue of whether the nonviable fetus is such a person, and the Constitution was silent on the question. As such, he said, this complex and irresolvable moral question should not be a legal decision but a legislative decision, just as are matters of war and peace, and the choice between socialism and capitalism.[112] The Court did not accept Fried's argument but instead overturned numerous restrictions imposed by the state legislature in Pennsylvania. Nonetheless, four justices dissented from the majority decision, including Chief Justice Warren Burger. The Court appeared to be one judge away from overturning *Roe*.

Two years after Reagan's reelection in 1984, a further opportunity to change the composition of the Court came when Chief Justice Burger, one of the members of the seven-person majority in *Roe*, retired. Seizing the opportunity, Reagan appointed Associate Justice William H. Rehnquist as chief justice, and he nominated a noted Roman Catholic conservative judge, Antonin Scalia, to the court. When Justice Lewis F. Powell stepped down on June 28, 1987, Reagan selected Judge Robert H. Bork of the Circuit Court of Appeals for the District of Columbia. Bork, a well-known conservative, drew the wrath of liberals in the Senate, feminists, and abortion supporters. He had written extensively about constitutional issues, sharply criticizing the "privacy" doctrine found in *Griswold* and *Roe*. Planned Parenthood took out a full-page newspaper advertisement that claimed, "Robert Bork is an extremist who believes you have no constitutional right to personal privacy."[113] After extensive televised hearings, the Senate defeated his nomination by a sharply divided vote of 58 to 42. Following Bork's defeat, Reagan turned to Judge Anthony Kennedy of the U.S. Circuit Court of Appeals; Kennedy won Senate confirmation after he assured the Senate that he accepted a constitutional right to privacy.

Although Congress thwarted some of these maneuverings, Reagan influenced the federal courts through his appointments. In his eight years in office, Reagan continued to ban Medicaid funds for abortions (as well as extending this ban to apply to organizations involved in international family planning). He had shifted the Court in a more antiabortion direction. His administration kept Planned Parenthood in turmoil with funding cuts and federal investigations. Nevertheless, contrary to Reagan's actions and rhetoric, the number of abortions continued to rise during his administration. When Reagan came into office, approximately 1.5 million abortions were performed each year in the United States, roughly three pregnancies in ten. When he left office, not much had changed. Attempts to overturn *Roe* had failed. When Democrats regained the House following the 1982 elections, social issues fell off the policy agenda. What had changed, however, was the intensity of the debate.

Beginning in the early 1980s, a dissident minority of antiabortion extremists turned to violence. Their absolutist views on abortion and their willingness to employ terrorist methods alienated and shocked the mainstream of the antiabortion movement.[114] While denounced by established leadership of the movement, extremists undertook a campaign to disrupt abortion clinics by conducting sit-ins, picketing physicians at their homes, harassing clinic employees, and, at times, resorting to more serious tactics, including the break-in and bombing of abortion clinics. For example, in 1980 Joseph Scheidler, a former Benedictine monk, was expelled from the Chicago-based antiabortion group Friends for Life after he continued to advocate "guerrilla" tactics in the "pro-life" struggle. He founded the Pro-Life Action League, which advocated violence as a political strategy. In his *Ninety-Nine Ways to Close an Abortion Clinic* (1984), he outlined a radical strategy of blocking access to clinics. While renouncing violence, Randall Terry's Operation Rescue launched massive demonstrations that blocked entrances to abortion clinics in Atlanta during the Democratic National Convention. Terry's carefully orchestrated "Siege of Atlanta" brought nearly two thousand antiabortion demonstrators to Atlanta to block an abortion clinic.

While these splinter groups largely used civil disobedience tactics modeled after those of civil rights protesters in the 1960s, they refused to denounce outright more violent forms of protest. Beginning in 1984, fire-bombings of abortion clinics escalated. Although eight clinic bombings were reported in the period between 1977 and 1983, in 1984 the number of incidents jumped to eighteen. President Reagan condemned this violence, but he refused to classify it as terrorism. As the violence escalated, however, the Bureau of Alcohol, Tobacco, and Firearms assigned fifty of its officers to its clinic violence team. In the next two years, 1985 and 1986, the number of bombings dropped to six, but these kinds of violent tactics divided the antiabortion movement, rallied feminists, and deeply alienated the American general public.

The election of 1988 brought the abortion issue into sharp relief within both political parties. Aware that he needed to win the right wing of his party to secure his bid for the presidency, Vice President George Bush reversed his stance by declaring that he had become an ardent foe of abortion. Bush operatives at the Republican convention strengthened antiabortion planks to the party platform, including calls to end funding of proabortion population organizations, supporting parental consent requirements for minors regarding the use of contraceptives, and prohibiting the use of aborted fetuses in scientific research. Bush's move to the right earned him the support of evangelist Pat Robertson, who had challenged Bush in the primaries.[115] After the election, Robertson ensured his place as a leader at the Republican table with the formation of the Christian Coalition, a nationwide organization of like-minded evangelical Christians.

When the Democrats met at their national convention, proabortion activists rallied to the party, intent upon preventing a Republican from spending another four years in the White House. As one feminist scholar, Jo Freeman, observed, "The Reagan years had been disastrous for women and four more years of Republican rule, would, at the very least, result in a Supreme Court that would limit women's options for decades to come."[116] Concerned that the Democrats might backpedal on controversial issues such as abortion, women activists lobbied for a tougher stance on the issue. They gained the support of the Democratic party's nominee, Governor Michael Dukakis of Massachusetts. The final party platform declared that reproductive choice should be guaranteed regardless of ability to pay. During the subsequent campaign, Dukakis countered Bush's call for "adoption not abortion" as a solution to unwanted pregnancies by repeatedly calling for constitutional protection for legalized abortion. Polls at the time showed that the majority of Americans supported legalized abortions, but only in certain circumstances. Among those voters who viewed abortion as the main issue of the campaign, Bush received overwhelming support.[117] When the final vote was tallied, Bush crushed his

Democratic opponent, winning 54 percent of the popular vote and 426 electoral votes to Dukakis's 112 electors.

Once in office, Bush promised to make America a "kinder, gentler nation." Two days after the election, however, the U.S. Justice Department filed an amicus curiae brief in *Webster v. Reproductive Health Services* (1989), urging the Court to use the case as an opportunity to overturn *Roe*. During the summer of 1988, in the midst of the heated presidential campaign, Assistant Attorney General William Bradford Reynolds had encouraged William L. Webster, attorney general of Missouri, to appeal a federal appellate court's overturning of the state's legislative restrictions on abortion. At issue was the constitutionality of Missouri's decree that life begins at conception, a requirement to test the fetus's state of development after twenty or more weeks of pregnancy, a prohibition of public employees and public facilities from performing an abortion unnecessary to save a pregnant woman's life, and a ban on the use of public funds for "encouraging or counseling" a woman to have an abortion, except when her life was in danger.[118]

With the Court appearing poised to reconsider the constitutional right to abortion, women unleashed massive efforts to protect reproductive rights. Kate Michelman, the executive director of NARAL, launched a national campaign that drew support from Planned Parenthood, the National Organization for Women, and the Fund for the Feminist Majority. The efforts to rally women to the threat posed by the pending *Webster* decision included a massive print and television advertising campaign that warned of returning abortion to the back streets and alleys. As the campaign reached a crescendo the Court was receiving forty thousand pieces of mail a day. Finally, on April 9, 1989, more than three hundred thousand marchers demonstrated in front of the Court in an attempt to apply public pressure.

Seventeen days later, on April 26, 1989, the Court convened to hear oral arguments on the case. Sitting in the courtroom were Norma McCorvey and Sarah Weddington, who had brought *Roe v. Wade* before the Court. William Webster represented the State of Missouri; Frank Susman represented Reproductive Health Services. In an unusual step, the Rehnquist Court granted the Bush administration, represented by former Reagan solicitor general, Charles Fried, ten minutes to present its case. On the last day of the term in July 1989, the Court announced its decision. Four members of the Court, Chief Justice William H. Rehnquist and Justices Antonin Scalia, Anthony Kennedy, and Byron White, appeared willing to overturn *Roe*, but they failed to muster the fifth vote. Nonetheless, Justice O'Connor joined her four colleagues in a concurrent separate opinion that found that none of the state's regulations unduly burdened a woman's right to obtain an abortion. (Justice Scalia also joined the five-member majority in upholding Missouri's regulations with a separate concurrent opinion.) Visibly upset by the decision, Harry A. Blackmun, William Brennan Jr., and Thurgood Marshall offered a joint dissent. *Roe* had survived, but barely, and its framework was shaken as state legislatures were encouraged to enact more restrictive regulations. The decision outraged abortion proponents and opponents alike, and it muddled the policy waters by leaving to the various states opportunities to test the limits of *Webster*. As Kate Michelman from NARAL graphically put it, "The Court has left a woman's right to privacy hanging by a thread and passed the scissors to the state legislators."[119] The decision only served as a catalyst for further litigation and intensified mobilization on both sides of the issue.[120]

In 1990 the National Conference of Catholic Bishops (NCCB), formerly the NCWC, decided to increase its efforts to end legalized abortion. That year, the NCCB selected John Cardinal O'Connor, a prominent conservative bishop, to head its Committee on Pro-Life Activities. Yet, even while selecting Cardinal O'Connor, the church and the National Right-to-Life Committee refocused its activities away from a human life amendment; instead it turned its attention to the states. This turn in political strategy away from a human rights amendment outraged groups such as Operation Rescue, which intensified its civil disobedience campaign. Other splinter groups, such as Advocates for Life and Defensive Actions, openly called for violent action against abortion clinics.

George Bush sought to support the antiabortion movement without condoning or encouraging the radical fringe. Within Congress, abortion proponents found some encouragement when both houses reauthorized a qualified Hyde amendment that allowed federal funding of abortions for poor women who became pregnant as a result of rape or incest. This liberalized version of the Hyde amendment was vetoed by Bush. Nonetheless, in 1991 U.S. Senator Alan Cranston (D-California) and Congressman Don Edwards (D-California) introduced the Freedom of Choice Act, which proposed prohibiting any state from enacting abortion restrictions before the time of fetal viability or at any time when a pregnant mother's life was in danger. The bill never reached the floor of either house for a vote, but Bush promised that he would veto such legislation if the occasion did arise. He further sought to shore up his support among antiabortion activists by instructing his solicitor general, Kenneth Starr, to defend the gag rule—the federal ban on abortion at federally funded family planning clinics.

As legal challenges to the gag rule worked their way through the federal courts, the loss of Lewis Powell from the Supreme Court presented Bush with an opportunity to complete the Reagan legal revolution. Supported by Senator Warren Rudman (R-New Hampshire) and his chief of staff, John Sununu, Bush nominated David Souter, an unknown federal judge from New Hampshire. Souter, unlike Bork or Scalia, had not left a paper trail of legal articles or speeches. Nonetheless, Bush was assured by insiders that Souter could be counted on to vote against abortion if it came before the Court. Although opposed by abortion activists, Souter easily won confirmation.

All eyes now turned to the Court when *Rust v. Sullivan* came before it. Souter came under a watchful eye on both sides. The case involved a legal challenge to the gag rule, which the Court upheld in a 5 to 4 vote. Souter appeared safe, but antiabortionist groups later found his voting record hard to decipher. In 1991, when Bush vetoed a congressional bill to suspend the gag rule, Congress proved unable to override his veto.[121]

Soon after the *Rust* decision, further bad news for the proabortion side came when Justice Thurgood Marshall, a steadfast liberal on the Court, announced his decision to resign. Bush nominated Clarence Thomas, another African-American (although of considerably different political orientation) to the Court. Thomas brought to his nomination a decidedly conservative public record. In arguably the bitterest nomination fight in the Court's history, Thomas barely won confirmation in the Senate. His appointment appeared to give antiabortionists a clear majority on the Court.

The ambiguity of *Webster* led to a new round of state restrictions as the tug-of-war between antiabortion activists and the courts continued. In 1989 Pennsylvania enacted one of the most restrictive abortion laws in the states, one that required compulsory antiabortion lectures by doctors, a twenty-four-hour delay in obtaining an abortion following the lecture, strict reporting requirements, spousal notification, and stringent parental consent for minors or judicial approval from a judge. Signed into law by the vocal antiabortion governor, Robert Casey, a Democrat, the Abortion Control Act drew immediate legal challenges from Planned Parenthood and over 150 other proabortion groups. By the time *Planned Parenthood of Southeastern Pennsylvania v. Casey* had worked its way through the federal courts, women's groups had mobilized to draw public attention to the case. On April 5, 1991, feminists sponsored a massive march in Washington, under the banner of March for Women's Lives, that drew over half a million marchers, the largest march by proponents of abortion in the capitol's history, rivaling the antiwar marches of the 1960s.

The Court reaffirmed the centrality of *Roe* by a slim majority. Employing the doctrine of "undue" burden developed by Justice O'Connor, the Court imparted greater leeway to the states to restrict abortion than had been articulated in *Webster*. At the same time, the Court, in its 184-page decision, rejected *Roe*'s trimester approach through the doctrine of "undue burden." As a result, *Casey* upheld all of Pennsylvania's restrictions except spousal consent. Nonetheless, while Rehnquist, White, Scalia, and Thomas said that *Roe* should be overturned, they failed to win over

O'Connor, Kennedy, or Souter. *Roe* remained the law of the land—somewhat bruised, still under attack, but standing.[122]

Clinton Reverses Republican Policies

For twelve years the Republicans had maintained control of the White House. During this time the composition of the Court had changed radically from the one that had issued *Roe* nearly twenty years earlier. At the same time, while public expenditures for family planning services on the federal and state levels increased by $154 million over the previous decade, when inflation was taken into account expenditures actually fell by one-third under Republican rule.[123]

As the 1992 presidential election approached, both sides mobilized to affect the outcome. "Pro-family" forces found added strength with the entrance of Pat Robertson's Christian Coalition into the election. Promising to bring 20 million grassroot evangelical Christian voters to the polls, the Christian Coalition, under its young, articulate director, Ralph Reed, spent approximately $10 million to influence the outcome of the presidential election, as well as supporting local and state candidates loyal to "pro-family" and antiabortion values.[124] Joining the Christian Coalition were other groups that also opposed abortion, including the Catholic Campaign for America, headed by Mary Ellen Bork, the wife of Robert Bork; former secretary of education, William Bennett; and longtime conservative Republican activist Phyllis Schlafly. The conservative Arthur DeMoss Foundation launched a nationwide television campaign, "Life, What a Beautiful Choice." While this advertising campaign was not overtly political, it focused attention on the abortion issue in an election year. Kate Michelman, head of NARAL, warned that Bush was getting ready to make abortion illegal.[125]

When the Democrats nominated William Clinton, the governor of Arkansas, the party decided to downplay social issues such as abortion and focus on the economy, which had experienced a downturn in Bush's last year. This tactic of avoiding the abortion issue became apparent when the convention refused to allow Pennsylvania's antiabortion governor, Robert Casey, the opportunity to address the convention. Nonetheless, the party platform continued to support legalized abortion and to support public funding for abortion in stronger terms than in its 1988 platform. Clinton clearly wanted to direct voters' attention away from the abortion issue, although the majority of Americans supported abortion in cases of trauma—incest, rape, and when a woman's life was in danger. For his running mate Clinton selected the moderate U.S. senator from Tennessee, Albert Gore Jr., who like Clinton had switched his position on abortion to a "pro-choice" stance.

In a well-organized campaign, Clinton rallied party workers under the banner "It's the Economy, Stupid." Focusing on the economy made sense given the economic recession at the time and the divisiveness of social issues such as abortion. Surveys showed that Americans continued to be sharply divided on abortion, with 47 percent of the voters agreeing with the statement "Abortion should not be restricted because it is a women's choice." Only 10 percent of the respondents agreed that abortion should never be allowed, and another 29 percent agreed with the statement "Abortion should be allowed only in cases of rape, incest, or to save the life of the mother." Another 14 percent of the voters accepted the moderate proabortion statement "Abortion should be allowed when a clear need exists."[126] While Clinton urged the electorate to vote with their pocketbooks, exit poll data suggested that attitudes toward abortion significantly influenced the final tally when more proabortion Republicans than antiabortion Democrats defected from their respective parties.[127]

Clinton immediately moved to overturn Republican antiabortion measures. On January 22, 1993, two days after his inauguration, Clinton commemorated the twentieth anniversary of *Roe v. Wade* by issuing five executive orders that overturned the Reagan-Bush gag rule on abortion counseling; the Reagan ban on fetal research by federally funded researchers; a ban on the importation of RU 486, a "morning-after" abortion drug; a ban on abortions in overseas military hospitals first imposed by Richard Nixon; and a Reagan-Bush ban on American aid to international family planning organizations that performed or counseled for abortions.[128] His most significant actions came shortly afterward with the appointment of two "pro-choice" justices to the Supreme Court, Stephen G. Breyer and Ruth Bader Ginsburg. Although publicly criticized by the Vatican for his abortion policy, Clinton remained steadfast in showing that he was a proabortion president willing to defend abortion rights.[129]

In the first two years of the first Clinton administration, spending for family planning increased dramatically by 11 percent, with federal and state expenditures for contraceptive supplies and services totaling $715 million in 1994. Of this total, funding for contraceptive sterilization amounted to $148 million, while $90 million was spent for abortion services. In this same period, Title X spending rose by 37 percent between 1992 and 1994. Medicaid family planning expenses increased only 4 percent, a sharp downturn in growth from previous years. State government continued to remain the primary source of public support for the 203,200 abortions provided in 1994 to low-income women, even though looser federal abortion funding guidelines permitted payment in cases of rape and incest. Still, federally funded abortions numbered only 282 cases.[130]

Meanwhile, frustrated antiabortion lobbyists stepped up their efforts to impose new restrictions on abortion. Antiabortion extremists, perceiving failure through established political means, undertook more radical actions, including bombings, arson, vandalism, and murder. Although these acts did not appear to be part of a well-coordinated campaign, such incidents shocked the American public and alienated even mainstream antiabortion groups. Statistics collected by the National Abortion Federation revealed growing violence against doctors and clinics performing abortions. In the period from 1977 to 1983 there were 15 arsons and 8 bombings of abortion clinics. From 1984 through 1992 there were 65 arsons and 28 bombings. In Clinton's first three years in office, violence escalated, with 22 arsons and 32 bombings. Most alarming, however, was the murder of 4 persons working at abortion clinics and the attempted murder of 8 others in 1994.[131]

In the face of these terrorist attacks, the National Organization for Women sought to employ the Racketeer Influenced and Corrupt Organizations Act (RICO), legislation originally intended by Congress to clean up labor unions from organized crime, against militant antiabortion protest groups. The link between the most extreme acts of violence against abortion doctors and clinics with these militant protest groups remained inconclusive, leading the author of RICO, Robert Blakey, to file an amicus curiae brief against the implementation of this legislation to restrain abortion protest groups. He was joined by leftist political groups, including lawyers from People for the Ethical Treatment of Animals (PETA) and the radical environmental group Earth First!, who feared that such legislation might be employed against their organizations as well. It made for strange politics. When their RICO suit appeared to be going nowhere, NOW and Planned Parenthood of Washington, D.C., and several Virginia abortion clinics filed suit under the Ku Klux Klan Act, legislation enacted by Congress in 1871 to curtail terrorist activities against newly freed slaves in the South. Once again it was left to the Court to decide the constitutionality of a serious division in the body politic. In *Bray v. Alexandria Women's Health Clinic* (1993), the Court ruled that RICO and the KKK Act did not apply to abortion protesters because their activities were not designed to discriminate against women as a class.

Shortly after the decision, on March 10, 1993, David Gunn, a physician working at a Florida abortion clinic, was gunned down by Michael Griffith, a member of Rescue America, a splinter antiabortion group. Attorney General Janet Reno, speaking on behalf of the Clinton administration, called for federal legislation to protect women from violence. Shortly afterward, the Freedom of Access to Clinic Entrances Act (FACE) was introduced in Congress in November 1993. While Congress debated the act, another physician, George Tiller, in Wichita, Kansas, was shot by Rochelle Shannon, who had traveled from her home in Oregon to commit the crime. Other violence followed when Paul Hill, a member of Defensive Action, shot and killed a physician and his escort while they were leaving a Pensacola, Florida, abortion clinic. Outraged by these acts of violence, Congress enacted FACE in May 1993, making it a federal crime to block access to reproductive health clinics or to harass or use violence against abortion patients or abortion personnel. This legislation offered protection from violence, but attempts to pass the Freedom of Choice Act became bogged down in congressional maneuverings and failed to muster support in the Senate.[132] The election of a Republican Congress in 1994 ensured that further legislation favorable to the proponents of abortion would be stymied.[133]

Indeed, the Republican-controlled 104th Congress considered a record number of abortion bills, 37 in all, of which 14 were passed, including a ban on abortions on military bases overseas, severely limiting Title X funds, and banning abortions for women in federal prisons.[134] Similar activity occurred on the state level, where 304 bills on abortion-related issues were introduced in thirty-eight states.[135] The most controversial legislation came with the Partial Birth Abortion Ban Act, legislation that prevented a late-term abortion procedure in which a fetus is extracted feet first and a catheter is used to deflate the fetus's head in order to facilitate the final step. The bill prevented the use of this procedure except to save the life of the mother. An intensive lobbying campaign by the National Right to Life Committee and the Roman Catholic hierarchy failed to prevent Clinton from vetoing the bill on April 8, 1996, after Congress refused to loosen the language that would have allowed the procedure to protect the health of the woman.

The presidential election of 1996 again placed the abortion issue before the American public, as the Republican candidate, Senator Robert Dole (R-Kansas), ran on an antiabortion platform. At the Republican convention, proabortion Republicans led by Ann Stone attempted to change the platform, but antiabortion forces in the party defeated these efforts. Running as an incumbent, President Clinton easily defeated Dole. A pronounced "gender gap," with women overwhelmingly voting for Clinton, suggested that the abortion issue hurt the Republicans. Antiabortionists within the Republican party argued that Dole had not clearly articulated the abortion issue to the American public in order to cater to female voters and because his own wife, Elizabeth Dole, supported legalized abortion.

In his next term Clinton confronted further controversy over abortion. On April 1, 1997, the Food and Drug Administration under Commissioner David Kessler announced that the Population Council had filed an application to sell RU 486 based on clinical trials in the United States and Europe.

The council established a private company, Advances in Health Technology, to manufacture the drug. RU 486 promised to avoid abortion restrictions found in nearly all the states in 1996. When the National Right to Life Committee, however, called for a boycott of the drug, the product was withdrawn from the market. Nonetheless, the promise of a "morning-after" pill suggested that the abortion war had entered into new territory.

Nor did the issue of partial birth abortion (or intact dilation and evacuation) simply vanish, although few expected that it would. The issue suddenly revived when Ron Fitzsimmons, executive director of the National Association of Abortion Providers, an organization representing more than two hundred independent abortion clinics, admitted that he had lied to the public and Congress when he said the procedure was rarely performed. Declaring that lying had made him "physically sick," he told the press, "I can't do it again." As the news media picked up the story, many Democrats who had opposed the earlier ban dissociated themselves from the procedure and privately admitted to reporters in off-the-record interviews that "they felt they had been set up by the pro-choice community."[136] Once again on the offensive, the antiabortion movement pushed through Congress, led by Senator Rick Santorum (R-Pennsylvania), the Partial Birth Abortion Act of 1997. Although the act was vetoed by Clinton in 1997, the issue revealed just how persistent and intractable abortion policy remained in American politics at century's end.

Behind the sound and fury, often overlooked in the cacophonous debate, significant changes had occurred. Within the antiabortion movement, many believed that the imminent overturning of *Roe v. Wade* remained highly unlikely; as a result, they called for political compromise on the national level, while obtaining legal restrictions of abortion on the state level.[137] Moreover, federal involvement in family planning had become established policy. Debate now focused on levels of funding, not complete withdrawal of federal participation from family planning programs.

More significantly, in the five decades after the end of the Second World War, American sexual mores and practices underwent a profound transformation. Few doubted that the new contraceptive technology and government involvement in family planning helped accelerate this sexual revolution. In this way, the dreams and efforts of a select group of philanthropists, social scientists, population activists, and feminists transformed public policy in the United States. They achieved their intentions and welcomed with little reservation the consequences of their actions.

Conclusion

Public policy must be judged on two levels: Did the policy meet the expectations and accomplish the goals its advocates said it would? What effects—intended or unintended—did the policy have on the larger scheme of things in society?

Any assessment of policy change in the United States needs to begin with the understanding that the process is by necessity political, often acrimonious, and frequently accompanied by the formation of opposition groups. Debate often proves shrill, contention rancorous, and conflict seemingly irreconcilable; yet this reflects the vibrancy of a mature democracy. Such discord illustrates the strength of the democratic process, even while it has a disquieting effect on the polity.

In the period from 1965 to 1974, policy experts and activists played a critical role in transforming federal family planning policy. Initially, the primary impetus for federal family planning policy came from those who believed that overpopulation threatened political, economic, and social stability in the United States and the world. Convinced that a burgeoning global population portended disaster for the world, policy experts and activists lobbied policy makers in Washington to initiate federally funded contraception programs. At first, policy actors focused their attention on creating international family planning programs, but this interest turned to domestic federal family planning with Lyndon Johnson's Great Society. As a consequence, federal family planning became an instrument to alleviate problems of poverty, rising welfare costs, and out-of-wedlock births. Government officials in HEW touted family planning as the most successful antipoverty program.

In the late 1960s and early 1970s, the emergence of the abortion issue shifted the impetus for family planning from a population issue to a rights concern involving the right of women to legalized abortion. The emergence of the abortion rights issue changed the tenor of political debate and created ideological divisions within the Democratic and Republican parties, thereby ending the bipartisan support in Congress for federal family planning programs. Coinciding with the growth of the feminist movement in the late 1960s, the composition of the advocacy movement for federal planning shifted from control by established interests in the philanthropic community to proabortion and antiabortion groups mobilized on the grassroots level. As a result, the abortion issue became part of a larger political debate concerning the role of women, the breakdown of traditional families, sexuality, welfare and social policy, and the general culture in American democratic society.

The early advocates of federal family planning in the postwar period were motivated by a simple goal—the reduction of the global rate of population growth.[1] They believed this could be achieved through the development of better, safer, and cheaper contraception and through active intervention by the federal government. Government and United Nations involvement in international family planning proved highly successful as well. The rate of population growth in the world slowed dramatically in the postwar period because of economic modernization as well as interventionist family planning programs.[2] In achieving this, the early advocates of federal involvement achieved a principal goal, in terms of both policy innovation and policy outcome. In 1950 the world's population stood at 2.5 billion; today it stands at 5.8 billion. Western Europe and North America experienced sharp declines in the overall rate of population growth during the four decades from 1950 to 1990. By the 1990s Europe's overall birthrate had fallen to below the replacement fertility rate—the rate of population growth required to maintain current population levels. Italy had a fertility rate of only 1.2 births per woman, followed by Spain and Germany, with fertility rates of 1.3. Ireland's fertility rate fell from 3.55 in 1977 to 1.87 in 1995. Births in the United States fell below the replacement rate as well, and without high immigration the United States would have experienced a sharp decline in its overall rate of population growth. In 1970 only nineteen nations, almost all in Europe and North America, experienced below-replacement rates of fertility, but by 1995 there were fifty-one countries with below-replacement rates.[3]

This change was so dramatic that by the mid-1990s many demographers expressed worry about the far-reaching consequences of this declining rate of population growth, leading to a disproportionately elderly population. Government officials fretted about the financial costs of maintaining an elderly population without a large base of younger, employed people. Moreover, this aging population will have the numerical power to exert power at the ballot box that will inevitably influence social policy in the future.[4]

While the rate of growth remained a serious problem in Asia and Africa, the astounding decline in the rate of population growth belied cataclysmic projections made earlier by demographers.[5] Much of this decrease came through massive investments in family planning. By 1990 an estimated 50 percent of couples in the world used contraceptives. In Western nations, as well as in China, approximately 80 percent of couples used contraceptives. Other regions of the world experienced lower percentages of contraceptive use—Latin America less than 60 percent, South Asia approximately 40 percent, and Africa less than 20 percent.[6] Nonetheless, a dramatic transformation of contraceptive usage had occurred throughout the world. While overpopulation remained a pressing concern among demographers, as well as among population and environmental activists, advocates of family planning took deserved credit that matters might have been worse without public intervention.[7]

Policy innovators proved equally successful in changing federal family planning policy within the United States. Beginning with the Draper report in 1959, family planning advocates persistently pressured government officials, Congress, and the White House to initiate family planning programs in the United States. The advent of Johnson's Great Society allowed policy experts and family planning activists to link federal antipoverty programs to federally funded contraceptive programs through state agencies and private organizations. While federal programs remained uncoordinated, contrary to the expectations of family planning activists, family planning became an established policy within the federal government, able to withstand sharp political attacks during the Reagan years. The efforts of a small group of men and women, drawn from the philanthropic foundation community and activist organizations, had succeeded in transforming public policy within the United States.

Moreover, population experts and activists, joined by feminists, successfully initiated reforms in abortion law on the state level in the 1960s. Although abortion law reform within the states was not one of uniform success, the Supreme Court's decision in *Roe v. Wade* established legalized abortion as a constitutional right.

Weighing the effects of these programs in terms of their specific policy goals presents the historian with a complex set of questions of what might have happened if family planning implementation had occurred through a single agency or if more funds had been committed to the programs. Clearly, federal family planning programs experienced mixed success. Nonetheless, family planning advocates believed that these programs would have enjoyed greater success if more funds had been allocated to them. Without sufficient funds, many women, especially among the poor, were denied full access to contraception, including birth control through artificial contraception, sterilization, and abortion. Moreover, advocates criticized federal family planning policy for relying primarily on Medicaid reimbursements to private health care providers. At the same time, federally funded family planning programs operated through a variety of federal, state, and community agencies instead of through a single, centralized federal agency or program that might have allowed for more efficient implementation. The politics of family planning and the federal nature of the American polity did not allow for the creation of a single agency, however. As a consequence, family planning policy was initiated incrementally and implemented through a variety of federal and state agencies and private organizations. Fearing a political backlash from the hierarchy of the Catholic Church and Catholic voters, Johnson cautiously established family planning programs through administrative fiat with HEW public health and maternal care programs and OEO antipoverty agencies. Even this approach caused complaints from Catholic bishops. The Catholic bishops divided among themselves in publicly condemning Johnson's initiatives, and in the end they settled for a modest policy of noncoercive implementation. Within these circumstances, however, any proposal to establish a single family planning agency within the federal government would have faced immediate political opposition. Instead, Congress enacted the first family planning legislation through the Social Security amendments in 1967. Under the Nixon administration in 1970, Congress enacted specific family planning legislation, but the emergence of a highly politicized debate over abortion, as well as budget constraints and Nixon's commitment to "New Federalism," prevented the establishment of a single federal agency devoted solely to national family planning policy.

Even without a centralized agency, family planning programs experienced internal problems that extended beyond the issue of external policy coordination or increased expenditures. Initially lacking organizational structures to deliver contraceptives, public and private family planning agencies found it difficult to reach their targeted populations. As a result, family planners experimented with various ways of delivering services, including public health agencies, private providers such as Planned Parenthood clinics, community-based antipoverty programs, and public hospitals. The Ford Foundation and the Population Council established demonstration programs in poor neighborhoods and at university hospitals. Nevertheless, family planners concluded that large numbers of people were not reached through these programs. Moreover, even when programs were made accessible, they experienced high turnover among their clients and discontinued use of contraceptives, and many within the targeted population were unresponsive to the programs. For example, the Ford Foundation–sponsored program in Baltimore found that the most sexually active female teenagers felt they did not need sex education because they already were well informed about sex. Political agitation within the black community only exacerbated difficulties in reaching poor black women through family planning programs. Although family planning programs reached tens of thousands of women, they failed to reach the levels of participation family planners had expected initially in setting up these programs. In the end, the Medicaid system proved to be a more effective way of reaching clients by allowing reimbursement to private providers.

Relying on recipients to use contraception on a regular basis created its own set of problems. Irregular, improper, and discontinued use of contraception continued to present family planners with a unique set of challenges. This led some activists to consider more coercive measures to enforce national family planning. Others within the medical and foundation community instead sought to develop contraceptives that placed less reliance on users. Long-lasting contraceptive implants and the "morning-after" pill were developed to address this problem. That better contraceptive technologies might have produced better results within these programs seems plausible, but this assumption does not change the general assessment of policy makers at the time that family planning implementation experienced serious internal problems.

A historical assessment of family planning policy needs to ask, What did policy makers intend to accomplish through federal intervention? Family planning advocates brought a variety of concerns to their call for government intervention in domestic contraceptive programs, including reproductive rights for women, overpopulation, maternal health, and reduction in welfare costs. One of the important traditions within the birth control movement, articulated by Planned Parenthood, was the advocacy of artificial contraception as a means of liberating women from the arbitrary controls of a male-dominated society. Yet the population movement brought together a number of people such as Hugh Moore and many within the Population Council, such as Bernard Berelson and Frank Notestein, who remained largely indifferent to this appeal for sexual freedom. As a result, arguments for federal family planning often gave only perfunctory attention to women's rights, and often ignored such arguments completely in lobbying the Johnson and Nixon administrations to initiate domestic family planning programs.

While the demand for federal family planning programs and legalized abortion became increasingly framed within the context of women's rights in the mid-1970s, the rhetoric used to promote federal family planning in the 1960s and early 1970s was linked primarily to antipoverty measures. Within the context of the Great Society and the War on Poverty, this argument allowed the formation of a policy coalition around the belief that federal involvement in contraception would reduce welfare costs and dependency. Issues such as overpopulation and reproductive rights, while remaining in the background, might have divided supporters and drawn opposition within Congress. As a consequence, advocates spoke of reducing levels of poverty, welfare costs, and rising out-of-wedlock births, which were associated with rapidly rising welfare expenditures. Such rhetoric continued to be used in later decades, as captured in one 1977 report that declared federal family planning had saved the government long-term costs by averting the birth of children who presumably would have ended up on the welfare rolls.[8]

The percentage of people living in poverty fell nearly by half during the 1960s, but much of this decline came from economic growth, job creation, and increased health and Social Security benefits for the elderly.[9] Poverty levels began to increase in the late 1970s, but there is little evidence that federal family planning contributed significantly to either the decrease of overall poverty levels in the 1960s or the increase in the 1980s. Moreover, the continued rise in the number of out-of-wedlock births throughout the postwar period belied the stated belief of policy makers that federal family planning would reduce this perceived problem. While critics charged that family planning programs encouraged promiscuity, which contributed to out-of-wedlock births, the rise in the number of such births began in the 1950s, well before the expansion of federal contraception programs, the development of oral contraception, or the expansion of the welfare state. Out-of-wedlock births proved to be a complex social phenomenon that occurred within the context of changing social and sexual mores in American society that could not be attributed solely to family planning programs or sex education programs.

Nonetheless, while such programs did not cause the increase in the number of out-of-wedlock births, family planning programs failed to provide an effective policy instrument in itself for decreasing the rate of births of unmarried women, as policy makers claimed they would with federal intervention. Proponents of federal family planning claimed with justification that contraception programs prevented an even higher increase in the number of out-of-wedlock births, but the number and rate of such births continued to climb rapidly even after the establishment of these programs. By 1980 public expenditures for family planning, including federal and state expenditures, reached a total of $350 million, falling to around $250 million per year throughout the rest of the decade through 1996 (in constant 1980 dollars including the costs of inflation). This meant that within a fourteen-year period, 1980 to 1994, approximately $250 million each year was expended on family planning programs. In short, a total of over $3.5 billion in constant dollars was spent with the purported purpose of reducing the number of out-of-wedlock births, yet such births continued to climb.[10] Matters might have been worse without federal family planning programs, but federal policy failed to achieve its explicit goal of reducing the rate of out-of-wedlock births or welfare dependency. Judged by its stated goals, family planning did not live up to its expectations. Of course, this should not be taken as an argument against the establishment of such programs. Many social programs fail to realize completely the aspirations of policy makers, yet these programs often better the lives of many individual recipients. Social policy needs to be evaluated within a larger context to assess whether other programs might have worked better or whether the benefits of such programs are worth the costs given society's other priorities.

However one evaluates federal family planning policy, out-of-wedlock births increased by 600 percent in the three decades from 1960 to 1990. In 1960 approximately 5 percent of all births in the United States were to unmarried women; by 1991 approximately 30 percent of births occurred out of wedlock. At the current rate, 40 percent of all births (and 80 percent of minority births) will occur out of wedlock by the turn of the century.[11] In 1990 six out of every ten teenagers who gave birth were unmarried, and among black teenagers the ratio was nine out of ten. Beginning in 1985 out-of-wedlock birthrates sharply rose among white teenage mothers, while out-of-wedlock births among black teenagers remained constant. As a result, 57 percent of all babies born to unwed teenagers were born to white mothers in 1990. This meant that of the total 360,615 births to women aged fifteen to nineteen, 204,053 births were to unmarried, white teenagers, while 145,682 were to blacks, and 10,910 to other races.[12]

While these figures alarmed many social commentators and policy makers, scholars such as sociologist Kristin Luker and historian Maris Vinovskis argued that out-of-wedlock births should be seen as a common historical phenomenon and not in itself a social problem. Out-of-wedlock births, Luker argued, reflected the changing nature of the family in contemporary America that allowed women greater freedom to produce children outside the bonds of marriage. The problem of out-of-wedlock births was not a problem in itself but a result of poverty. As she observed, "Poverty is not exclusively or even primarily limited to single mothers; most single mothers are not teenagers; many teenage mothers have husbands or partners; and many pregnant teenagers do not become mothers." While she agreed that "the rates of pregnancy and childbearing among teenagers are a serious problem, ... early childbearing doesn't make women poor; rather, poverty makes women bear children at an early age." She concluded, "Society should worry not about some epidemic of 'teenage pregnancy' but about the hopeless, discouraged, and empty lives that early childbearing denotes."[13]

Others argued, however, that the breakdown of the traditional family and the increase in single-parent families had led to a frightening social crisis in contemporary America that perpetuated poverty, juvenile delin-

quency, welfare dependency, child poverty, and problems in the inner city.
Sociologist David Popenoe maintained that a divorce rate of 50 percent in
first marriages, the rapid rise of nonmarital cohabitation, and out-of-
wedlock births had eroded traditional family values and had led to social
disaster. Citing a large body of social science evidence, he found that
children who grew up in single-parent homes were disadvantaged economically, educationally, and socially. Children from such families, he
argued, were twice as likely to drop out of high school, 2.5 times as likely
to become teen mothers, and 1.4 times as likely to drop out of school and
become unemployed. Furthermore, he maintained that the "loss of
economic resources accounts for about 50 percent of the disadvantages
associated with single parenthood." In addition, the relationship of single-
parent families to poor school achievement, and child abuse had been
proved "again and again in the [social science] literature."[14] Similar arguments appeared in David Blankenhorn's *Fatherless America: Confronting
Our Most Urgent Social Problem* (1995), which concluded that single-parent
families signified "nothing less than a culture gone awry." Like Popenoe,
Blankenhorn linked single-parent families to jumps in crime rates, out-of-
wedlock childbearing, children growing up in poverty, youth violence,
unsafe neighborhoods, and domestic violence.[15]

Such arguments reflected a larger cultural debate about social and family values in contemporary America that extended beyond federal family
planning policy per se. Nonetheless, Popenoe and Blankenhorn implied
that family planning had failed to address these larger social and cultural
problems. Patrick F. Fagan, a former official in the Bush administration,
specifically challenged current federal family planning for not addressing
these larger problems. Like Popenoe and Blankenhorn, Fagan argued that
the "soaring rates of divorce and out-of-wedlock births" were destroying
the "basic social institutions of society" and creating "more welfare dependence, more crime, more health and behavioral problems, and lower educational achievement." He called for welfare reform, federal policies to
strengthen traditional family and religious values, and a correction in family planning programs to change teenagers' attitudes toward early sexual
activity. He also called for federal family planning policy to promote sexual abstinence educational programs, citing a federal study in 1985 that
showed that among female teenagers taking abstinence courses "pregnancy rates have been reduced by over 40 percent when compared to girls
who have not taken the classes. By contrast, programs promoting contraception often increase pregnancy rates."[16] In addition, Fagan urged
Congress to enact legislation that encouraged adoption through tax credits
and to maintain the Hyde amendment to discourage abortion.

In the late 1960s the movement for legalized abortion changed the
nature of the family planning debate by extending it to a rights issue. The

abortion reform movement proved remarkably successful on the state level in enacting liberalized abortion legislation. Although this success was not uniform within the states, women activists and advocates of abortion reform, including activists in NARAL, Planned Parenthood, and ZPG, changed abortion law within the majority of states in this period. By lobbying on the state level, abortion advocates showed that dramatic policy change could occur through well-conducted political campaigns. In 1973 this effort culminated in *Roe v.Wade*. Legalized abortion became a constitutional right of women and families.

Although abortion advocates transformed abortion policy in the United States, they enjoyed less success in pressuring Congress to provide funds to allow poor women to exercise this constitutional right. Through the Hyde amendment, Congress imposed restrictions on the use of Medicaid funds for abortions. The Clinton administration lifted many of the antiabortion restrictions imposed by the Reagan and Bush administrations, but legislation such as the Freedom of Choice Act failed to win support in Congress. The mobilization of antiabortion groups and the polarization of the abortion issue in the Republican and Democratic parties blocked further policy change. Legalized abortion remained the law of the land, but federal funding to support this right remained restricted. Furthermore, many state legislatures imposed regulations that placed stringent guidelines on abortion procedures. Although the courts overturned many state regulations, other restrictions were upheld by subsequent court rulings.

The result was political stalement: abortion remained a constitutional right, but Congress refused to support this right with federal funds. After Congress's failure in the early years of the Reagan administration to enact legislation that would have overturned *Roe v. Wade*, few antiabortion activists believed that constitutional change would occur in the immediate future without a change in the composition of the Supreme Court. This appeared to be a remote possibility under the Clinton administration, and many doubted that it would occur even with a new Republican administration. Legalized abortion appeared to have become an accepted part of national life. Advocates of legalized abortion, therefore, achieved a major policy goal—the legalization of abortion—but failed to overcome congressional opposition to funding abortion through Medicaid and other welfare policies. Without federal funding for abortions, policy implementation remained incomplete.

The mobilization of democratic abortion and antiabortion groups changed the nature of the debate into a fight over rights, but it also changed those involved in the abortion debate by mobilizing new groups organized on the grassroots level. In the meantime, the population movement underwent significant changes as philanthropic foundations such as the Population Council and the Ford Foundation shifted their research and service focus away from specific population concerns to larger issues of economic development, reproductive rights, and the status of women in developing countries.[17] While groups such as ZPG, the Population Crisis Committee, and the Population Reference Bureau continued their involvement in population issues, environmental concerns—although related to overpopulation—became paramount.

At the same time, the population movement divided over issues such as immigration. Typical of the division, the Federation for American Immigration Reform (FAIR) was founded in 1979 when the Sierra Club and ZPG refused to endorse immigration restrictions. FAIR leaders argued that immigration to the United States threatened the resources and environment of the nation. They linked immigration, both legal and illegal, to social justice concerns. Furthermore, FAIR believed that the population increase in the United States from Mexico and other parts of the Third World threatened to change the nature of America within a century, and that continued immigration was a prescription for social injustice, the promotion of an underclass in the nation, further ethnic division, and the displacement of American workers, especially among African-Americans, by exploited and underpaid illegal immigrants.[18]

While the population movement underwent significant change, Planned Parenthood experienced a crisis of leadership. In 1993 Faye Wattleton resigned as president and was replaced by Pamela Maraldo. Many local affiliates believed that Wattleton had dragged the organization "unnecessarily into the abortion controversy."[19] Underlying this controversy, Planned Parenthood experienced financial problems as many women increasingly relied on private physicians for contraceptive prescriptions. Furthermore, congressional restrictions on funding organizations that provided abortion services hurt local PPFA chapters. Under Maraldo, a former official for the National League of Nursing, Planned Parenthood tried to change the focus of the organization from reproductive health care to general family medicine.[20] After continued clashes with the board of directors over this new agenda, Maraldo resigned two years after accepting the presidency. In 1996 Gloria Feldt, an abortion activist from Odessa, Texas, and Phoenix, Arizona, where she headed PPFA local affiliates, assumed the presidency of PPFA. She promised to return the organization to its traditional interest in reproductive rights and reproductive health care. She felt that PPFA's mission was one of "advocacy to ensure that everyone can get family planning and reproductive health-care services and education." Declaring that Planned Parenthood had not been visible in recent years in "leading the charge for reproductive rights and reproductive health," she promised to combat the "conservative onslaught" against legalized abortion. "It's about when we're going to be a nation," she said, "that embraces knowledge and education about responsible sex, as opposed to trying to keep people ignorant about it. I think the abortion debate is not about abortion at all. . . . it's more about the future of women and children and families in this country."[21]

Feldt voiced the anxieties of abortion activists and many women that reproductive rights were threatened in the conservative climate of the 1990s. Abortion symbolized, as Feldt said, the rights and status women had gained through struggle over the previous three decades. Feminists such as Susan Faludi argued that a backlash against women had become apparent in American culture.[22] Signs of this backlash were found in the violence against abortion doctors, the prominence of the Christian Right in the Republican party, the changing composition of the Supreme Court, the *Webster* decision, the failure of the Freedom of Choice Act in Congress, and partial birth abortion legislation that only Clinton's veto had prevented from becoming law.

The antiabortion activists felt equally pessimistic. From their perspective, the political fight had gone against them. They viewed recent Supreme Court decisions as victories for the abortion movement. In the end, the Supreme Court had not overturned *Roe*; the number of abortions in the United States had continued to rise since the 1970s; antiabortionists had been ostracized by the Democratic party; and the Republican party appeared divided on the issue, and talk of the "gender gap" portended a reversal of the party's antiabortion position. State legislation to restrict the number of abortions had been overturned to all extents and purposes by activist judges. The media seemed hostile, portraying antiabortionists as fanatics and members of the Christian Right as bigoted extremists.

In this context, many spoke of a "cultural war."[23] Underlying this cultural divide was a deeper conflict between fundamental and irreconcilably different moral visions of the meaning of human life and human sexuality. Apparent changes in sexual mores within American culture accentuated these differences that accompanied what became known as the "sexual revolution." This cultural division entailed fixed and intransigent positions over abortion, reproduction technology, the place of the traditional family, and religious values. Given these apparently disparate moral visions, political and cultural compromise became impossible.[24]

In a broader sense, however, talk of a "cultural war" and a "sexual revolution" proved misleading. Although this language captured the polarized nature of the abortion debate, surveys showed that Americans were not divided into distinct camps with opposed positions on a broad range of issues. Social science surveys showed that about 20 percent held strongly orthodox religious beliefs; another 20 percent described themselves as theologically liberal. This left roughly 60 percent of Americans occupying the middle ground. Furthermore, survey data revealed that those Americans who described themselves as "religiously orthodox" were no more politically conservative than those who described themselves as "religiously liberal." On issues such as racial equality, religious conservatives and religious liberals were "progressive" in supporting antidiscrimination and equal opportunity measures. The religiously orthodox tended to be more "progressive" on more economic issues than were religious liberals. That is, religious conservatives were not necessarily inclined to support conservative fiscal policies or probusiness tax policies. Religion remained an important source of political division in the United States, but this religious divide primarily affected gender- and family-related issues of schooling, sexuality, reproductive rights, and women's involvement in the family and the workplace.[25] Thus, while clear differences existed in religious perspectives, they did not translate readily into specific political and social attitudes. A "cultural war" existed on issues related to schooling, sexuality, gender roles, and reproductive rights, but the political implications of this divisiveness did not determine party affiliation or voting behavior. In fact, since the 1970s Americans became more unified in their attitudes toward racial integration, crime and justice, and gender equality.[26]

This agreement about racial integration and social justice issues qualifies the nature of the "cultural war" in the United States. Although opinion remained sharply divided on the abortion issue, Americans had more in common with one another than they differed on matters concerning sexual attitudes and practices. By 1990 most Americans used artificial contraception. There was little difference among Protestants, Catholics, and Jews in overall contraceptive practice, with about three of five women in each religious group using artificial contraception. The prevalence of contraception ranged from 59 percent among Catholic women to 62 percent among Jewish women. While Protestants relied more heavily on sterilization than any other form of contraception (32 percent), Catholic women were more likely to use the pill (33 percent), and Jewish women were more likely to use the diaphragm (27 percent). Among Protestants, black women relied more heavily than white women on the pill or on sterilization. Among Catholics, Hispanics were less likely than blacks or whites to use the pill, and were almost twice as likely as all whites to rely on tubal ligation.[27] The debate over contraception, if it ever was an issue, appeared to have been settled as the twentieth century drew to a close.

Similarly, American sexual mores showed surprisingly little change in practice among older adults, although significant changes in sexual practices were apparent among teenagers. Tom Smith, director of the General Social Survey Project at the University of Chicago, reported in 1991 that

97 percent of adult Americans had had intercourse since the age of eighteen. About one-fifth of the respondents in social surveys in 1989 reported not having had sexual partners during the previous year. Moreover, 1.5 percent of married people reported having had a sexual partner other than their spouse in the previous year. Faithfulness within marriage was widely accepted, with about three-fourths of Americans believing that sexual relations with someone other than one's spouse was always wrong. Nonetheless, the number of partners in the previous year was highest among those between the ages of eighteen to twenty-nine (the mean number of partners the previous year standing at 1.76), followed by those aged forty to forty-nine (with the mean number of partners at 1.27).

Smith found that about 2 percent of sexually active adults reported being exclusively homosexual or bisexual during the year preceding the survey, and 5 to 6 percent had been exclusively homosexual or bisexual since the age of eighteen. This last finding drew immediate criticism from gay rights activists, who argued that the incidence of homosexual and bisexual activity was underreported.[28]

Whether or not this was the case, Americans generally disapproved of homosexuality, but this attitude was clearly changing. When asked in 1973 whether homosexual relations were always wrong, close to 80 percent of Americans declared they were, while only about 10 percent agreed they were not wrong. By 1997 the trend was toward acceptance of homosexuality. When asked in 1997 about their attitudes toward homosexuality, 71.9 of respondents said it was always wrong, 5.0 percent said it was almost always wrong, 6.8 felt it was wrong only sometimes, and 16.3 percent felt it was not wrong on any occasion. While disapproval remained high, fewer Americans felt that homosexuality was always wrong, and more Americans felt that it was not wrong without qualification. This attitudinal change was further evidenced in attitudes toward homosexuals teaching in college. This practice had met with general disapproval in the early 1970s, with close to a majority of Americans believing that homosexuals should not be allowed to teach, while by 1996 close to 80 percent of Americans believed that homosexuals should be allowed to teach in college.[29]

However staid married couples were, Smith reported that 7 percent of all adults during the year 1989 engaged in sexual behavior—multiple sex partners, exclusively male homosexual or bisexual sexual relations—that placed them at risk of contracting AIDS. Moreover, he found 33 percent had engaged in relatively risky behavior at some time since age eighteen. While Americans believed in monogamy as a moral ideal—this was practiced by the vast majority of spouses at least on a year-to-year basis—attitudes were changing among younger people. Those under the age of thirty tended to have more frequent sex and sex with multiple partners.

This change in behavior was accompanied by increased social acceptance of premarital sex.[30]

This evidence suggests that the sexual revolution had not occurred with the speed and depth that many assumed. Nonetheless, American sexual mores and practices were changing at a persistent pace. Whether the early advocates of federal family planning who began their work in the immediate aftermath of the Second World War would have welcomed this quiet sexual revolution in its entirety is doubtful. Bernard Berelson and Frank Notestein expressed doubts over some aspects of this revolution, especially concerning abortion as a means of birth control. Others, such as John D. Rockefeller 3rd, welcomed and encouraged this sexual revolution, including the legalization of abortion and homosexual rights.

Still, the family planning movement had accomplished much from a policy perspective. Intervention by governments and international organizations such as the United Nations had contributed significantly to a reduction in the rate of population growth in many parts of the world. By the 1990s, federal family planning had become established policy. Although federal contraceptive programs failed to meet the intentions of policy makers in addressing fully the problem of out-of-wedlock births and reduction of welfare costs and dependency, large numbers of poor women had received and continued to receive contraception funded through federal programs. Abortion had been legalized as a constitutional right for all women, even though Congress restricted federal funds for abortions. Moreover, Americans practiced artificial birth control in overwhelming numbers. Even with the insurgence of political and fiscal conservatism in the 1980s and the growth of the Christian Right in politics, a liberal sexual culture had been created. The emergence of political conservatism that occurred in the midst of a sexual revolution created a radical dichotomy between political culture and social/sexual culture.

This apparent discrepancy between politics and culture led to political conflict, cultural tension, and social acrimony, but such incongruities are inherent in any period of technological, social, and cultural transition. Perhaps such contradictions between ideals and practices, tradition and transition, politics and society have been apparent in America since its inception as a nation. Nonetheless, policy shifts do occur through the concerted efforts of individuals and social movements, as seen in the course of federal family planning in America, but such changes lead to unintended social consequences and leave policy makers with new sets of problems that in the end can only be resolved through honest intellectual debate and public discourse within the democracy.

Notes

Chapter 1

1. Harold G. Moulton, *Controlling Factors in Economic Development* (Washington, D.C., 1949).

2. An excellent account of the John D. Rockefeller 3rd philanthropic work in relation to his family is found in John Ensor Harr and Peter Johnson, *The Rockefeller Conscience: An American Family in Public and in Private* (New York, 1991).

3. DonaldMcLean to John D. Rockefeller 3rd, February 1, 1952, RG 2, Box 45, Rockefeller Foundation Papers, Rockefeller Archives, Tarrytown, New York (hereafter, RA).

4. For a general discussion of eugenics in reform thought, see Daniel J. Kelves, *In the Name of Eugenics* (New York, 1990); Mark Heller, *Eugenics: Hereditarian Attitudes in American Thought* (New Brunswick, N.J., 1963); and Donald K. Pickens, *Eugenics and the Progressives* (Nashville, Tenn., 1968). Other useful, more specialized studies are found in Marouf A. Hasian Jr., *The Rhetoric of Eugenics in Anglo-American Thought* (Athens, Ga., 1966). Especially important is Edward J. Larson, *Sex, Race, and Science: Eugenics in the Deep South* (Baltimore, 1995).

For the complex relationship between the eugenics movement, feminism, and the birth control movement, see David M. Kennedy, *Birth Control in America: The Career of Margaret Sanger* (New Haven, Conn., 1970); Linda Gordon, *Woman's Body, Woman's Right: Birth Control in America* (New York, 1996); James Reed, *The Birth Control Movement and American Society: Private Vice to Public Virtue*, rev. ed. (Princeton, N.J., 1983); Ellen Chesler, *Woman of Valor: Margaret Sanger and the Birth Control Movement in America* (New York, 1992); and Carole R. McCann, *Birth Control Politics in the United States, 1916–1945* (Ithaca, N.Y., 1994).

5. Important books written in the immediate postwar years include Guy Irving Burch and Elmer Rindell, *Population Roads* (New York, 1945); Fairfield Osborn, *Our Plundered Planet* (New York, 1946) and *The Limits of Earth* (New York, 1953); and Robert Cook, *Human Fertility* (New York, 1951).

6. "William Vogt," *Current Biography, 1953* (New York, 1953), 638–639. Also "William Vogt, Former Director of Planned Parenthood, Is Dead," *New York Times*, July 12, 1968, 31.

7. William Vogt, *Road to Survival*, with an introduction by Bernard Baruch (New York, 1948), 42, 146–151, 218, 282–283.

8. For Fairfield Osborn, see Andrew Jamison and Ron Eyerman, *Seeds of the Sixties* (Berkeley, 1994), 64–103; and "Fairfield Osborn," *Current Biography, 1949* (New York, 1949), 463–464.

9. John Ensor Harr and Peter Johnson, *The Rockefeller Conscience* (New York, 1991) 3–26; also Peter Collier and David Horowitz, *The Rockefellers: An American Dynasty* (New York, 1976), especially 193–198.

10. This perspective found early expression in an internal Rockefeller Foundation memorandum circulated in 1952 that declared, "We need to see birth control in expansive terms." Birth control should be interrelated to increasing food supply, improving health, and developing education. This entailed the development of a "cheap and effective pill, as well as increasing food from the sea, solar power, and developing genetic mechanisms that affect the yield of crop plants." Warren Weaver, Memorandum, January 1, 1952, RG 2, Box 1, RA.

11. Population Council, *The Population Council: A Chronicle of the First Twenty-Five Years, 1952–1977* (New York, 1978), 10–17.

12. Spellman's reaction is discussed in a lengthy memorandum written by Frank W. Notestein and Bernard Berelson in 1969. Because this twenty-eight-page memorandum is not documented, the Catholic influence on defeating the "population" proposal must remain hearsay, however plausible. Frank W. Notestein and Bernard Berelson, "The Foundations and Population" (Confidential), October 1969, Joan Dunlop Papers, Box 2, RA.

13. Detlev Bronk had been elected to the presidency of the National Academy of Sciences after an unprecedented floor fight with James B. Conant. Seen as a proponent of arms control with the Soviet Union, Conant was defeated by a group of scientists from the Berkeley Radiation Laboratory, including Wendell Latimer, Edward Teller, Ernest Lawrence, and Luis Alvarez, that advocated the development of the hydrogen bomb. Later Bronk played a critical role in reorganizing the Rockefeller Institute into the Rockefeller University.

14. Quoted from an interview with Detlev Bronk by Peter Collier and David Horowitz; see Collier and Horowitz, *The Rockefellers*, 287.

15. Donald McLean to Files, June 25, 1952, RG 2, Box 45, RA.

16. A detailed record of the conference is found in RG 2, Box 47; and the Rockefeller Foundation Papers, RG 3.2, Box 57, RA.

17. "Documentation for the Conference on Population Problems, Williamsburg Inn, Williamsburg, Virginia (June 20–22, 1952)," p. 33, RG 2, Box 45, RA.

18. Donald McLean to John D. Rockefeller 3rd, January 29, 1952, Rockefeller Foundation, RG 2, Box 45, RA.

19. "Documentation of the Conference on Population Problems, June 22, 1952, 10–44," RG 2, Box 45, RA.

20. Thomas Parran to John D. Rockefeller 3rd, October 28, 1952, RG 2, Box 45, RA.

21. John D. Rockefeller 3rd to Detlev W. Bronk, October 15, 1952, RG 2, Box 45, RA.

22. John D. Rockefeller 3rd to Nelson Rockefeller, September 3, 1953, RG 2, Box 45, RA.

23. Donald McLean to John D. Rockefeller 3rd, September 8, 1952, RG 2, Box 45, RA.

24. Population Council, *The Population Council*, 21–41. For specific funding during this period, see Frederick Osborn, Memorandum, July 1, 1958, RG 2, Box 45, RA.

25. Included on this advisory board were Kingsley Davis, Philip M. Hauser, Clyde V. Kiser, Frank Lorimer, Frank Notestein, and P. K. Whelpton. In 1954 Dudley Kirk, a former State Department official, accepted the directorship of demography at the council. Three years later W. Parker Mauldin, a demographer who had served as chief of the Foreign Manpower Research Office in the U.S. Bureau of the Census, joined the staff.

26. The Population Council funded programs at Columbia University, Princeton University, the University of Chicago, the University of Michigan, Dartmouth College, the University of Minnesota, Boston University, Cornell University, and the University of Pennsylvania. The early years of the council are recounted in Population Council, *The Population Council*.

27. John Sharpless, "The Rockefeller Foundation, the Population Council, and the Groundwork for New Population Policies," *Rockefeller Archive Center Newsletter*, Fall 1993, 1–4.

28. Suzanne A. Onotaro, "The Population Council and the Development of Contraceptive Technologies," *Research Reports from the Rockefeller Archives Center* Spring 1991: 1–2; John B. Sharpless, "The Rockefeller Foundation, the Population Council, and the Groundwork for New Population Policies," *Rockefeller Archive Center Newsletter*, Fall 1993, 1–4.

29. Frederick Osborn to John D. Rockefeller 3rd, July 13, 1959, RG 2, Box 45, RA.

30. "Frank Wallace Notestein," in *Who's Who* (New York, 1963), 2323.

31. Population Council, *The Population Council*, 41–68.

32. Montgomery S. Bradley to Files, July 12, 1961, Rockefeller Brothers Fund, Box 87, RA.

33. Population Council, Minutes of Staff Meeting, May 11, 1962, Population Council, Box 128, RG 1V3 4.6 (unprocessed), RA.

34. Ford Foundation, "Population Problems" (internal memorandum from Ford), March 30, 1960, RG 2, Box 46, RA; and Frederick Osborn, "American Foundations and Population Problems," April 8, 1965, Osborn Papers, American Philosophical Society (hereafter cited as APS). For a full discussion of the Ford Foundation's involvement in family planning through 1977, see Oscar Harkavy, "The Foundation's Strategy for Work on Population" (confidential), June 1977, Harkavy File, Ford Foundation Archives (hereafter cited as FA).

35. For details of these gifts for the Commonwealth Fund, see Malcolm P. Aldrich to John D. Rockefeller 3rd, November 20, 1961, RG 2, Box 46; for Scaife Foundation and Scaife gifts given by Cordelia Scaife May, see John D. Rockefeller 3rd, November 29, 1961, RG 2, Box 46; for the Carnegie Institute and the Milbank Memorial Fund, see Frederick Osborne to John D. Rockefeller, October 18, 1956, RG 2, Box 46; and the Avalon Foundation, see York Allen to Rockefeller Brother Fund Files, November 10, 1960, Rockefeller Brothers Fund, Box 87, RA.

36. Frederick Osborn, "American Foundations and Population Problems," April 8, 1965, Osborn Papers, APS.

37. The development of these programs is described in the annual reports of the Population Council (1959–1965) and discussed in a lengthy memorandum by Frederick Osborn, "American Foundations and Population Problems, April 8, 1965, Osborn Papers, APS. The prospects for Latin America and Africa are found in Population Council, "Excerpt of Minutes of Docket Conference with the Ford Foundation," Population Council (unprocessed), RA.

38. The role of Scaife funds and the following discussion are drawn from council annual reports from 1962 to 1969 and from Frank Notestein, "Report on the Activities of the Population Council Made Possible by Gifts Received Through the Generosity of the Scaife Family" (1969), Frank Notestein Papers, Box 9 (unprocessed), Princeton University.

39. The use of the IUD was deemed a success in Taiwan and Korea. In 1962 the Taiwanese government invited the Population Council to set up an experimental family planning program in Taichung through a "prepregnancy health" clinic. Shortly afterward, an islandwide program was launched on a "quasi-private" basis, with the major funding coming from the government. Within a few years, the council reported, the birth rate dropped, with more than a third of women of childbearing age practicing modern contraception or sterilization. Notestein concluded, "Taiwan has shown the world that birth control programs can speed the reduction of the birth rate even in the strong familial societies of the Orient. Taiwan is an excellent demonstration of the usefulness of private and quasi-public institutions in leading the way on controversial issues before open government support becomes possible." Taiwan adopted a formal family

planning policy in 1968, but family planning in Korea received government support from its inception. Although Korea had a less well educated and poorer population than did Taiwan, the council found that its birthrate also dropped, with more than a third of women of childbearing age practicing birth control. Ibid.

40. John D. Rockefeller 3rd, "The Reminiscences of John D. Rockefeller, 3rd," Columbia University Oral History, Columbia University, 1964), 268–271.

41. Bernard Berelson, *The Population Council: 1952–1964* (July 1965), Population Council, Berelson Files (unprocessed), RA.

42. Bernard Berelson, "Communication Research Program," January 25, 1962, Population Council, Berelson Files, RA.

43. CIB to WW, October 22, 1948, Rockefeller Foundation Papers, RG3.2, Box 57, RA.

44. Lawrence Lader, *Breeding Ourselves to Death* (New York, 1971), 7.

45. Hugh Moore, Interview with Franklin D. Roosevelt, December 30, 1938, Box 1, Hugh Moore Papers, Princeton University.

46. "Clark M. Eichelberger," *Current Biography, 1947* (New York, 1947), 191; and "Clark M. Eichelberger Dies at 83; Led American U.N. Association," *New York Times*, January 27, 1980. Also Robert Divine, *The Reluctant Belligerent* (New York, 1979). For the National Peace Conference, see Rev. John Nevin Sayre's obituary in the *New York Times*, September 16, 1977.

47. Moore's involvement in Americans United for World Organization is traced in Ernest Martin Hopkins to Hugh Moore, November 17, 1955, Moore Papers, Box 1. His views on Wallace are found in Hugh Moore to Samuel Guy Inman, November 4, 1946, Moore Papers, Box 1, Princeton University.

48. Hugh Moore to Malcom W. Davis, Carnegie Endowment for International Peace, November 10, 1949, Moore Papers, Box 2, PrincetonUniversity.

49. Hugh Moore to Frank G. Boudreau, November 9, 1948; Frank G. Boudreau to Hugh Moore, November 8, 1948; Moore Papers, Box 2, Princeton University.

50. Sabra Holbrook to Hugh Moore, November 10, 1953, Box 3, Moore Papers.

51. For Griessemer's work on the Constitution, see Thomas O. Griessemer to C. P. Blacker, July 29, 1953, Moore Papers, Box 3, Princeton University. The relationship between Mrs. Pillsbury and Moore is traced in a series of letters, including Mrs. Philip W. Pillsbury to Hugh Moore, November 18, 1953; Hugh Moore to Mrs. Philip Pillsbury, November 21, 1954; and Hugh Moore to Mrs. Philip Pillsbury, December 7, 1953; Moore Papers, Box 3, Princeton University.

52. Hugh Moore, Confidential Memorandum, "Population Action Now," February 1, 1954, Box 1, Moore Papers; and Hugh Moore to Joseph W. Ayer, December 3, 1968, Moore Papers, Box 3, Princeton University.

53. Quoted in Lader, *Breeding Ourselves to Death*, 14.

In organizing the World Population Emergency Campaign, Moore enlisted the support of leading financial and industrial leaders, including Eugene Black, World Bank; Will Clayton, cotton magnate and former under secretary of state; General William H. Draper Jr., chairman of Combustion Engineering; Marriner S. Eccles, chairman of the Federal Reserve Board; Rockefeller Prentice, John Rockefeller 3rd's cousin; Thomas S. Lamont, Morgan Guaranty Trust Company; Fowler McCormick, chairman of International Harvester; and Lammot duPont Copeland, chairman of E. I. duPont & Co.

54. Ibid., 5.

55. Hugh Moore Fund, *The Population Explosion* (New York, 1954); and Hugh Moore, Will L. Clayton, and Ellsworth Bunker to John D. Rockefeller 3rd, November 26, 1954, RG 2, Box 45, RA.

56. He wrote to Will Clayton, "I read the pamphlet to my wife. We share similar concerns." At the same time, staff members at the council felt that anticommunism

should not be linked to population policy, although it had value in arousing the public's interest in the issue. Rockefeller and the staff at the Population Council emphasized that the population issues should be placed on a scientific and humanitarian basis. John D. Rockefeller to Will Clayton, May 29, 1957, Box 46, RG 2; and Staff Minutes, Population Council, February 5, 1957, Population Council Papers (unprocessed), RA.

57. Montgomery S. Bradley to Rockefeller Brothers Fund General Files, September 8, 1960, Rockefeller Brothers Fund, Box 4, Series 4, RA.

58. Quoted in Lader, *Breeding Ourselves to Death*, 11.

59. See chapter 2 for a full discussion of the Population Crisis Committee.

60. Reed, *The Birth Control Movement and American Society* (rev. ed. Princeton, N.J., 1983), 294.

61. Gamble's career in the birth control movement is described in ibid., 225–277, on which the following discussion relies.

62. Clarence J. Gamble to John D. Rockefeller 3rd, May 16, 1935, RG 2, Box 1, RA.

63. This testing program won the support of the Rockefeller Foundation. See Arthur W. Packard to John D. Rockefeller 3rd, June 9, 1937, RG 2, Box 1, RA.

64. Gunnar Myrdal, *An American Dilemma: The Negro Problem and Modern Democracy*, 2 vols. (New York, 1944), 179.

65. For a more detailed and revealing account of Gamble's involvement in Puerto Rico, see Annette B. Ramierz de Arellano and Conrad Seipp, *Colonialism, Catholicism, and Contraception: A History of Birth Control in Puerto Rico* (Chapel Hill, N.C., 1983), 45–62.

66. A useful essay on American involvement in the Caribbean is Louis A. Perez Jr., "Intervention, Hegemony, and Dependency: The United States in the Caribbean, 1898–1980," *Pacific Historical Review* 51 (May 1982): 165–194.

67. Arellano and Seipp, *Colonialism, Catholicism, and Contraception*, 26.

68. Quoted in ibid., 34.

69. Gamble's work in Puerto Rico was described by him in a detailed letter to the Rockefeller Foundation, Clarence J. Gamble to Arthur W. Packard, May 13, 1937, RG 2, Box 1, RA.

70. B. E. Washburn to W. A. Sawyer, June 18, 1937, RG 2, Box 1, RA.

71. Phyllis Page to Arthur W. Packard, September 21, 1937, Rockefeller Foundation, OMR folder, Birth Control, RA.

72. Quoted in Arellano and Seipp, *Colonialism, Catholicism, and Contraception*, 48.

73. Kennedy, *Birth Control in America*, 262–263.

74. Reed, *The Birth Control Movement and American Society*, 247–254.

75. As early as 1909 a German gynecologist, Ernst Grafenberg, began to develop an intrauterine contraceptive device made of a ring of silk gut and silver wire. Unfortunately, the device often caused excessive menstrual periods and cramps. Sometimes the effects of the coil were even more dangerous, leading to severe pelvic inflammatory disease, which before the development of antibiotics could be fatal. See ibid., 272–277.

76. Quoted in ibid., 305.

77. The development of the pill is described in great detail in Bernard Asbell, *The Pill: A Biography of the Drug That Changed the World* (New York, 1995), especially 3–213; Paul Vaughan, *The Pill on Trial* (New York, 1970); and Carl Djerassi, *The Pill: Pygmy Chimps and Degas' Horse* (New York, 1992).

78. Christopher Tietze outlined contraceptive research on the island in the immediate postwar years in a lengthy memorandum to the Rockefeller Foundation, Arthur W. Packard to General Files, October 24, 1946, RG 2, Box 1, RA.

79. Arthur Packard to Files, "Regarding Telephone Conversation with Frederick Osborn," January 24, 1947, RG 1, Box 1, RA.

80. Still, it is worth noting that not all population activists were sanguine about the

prospects of the pill and the IUD. Hugh Moore, for one, continued to believe that "sterilization is one of the most likely means of controlling the population explosion. More likely, in my view, than the much publicized pill." Moore was an active supporter for the Human Betterment Association for Voluntary Sterilization. Hugh Moore to Winthrop W. Aldrich, November 25, 1963, Box 1, Moore Papers, Princeton University.

81. John D. Rockefeller 3rd to Frederick Osborn, May 15, 1958, RG 2, Box 45, RA.

82. "William Henry Draper," *Current Biography, 1952* (New York, 1952), 161–162; and "Proper Public Servant: William Henry Draper, Jr.," *New York Times*, March 23, 1959, 23.

Key members of the Draper committee included John J. McCloy, former high commissioner for Germany; and General Alfred Gruenther, former supreme allied commander in Europe.

83. William Draper to Frederick Brown, December 27, 1963, Population Council, Box 107, RA.

84. Hugh Moore to William Draper, July 9, 1965; and William H. Draper to Hugh Moore, February 13, 1963, Moore Papers, Box 3, Princeton University.

For a perspective of this meeting from the point of view of the population movement, see Lader, *Breeding Ourselves to Death*, 15–20.

85. Robert Cook to Frederick Osborn, June 4, 1959; and Staff Diary Notes, May 21, 1959, Population Council, Box 99 (unprocessed), RA.

86. President's Committee to Study the United States Military Assistance Program, *Letter to the President of the United States from the President's Committee to Study the United States Military Assistance Program and the Committee's Final Report; Conclusions Concerning the Mutual Security Program* (Washington, D.C., August 17, 1959), 1.

87. President's Committee to Study the United States Military Assistance Program, *Composite Report of the President's Committee to Study the United States Military Assistance Program*, vol. 1 (Washington, D.C., August 17, 1959), 94–98.

88. Eisenhower quoted in "A Single Agency for Economic Aid Urged in Report," *New York Times*, July 24, 1959, 1. For debates over military assistance and foreign aid, see "Aid Bill Is Passed by House, 279–136," *New York Times*, July 30, 1959, 1; and "President's Adviser Decries Aid Defeat," *New York Times*, March 23, 1959, 10.

89. "Catholics Oppose Use of AID Funds for Birth Control," *New York Times*, November 26, 1959, 1, 43.

90. "Kennedy Opposes Advocacy by U.S. of Birth Control," *New York Times*, November 28, 1959, 1.

91. "Several Democratic Contenders Give Views on Birth Control Aid," *New York Times*, November 29, 1959, 43.

92. James Reston, "The Religious Issue That Won't Go Away," *New York Times*, November 29, 1959, 4:10.

Governor Nelson Rockefeller came out in favor of family planning assistance to nations that requested it. Arthur Krock discusses the politics of the Draper report in "Welcome Change from the Hush-Hush Stage," *New York Times*, December 1, 1959, 38.

93. Dwight D. Eisenhower, *Public Papers of the Presidents of the United States: Dwight D. Eisenhower, 1959* (Washington, D.C., 1960), 787–788. Also, "Eisenhower Bars Birth-Control Help," *New York Times*, December 3, 1959, 1; and Arthur Krock, "President and the Bishops Agree," *New York Times*, December 3, 1959, 6:4, 5.

94. See "Parenthood Unit Scores U.S. Stand," *New York Times*, December 4, 1959, 16; "Bishop Pike Scored by Catholic News," *New York Times*, December 5, 1959, 16:2.

95. After leaving office, Eisenhower came to believe that the population problem was one of the "most critical problems facing mankind," warning of "riotous explosions" at home and abroad unless the problem was faced head-on. As a result, in 1965 he was willing to support family planning programs. He recommended that if family

planning was not tied to welfare, "then history will rightly condemn us." We find ourselves, he wrote, in a "curious position of spending money with one hand to slow up
population growth among responsible families and with the other providing financial
incentives for increased production by the ignorant, feeble-minded or lazy." Dwight D.
Eisenhower to Senator Ernest Gruening, June 18, 1965, Post-Presidential Files,
1961–1969, Dwight D. Eisenhower Presidential Library.

Also Clifford Roberts to William H. Draper, February 28, 1966, Special Names
Series, Box 16; William H. Draper to Dwight D. Eisenhower, March 6, 1964, Office
Files, Box 33; William H. Draper to Dwight D. Eisenhower, September 28, 1964,
Office Files, Box 33; William H. Draper to Dwight D. Eisenhower, November 18,
1964, Office Files, Box 33; William H. Draper to Dwight D. Eisenhower, December 8,
1964, Office Files, Box 33; William H. Draper to Dwight D. Eisenhower, December
21, 1963, Office Files, Box 33; William H. Draper to Dwight D. Eisenhower, Decem-
ber 26, 1964, Office Files, Box 33; Dwight D. Eisenhower to William H. Draper,
December 30, 1963, Office Files, Box 33; Dwight D. Eisenhower to H. J. Porter,
November 20, 1964, Office Files, Box 49, Eisenhower Library.

96. Hugh Moore to John D. Rockefeller 3rd, December 1, 1959, RG 2, Box 44, RA.

97. This survey revealed that birth control was available to women for postpartum
checkups in Alabama, Mississippi, North Carolina, and Virginia. PPFA local affiliates
were cooperating with state health departments in Florida, Georgia, and South
Carolina. Local public health units with "child spacing" clinics were found in California
at a clinic in Huntington Park, the Santa Monica County Health Clinic, the San
Fernando Mothers Clinic, and the Family Planning Clinic in Tulare County. Clinics
were found in Delaware in Georgetown, Delaware. Illinois listed a clinic administered
through the Champaign-Urbana Public Health Office. PPFA worked with Missouri
health officials in postpartum clinics at three sites in rural areas. The University of
Arkansas established a demonstration clinic financed by Winthrop Rockefeller. Miram
F. Garwood to William Vogt, July 5, 1955, Public Health File, Planned Parenthood of
America Papers (hereafter cited as PPFA).

98. Miram F. Garwood to William Vogt, "Relationship of Planned Parenthood to
Public Health," July 4, 1956, PPFA Subject File, Public Health, PPFA; and "Tentative
Outline for Approach to Health and Welfare Officials by PPFA Consultants" (1955),
PPFA Subject File, Public Health, PPFA.

99. William Vogt to Hugh Moore, June 14, 1960, PPFA Subject File, Hugh Moore
from 1959, PPFA.

100. Mary S. Calderone to Cass Canfield, June 24, 1960, PPFA National File, Cass
Canfield, PPFA.

101. Population Council, Minutes of the Population Council, April 5, 1962,
Population Council, RG IV3 B4.6, Box 128 (unprocessed), RA.

102. Cass Canfield to Frank Notestein, June 6, 1962, Population Council, RG IV3
B4.6, Box 122 (unprocessed), RA.

103. Hugh Moore to William H. Draper, April 26, 1962, Moore Papers, Box 3,
Princeton University.

104. Moore's attitude toward the Kennedy administration and his campaign to
arouse elite and public opinion is found in his correspondence with William Draper.
See Hugh Moore to William Draper, April 26, 1962; Hugh Moore to William Draper,
May 21, 1962; and William Draper to Hugh Moore, May 31, 1962; and William
Draper to Moore, June 1, 1962; Moore Papers, Box 3, Princeton University.

105. These lobbying efforts are discussed in a Population Council memorandum,
DK to FWN, February 20, 1962, Population Council, RG IV3 B4.6 (unprocessed), Box
122, RA; and William H. Draper to Winfield Best, June 18, 1962, PPFA Subject File,
Draper from 1960, PPFA.

106. Winfield Best to William Draper, July 18, 1963, PPFA.

107. John Rock, *The Time Has Come* (New York, 1963).

108. Hugh Moore to William H. Draper, August 21, 1963, Box 4, Moore Papers, Princeton University.

109. Hugh Moore to William H. Draper, February 25, 1963, Box 3, Moore Papers, Princeton University.

110. Mary Calderone to William Draper, June 4, 1962, PPFA Subject File, Draper from 1960, PPFA.

111. Bernard Berelson to Edward Solomon, August 13, 1963, Population Council, Organization File, Box 107, RF; and Dudley Kirk to Alan F. Guttmacher, September 23, 1963, Population Council, Organization File, Box 107, RA.

112. Frederick Osborn to Miss Harris, June 22, 1963, Frederick Osborn Papers, APS.

Chapter 2

1. Lyndon Baines Johnson, *Public Papers of the Presidents: Lyndon Baines Johnson, 1965*, vol. 2 (Washington, D.C., 1966), 635–650.

Johnson's speech was written by Daniel Moynihan, from Harvard University and working on-leave at the Labor Department. Three months prior to Johnson's speech, Moynihan had drafted a report on the black family issued by the Office of Policy Planning and Research. The Moynihan report traced the historic poverty of blacks to the breakdown of the black family structure, which had resulted from years of degradation and discrimination. Johnson's address and report soon came under attack from civil rights activists and black leaders, who accused the administration of being racist and insensitive. The furor caused by the address and the report revealed the serious problems the administration faced in convincing blacks and political activists of the sincerity of its antipoverty and family planning programs. For the Moynihan report, see Lee Rainwater and William L. Yancey, eds., *The Moynihan Report and the Politics of Controversy* (Cambridge, Mass., 1967).

There is an extensive literature on welfare in the Great Society. A beginning point is Michael Harrington, *The Other America* (New York, 1972). A sympathetic overview of the Great Society is found in Irving Bernstein, *Guns or Butter* (New York, 1996), while James Patterson provides a more balanced account in *Grand Expectations: United States, 1945–1974* (New York, 1996). For detailed studies of welfare policy, see Sar A. Levitan and Robert Taggart, *The Promise of Greatness* (Cambridge, Mass., 1976); Robert D. Plotnick and Felicity Skidmore, *Progress Against Poverty: A Review of the 1964–1974 Decade* (New York, 1975); Robert H. Haveman, ed., *A Decade of Federal Antipoverty Programs: Achievements, Failures and Lessons* (New York, 1977); and David Zarefsky, *President Johnson's War on Poverty* (University, Ala., 1986). The Office of Economic Opportunity is discussed by Stephen Goodell and Bennet Shiff, *The Office of Economic Opportunity During the Administration of President Lyndon B. Johnson, 1963–1969* (Washington, D.C., 1973).

2. Some of these problems came from a general concern about the side effects of oral contraceptives and IUDs and the permanent consequences of sterilization. Indications of the adverse side effects of IUDs are found in Louis Hellman, "United States Food and Drug Administration: Report on Intrauterine Devices by the Advisory Committee on Obstetrics and Gynecology," *Family Planning Perspectives*, I (March 1968): 12–15. While this report found IUDs generally safe, it noted, "The prevalence of PID [pelvic inflammatory disease] in the entire female population is not known exactly but it is very likely considerable; the disease is more common among the socially and economically deprived" (14).

3. Dr. Philip R. Lee, "Oral History," January 18, 1969, Lyndon Baines Johnson Library (hereafter cited as LBJ Library), Austin, Texas.

4. For a laudatory biographical portrait of Shriver that traces his early years before he joined the Kennedy administration, see Arthur Jones, "R. Sargent Shriver, Jr.: Biographical Portrait," *U.S. Catholic Historian* 7 (Winter 1988): 39–54.

5. Phyllis Piotrow to Hugh Moore, November 19, 1965, Box 17, Moore Papers, Princeton University.

6. In part, this effort aimed to counter what population activists perceived as a prevailing pro-growth, large-family ethos in America, often encouraged by "big business," which inaccurately believed population growth meant expanded markets. This pro-growth, large-family perspective, indeed, was found in business circles. For example, see "Rocketing Birth: Business Bonanza," *Life*, June 16, 1958, 83–89. Just how pervasive this belief was among corporate leaders remained unclear, however. Nonetheless, many population activists saw American business as encouraging this "dangerous" notion that population growth was healthy for the economy.

7. *The Reader's Guide to Periodical Literature* lists 60 articles on population from March 1959 to February 1965, 72 articles from March 1965 to February 1969, and 99 articles from March 1969 to February 1973, including 30 articles in a one-year period (March 1969 to February 1970) and another 39 articles in the following year (March 1970 to February 1971). Typically these articles include "Avalanche of Babies," *Newsweek*, April 27, 1959, 67–69; "Luxuries to Vanish with Population Growth?" *Science Digest*, July 1959, 5; "Are We Overworking the Stork?" *Parents Magazine*, October 1961, 72–73; "Population Problems and the Church," *Christian Century*, July 6, 1962, 710–12; "Population Explosion Demands Worldwide Action," *Christian Century*, January 8, 1964, 43–46; "What the Population Explosion Means to You," *Ladies' Home Journal*, June 1963, 59–64; "Why Americans Must Limit Their Families," *Redbook*, August 1963, 30–38; "Intelligent Woman's Guide to the Population Explosion," *McCall's*, February 1965, 32–40; "Tax on Babies to Limit Population?" *U.S. News and World Report*, January 31, 1966, 11; D. Lyle, "Human Race Has, Maybe, Thirty-five Years Left," *Esquire*, September 1967, 116–118; William H. Draper, "Overpopulation: Threat to Survival," *Parents Magazine*, August 1967, 30; A. T. Day, "Population Increase: A Grave Threat to Every American Family," *Parents Magazine*, October 1969, 56–71; L. Lader, "Laws to Limit Family Size," *Parents Magazine*, October 1970, 58–61; and C. Panati and M. Lord, "Population Implosion," *Newsweek*, December 6, 1976, 58.

8. For a review of this literature, see "Overpopulation," in *The Encyclopedia of Science Fiction*, 2d ed., ed. John Clute and Peter Nicholls (New York, 1993), 901–902.

9. Paul R. Ehrlich, *The Population Bomb* (New York, 1968), 132–142, 176–198.

10. Relevant polling data are found in George Gallup and Associates, *The Gallup Poll*, 1654, 1785–1786, 1822–1823, 1915–1916, 1936–1937, 2157–2158, 2299–2300.

11. For social life in the fifties, see John P. Diggins, *The Proud Decades* (New York, 1988); James Gilbert, *Another Chance: Postwar America, 1945–1985* (New York, 1981); Paul Carter, *Another Part of the Fifties* (New York, 1983). For women and sexual changes, see William Chafe, *The American Woman* (New York, 1972); Carl Degler, *At Odds* (New York, 1980); John D'Emilio and Estelle Freedman, *Intimate Matters: A History of Sexuality in America* (New York, 1988); and Elaine Tyler May, *Homeward Bound* (New York, 1987).

12. Alfred Kinsey et al., *Sexual Behavior in the Human Male* (Philadelphia, 1948); Kinsey et al., *Sexual Behavior in the Human Female* (Philadelphia, 1953). Two favorable biographies of Kinsey written by two of his research assistants are Cornelia V. Christenson, *Kinsey: A Biography* (Bloomington, Ind., 1971), and Wardell B. Pomeroy, *Dr. Kinsey and the Institute for Sex Research* (New York, 1972). For a revealing account of

Kinsey's biases, see James H. Jones, *Alfred C. Kinsey: A Public/Private Life* (New York, 1997).

13. An insightful critique of *Playboy* and its readers is offered by Barbara Ehrenreich, *The Hearts of Men: American Dreams and the Flight from Commitment* (Garden City, N.Y., 1983), 42–51.

14. Bishop Kennedy is quoted in "Morality: The Second Sexual Revolution," *Time*, January 24, 1964, 54–59. Also Peter Bertocci, "Extramarital Sex and the Pill," *Christian Century*, February 26, 1964, 267–270. Bertocci, a Boston University psychologist, maintained that "sex, both within and outside marriage, decreases in quality of satisfaction to the extent that the sexual act cannot express or symbolize other values in the lives of those concerned" (268). He felt that the pill perpetuated this problem.

15. Helen Gurley Brown, *Sex and the Single Girl* (New York, 1962), 225–226.

16. Lawrence Lipton, *The Erotic Revolution: An Affirmative View of the New Morality* (Los Angeles, 1965).

17. "The Morals Revolution on the U.S. Campus," *Newsweek*, April 6, 1964, 52–59; also Steven Spencer, "Birth Control Revolution," *Saturday Evening Post*, January 15, 1966, 21–25, 66–70. An excellent overview of research into premarital sexual relations in this decade is found in Kenneth L. Cannon and Richard Long, "Premarital Sexual Behavior in the Sixties," *Journal of Marriage and Family* 33 (February 1971): 36–49.

18. Robert R. Bell and Jay B. Chaskes, "Premarital Sexual Experience Among Coeds, 1958 and 1968," *Journal of Marriage and Family* 32 (February 1970): 81–88. Similarly, another team of medical doctors found that the fear of pregnancy no longer deterred teens from premarital sexual intercourse. See Sadja Goldsmith et al., "Teenagers, Sex, and Contraception," *Family Planning Perspectives* 14 (January 1972): 32–38.

19. Cannon and Long, "Premarital Sexual Behavior in the Sixties," 36–49.

20. Howard Hoyman, "Sex and American College Girls Today," *Journal of School Health* 37:2 (February 1967): 54–62.

21. For an insightful discussion of *Griswold*, see David J. Garrow, *Liberty and Sexuality: The Right to Privacy and the Making of Roe v. Wade* (New York, 1994), 240–269.

22. The following discussion of the sexual revolution among students, hippies, and homosexuals draws from John D'Emilio and Estelle B. Freedman's important book, *Intimate Matters: A History of Sexuality in America* (New York, 1988), 301–326.

23. An excellent overview of black attitudes toward family planning is found in Robert G. Weisbord, "Birth Control and the Black Americans: A Matter of Genocide?" *Demography* 10:4 (November 1973): 571–590; also, J. Mayone Stycos, "Opinion and Population Problems: Some Sources of Domestic and Foreign Opposition," in *Rapid Population Growth: Consequences and Policy Implications*, ed. National Academy of Science (Baltimore, 1971). Jessie M. Rodrique argues that the African-American community historically supported family planning prior to the Second World War in "The African-American Community and the Birth Control Movement, 1918–1942" (Ph.D. diss., University of Massachusetts, 1991; microfilm).

The Black Muslim newspaper, *Muhammad Speaks*, aimed a barrage of feature articles, editorials, and cartoons at family planning during these years. For example, see Tynetta Denear, "Family Most Powerful Unit in Islam," *Muhammad Speaks*, May 1962; Cartoon: "Planning No Future for You," *Muhammad Speaks*, June 1962; "World Hits Three Billion, Power Shifts," *Muhammad Speaks*, July 1962; Cartoon: "The Plan: Keep Africa White," *Muhammad Speaks*, July 15, 1962; "Negro Growth Tops Whites in 50 Cities," *Muhammad Speaks*, August 31, 1962; "Expert Says Illegitimacy Is Not Tied to Relief Check," *Muhammad Speaks*, September 30, 1962; "Fountain of Youth May Slow-Down Aging Process," *Muhammad Speaks*, November 15, 1962; "White Clinic Sterilizes More Negro Women!" "Birth Control Death Plan!" "Sterilization Plot in Virginia Halts Birth of Negroes," and "Catholic Archbishop Strikes at Warrenton Sterilization Project,"

Muhammad Speaks, December 15, 1962; "Beware False Prophets" and "Ok's Plot to Curtail Negro Births," *Muhammad Speaks,* December 30, 1962; "Would Take Away Children, Cast Their Parents Adrift," *Muhammad Speaks,* January 15, 1963; and "Sees Family Planning as Routine Matter in Future," *Muhammad Speaks,* March 18, 1963.

24. For PPFA relations with the civil rights movement, see "Reaffirmation Resolution, National Urban League Delegate Assembly, Philadelphia, August 23, 1966, and Naomi T. Gray to Mrs. Harriet Pilpel, June 27, 1966, Subject File, Urban League, PPFA Papers; Alan F. Guttmacher to Cecil New, March 7, 1966, PPFA Subject File, Negro File, PPFA.

25. Wylanda B. Colwes to Alan F. Guttmacher, June 19, 1962, Subject File, Negro File, PPFA.

26. This heated conference is reported by Elsie Jackson, PPFA field consultant. Elsie Jackson to Alan F. Guttmacher, April 4, 1966, Subject File, Negro File, PPFA.

27. A copy of the pamphlet is found in PPFA Subject File, Negro file, PPFA. For a meeting between Thompson and PPFA officials, see Wylanda B. Colwes to Alan F. Guttmacher, March 28, 1966, PPFA Subject Files, Negro File, PPFA.

28. Administrative Board of the National Catholic Welfare Conference, press release, November 14, 1966, Central Files, Welfare, Box 1, LBJ Library.

29. Charles L. Schultze to Joseph Califano, June 10, 1967, Central Files, Welfare, Box 2, LBJ Library.

30. Many in the population movement had not forgotten that a threatened boycott by the Catholic Church hierarchy of *Woman's Day* in 1961 had forced Ortho, a pharmaceutical company that had pioneered in developing the pill, to withdraw its advertising from the magazine. Population Council, Staff Minutes, December 19, 1961, Population Council Papers (unprocessed), RA.

31. For example, as early as the summer of 1962, Cass Canfield reported that he had traveled to Rome, where he had met with a group of Jesuits and other priests. All agreed, Canfield reported, that there was a population problem, although some felt there was a food supply problem in the developing nations. One Jesuit, Roberto Tucci, said that Catholics were permitted to use a steroid coil for the purpose of regularizing the menstrual cycle; Canfield commented, "In practical terms this attitude would seem to open a rather large door since most women, having started to use the pill with the blessing of the Church, would be likely to continue to do so." Frederick Osborn to Frederick Notestein, "Report of Luncheon with Cass Canfield," July 9, 1962, Population Council Papers (unprocessed), Box 122, RA.

Typical of these rumors was a report made by Bernard Berelson that read, "A research associate in Stockholm has an uncle who is the Pope's personal dentist. The word is that family planning is to be left to the couple after consultation with their parish priests and methods are to be left to the woman and her doctor. It all sounds too good to be so." Barney Berelson to Frank Notestein, July 19, 1966, Berelson Files, Population Council Papers (unprocessed), RA.

32. Richard N. Garner to Douglass Cater, December 3, 1965, Douglass Cater File, Box 15, LBJ. Also Joseph Califano to the President, November 15, 1966, Central Files, Welfare, LBJ Library.

For changing attitudes in the Catholic press, see James Hitchcock, "The American Press and Birth Control: Preparing the Ground for Dissent," Hitchcock *Years in Crisis* (San Francisco, 1984), 84–102.

33. Included at this luncheon were Bernard Berelson, David Ogilvy, Robert Coughlan, Norman Cousins, Theodore Waller, and John Fischer. Winfield Best to Cass Canfield, June 4, 1963, PPFA Subject File, Canfield from 1960, PPFA.

34. Thomas E. Blantz, C.S.C., *George N. Shuster: On the Side of Truth* (Notre Dame, Ind., 1993), 314–324, quotation on 314.

35. For PPFA's role in planning the conference, see Cass Canfield to George Shuster, September 25, 1962, 1st Conference Folder (1962), University of Notre Dame Archives (hereafter cited as ND); and Cass Canfield to William H. Draper, September 17, 1962, Subject File, Draper from 1960, PPFA.

Details of Population Council and Ford Foundation sponsorship of the conferences are found in "Application to Ford for Conference on Population Problems, June 5, 1963, in Conference on Population Problems Folder, ND.

Shuster's response is found in press release, "Summer Conference on Population Question Planned at Notre Dame," May 13, 1964, Conference on Population Problems File (1963), ND.

36. Winfield Best to Cass Canfield, March 25, 1966, PPFA Subject File, Canfield, PPFA.

37. This controversy is traced in a series of newspaper clippings with attached memorandums located in the University of Notre Dame Archives. See John Cogley, "Contraception Exclusive," *New York Times*, September 27, 1965; "37 Catholics Ask New Birth Control View," *Chicago Tribune*, September 28, 1965; "Birth Control Endorsement Report False, Says Priest," *Des Moines Register*, October 17, 1965; "Birth Control Report Reaches Commission," *Providence Journal*, October 8, 1965; George Shuster to Jim Murphy, October 4, 1965; Theodore Hesburgh to George Shuster, October 4, 1965; Jim Murphy to George N. Shuster, October 4, 1965; George Shuster to George Henri do Riedmatten, O.P. March 22, 1965, Population Problems Conference Files, ND.

38. Russell Kirk, "Let's Be Sexumenical," *National Review*, December 26, 1967, 1430.

39. Rev. Theodore Hesburgh to Robert West, May 13, 1965, Theodore Hesburgh Papers, Rockefeller Foundation File, ND.

40. See an exchange of letters concerning Hesburgh's first appointment to the board. Rev. Theodore Hesburgh to John D. Rockefeller 3rd, January 30, 1961; Rev. Theodore Hesburgh to Flora M. Rhind, December 13, 1966; and Kellum Smith Jr. to Fr. Theodore Hesburgh, April 14, 1966, Rockefeller Folder, Hesburgh Papers, ND.

41. "University of Chile Postpartum Family Planning" (1966), Rockefeller Board Folder, Fr. Theodore Hesburgh Office Files, ND.

42. John M. Weir to Father Ted Hesburgh, February 25, 1966, Rockefeller Board Folder, Hesburgh Office Files, ND; also Albert Ravenholt, "Sacred Cows of India Are Coil Device Target," *Washington Post*, December, 14, 1966.

43. John D. Rockefeller 3rd to Fr. Theodore Hesburgh, April 15, 1965; Hesburgh to Rockefeller, April 23, 1965; Fr. Theodore Hesburgh to John D. Rockefeller 3rd, May 19, 1965; Hesburgh to Rockefeller, May 25, 1965; Rockefeller to Pope Paul VI, July 16, 1965; Hesburgh to Rockefeller, July 27, 1965; Rockefeller to Hesburgh, July 29, 1965; Hesburgh to Rockefeller, October 2, 1965; Rockefeller to Amleto Cardinal Ciocognani, Secretary of State, Vatican, June 7, 1967; Rockefeller Correspondence, Hesburgh Office Files, ND.

44. Bernard Berelson to File, April 30, 1965, Berelson File, Population Council Papers, RA.

Cordial relations with Moyers quickly developed. In 1965 Population Council staff member Raymond Lamontagne, writing on the behalf of Rockefeller, thanked Moyers for his work: We are "most appreciative for the real interest and concern which you express on the subject [population]" and we feel our views have been given a solid hearing. Raymond Lamontagne to Bill Moyers, June 28, 1965, Central Files, Welfare, Box 5, LBJ Library.

45. John D. Rockefeller 3rd, "The Reminiscences of John D. Rockefeller, 3rd," Columbia Oral History Project (Columbia University, 1964), 268–271.

Rockefeller suggested that he should work with key national leaders, while the council traveled "the lower road of administrative and technical action." At the same time, Rockefeller said that five other groups should be targeted: labor unions, industry, hospitals, medical care plans, and Negro leadership organizations. Through his position and contacts he could quietly bring the key leaders together and "gently urge them further down the right road." John D. Rockefeller 3rd to Frank W. Notestein, October 11, 1964; and Frank W. Notestein and Bernard Berelson to John D. Rockefeller 3rd, October 15, 1964, Berelson Files, Population Council Papers (unprocessed), RA.

46. The exact figures reveal that gifts to the council increased sharply from 1959 through 1964, largely because of Ford Foundation contributions:

Donor	1952–1958	1959–1964	TOTAL
Ford Foundation	1 million	8.4 million	9.4 million
JDR 3rd	1.8 million	974,000	2.8 million
Rockefeller Foundation	—	1.6 million	1.6
Rockefeller Brothers Fund	540,000	1.5	1.6
JDR III Trusts	750, 000	1.1	1.8
Mrs. Rockefeller, Jr.	—	85,231	85,231
Mrs. Jean Mauze	—	272,543	272,543
Mrs. May		509,769	509,769
Mrs. Alan M. Scaife		2.1 million	2.1 million
Avalon Foundation	—	260,000	260,000
Commonwealth	—	150,000	150,000
Carnegie		123,281	123,281

Source: Bernard Berelson, Annual Report File (1965), Bernard Berelson Papers, Unprocessed, RF. Also "Ford Foundation's Activities in Population," August 1968, Population Program File, FA.

47. While Moore shared Rockefeller's concern that not enough was being done, he blamed the "timidity" of the Population Council for much of the lack of resolve. He was joined in this perception by William Draper. Both lamented that the Population Council remained "too optimistic" about the population crisis. Furthermore, both felt that scare tactics needed to be used to motivate policy makers and the people to act immediately. Given the nature of the crisis, immediate action by the federal government was called for, comparable to a "Manhattan Project" to control population growth internationally and domestically. William Draper to Hugh Moore, November 22, 1965, Moore Papers, Box 17, Princeton University.

Even as late as 1968, Moore continued to accuse the Population Council of being too conservative in its approach to the population issue. He wrote to a supporter: "My only disagreement with Frank Notestein is that he tends to suggest that maybe things are going to come out alright—which I seriously doubt. I think people really need to be scared." Hugh Moore to Joseph W. Ayer, December 3, 1968, Moore Papers, Box 17, Princeton University.

48. In creating this new organization, Moore called on many of his friends associated with past causes, including Harper and Row publisher, Cass Canfield; General William Draper; New York political activist Mrs. John L. Loeb; dean of the School of Foreign Relations at Georgetown University, William Moran Jr.; banker and relative to the Abbey Aldrich Rockefeller side of the family Rockefeller Prentice; pollster journalist Elmo Roper; Pittsburgh philanthropist Mrs. Cordelia Scaife May; and Scaife Foundation

representative A. W. Schmidt. Additional financial support came from Ellsworth Bunker, Will Clayton, Joseph Sunnen, Max Ascoli, Lamont duPont Copeland, and Marriner Eccles.

49. John D. Rockefeller 3rd to Hugh Moore, June 22, 1965, Moore Papers, Box 17, Princeton University.

50. Hugh Moore, Memorandum, April 1, 1966, Moore Papers, Box 17, Princeton University.

51. Hugh Moore to Bill Draper, August 10, 1965, Moore Papers, Box 17, Princeton University.

52. Hugh Moore, Memorandum, October 6, 1965, Moore Papers, Box 17, Princeton University.

53. Hugh Moore to Russell H. Bennett, November 29, 1965, Moore Papers, Box 18, Princeton University.

54. In describing his feelings toward Keating and Nelson Rockefeller in 1965, he added that he had read that the next likely Democratic presidential candidates were Humphrey and Bobby Kennedy. "The mere prospect," he bluntly declared, "sends chills down my spine." Hugh Moore to Arthur Krock, February 21, 1966; and Hugh Moore to Russell Bennett, November 29, 1965, Moore Papers, Box 17, Princeton University.

55. Ibid.

56. Winfield Best to Cass Canfield, March 25, 1966, Canfield Subject files, PPFA.

57. Rockefeller Prentice agreed with Moore that in order to launch a "Manhattan scale project" to reduce population Congress needed to be educated, but he wondered whether unnecessary tensions had been created with PPFA. Rockefeller Prentice to William Draper, January 15, 1966, PPFA Subject File, Draper 1964, PPFA.

58. Hugh Moore to Arnold H. Maremont, July 21, 1967, Box 17, Moore Papers, Princeton University.

59. Minutes of the Executive Group of PCC, August 4, 1965, PPFA Subject File: Population Crisis Committee Correspondence from 1965, PPFA.

In fact, PCC hoped from the outset to receive tax-exempt status from the Internal Revenue Service as an "educational" organization. PCC was incorporated as a "non-profit" organization in December 1965, but the IRS ruled that PCC, as a lobbying organization, was not eligible for tax-exempt status. The PCC sought to overcome this ruling in a strategy laid out by PCC lobbyist Justin Blackwelder. Writing to Cass Canfield, Blackwelder noted, "If you ask most lawyers including our own if we can get tax exemption under 501 (C) they would all agree that it could not be done. We are a lobbying organization, as stated in our application. But it can be done and has been done as evidenced in the Atlantic Union Committee for years. It had no purpose other than lobbying. It so stated and I worked for it as a lobbyist. We received revenue of nearly half a million dollars, but tax exemption was granted retroactively. Many of our large contributors refiled for previous years and received the deduction. Elmo [Roper] and Justice Roberts felt we could not get tax exemption. I obtained tax exemption for a similar organization in 1955, also retroactive. In 1956, Senator Bricker, at the insistence of Dean Clarence Manion, wrote to Internal Revenue demanding removal of Atlantic Union Committee tax status be revoked, but IRS said it could not be revoked." In the end, Blackwelder's efforts to lobby the IRS failed. Justin Blackwelder to Cass Canfield, July 7, 1966, PPFA Subject File: Population Crisis Committee Correspondence from 1965, PPFA.

60. Alan F. Guttmacher, Confidential Meeting Notes, December 10, 1963, Population Council Papers (unprocessed), Box 107, RA.

61. Hugh Heclo, "Issue Networks and the Executive Establishment," in *The New American Political System*, ed. Anthony King (Washington, D.C., 1980).

62. Cass Canfield to Bernard Berelson, November 23, 1964, Berelson File, Population Council Papers (unprocessed), RA.

63. Busby's suggestion that Mrs. Albert Lasker be included in a possible meeting with Johnson was not explained, although one reason might be that the Laskers were heavy contributors to the Democratic party.

64. Bernard Berelson to John D. Rockefeller 3rd, December 2, 1964, Berelson File, Population Council Papers (unprocessed), RA.

65. Horace Busby to Bernard Berelson, December 10, 1964, Berelson File, Population Council Papers (unprocessed), RA.

66. John D. Rockefeller 3rd to McGeorge Bundy, November 10, 1964, Berelson File, Population Council Papers (unprocessed), RA.

67. For meetings between the administration and the population lobby, see Dean Rusk to the President, November 20, 1964, National Security Files, Population; Jack Valenti to McGeorge Bundy, December 4, 1964; Perry Barber to Jack Valenti, December 3, 1964; Jack Valenti to William Draper, November 24, 1964; William Draper to Jack Valenti, November 19, 1964; Ralph A. Dungar to Anthony Celebrezze, June 27, 1964; Leon A. Schertler to Bill D. Moyers, November 24, 1964, all in Box 1, Central Files, Welfare, LBJ Library. Also, for an insight into the lobbying strategy that was developed at a dinner hosted by John D. Rockefeller 3rd attended by Berelson, Canfield, Draper, Notestein, Detlev Bronk, and State Department official Robert Barnett, see Cass Canfield to W. Best, October 22, 1964, PPFA Subject File: Cass Canfield, PPFA.

68. General William H. Draper to General Dwight D. Eisenhower, December 8, 1964, and General William H. Draper to General Dwight D. Eisenhower, December 26, 1964, in Office of Dwight D. Eisenhower, Box 33, Eisenhower Library.

69. Nan Tucker McEvoy to Douglas Cater, December 20, 1964, Speech Files, Box 133, LBJ Library.

70. "Draft Statement of Speech Draft 1," December 31, 1964; "Teletype from Mr. Goodwin to Mr. Busby for Presidential Draft #3" (n.d.); Benjamin Read to Bill Moyers, December 30, 1964, White House Central Files, Box 136, LBJ Library. For the final version of the speech, see Lyndon Baines Johnson, "Annual Message to the Congress on the State of the Union," January 4, 1965, *Public Papers of the Presidents of the United States: Lyndon B. Johnson, 1965* (Washington, D.C., 1966), 4.

71. William Draper to Lyndon Baines Johnson, January 17, 1966, Central Files, Box 1 LBJ Library.

72. During the presidential campaign, the Republican Citizens Committee called for the U.S. Public Health Service to provide appropriate leadership and assistance to state and local health departments in offering family planning advice and services to disadvantaged citizens. For the White House view of this, see Dean Rusk to the President, November 20, 1964, National Security Files: Population, LBJ Library. For the Draper-Notestein platform statement, see William Draper to Winfield Best, March 31, 1964; and William Draper to Robert W. McCormick, March 31, 1964, PPFA Subject File: Draper from 1964, PPFA.

73. Dean Rusk to the President, November 20, 1964, National Security Files: Population, LBJ Library.

74. For the details of the comedy of errors concerning Rockefeller's plans to meet with the president, see Jack Valenti to McGeorge Bundy, December 4, 1964; Perry Barber to Mr. Valenti, December 3, 1964; Perry Barber to Jack Valenti, November 30, 1964; Jack Valenti to the President, November 24, 1964; Jack Valenti to the President, November 23, 1964; William Draper to Jack Valenti, November 19, 1964, Central Files, Welfare, Box 1 LBJ Library.

75. John D. Rockefeller 3rd to McGeorge Bundy, April 28, 1965; John D. Rockefeller 3rd to Lyndon Baines Johnson, March 3, 1965; McGeorge Bundy to Mr. Jack Valenti, March 7, 1965; Jack Valenti to Lyndon Baines Johnson, March 9, 1965; Jack Valenti to McGeorge Bundy, March 11, 1965; McGeorge Bundy to John D. Rockefeller 3rd, March 16, 1965; Central Files, Welfare, Box 1 LBJ Library.

76. Lyndon Baines Johnson to Douglass Cater, December 5, 1966, Cater Files, Box 66, LBJ Library.

77. John D. Rockefeller 3rd to Douglass Cater, October 21, 1966, Duggan File, LBJ Library.

78. Richard Day to Alan Guttmacher, April 12, 1965, PPFA Subject File, Children's Bureau, PPFA. Dorothea Andrews to Carl Zimmerman, November 5, 1966, Box 1143, Children's Bureau, NA.

79. Phyllis Piotrow, Summary of United States Government Policies in the Field of Population, July 21, 1965, Moore Papers, Box 17, Princeton University.

80. The White House perception of Congress is found in Douglass Cater to the President, December 6, 1966, Central Files, Welfare, Box 1, LBJ Library.

81. Douglass D. Cater to the President, March 30, 1965, Douglass Cater File, Box 66, LBJ Library.

82. Ibid.

83. Ibid. Also see attached to Cater's memorandum, "Family Planning and Birth Control Activities Under Community Action Programs," March 3, 1965.

84. See I. Jack Fasteau, Program Coordinator for OEO, to Dr. William Steward, Health and Medical Affairs, Public Health Service, March 15, 1965, Box 96, and Arthur J. Lesser, Children's Bureau, Memorandum, March 17, 1965, Children's Bureau Papers, National Archives (hereafter cited as NA).

85. Association for Voluntary Sterilization, "Sargent Shriver Charged with Counting Angels on Head of a Pin," Press release, August 25, 1966, Box 995, Children's Bureau Papers, NA.

86. Rowland Evans and Robert Novak, "Birth De-Control," unidentified column, April 10, 1965, Douglass Cater File, Box 66, LBJ Library.

87. Joseph A. Kershaw to Harry C. McPherson, October 19, 1965 Files (microfilm), Reel 3, LBJ Library.

88. Joseph A. Kershaw to Donald Baker, October 20, 1965, OEO Files (microfilm), Reel 3, LBJ Library.

89. Quoted in William B. Ball, "Population Control: Civil and Constitutional Concerns," in *Religion and Public Order*, ed. Donald A. Grannella (N.Y. 1971), 128–169, especially 129.

90. Harry C. McPherson Jr. to the President, January 5, 1966; Harry C. McPherson to Bill Moyers, January 28, 1966; Douglass Cater file, Box 66; LBJ Library.

91. Douglass Cater to the President, November 29, 1966, Douglass Cater File, Box 66, LBJ Library.

92. Harry C. McPherson to Bill Moyers, January 28, 1966, Douglass Cater File, Box 66, LBJ Library.

93. Douglass Cater, "Family Planning Services in Public Health Programs," September 1966, Douglass Cater File Box 66, LBJ Library.

94. Johan W. Eliot and Leslie Corsa Jr., "Family Planning Activities of Official Health and Welfare Agencies, United States, 1966," *American Journal of Public Health* 58: 4 (April 1968): 700–712.

95. An overview of family planning programs operating at the state level is found in George W. Perkins and David Radel, *Current Status of Family Planning Programs in the United States* (New York, 1966), located in the Ford Foundation Archives.

96. U.S. Department of Health, Education, and Welfare, "Report on Family Planning: U.S. Department of Health, Education, and Welfare Activities of the U.S. Department of HEW," *Family Planning, Fertility, and Population Dynamics* (September 1966) (Washington, D.C., 1966).

97. See chapter 1 for Gamble's efforts in the South. Also Edward J. Larson, *Sex, Race, and Science: Eugenics in the Deep South* (Baltimore, 1995). For state programs, see

Arthur J. Less, Memorandum, July 25, 1967, Children's Bureau Records, Box 1142; and Joseph H. Meyers, Commissioner of Welfare to Mr. Wilbur Cohen, July 19, 1967, Children's Bureau Records, Box 1142, NA.

98. Lyndon Baines Johnson, *Public Papers of Lyndon B. Johnson, 1967*, vol. 1 (Washington, D.C., 1968), 11.

99. U.S. Congress, Senate Committee on Finance, *Social Security Amendments of 1967: Hearings on H.R. 10280* (Washington, D.C., 1967).

100. The administration's involvement in this legislation is found in James Jones to Harry McPherson, April 4, 1967, Box 165; Wilbur J. Cohen to Lyndon Baines Johnson, July 14, 1967, Box 164; and Douglass Cater to Joseph Califano, December 22, 1967, Legislative Files, Box 164, LBJ Library.

For an excellent discussion of the legislative history of these amendments, see Edward Berkowitz, *Mr. Social Security: The Life of Wilbur J. Cohen* (Lawrence, Kans., 1995), 252–262; and Irving Bernstein, *Guns or Butter: The Presidency of Lyndon Johnson* (New York, 1996).

101. For Rockefeller's involvement in this legislation, see Douglass Cater to John D. Rockefeller 3rd, May 8, 1968, Ervin Duggan Office Files, Box 12, LBJ Library.

102. Ernest Gruening to LBJ, Telegram, March 29, 1967; Phillip S. Hughes to McPherson, February 1, 1967; Ernest Gruening to Lyndon B. Johnson, February 3, 1967; Harry C. McPherson to Lyndon Baines Johnson, January 10, 1967; James R. Jones to Harry S. McPherson, April 4, 1967; Wilbur J. Cohen to Lyndon Baines Johnson, July 14, 1967, in Legislative Files, Box 164; and Wilf Rommel to Harry C. McPherson, September 30, 1966; Legislative Files, Box 165, LBJ Library. Also U.S. Congress, *Hearings Before the Subcommittee on Employment, Manpower and Poverty*, 89th Cong., 2d sess., May 10, 1966 (Washington, D.C., 1966).

103. Phillip S. Hughes to Harry McPherson, February 1, 1967, Legislative Files, Box 164, LBJ Library. Also U.S. Congress, *Social Security Amendments of 1967: Hearings Before the Committee on Finance*, U.S. Senate, 90th Cong., 1st sess., August 22, 23, and 24, 1967 (Washington, D.C., 1967).

104. Oscar Harkavy, Frederick S. Jaffe, and Samuel M. Wishik, "Implementing DHEW Policy on Family Planning and Population: A Consultant's Confidential Report," September 1967, Oscar Harkavy File, Ford Foundation Library.

105. Office of Economic Opportunity, *Family Planning* (Washington, D.C., March 1969), 2.

106. John W. Gardner, "Family Planning Policy," January 1968, Douglass Cater Files, Box 66, LBJ Library. Also Mrs. E. Switzer to Katherine B. Oettinger, January 22, Children's Bureau Files, Box 1142, National Archives; Katherine B. Oettinger, "Family Planning Program Objects," Douglass Carter Files, Box 66, LBJ Library; and Philip R. Lee, "Report of the Special Study Group on the Provision of Family Planning Services," October 1968, Wilbur Cohen File, LBJ Library.

107. Department of Health, Education, and Welfare, "Report on Family Planning Activities: A Report to the House Committee on Appropriations" (1968), Ervin Duggan Office Files, Box 12, LBJ Library.

108. Dr. Carl S. Schultz to HEW Secretary, "Constraints in the Development of Domestic Family Planning Services," July 29, 1968, Children's Bureau Records, Box 1142; and Dr. Arthur J. Lesser, "Family Planning, Present and Proposed Activities, FY 1968–1968," (n.d. 1968?), Children's Bureau Records, Box 1143, NA.

109. Judith Black, "The Fallacy of the Five Million Women: A Reestimate," *Demography* 9:4 (November 1972): 569–588.

110. For discussions of out-of-wedlock births during this period, see Clark E. Vincent, *Unmarried Mothers* (New York, 1961); Vera Shlakman, "Unmarried Parenthood: An Approach to Social Policy," *Social Casework* 47 (1966): 497–498; Major Mary

E. Verner, "Administrative Concepts in Comprehensive Services for Unmarried Parents," in National Council on Illegitimacy, *Unmarried Parenthood: Clues to Agency and Community Action* (New York, 1967); and Ellen Winston, *Unmarried Parents and Federal Programs of Assistance* (Washington, D.C., 1966). For an early expression of this concern with out-of-wedlock births and welfare dependence, see U.S. Department of Health, Education, and Welfare, *Illegitimacy and Its Impact on the Aid to Dependent Children Program* (Washington, D.C., 1960), which reported a steady rise in out-of-wedlock births among teenagers since 1940.

A detailed examination of teenage out-of-wedlock births from 1940 through 1968 is provided by demographer Phillips Cutright, who reported the following increases in teenage out-of-wedlock birthrates:

Illegitimate Births per 1,000 Unmarried Women Aged 14, 15–17, 18–19 and 15–19 by Color, United States, 1940–1968

Color/Age	1940	1950	1960	1968
Nonwhite				
14	13	19	20	21
15–17	38	53	56	67
18–19	61	93	114	112
15–19	45.5	65.6	73.9	82.0
White				
14	0.5	0.8	1	1
15–17	2	3	4	6
18–19	5	8	12	17
15–19	3.5	5.1	6.6	9.7
Total white and nonwhite				
15–19	8.3	12.8	15.6	19.8

Source: Phillips Cutright, "The Teenage Sexual Revolution and the Myth of an Abstinent Past," *Family Planning Perspectives* 4:1 (January 1972): 24–31.

A feminist perspective on out-of-wedlock births in America in the postwar period prior to *Roe v. Wade* is offered in Rickie Solinger, *Wake Up Little Susie: Single Pregnancy and Race Before Roe v.Wade* (New York, 1992). For a discussion of the historical and policy implications of adolescent pregnancy after *Roe*, see Maris A. Vinovskis, *An "Epidemic" of Adolescent Pregnancy: Some Historical and Policy Considerations* (New York, 1988). Other secondary sources include Marian J. Morton, *Sin No More: Social Policy and Unwed Mothers in Cleveland, 1855–1990* (Columbus, Ohio, 1993); Agnes K. Hanna, "Changing Care of Children Born Out-of-Wedlock," in *Children and Youth in America: A Documentary History*, Vol. 3, *1933–1973*, ed. Robert H. Bremner (Cambridge, Mass. 1974); Peter Laslett et al., eds., *Bastardy and Its Comparative History* (Cambridge, Mass. 1980); Kristin Luker, *Conspicuous Conception* (New York, 1997); and Prudence Mors Rains, *Becoming an Unwed Mother: A Sociological Account* (Chicago, 1971). Comparative studies that focus on contemporary out-of-wedlock births are found in Lewellyn Hendrix, *Illegitimacy and Social Structures: Cross-Cultural Perspectives on Nonmarital Birth* (Westport, Conn., 1996); and Elsie F. Jones, *Teenage Pregnancy in Industrialized Countries* (New Haven, Conn. 1996).

111. Arthur J. Less, "Children's Bureau Family Planning Programs," October 3, 1967, Children's Bureau Records, Box 1143, NA.

112. Representative Paul H. Todd to Mrs. Katherine Oettinger, August 6, 1966, Children's Bureau, Box 993, NA.

113. There is extensive correspondence in the Johnson Library concerning Rockefeller's "World Leaders Statement on Population." See Raymond A. Lamontagne to Douglass Cater, November 23, 1966, Box 66; Douglass Cater to Lyndon Baines Johnson, December 2, 1966, Box 66; John D. Rockefeller to Hon. John W. Garner, October 3, 1967, Box 66, all in Cater File, LBJ Library. Also Philander P. Claxon Jr. to Douglass Cater, August 4, 1967, Central Files, Welfare, Box 7; A. Cosign to John D. Rockefeller 3rd, September 16, 1967, National Security Files, Box 38; John D. Rockefeller 3rd to Mr. Cosign, October 9, 1967, Central Files Welfare, Box 2; Dean Rusk to Lyndon Baines Johnson, June 28, 1967, Box 16; Philander P. Claxon Jr. to Douglass Cater, June 23, 1967, Box 16, Cater File; and "Statement on Population by World Leaders," October 13, Central Files, Welfare, Box 2, LBJ Library.

114. John D. Rockefeller 3rd to the President, May 26, 1967, Cater File, Box 16. Further background on the proposed commission is found in Phillip R. Lee to Wilbur Cohen, June 27, 1968, Wilbur Cohen File, LBJ Library.

115. Charles L. Schultze to Joseph Califano, June 10, 1967, Central Files, Welfare, Box 2; Philip R. Lee to Douglass Cater, February 26, 1968, Cater File, Box 66, LBJ Library.

116. Douglass Cater to the President, May 22, 1968, Cater File, Box 66, LBJ Library.

117. Formula family grants through the Maternal and Child Health Services increased from $1.5 million in 1965 to $2.5 million in 1968. Special project grants for maternity and infant care rose from $350,000 in 1965 to $6.3 million in 1968.

118. Douglass Cater to John D. Rockefeller 3rd, May 8, 1968; and "DHEW Report on Family Planning," May 1968; Duggan Office Files, Box 12, LBJ Library.

119. The workings of the committee are found in Ben Wattenberg to the President, November 15, 1968, Office Files of Ervin Duggan, Box 12; Ervin Duggan to the President, January 6, 1969, Central Files, Welfare, Box 382; Press Release, "Exchange of Remarks Between the President and Secretary Cohen and John D. Rockefeller 3rd," January 7, 1968, Office Files of Ervin Duggan, Box 12; and Katherine Oettinger to Douglass Cater, July 25, 1968, Cater File, Box 66; and Harry McPherson to President, February 23, 1977, Central File, Welfare, Box 2, LBJ Library.

Chapter 3

1. J. Mayone Sycos, "Opinion, Ideology, and Population Problems: Some Sources of Domestic and Foreign Opposition," in National Academy of Sciences, *Rapid Population Growth: Consequences and Policy Implications* (Baltimore, 1971).

2. Leslie Corsa, "United States: Public Policy and Programs in Family Planning," *Studies in Family Planning*, 5 (March 1968): 2–3.

3. An excellent and detailed overview of family planning programs, broken down on a state level, prior to Nixon's election and during his first year in office is provided in Joy G. Dryfoos, Frederick S. Jaffe. "Eighteen Months Later: Family Planning Services in the United States, 1969," *Family Planning Perspectives* 3:2 (April 1971): 29–44.

4. F. S. Jaffe, "Family Planning and the Medical Assistance Program," *Medical Care* 6:1 (January–February 1968); quoted in Jeannie I. Rosoff, "Medicaid, Past and Future," *Family Planning Perspectives* 4:3 (July 1972): 26–33, especially 26.

5. Ibid., 29.

6. Drawing from OEO sources, Levitan reported the following delegation of family planning grants in fiscal 1968:

Agency	Number	Percentage
Total	159	100
Planned Parenthood–World Population	63	40
Health departments	25	16
Hospitals	2	1
Other	8	5
CAA	16	38

Source: Sar A. Levitan, *The Great Society's Poor Law: A New Approach to Poverty* (Baltimore, 1969), 207–213.

7. Sar A. Levitan and Judith LaVor, "The Reluctance of Uncle Sam's Bureaucrats to Fight Poverty with 'The Pill,' " *Poverty and Human Resources Abstracts* 4:5 (September–October 1969): 28–34.

8. Joan Hoff, in her revisionist history of the Nixon administration, downplays Daniel Moynihan's role in domestic affairs, but archival evidence suggests that he played a critical role in promoting family planning in the Nixon administration. He helped draft the legislation, guided it through Congress, and then served as a presidential liaison to the Rockefeller Commission on Population Growth and the American Future. It should be noted that Hoff does not discuss family planning policy in the Nixon administration. Joan Hoff, *Nixon Reconsidered* (New York, 1994), especially 119–129. For the inner workings of the administration, see A. James Reichley, *Conservatives in the Age of Change: The Nixon and Ford Administrations* (Washington, D.C., 1989); and Rowland Evans and Robert D. Novak, *Nixon in the White House: The Frustration of Power* (New York, 1970).

9. The Population Council held two extended discussions of the encyclical and its possible effects on the administration and family planning domestically and internationally. Population Council, Minutes of Meeting of Principal Officers, August 5 and August 12, 1968, Population Council Papers (unprocessed), RA.

10. U.S. Congress, *National Party Platforms*, vol. 2 (1960–1976) (Washington, D.C., 1976), 759.

11. Although this letter is not found in the Nixon administration archives, a copy was sent to William Draper at the Population Crisis Committee, and the Population Council. Oscar Harkavy to General William H. Draper, Population Crisis Committee, January 22, 1969, Population Council Papers, RA.

12. Cass Canfield organized a political support committee, The Friends of Senator Ernest Gruening, that included Alan F. Guttmacher, George N. Lindsay, Hugh Moore, Stewart Mott, Aldoph W. Schmidt, and Paul H. Todd Jr. Cass Canfield to Hugh Moore, May 6, 1968, Moore Papers, Box 107, Princeton University.

13. Strategy for influencing the new administration is outlined in Bernard Berelson to John D. Rockefeller 3rd, December 26, 1968; and Nan Tucker McEnvoy to John D. Rockefeller 3rd, February 28, 1969, John D. Rockefeller 3rd Papers (unprocessed), RA.

14. For insights into Congress in 1968, see Donald C. Bacon, Roger A. Davidsen, and Morton Keller, eds., *Encyclopedia of the U.S. Congress* (New York, 1995), 680 (Bush), 1040 (Gruening), 1183 (Javitts), 1327 (Magnusen), and 1964 (Yarborogh). Bush's role in Congress has not been fully explored, but for a beginning Barbara Sinclair offers some

background to his congressional career in "Governing Unheroically (and Sometimes Unappetizingly): Bush and the 101st Congress," in *The Bush Presidency: First Appraisals*, ed. Bert A. Rockman and Colin Campbell (New York, 1991), 155–184.

15. Bernard Berelson, Memorandum Regarding Conversation with Carl Shultz, March 10, 1969, RG 5, RA.

16. Insight into Daniel Moynihan's role in the Nixon administration is found in Stephen Hess, "Moynihan: The Federal Executive," unpublished talk at the Woodrow Wilson International Center for Scholars, March 17, 1997, on file at the Wilson Center.

17. John D. Rockefeller 3rd to Daniel Moynihan, February 13, 1969, RG5, RA; Rockefeller to Daniel Moynihan, March 26, 1969, John D. Rockefeller 3rd Papers (unprocessed), RA.

18. John D. Rockefeller 3rd to Lee A. DuBridge, March 26, 1969, John D. Rockefeller 3rd Papers (unprocessed), RA.

19. John D. Rockefeller 3rd to Lee DuBridge, February 11, 1969, John D. Rockefeller 3rd Papers (unprocessed), RA.

20. John D. Rockefeller 3rd to Daniel Moynihan, March 26, 1969; John D. Rockefeller 3rd to the President, March 26, 1969, John D. Rockefeller 3rd Papers (unprocessed), RA.

21. Paul R. Ehrlich, *The Population Bomb* (New York, 1968). Also see Leon F. Bouvier, "Which Way Population Growth: Baby Boom or Baby Bust?" *Vital Issues* 22 (January 1973): 1–4.

22. See chapter 5 for a discussion of the growing sentiment that radical measures needed to be undertaken to control population growth in the United States.

23. John D. Rockefeller 3rd to Frank Notestein, June 30, 1969, with enclosed press release, John D. Rockefeller 3rd Papers (unprocessed), RA.

24. For a summary of the population movement at this time, see Carol T. Foreman to Bernard Berelson, October 26, 1973, Bernard Berelson Papers, Organizational File, RA.

25. Richard M. Nixon, "Special Message to Congress on Problems of Population Growth," July 18, 1969, in *Public Papers of the Presidents of the United States: Richard Nixon, 1969* (Washington, D.C., 1971), 521–530.

26. Ibid., 521–531.

27. John D. Rockefeller 3rd to Richard M. Nixon, July 18, 1969, John D. Rockefeller 3rd Papers (unprocessed), RA.

28. PL 91–572 and PL 213.

29. PL 91–572.

30. Phyllis Tilson Piotrow, *World Population Crisis: The U.S. Responds* (New York, 1973), 75, 92. Also Helen Silverberg, "State-Building, Health Policy, and the Persistence of the American Abortion Debate," *Journal of Policy History* 9:3 (1997): 1–29.

31. This bipartisan support for family planning was noted in "Government Seeks Ways to Limit Population Growth," *Congressional Quarterly* (July 12, 1970): 26: 1554–1557. Population activists, too, were impressed with the rare "unanimity" in the congressional hearings. See Richard Lincoln, "S.2108: Capital Hill Debates the Future of Population and Family Planning," *Family Planning Perspectives* 2:1 (January 1970): 6–12.

32. U.S. Senate, *Family Planning and Population Research Act (1970): Hearing Before the Subcommittee on Health of the Committee on Labor and Public Welfare*, 91st Cong., 2d sess., S. 2108 and S. 3219, December 8, 9, 1969, and February 19, 1970 (Washington, D.C., 1970), 22.

33. Ibid., 25–30.

34. Ibid., 119–141.

35. U.S. Congress, *Family Planning Services: Hearings Before the Subcommittee on*

Health and Human Welfare of the Committee on Interstate and Foreign Commerce, 91st Cong., 2d sess., HR 15159, HR 9107, HR 9109, HR 15691, HR 1123, and HR 2108, August 3, 4, 7, 1970 (Washington, D.C., 1971), 217–219. Also Lincoln, "S.2108," 6–12; and *U.S. Code: Congressional and Administrative News*, 91st Cong., 2d sess. (1970), 3: 5068–5082.

36. Silverberg, "State-Building, Health Policy, and the Persistence of the American Abortion Debate," argues that Catholic opposition significantly changed the final version of the bill. A close reading of the hearings, as well as private correspondence concerning the bill, which Silverberg did not undertake, shows that Tydings had dropped his proposal for a categorical grants program upon the request of HEW secretary Finch. Furthermore, both the Senate and House versions of the bill excluded federal support for abortions from the outset. There is no evidence, contrary to Silverberg, that the Catholic hierarchy directly influenced the bill. In 1969–1970, federal funding for abortion drew little support within Congress or the general public, and any proposal for such a measure would have jeopardized the entire bill. Finally, while Silverberg argues that proabortion groups were not well organized, she does not provide any evidence for her assertion that antiabortion groups were better organized.

37. "P.L. 91–572, Milestone U.S. Family Planning Legislation, Signed into Law," *Family Planning Perspectives* 3:1 (January 1971): 2–3. Also Silverberg, "State-Building, Health Policy, and the Persistence of the American Abortion Debate," Kristin Luker, *Dubious Conceptions: The Politics of Teenage Pregnancy* (Cambridge, 1996), 59; and Simone M. Caron, "Race, Class, and Reproduction: The Evolution of Reproductive Policy in the United States, 1800–1989" (Ph.D. diss., Clark University, 1989), 34–35.

38. John D. Rockefeller 3rd to Daniel Moynihan, August 25, 1969; John D. Rockefeller 3rd to William Dawson, October 10, 1969; William Dawson to John D. Rockefeller 3rd, October 27, 1969; and John D. Rockefeller 3rd to John Blatnick, October 3, 1969. Also Thomas B. Littlewood, *The Politics of Population Control*, John D. Rockefeller 3rd Papers (unprocessed), RA (Notre Dame, 1977).

39. Ronald Freed to John D. Rockefeller 3rd, October 1, 1969, John D. Rockefeller 3rd Papers (unprocess), RA.

40. Hugh Moore to A. W. Schmidt, December 31, 1970, Box 17, Moore Papers, Princeton University.

41. The Rockefeller Commission is discussed by Charles F. Westoff, "The Commission on Population Growth and the American Future: Origins, Operations and Aftermath," in *Sociology and Public Policy: The Case of Presidential Commissions*, ed. Mirra Komarovsky (New York, 1975), 43–60.

42. See Chapter 6 for a full discussion of the committee.

43. This was an increase of $129 million, including most significantly $30 million for project service grants, $10 million for grants to states, $30 million for research, $2 million for training, and $750,000 for information and educational materials. Jeanie I. Rosoff, Memorandum, Hugh Moore Papers, Box 17, Princeton University.

44. Joy G. Dryfoos and Frederick S. Jaffe, "Eighteen Months Later," 29–43.

45. For the erosion of the federal system during the Johnson and Nixon administrations, see Martha Derthick, "Crossing Thresholds: Federalism in the 1960s," *Journal of Policy History* 8:1 (1996): 64–81. Contrary to the view that the Nixon administration dismantled, or attempted to dismantle, federal government powers through his "creative federalism," Derthick shows that state powers were weakened in this period. In doing so, she casts a new meaning on what scholars have described as the "New Federalism" as it emerged in this period. New Federalism, as a reform idea and structure as proposed by its proponents, was a system that sought to balance federal mandates and funding with state and local interests. See Timothy Conlon, *New Federalism: Intergovernmental Reform from Nixon to Reagan* (Washington, D.C., 1988).

46. Peter Dobkin Hall, *Inventing the Nonprofit Sector and Other Essays on Philanthropy, Voluntarism, and Nonprofit Organizations* (Baltimore, 1992), 7.

47. These figures are drawn from Lester M. Salamon, *America's Nonprofit Sector: A Primer* (Baltimore, 1992), 45–46. For an excellent overview of the emergence of the modern welfare state, see Edward D. Berkowitz, *America's Welfare State: From Roosevelt to Reagan* (Baltimore, 1991).

48. The role of nonprofit institutions in the modern welfare state has only begun to be explored by scholars. An excellent starting point for understanding the new welfare state is provided by the following: Neil Gilbert, *Capitalism and the Welfare State: Dilemmas of Social Benevolence* (New Haven, Conn., 1983); Hall, *Inventing the Nonprofit Sector*; and Shelia B. Kameron and Alfred J. Kahn, *Privatization and the Welfare State* (Princeton, N.J., 1989). An important study of the nonprofit sector is Eleanor L. Brilliant, *The United Way: Dilemmas of Organized Charity* (New York, 1990). Also Steven R. Smith and Michael Lipskey, *Nonprofits for Hire: The Welfare State in the Age of Contracting* (Cambridge, 1993); Salamon, *America's Nonprofit Sector*; Lester M. Salamon and Alan J. Abramson, *The Federal Budget and the Nonprofit Sector* (Washington, D.C., 1982). Useful essays on the nonprofit sector are found in Lester M. Salamon, ed., *Beyond Privatization: The Tools of Government Action* (Washington, D.C., 1989); and W. W. Powell, ed., *The Non-Profit Sector: A Research Handbook* (New Haven, Conn., 1988).

49. Office of Economic Opportunity, *Family Planning* (Washington, D.C., March 1969), 2.

50. For a discussion of problems of family planning in this period of expansion, see Dr. Carl S. Schultz to HEW Secretary, "Constraints in the Development of Domestic Family Planning Services," July 29, 1968, Children's Bureau Records, Box 1142; and Arthur J. Less, "Family Planning, Present and Proposed Activities, FY 1968–1969" (n.d.), Children's Bureau Records, Box 1143, NA.

The problems of program delivery and appraisal of programs in eight major metropolitan cities—Atlanta, Baltimore, Cleveland, Kansas City, Los Angeles, Newark, Pittsburgh, and St. Louis—is discussed by Joy G. Dryfoos, "Planning Family Planning in Eight Metropolitan Areas," *Family Planning Perspectives* 3:1 (January 1971): 11–15.

51. Sar Levitan, *The Great Society's Poor Law* (Baltimore, 1969), 209–213.

52. Lynn C. Landman, "West Virginia's Approach to a Statewide Family Planning Program," *Family Planning Perspectives* 2:4 (October 1970): 21–24.

53. Ronald W. O'Connor, "Planning and Implementing a Large-Scale Family Planning Program in Georgia," *American Journal of Public Health* 60 (January 1970): 78–86. Also, on Georgia family planning, specifically a discussion of contraceptive methods, see Hazel A. Hutchenson and Nicholas H. Wright, "Georgia's Family Planning Program," *American Journal of Nursing* 68:2 (February 1968): 332–335.

54. U.S. Congress, *Treasury Department Report on Philanthropy*, House Committee on Ways and Means, 8901, February 2, 1965 (Washington, D.C., 1965).

55. John Ensor Harr and Peter J. Johnson, *The Rockefeller Conscience: An American Family in Public and Private* (New York, 1991), 289–300; and Waldemar Nielson, *The Big Foundations* (New York, 1972).

56. Ford Foundation, "The Foundation's Strategy for Work on Population," Confidential Memorandum, June 1977, FA.

57. Ford Foundation, "Policy Paper on Population," March 28/29, 1963, FA.

58. Gordon W. Perkins and David Radell, *Current Status of Family Planning Programs in the United States* (New York, 1966).

59. Ford Foundation, "Ford Foundation's Activities in Population," August 1968, Oscar Harkavy files, FA.

60. Joseph D. Beasley, Ralph F. Frankowski, and C. Morton Hawkins, "The Orleans Parish Family Planning Demonstration Program: A Description of the First

Year," *Milbank Memorial Fund Quarterly* 47 (July 1969): 225–253; "The United States: The New Orleans Parish Family Planning Demonstration Program," *Studies in Family Planning* 25 (December 1967): 5–9; and "Family Planning Campaign—The Louisiana Story," *U.S. News and World Report*, July 28, 1969, 55–57.

61. For a fascinating account of Beasley and the Louisiana family planning program, see Martha C. Ward, *Poor Women, Powerful Men: America's Great Experiment in Family Planning* (Boulder, Colo., 1986). This discussion draws heavily from Ward's fine account of the Louisiana family planning program. Also Littlewood, *The Politics of Population Control*, 88.

62. Ford Foundation, "Ford Foundation's Activities in Population," August 1968, Harkavy files; FA. "Tulane University; Partial Support of a Family Planning Demonstration Program for New Orleans and State of Louisiana," March 30, 1970, RG 6700140 (microfilm), FA. Also U.S. Senate, *Family Planning and Population Research, 1970* (Washington, D.C., 1970), 66–70.

63. David Bell to McGeorge Bundy, "Support to Family Planning Programs: Demonstration of New Orleans and Louisiana Family Planning," June 32, 1972, FA.

64. Ward, *Poor Women*, 73.

65. Ibid., 82–83.

66. Ibid., 91–97, quotation on 93.

67. Ford Foundation, "Planned Parenthood of New York City, Inc.," January 28, 1968, PPNYC file, 1163, FA.

68. The proposal illustrates the various personnel needs of family planning programs. The request called for the hiring of six technical assistant staff positions, a senior technical consultant, two training specialists, a community education technician, and a consultant to develop a training curriculum.

69. "Planned Parenthood of New York City, January 28, 1968," PPNYC File, RG 68000770, (microfilm), FA.

70. Planned Parenthood of New York City, "Family Planning in New York City: Recommendations for Action," *Family Planning Perspectives* 2:4 (October 1970): 25.

71. Davidson R. Gwatkin to Oscar Harkavy, April 30, 1968, PPNYC File, RG 68000770 (microfilm), FA.

72. Ford Foundation, Planned Parenthood Association of Maryland, Inc. Supplemental Grant for an Education and Contraceptive Service Program for Teenagers in Cooperation with Baltimore Urban League and Johns Hopkins University, February 28, 1971, RG 6800200 (microfilm), FA.

73. Ibid.

74. Robert S. Wickham to Oscar Harkavy, Evaluation of Grant, 680–0200, August 29, 1975, FA.

75. Department of Health, Education, and Welfare, *Child Health and Human Development: Research Progress. A Report to the National Institute of Child Health and Human Development* (Washington, D.C., 1972), 42–44; and Richard Albert Rielly, "Family Planning Service Programs: An Operation Analysis of the City of St. Louis, Missouri" (Ph.D. diss., School of Medicine, Washington University, 1972).

76. U.S. Department of Health, Education, and Welfare, *Family Planning Service Programs: An Operational Analysis* (Washington, D.C., 1970), 73. Also Howard C. Taylor, "A Family Planning Program Related to Maternity Service," *American Journal of Obstetrics and Gynecology* 44 (July 1966): 726–731.

77. Population Council, "Summary of Meeting to Consider the Proposal for Family Planning via Medical Schools," April 5, 1968; "Minutes of June 28th Meeting at the University Club to Review a Proposal to Bring Family Planning to the Urban Poor via the Medical Schools," June 28, 1967; and "Summary of Meeting to Consider the Proposal of Family Planning," August 18, 1968, OEO-Postpartum Program Files, Population Council Papers (unprocessed), RA.

78. Population Council, "Family Planning via Medical Schools: A Proposal Prepared by the Population Council," November 1968, in OEO-Postpartum Program Files, Population Council Papers (unprocessed), RA.

79. Ibid.

80. Philip R. Lee to Bernard Berelson, June 26, 1968; "Summary of Meeting to Consider the Proposal on Family Planning Via the Medical Schools," May 28, 1968; Bernard Berelson to Philip Lee, May 29, 1968; and Bernard Berelson to Files: Telephone Conversation with Katherine Oettinger, April 16, 1968; OEO-Postpartum Program Population Council Papers (unprocessed), RA.

81. Population Council, "Summary of Meeting to Consider the Proposal on Family Planning Via the Medical Schools," May 28, 1968; Bernard Berelson to Philip R. Lee, May 29, 1968; Bernard Berelson to Files, Telephone Conversation with Katherine Oettinger, April 15, 1968; OEO-Postpartum Program File, Population Council Papers (unprocessed), RA.

82. Bernard Berelson to Files, Telephone Conversation with Katherine Oettinger, April 15, 1968, OEO-Postpartum Program File, Population Council Papers, RA.

83. George Contis to Frank Shubeck, November 21, 1969; and Cliff Peace to Joel Monague, "Impasse on OEO Program," December 1, 1970, OEO-Postpartum Program File, Population Council Papers (unprocessed), RA.

84. WBW to BB, February 24, 1970, Population Council Papers (unprocessed), RA.

85. Westinghouse Learning Corporation, "The Office of Economic Opportunity, Population Council, Medical Schools, Family Programs Assessment, Summary Report, 1970," in OEO/Postpartum Program File, Population Council Papers (unprocessed), RA.

86. United Black Front, *An Analysis of Our Community Trinity: Health, Education and Labor. As It Affects Us, with an Emphasis on Health and Education* (n.d., 1970?), copy in OEO-Postpartum File, Population Council Papers (unprocessed), RA.

87. Population Council, Progress Report, June 15, 1969 to December 31, 1969, Population Council Papers, RA.

88. Hugh B. Davis, "Transcript of Speech," (1971), OEO-Postpartum Files, Population Council Papers (unprocessed), RA.

89. Bernard Berelson to Donald Rumsfield, November 9, 1970, Population Council/OEO files, Population Council Papers (unprocessed), RA.

90. Memorandum (WBW to Bernard Berelson), February 24, 1970, OEO-Postpartum Program File, Population Council Papers (unprocessed), RA.

Chapter 4

1. For an earlier example of the feminist critique of population control and the failure of family planners to place the use of "the pill" in a larger perspective of women's health, see Barbara Seaman, *The Doctor's Case Against the Pill* (Alameda, Calif., 1969). For later examples of feminist critiques of population control, see Claudia Dreifus, *Seizing Our Bodies: The Politics of Women's Health* (New York, 1977); and Betsy Hartmann, *Reproduction Rights and Wrongs: The Global Politics of Population* (New York, 1987). In her history of the birth control movement, Linda Gordon (*Woman's Body, Woman's Right: Birth Control in America* [New York, 1976]) offers a nuanced, dialectical feminist/Marxist analysis that sharply differentiates birth control as a woman's right from contraceptives as an instrument of birth control. Gordon later developed her critique of Malthusianism and birth control in Linda Gordon, "Malthusianism, Socialism, and Feminism in the United States," *Journal of European Ideas* 4:2 (1983): 203–214. Also of interest is a feminist critique of oral contraceptives in Selig Greenberg, "The Pill," *The Progressive* 33 (February 1969): 34–37.

An important reply to the feminist critique of population control is Ruth Dixon-Mueller, *Population Policy and Women's Rights: Transforming Reproductive Choice* (Westport, Conn., 1993).

2. Garry Wills, "Catholics and Population," *National Review*, July 27, 1965, 643–644; Garry Wills, "Catholics and Population: A Defense," *National Review*, October 19, 1965, 993–994; and William F. Buckley Jr., "The Birth Rate," *National Review*, March 23, 1965, 231. Also, Patrick Allitt, *Catholic Intellectuals and Conservatives in America, 1950–1985* (Ithaca, N.Y., 1993), 172.

3. John Ford, S.J., "What Would Be the Doctrinal and Pastoral Tendencies in This Country?" (1965), National Catholic Welfare Conference papers (NCWC), Box 86, Catholic University of America Archives, Washington, D.C. (hereafter NCWC).

4. John Rock, *The Time Has Come: A Catholic Doctor's Proposal to End the Battle over Birth Control* (Ithaca, N.Y., 1963).

5. Buckley, "The Birth Rate," 231.

6. For the history of contraception, see John M. Riddle, *Contraception and Abortion from the Ancient World to the Renaissance* (Cambridge, Mass. 1992). Also Norman E. Himes, *Medical History of Contraception* (Baltimore, 1936); Angus McLaren, *Birth Control in Nineteenth-Century England* (New York, 1978), and Peter Fryer, *The Birth Controllers* (London, 1965). Kristin Luker emphasizes the "controversial" and changing nature of contraception and abortion within Roman Catholic doctrine in *Abortion and the Politics of Motherhood* (Berkeley, 1984), 3–39. While showing that the Roman Catholic position on these matters underwent change, John T. Noonan Jr. suggests greater theological consistency in his work, including *Contraception: A History of Its Treatment by the Catholic Theologians and Canonists* (Cambridge, Mass., 1965), and "Contraception," *New Catholic Encyclopedia*, vol. 6 (New York, 1967), 271–275. Also see John T. Noonan Jr., "An Almost Absolute Value in History," in *The Morality of Abortion: Legal and Historical Perspectives*, ed. John T. Noonan Jr. (Cambridge, 1978); and John Connery, *Abortion: The Development of the Roman Catholic Perspective* (Chicago, 1977). Also useful is Louis Dupre, *Contraception and Catholics* (Baltimore, 1964); and J. C. Ford and G. A. Kelly, *Contemporary Moral Theology*, vols. 1–2, (Westminster, Md., 1958–1963). An important discussion of contemporary contraceptive practices with a comparative framework is found in Marilyn Jane Field, *The Comparative Politics of Birth Control: Determinants of Policy Variation and Change in the Developed Nations* (New York, 1983).

7. This discussion of Catholic attitudes to the family and quotations are drawn from Jeffrey M. Burns, *American Catholics and the Family Crisis, 1930–1962: An Ideological and Organizational Response* (New York, 1988).

8. John C. Ford and George Kelly, *Contemporary Moral Theology*, vol. II, *Marriage Questions* (Westminster, Md., 1963); and John L. Thomas, *Marriage and Rhythm* (Westminster, Md., 1958). Also, for an excellent summary of the Catholic position on the rhythm method, see John L. Thomas, "Rhythm (Period Abstinence)," in *New Catholic Encyclopedia* (New York, 1967), 464–466.

9. Quoted in Philip Gleason, *Speaking of Diversity: Language and Ethnicity in Twentieth-Century America* (Baltimore, 1992), 209.

10. For a discussion of Seldes's *Catholic Crisis* (New York, 1939), see Gleason, *Speaking of Diversity*, 209. Also of interest, however, is Seldes's earlier *You Can't Print That! The Truth Behind the News* (Garden City, N.Y., 1929), which associated Roman Catholicism with both fascism and communism.

11. For a discussion of Catholics' relationship to liberalism, see Philip Gleason, "American Catholics and Liberalism, 1789–1960," in *Catholicism and Liberalism: Contributions to American Public Philosophy*, ed. R. Bruce Douglass and David Hollenbach (Cambridge, Mass. 1994), 45–75. Also useful on Catholics and pluralism is Gleason, *Speaking of Diversity*, especially 207–231. For modernism, see R. Scott Appleby, "*Church*

and Age Unite!" The Modernist Impulse in American Catholicism (Notre Dame, Ind., 1991). A highly readable biography of one of the leading Americanists is found in Marvin R. O'Connell, *John Ireland and the American Catholic Church* (St. Paul, Minn., 1988). Also worth reading are Thomas T. McAvoy's *The Great Crisis in American Catholic History, 1895–1900* (Chicago, 1957); and David P. Killen, "Americanism Revisited: John Spalding and *Testem Benevolentiae*," *Harvard Theological Review* 66 (October 1973): 413–454.

Any full understanding of the American Catholic Church and its perception of itself in a pluralistic society must begin with John Courtney Murray, most notably *We Hold These Truths* (New York, 1960), as well as John Courtney Murray, *Religious Liberty: Catholic Struggles with Pluralism* (Louisville, Ky., 1993), and *Bridging the Sacred and the Secular* (Washington, D.C., 1994). Also see Donald E. Pelotte, *John Courtney Murray: Theologian in Conflict* (New York, 1976); Thomas P. Ferguson, *Catholic and American: The Political Theology of John Courtney Murray* (Kansas City, Mo., 1993); and J. Leon Hooper's more abstract book, *The Ethics of Discourse: The Social Philosophy of John Courtney Murray* (Washington, D.C., 1986). A useful and readable survey of church-state relations is found in Alec R. Vidler, *The Church in an Age of Revolution: 1789 to the Present Day* (London, 1971). Also, drawing upon the work of Murray, the Jesuit theologian Francis Canavan, S.J., examined the relationship between law and morals, especially in regard to birth control, euthanasia, and homosexuality, in "Law and Morals in a Pluralistic Society," *Catholic Mind*, April 1966, 49–55.

Still, in some ways, John Courtney Murray's writings provided little direct guidance on the abortion issue. Because he believed that legalized abortion could not occur in America, he did not directly discuss this issue and its ramifications for a pluralistic society.

12. It is worth noting that Father Ryan was strongly opposed to artificial birth control, however. For Ryan's thought on social justice, see F. L. Broderick, *Right Reverend New Dealer: John A. Ryan* (New York, 1963). John A. Ryan's thought is best articulated in John A. Ryan and Francis J. Boland, *Catholic Principles of Politics* (New York, 1940). Also, on progressive Catholicism, see Robert D. Cross, *The Emergence of Liberal Catholicism in America* (reprint, New York, 1997); Aaron Abell, *American Catholicism and Social Action: A Search for Social Justice* (Notre Dame, Ind., 1960); and David O'Brien, *American Catholics and Social Reform: The New Deal Years* (Oxford, 1968). Elizabeth McKeown discusses the National Catholic Welfare Conference in *War and Welfare: American Catholics and World War I* (New York, 1988).

13. Bishops of the United States, "Explosion or Backfire" (1959), Box 86, NCWC. Also see "Digest of Memorandum," January 28, 1958, which expressed concern that "birth control advocates are carrying on an unremitting effort to popularize their cause" Box 85, NCWC.

14. See William J. Gibbons, S.J., *Population Resources and the Future* (New York, 1961); Thomas K. Burch, "Facts and Fallacies About Population Growth," *Catholic World*, July 1960; and Joseph Gremillion, "Meeting Expanding Food Needs," *Catholic World*, July 1960.

15. Most Reverend Egidio Vagnozzi to Msgr. Paul Tanner, September 23, 1961; Rev. Paul Tanner to Most Rev. Egidio Vagnozzi, September 29, 1961; and Harmon Burns Jr. to Msgr. P. Tanner, September 27, 1961, Box 86, NCWC .

16. The initial NIH report, "Research on Birth and Population Control," was suppressed at the urging of the bishops, and a revised report, "A Survey of Research in Reproduction as Related to Population Control," was written in consultation with Father John C. Knott. The revised report did not recommend a specific allocation of funds for future projects as the original had proposed. On the revision of the NIH report, see David Broder, "Report Languishes: Fertility Study Points Up Delicate

Policy Question," *Washington Star*, April 25, 1962. The bishops' discussion of this report is found in Francis Hurley to Paul Tanner, July 9, 1962; and Hurley to Tanner, December 7, 1962, Box 93, NCWC. The Fulbright amendment to the Foreign Assistance Act was modified in conference and limited funding only to research. For the Fulbright amendment, see William Consedine to Msg. Paul Tanner, October 4, 1963; and Paul Tanner to Senator William Fulbright, October 4, 1963, Box 86, NCWC.

17. Mr. William Consedine to Monsignor Francis Hurley, March 19, 1964, Box 86, NCWC. For an overview of Catholic involvement in American politics, see Mary T. Hanna, *Catholics and American Politics* (Cambridge, Mass., 1979). A traditionalist critique of the American Catholic Church and birth control, as well as liberal culture is found in E. Michael Jones, *John Cardinal Krol and the Cultural Revolution* (South Bend, Indiana 1995), especially 227–301.

18. David J. Garrow, *Liberty and Sexuality: The Right to Privacy and the Making of Roe v. Wade* (New York, 1994), 196–269.

19. Indeed, earlier, when Baird was arrested for distributing contraceptives in Hempstead, New York, in 1965 (later dismissed), William Buckley, who was running as the Conservative party candidate for mayor against John Lindsay, wrote a letter to Baird supporting his activities. Ibid., 373–374, 410, 457, 517–520.

20. See, for example, Albert C. Saunders, "Birth Control: The Issue and the Reality," in *Religion and the Public Order*, ed. Donald A. Giannella (New York, 1965), 204–236.

21. Francis Hurley to Paul Tanner, January 13, 1965; and C. Joseph Nuesse to Paul Tanner, January 14, 1965, Box 86, NCWC.

22. Monsignor Francis T. Hurley to Archbishop O'Boyle, August 14, 1965, Box 93, NCWC.

23. "Testimony of William B. Ball, General Counsel of the Pennsylvania Catholic Welfare Committee Before the Subcommittee on Foreign Aid Expenditures of the Senate Government Operations Committee," Press release, August 24, 1965, Box 93, NCWC.

24. Harmon Burns to William Consedine, August 25, 1965, Box 93, NCWC; also Harmon Burns to William Consedine, September 11, 1965, Box 86, NCWC.

25. Robert B. Fleming to William B. Ball, September 23, 1965, Box 86, NCWC.

26. William B. Ball, NCWC Policy on Government Birth Control, November 8, 1965, Box 93, NCWC.

27. William Consedine to files, December 15, 1965, Box 94, NCWC; and William Ball to Patrick O'Boyle, December 14, 1965, Box 95, NCWC.

For other meetings with Shriver and discussions within the NCWC, see Paul Tanner to Most Rev. Patrick O'Boyle, March 11, 1965, Box 86, NCWC; Francis Hurley to Paul Tanner, August 23, 1965, Box 93, NCWC; and Memorandum, "Sargent Shriver, Economic Opportunity Act of 1964, and Birth Control," February 26, 1965, Box 95, NCWC.

28. Russell Kirk to Bill Ball, December 7, 1965, Box 93, NCWC.

29. Minutes, Informal Minutes of NCWC Coordinating Committee on Economic Opportunity, February 4, 1965, Box 98, NCWC.

30. Paul Connolly to Patrick A. O'Boyle, March 8, 1965, Box 93, NCWC.

31. Press Clipping, Rowland Evans and Robert Novak, "Inside Report: Birth Control Battle," November 12, 1965, Box 86, NCWC. Also "A Curious View," *Washington Evening Star*, November 17, 1965, Box 86, NCWC.

32. Francis Hurley to Paul Tanner, November 17, 1965, Box 86, NCWC.

33. Draft Statement, "Family Planning and Public Policy," March 19, 1965, Box 95, NCWC.

34. Birth Control Notes, November 3, 1966, Box 93, NCWC.

35. James Francis Cardinal McIntyre to Archbishop O'Boyle, November 30, 1965, Box 93, NCWC.

36. Similarly, Richard A. McCormick, S.J., another leading theologian, told the bishops that he felt the statement did not make very clear the principles that allowed the church to support the expenditures of public funds for something the church held immoral. The idea of civil religious division as constituting a reason for exception, as maintained in the draft, appeared to him as hypocritical. Francis J. Connell at Holy Redeemer College wondered how much weight should be given to majority opinion. For example, he noted, "Many people in the South today disagree with us on the matter of equality for Negroes. Our protests are certainly leading to civil division in our country, but ... are we going to give up without a struggle and say that we don't wish to impose our views on those who differ from us?" Still, he could not come up with a reasonable principle for the church condemning artificial contraception while at the same time, in effect, accepting federally supported family planning. John Courtney Murray to Francis Hurley, March 27, 1965, Box 95, NCWC; Richard A. McCormick, S.J., to Francis Hurley, March 27, 1965, Box 95, NCWC; and Francis J. Connell to Msgr. Hurley, March 23, 1965, Box 95, NCWC. Also, see Francis Canavan, S.J., to Msgr. Hurley, March 25, 1965, Box 95; Richard McCormick to Francis Hurley, March 25, 1965, Box 95, NCWC.

37. The notable exception, however, was Father Robert F. Drinan, professor at Boston College School of Law, who was to run successfully for Congress a few years later. He argued that the government was justified in "adopting a role of advocacy as to the necessity of family planning and family limitation." Robert F. Drinan to Francis Hurley, March 24, 1965, Box 95, NCWC. A controversial account of Drinan's later role on the abortion issue is found in James Hitchcock, "The Strange Political Career of Father Drinan," *Catholic World Report*, July 1996, 38–45.

38. Laurence Cardinal Shehan to Archbishop O'Boyle, September 3, 1965, Box 86, NCWC; Archbishop O'Boyle to Egidio Vagnozzi, September 4, 1965, Box 86, NCWC; and Francis Hurley to Rev. Geno Baroni, May 14, 1965, Box 95, NCWC.

39. Francis Hurley to James Norris, May 20, 1965, Box 95, NCWC.

40. Most Reverend Patrick A. O'Boyle, "Birth Control and Public Policy," August 29, 1965, Box 86, NCWC. E. Michael Jones, *John Cardinal Krol* is especially useful in understanding the Catholic hierarchy at this point, especially 280–281.

41. Francis Hurley to Msgr. John E. Molan, December 7, 1965, Box 93, NCWC.

42. Francis Hurley to Most Rev. William E. Cousins, May 26, 1965, Box 99, NCWC; Thomas D. Hinton to Theodore Berry, June 2, 1965, Box 93, NCWC; Thomas D. Hinton to Most Rev. William E. Cousins, June 5, 1965, Box 93, NCWC; Dr. John J. Breen to Archbishop William Cousins, May 18, 1965, Box 93, NCWC.

43. "Racial Motive Is Discounted in Birth Control," *Philadelphia Inquirer*, January 7, 1966, Box 93, NCWC.

44. Press Release, Catholic Welfare Bureau, "Family Planning Project Is Killed," March 3, 1966, Box 93, NCWC.

45. William B. Ball, Memorandum of Law and Authorization Under the Economic Opportunity Act for Expenditure of Public Funds to Support Birth Control Programs, February 4, 1966, Box 93, NCWC. Also William Consedine to Donald M. Baker, February 4, 1966, Box 93, NCWC.

46. Most Rev. Walter W. Curtis to Paul Tanner, February 10, 1966, Box 93, NCWC.

47. NCWC, Minutes of the Staff Meeting, February 4, 1966, Box 93, NCWC.

48. "Conservative to Head Birth Study," *Boston Morning Globe*, March 3, 1966; "Two Americans on Birth Control Study Commission," *New London*, March 7, 1966; clippings in Barrett papers, ND.

268 *Notes*

49. Quoted in Robert Blair Kaiser, *The Politics of Sex and Religion: A Case History in the Development of Doctrine, 1962–1984* (Kansas City, Mo., 1985), 80.

50. Quoted in Ibid., 163.

51. Robert G. Hoyt, *The Birth Control Debate* (Kansas City, Mo., 1968). Also Kaiser, *The Politics of Sex and Religion*, 182.

52. The Curran issue is discussed by Philip Gleason, *Contending with Modernity: Catholic Higher Education in the Twentieth Century* (New York, 1995), 312–313. For a critical perspective on the Curran controversy, see George A. Kelly, *The Battle for the American Church* (Garden City, N.Y., 1979), 57–99.

53. The encyclical, *Humanae Vitae*, is reprinted in full in *Catholic Almanac* (New York, 1969), 97–105.

54. "The Catholic Church and Birth Control," *U.S. News and World Report*, August 12, 1968, 38–39.

55. Hugh Moore to Ellsworth, August 5, 1968, Hugh Moore Papers, Box 17, Princeton University.

56. Father John O'Brien to Hugh Moore, September 10, 1968; Hugh Moore to Father John O'Brien, September 5, 1968; Harold Bostrom to Hugh Moore, August 5, 1968; Harold Bostrom to Hugh Moore, September 12, 1968; and Harold Bostrom to Hugh Moore, July 30, 1968; Hugh Moore Papers, Box 17, Princeton University.

57. John T. Noonan Jr. took a leading role in articulating the theological argument against the church's position on artificial birth control, even before the *Humanae Vitae* was issued. See "Authority, Usury and Contraception," *Cross Currents* 16 (Winter 1966): 71–75. Also Noonan, "Natural Law, the Teaching of the Church and Contraception," *American Journal of Jurisprudence* 25 (1980): 16–37. *Humanae Vitae* was defended in John C. Ford, S.J., and Germain Griez, "Contraception and the Infallibility of the Ordinary Magisterium," *Theological Studies* 39 (1978): 258–312. For a response to Noonan, see Joseph Boyle, "Human Action, Natural Rhythms, and Contraception: A Response to Noonan," *American Journal of Jurisprudence* 26 (1981): 32–46.

58. "Catholic Church Moves Toward Biggest Crisis in 400 Years," *U.S. News and World Report*, September 30, 1968, 66–67.

59. One survey conducted by University of Notre Dame sociologist Donald Barrett reported that almost half of the Catholic diocesan priests in the United States disagreed with the encyclical; see "U.S. Priests Split over Papal Edict," *Austin Statesman*, October 8, 1965, in Hugh Moore Papers, Box 17, Princeton University. Reaction to the encyclical is summarized in "Encyclical Comments and Reactions," *Catholic Almanac* (New York, 1969), 107–119. Also Jay Dolan, *The American Catholic Experience: A History from Colonial Times to the Present* (Garden City, N.Y., 1985), 434–436; Thomas W. Spaulding, *The Premier See: A History of the Archdiocese of Baltimore, 1789–1989* (Baltimore, 1979), 462; C. Joseph Nuesse, *The Catholic University of America: A Centennial History* (Washington, D.C., 1990), 401–16; and George A. Kelly, *The Battle for the American Church* (Garden City, N.Y., 1979); Daniel Callahan, ed., *The Catholic Case for Contraception* (New York, 1969); F. V. Joannes, ed., *The Bitter Pill: Worldwide Reaction to the Encyclical* Humanae Vitae (Philadelphia, 1970); and Norman St. John–Stevas, *The Agonizing Choice: Birth Control, Religion, and the Law* (Bloomington, Ind., 1971). Alan Guttmacher contrasted the Protestant views of contraception in *Birth Control and Love: The Complete Guide to Contraception* (New York, 1969).

60. Andrew M. Greeley, *Priest in the United States: Reflections on a Survey* (Garden City, N.Y., 1973), 193; Greeley, *The Catholic Myth: The Behavior and Beliefs of American Catholics* (New York, 1990). Also Richard A. Schoenherr and Lawrence A. Young, *Full Pews and Empty Altars: Demographics of the Priest Shortage in the United States Catholic Dioceses* (Madison, Wis., 1993); Peter McDonough, *Men Astutely Trained: A History of the Jesuits in the American Century* (New York, 1992); and Kelly, *Battle for the American Church*, 236.

61. Charles F. Westoff and Elise F. Jones, "The Secularization of U.S. Catholic Birth Control Practices," *Family Planning Perspectives* 9:5 (September/October 1977): 203–207.

62. Gleason, *Confronting Modernity*, 313. Also Charles E. Curran et al., *Dissent in and for the Church: Theologians and* Humanae Vitae (New York, 1969); John F. Hunt and Terrence R. Connelly, *The Responsibility of Dissent: The Church and Academic Freedom* (New York, 1969); and Janet E. Smith, Humanae Vitae: *A Generation Later* (Washington, D.C., 1991).

63. For an excellent study of the history of abortion in the United States, see James C. Mohr, *Abortion in America: The Origins of National Policy, 1800–1900* (New York, 1978); also Leslie Reagan, relying heavily on court records in Illinois, provides a detailed account of the enforcement of abortion laws in her *When Abortion Was Against the Law: Women, Medicine and the Law, 1867–1973* (Berkeley, 1996). Reagan maintains that most abortions remained a relatively safe operation performed by doctors in clinical settings until the late 1950s, when they were driven underground by the enforcement of state antiabortion laws.

64. Suzanne Staggenborg, *The Pro-Choice Movement: Organization and Activism in the Abortion Conflict* (New York, 1991). The following discussion of the pro-choice movement draws from this study, as well as from Garrow, *Liberty and Sexuality*. It is worth noting that Garrow's exhaustive account of the legal struggle over abortion discounts the important role played by population activists within the proabortion movement, especially on the state level. Staggenborg describes more fully the politics of the movement.

65. Reagan, *When Abortion Was Against the Law*, 5–6. This discussion of abortion law and practice before 1960 is drawn from Reagan's provocative research.

66. Ibid., 23–24.

67. Ibid., 133–147.

68. Leslie Reagan, in her well-researched study of abortion practices before *Roe*, argues that this repression should be attributed to the "far-reaching effects of 'McCarthyism.'" She maintains, "The state's surveillance of abortion in this period is another aspect of the political and cultural attack on critical thought and behavior. McCarthyism was devoted not only to eradicating the Communist Party, but to destroying the labor, peace, and interracial movements." Given that McCarthy, although a Catholic, did not make abortion a focal point of his politics, it appears specious to accuse anticommunism or McCarthyism of directly affecting how local hospitals enforced guidelines or how local prosecutors, often looking for political headlines, operated on the local level. This tendency to impugn McCarthyism for every perceived and actual ill in the 1950s substitutes rhetoric for historical analysis. Furthermore, Reagan shows that this repression of legalized abortion began during the Second World War, well before Joseph McCarthy had emerged as a leading political figure or before the anticommunist crusade. How McCarthyism, therefore, should considered the cause of this repressive climate remains a historical puzzle in her analysis. Surely, the conservatism of the 1950s must have contributed to the backlash against legalized abortion, but the 1940s were not a conservative decade. Promotion of maternity and a concern with the breakup of the family, created by the divorce, war, and perceived juvenile delinquency, occurred during the war, especially after 1943. How these anxieties were linked to abortion in explicit ways needs fuller historical analysis. Ibid. 163, 193–215.

69. Staggenborg, *The Pro-Choice Movement*, 13–37; and Marvin Olasky, "Engineering Social Change: Triumphs of Abortion Public Relations from the Thirties Through the Sixties," *Public Relations Quarterly* 33 (1988): 17–21.

70. Sherri Finkbine, "The Lesser of Two Evils," in *The Case for Legalized Abortion Now*, ed. Alan Guttmacher (Berkeley, 1967), 12–25; Raymond Tatalovich and Byron W. Daynes, *The Politics of Abortion* (New York, 1981), 45–46.

71. The early history of the abortion reform/repeal movement is discussed James C.

Mohr, *Abortion in America: The Origins and Evolution of National Policy* (New York, 1978); Lawrence Lader, *Abortion II: Making the Revolution* (Boston, 1973); Malcome Potts, Peter Diggory, and John Peel, *Abortion* (Cambridge, Mass., 1977); and Raymond Tatalovich and Byron W. Daynes, *The Politics of Abortion: A Study of Community Conflict in Public Policy Making* (New York, 1981).

72. These states were Arkansas, California, Colorado, Delaware, Florida, Georgia, Kansas, Maryland, Mississippi, North Carolina, New Mexico, Oregon, South Carolina, and Virigina. Tatalovich and Daynes, *The Politics of Abortion*, 24.

73. Quoted in David Garrow, *Liberty and Sexuality*, 104.

74. Ibid., 306.

75. Lader had worked for the Hugh Moore Fund in the 1960s. See Hugh Moore to Robert Willison, September 1, 1972, Hugh Moore Papers, Box 17, Princeton University.

76. Staggenborg, *The Pro-Choice Movement*, 18–21; and for a more detailed account of NARAL activities, Garrow, *Liberty and Sexuality*, 335–338. Lawrence Lader provides a personal perspective of these early activities in his *Abortion II*.

77. Gordon, *Woman's Body, Woman's Right*; Ellen Chesler, *Woman of Valor: Margaret Sanger and the Birth Control Movement in America* (New York, 1992); David M. Kennedy, *Birth Control in America: The Career of Margaret Sanger* (New Haven, Conn., 1970); James Reed, *The Birth Control Movement and American Society: From Private Vice to Public Virtue* (Princeton, N.J., 1983); and Garrow, *Liberty and Sexuality*; and Carole R. McCann, *Birth Control Politics in the United States, 1916–1945* (Ithaca, N.Y., 1984).

78. Lader, *Abortion II*, 37; Garrow, *Liberty and Sexuality*, 343–344. Also, for a fascinating account of this fight, see Flora Davis, *Moving the Mountain* (New York, 1991), 52–59, 66–68. Also Maren L. Carden, *The New Feminist Movement* (New York, 1974), 104–135; Jo Freeman, *The Politics of Women's Liberation* (New York, 1975), 71–102; Barbara S. Rothman, *Woman's Proper Place* (New York, 1978), 244–246; Leila Rupp and Verta Taylor, *Survival in the Doldrums* (New York, 1983), 179–186; and Winifred S. Wandersee, *On the Move* (Boston, 1988), 36–55.

79. Staggenborg, *The Pro-Choice Movement*, 41–42. Especially useful is Judith Hole and Ellen Levine, *Rebirth of Feminism* (New York, 1971). Also Ellen Willis, *Up from Radicalism* (New York, 1971), especially 117–118. For radical feminism, although this history tends toward the doctrinal, see Alice Echols, *Daring to Be Bad: Radical Feminism in America, 1967–1975* (Minneapolis, Minn., 1989).

80. A good study of the movement to reform abortion law in Hawaii is found in Patricia G. Steinhoff and Milton Diamond, *Abortion Politics: The Hawaii Experience* (Honolulu, 1977).

81. Andrew H. Merton, *Enemies of Choice: The Right to Life Movement and Its Threat to Abortion* (Boston, 1981), 51–58.

82. Barbara Hinkson Craig and David M. O'Brien, *Abortion and American Politics* (Chatham, N.J., 1993), 73–75.

83. For a succinct history of the antiabortion movement, see Keith Cassidy, "The Right to Life Movement," in *The Politics of Abortion and Birth Control in Historical Perspective*, ed. Donald T. Critchlow (University Park, Pa., 1996), 128–159. The following discussion on the antiabortion movement relies heavily on Cassidy, but Michael Cuneo (*Catholics Against the Church: Anti-Abortion Protest in Toronto, 1969–1985* [Toronto, 1989]) provides many insights into the movement. For two journalistic accounts of the movement, see Merton, *Enemies of Choice*; and Connie Paige, *The Right to Lifers: Who They Are, How They Operate, Where They Get Their Money* (New York, 1983). There is a developing monographic literature on the antiabortion movement; see James Kelly, "Seeking a Sociologically Correct Name for Abortion Opponents," in *Abortion Politics in the United States and Canada* (Westport, Conn., 1994), 14–40; James R. Kelly,

"Beyond the Stereotypes: Interviews with Right-to-Life-Pioneers," *Commonweal*, November 20, 1981, 654–659; Kelly, "Toward Complexity: The Right to Life Movement," *Research in the Social Scientific Study of Religion* 1 (1989): 83–107; Timothy A. Byrnes and Mary C. Segers, eds., *The Catholic Church and the Politics of Abortion: A View from the States* (Boulder, Colo., 1992); Amy Fried, "Abortion Politics as Symbolic Politics: An Investigation into Belief Systems," *Social Science Quarterly* 69 (1988): 137–154; and Mary Jo Neitz, "Family, State, and God: Ideologies of the Right-to-Life Movement," *Sociological Analysis* 42 (1981): 265–276. Useful on abortion issues in state politics, especially New York, is Robert J. Spitzer, *The Right to Life Movement and Third Party Politics* (Westport, Conn., 1987). Also useful is Faye D. Ginsburg, *Contested Lives: The Abortion Debate in an American Community* (Berkeley, 1989), especially 23–76. James Davison Hunter, *Before the Shooting Begins: Searching for Democracy in America's Culture War* (New York, 1994), places the abortion debate in a larger context of cultural polarization.

84. Merton, *Enemies of Choice*, 43–47.

85. Paige, *The Right to Lifers*, 58–60.

86. These "progressive" antiabortionists are discussed in ibid., 64–70.

87. Katherine Rahl, a Planned Parenthood activist, attended the third annual convention of the Right to Life Committee and reported to David Lelewer, John D. Rockefeller 3rd's associate, that Fred Mecklenburg in his keynote address, "re-affirmed his position as a Planned Parenthood physician." Rahl reported that Mecklenburg was concerned with problems of distribution of family planning services—getting individual families to regulate family size and accept sexual responsibility. He reminded the right-to-life people that they should not object to Dr. Beasley's work. Katherine Rahl, "Report on Third Annual National Right to Life Committee Meeting, Philadelphia, Pa., June 16–18, 1972" (1972), David Lelewer Papers, Box 1, RA.

88. Ginsburg, *Contested Lives*, 44; and Peter Leahy, "The Anti-Abortion Movement: Testing a Theory of the Rise and Fall of Social Movements" (Ph.D. diss., Syracuse University, 1975).

89. Constance Balide, Barbara Danziger, and Deborah Spitz, "The Abortion Issue: Major Groups, Organizations and Funding Sources," in *The Abortion Experience*, ed. Howard J. Osofsky and Joy D. Osofsky (Hagerstown, Md., 1973), 496–529; and Mary T. Hanna, *Catholics and American Politics* (Cambridge, Mass., 1967).

90. Not surprisingly, 93 percent of NARAL's members supported the Equal Rights Amendment, while only 9 percent of NRLC's members supported it. Nonetheless, while 95 percent of NARAL's members approved of women having an equal role with men in business, industry, and government, the great majority of NRLC's members (71 percent) approved of this as well. This composition of abortion and antiabortion activists is found in Donald Granberg, "The Abortion Activists," *Family Planning Perspectives* 13:4 (July/August 1981): 157–163.

91. Paige, *The Right to Lifers*, 43–44. For the Southern Baptist position, see Nancy Tatom Ammerman, *Baptist Battles: Social Change and Religious Conflict in the Southern Baptist Convention* (New Brunswick, N.J., 1990), 101.

92. The Mormon position on abortion is discussed by Daniel H. Ludlow, *The Church and Society: Selections from the Encyclopedia of Mormonism* (Salt Lake City, Utah, 1992), 1.

93. Patrick Allitt, *Catholic Intellectuals and Conservative Politics in America, 1950–1985* (Ithaca, N.Y., 1993), 163–166.

94. For these demonstrations see, "Sons of Thunder," *Triumph*, March 1970, 8; "Editorial," *Triumph*, July 1970, 8–9. These demonstrations are described by Allitt, *Catholic Intellectuals and Conservative Politics*, 148–154.

95. William F. Buckley, "Abortion," *National Review*, June 30, 1970, 658–59; also

quoted by Allitt, *Catholic Intellectuals and Conservative Politics*, 154. Earlier Buckley had written that the case for protecting the rights of unborn children must be "persuasive rather than coercive," noting that "the law, in effect, does not recognize an unborn child as a human entity, possessing rights—which is why penalties against illegal abortions are less than those against murder." William F. Buckley Jr., "The Catholic Church and Abortion," *National Review*, April 5, 1966, 308.

In 1971 Patricia Bozell, Buckley's sister, physically attacked feminist Ti-Grace Atkinson, who in an inflammatory address at Catholic University of America speculated out loud that the Virgin Mary might have had a better sex life if she had been "knocked up" by a man instead of by God Almighty. Upon hearing this, Bozell rushed onto the stage and slapped Atkinson. Bozell was then restrained and arrested. See Allitt, *Catholic Intellectuals and Conservative Politics*, 153; and "Free Speech and Catholic University: Ti-Grace Affair," *America*, March 27, 1971, 306.

96. George Gallup, *The Gallup Poll* (New York, 1985), 1985. Elizabeth Adell Cook, Ted G. Jelen, and Clyde Wilcox provided a detailed assessment of polling and survey material concerning public opinion on abortion from 1972 through 1992 in their *Between Two Absolutes: Public Opinion and the Politics of Abortion* (Boulder, Colo., 1992). This study is essential for understanding divisions in public opinion concerning abortion.

97. Gallup, *The Gallup Poll*, 2225–2226, 2274.

98. Only in 1974, after *Roe v. Wade*, did George Gallup provide a complete breakdown of his respondents by sex, race, education, region, and income. See Gallup, *The Gallup Poll*, 379. A sophisticated discussion of blacks' attitudes toward abortion, based on religious attitudes, education, and age, is offered in Cook, Jelen, and Wilcox, *Between Two Absolutes*, 44–48, 114–124. Rosalind Petchesky, in *Abortion and Woman's Choice* (Boston, 1990), emphasizes the importance of black leadership in shaping African-American opinion.

99. *National Right to Life News*, August 18, 1980, quoted in Paige, *The Right to Lifers*, 101.

100. A useful summary of African-American opposition to family planning is found in Robert G. Weisbord, "Birth Control and Black Americans: A Matter of Genocide?" *Demography* 10, (November 1973): 571–590. An eloquent defense of abortion reform aimed at countering opposition within the African-American community was made by Mary Treadwell, a black activist in Washington, D.C. See Mary Treadwell, "Is Abortion Black Genocide?" *Family Planning Perspectives* 4:1 (January 1972): 4–5. Also, for a defense of family planning as nonracist, see Raymond Pace Alexander, "Medico-legal Aspects of Contraception," *New York State Bar Journal* 41 (October 1969): 476–479.

It is important to note that Jesse Jackson reversed his opposition to abortion during his presidential campaign in 1988. He declared, "We oppose any attempts to repeal a woman's right to choose and must make sure that poor women have the same reproductive rights available to them as the rich—including Medicaid funding of abortion and the enforcement of informed consent laws to prevent involuntary sterilization." Quoted in Frank Clemente and Frank Watkins, eds., *Keep Hope Alive: Jesse Jackson's 1988 Presidential Campaign* (Boston, 1989), 166.

101. For example, in a controversial article written for *Ebony* magazine, comedian Dick Gregory argued that blacks should have large families as a way of avoiding "genocide." His article elicited numerous letters from readers. See Dick Gregory, "My Answer to Genocide," *Ebony*, October 1971, 66–70, 72. Readers responded in the next issue, November 1971, 16–18, 20, 22, 28.

102. Mary Smith, "Birth Control and the Negro Women," *Ebony*, March 1968, 29–37.

103. Quoted in Robert Weisbord, "Birth Control and Black Americans," *Demography*, 581.

104. Merton, *Enemies of Choice*, 26; also *New York Times*, August 5, 1963, 12.

105. Weisbord, "Birth Control and Black Americans," 584–586; Merton, *Enemies of Choice*, 26.

106. Van Keys, "Thoughts for Negroes," *Black Panther*, March 9, 1969, 1.

107. Quoted in Weisbord, "Birth Control and Black Americans," 580.

108. Toni Cade, "The Pill: Genocide or Liberation?" in *The Black Woman: An Anthology*, ed. Toni Cade (New York, 1970), 162–169, especially 162, 167.

109. For an eloquent expression of this argument, expressed a decade later, see Angela Davis, *Women, Race, and Class* (New York, 1981), especially 202–222.

110. Jack Slater, "Sterilization: Newest Threat to the Poor," *Ebony*, October 1973, 150–156. Charges of racism are raised in Herbert Aptheker, "Racism and Human Experimentation," *Political Affairs* 53, (February 1974): 48–59; and Aptheker, "Sterilization, Experimentation, and Imperialism," *Political Affairs* 53, (January 1974): 37–49. A detailed account of federally funded sterilization is found in Thomas M. Shapiro, *Population Control Politics: Women, Sterilization, and Reproductive Choice* (Philadelphia, 1985). Shapiro, an activist, dramatically details how feminists became involved in a campaign to restrict and regulate involuntary sterilization.

111. U.S. Senate, Hearings, Subcommittee on Health, Senate Committee on Labor and Public Welfare, *Quality of Health Care—Human Experimentation, 1973*, July 10, 1973, part 4. For Hern's statement, see especially 1496–1552.

112. Denton Vaughan and Gerald Sparer, "Ethnic Group and Welfare Status of Women Sterilized in Federally Funded Family Planning Programs, 1972," *Family Planning Perspectives* 6:4 (Fall 1974): 224–229.

113. The politics of the White House concerning sterilization policy is discussed by Thomas Littlewood, *The Politics of Population Control* (Notre Dame, Ind., 1977), 107–133. Also see, Claudia Dreifus, "Sterilizing the Poor," *The Progressive* 39 (December 1975): 13; Mark Bloom, "Sterilization Guidelines: 22 Months on the Shelf," *Medical World News*, November 9, 1973, 12. For black reaction to sterilization, see Alyce Gullattee, "The Politics of Eugenics," in *Eugenic Sterilization*, ed. Jonas Botitscher (Springfield, Ill., 1973). Also Julius Paul, "The Return of Punitive Sterilization Proposals: Current Attacks on Illegitimacy and the AFDC Program," *Law and Society Review* 3:1 (August 1968), 77–106. For the Nixon White House, see John H. Kessel, *The Domestic Presidency: Decision-Making in the White House* (North Scituate, Mass., 1975). For a later discussion of sterilization policy, see Patricia Donovan, "Sterilization and the Poor: Two Views on the Need for Protection from Abuse," *Family Planning/Population Reporter* 5: 2 (April 1976): 28.

114. Insight into state campaigns from the point of view of the population movement is found in Hugh Moore to William H. Draper, August 28, 1972; and Larry Lader to Hugh Moore, April 21, 1970, Hugh Moore Papers, Box 17, Princeton University. David Garrow discusses the state campaigns in *Liberty and Sexuality*, 579.

115. An insightful account of the abortion fight in North Dakota is provided by Ginsburg, *Contested Lives*, 64–72.

116. Quoted in Garrow, *Liberty and Sexuality*, 579. Garrow provides a dramatic account of the Michigan and North Dakota referendum and its effect on the abortion repeal movement; see especially 566–567, 577–579. Garrow provides an encyclopedic history of the abortion reform movement that details both the political and the legal struggle over abortion rights.

117. Larry Lader to Hugh Moore, August 22, 1972, Hugh Moore Papers, Box 17, Princeton, University. Also, for Lader's earlier appraisal of the state battles over abortion, see Larry Lader to Hugh Moore, April 21, 1970, Hugh Moore Papers, Box 17, Princeton University.

274   *Notes*

Chapter 5

1. For example, Karen O'Connor finds that the abortion controversy was "triggered" by *Roe v. Wade*. See O'Connor, *No Neutral Ground? Abortion Politics in an Age of Absolutes* (Boulder, Colo., 1996), 3. For a detailed account of the struggle on the abortion issue on the state level preceding *Roe*, see David Garrow's exhaustive account, *Liberty and Sexuality* (New York, 1994), 335–338.

2. Richard M. Nixon, "Statement by the President on the Report of the Commission on Population Growth and the American Future," May 5, 1971, *Public Papers of the Presidents: Richard M. Nixon*, vol. 2 (Washington, D.C., 1971), 576–577.

3. O'Connor, *No Neutral Ground*, 44.

4. Joseph Sunnen to Hugh Moore, November 5, 1968; and Hugh Moore to William H. Draper, August 28, 1972; Moore Papers, Box 17, Princeton University.

5. For Moore's relationship with Lader, see Hugh Moore to Robert Willison, September 1, 1972; Lawrence Lader to Hugh Moore, August 22, 1972; and Lawrence Lader to Moore, April 21, 1970; Moore Papers, Box 17, Princeton University.

6. Hugh Moore to Joseph W. Ayer, December 3, 1968, Moore Papers, Box 17, Princeton University.

7. Hugh Moore to Emerson Foote, January 5, 1968, Moore Papers, Box 17, Princeton University.

8. The advertisement appeared on March 10, 1968, in the *New York Times* and on March 13 in the *Washington Post*.

9. George N. Lindsay to Marriner S. Eccles, March 15, 1968, Hugh Moore Papers, Box 17, Princeton University.

10. Donald Strauss to Harold Bostrom, March 15, 1968; Harold W. Bostrom to William Draper, March 19, 1968, Moore Papers, Box 17, Princeton University.

11. Resolution of Planned Parenthood-World Population, Executive Committee, March 14, 1968; and press release, "George Lindsay Statement in Response to 'Have You Ever Been Mugged Today,'" March 11, 1968; Moore Papers, Box 17, Princeton University.

12. Publicly, Draper supported the advertisement, telling Lindsay, "I can see objections to the ads, but I see no advantage in exaggerating these objections by strained interpretations." Behind the scenes, Moore apologized to Draper, telling him he thought Draper, as an executive member of the PCC, would agree to the ad. William Draper to George N. Lindsay, March 25, 1968; William Draper to Hugh Moore, March 23, 1968; and Hugh Moore to Bill Draper, April 8, 1968; Moore Papers, Box 17, Princeton University.

13. Hugh Moore to John Rock, March 28, 1965, Moore Papers, Box 17, Princeton University.

14. Harold Bostrom to George N. Lindsay, March 27, 1968, Hugh Moore Papers, Box 17, Princeton University.

15. Hugh Moore to Harold Bostrom, April 7, 1969; and Harold Bostrom to George Lindsay, April 17, 1969; Moore Papers, Box 17, Princeton University.

16. Hugh Moore to Cass Canfield, December 10, 1969, Moore Papers, Box 17, Princeton University.

17. Harold Bostrom to Hugh Moore, December 15, 1969, Moore Papers, Box 17, Princeton University.

18. Lawrence Lader, *Breeding Ourselves to Death* (New York, 1971), 80–82.

19. Harold Bostrom to Hugh Moore, August 20, 1972, Moore Papers, Box 17, Princeton University.

20. Kingley Davis, "Population Policy: Will Current Programs Succeed?" *Science*, November 10, 1967, 730–739; reprinted in Daniel J. Callahan, ed., *The American Population Debate* (New York, 1971), 227–258. All quotations are from Callahan.

21. Ibid., 225, 235, 238, 247, 254.

22. Melvin M. Ketchel, "Should Birth Control Be Mandatory?" *Medical World News*, October 18, 1968, 66–71. Also Melvin M. Ketchel, "Fertility Control Agents as a Possible Solution to the World Population Problem," *Perspectives in Biology and Medicine*, 11, (Summer 1968), 687–702.

23. The argument that the decline in the birthrate was only an aberration is expounded in Lawrence A. Mayer, "U.S. Population Growth: Would Fewer Be Better?" *Fortune*, June 1970, reprinted in Daniel Callahan, ed., *The American Population Debate*, 3–20.

24. Ronald M. Baker, "Population Control in the Year 2000: The Constitutionality of Placing Anti-Fertility Agents in the Water Supply," *Ohio State Law Journal* 32 (Winter 1971): 108–118. This argument found support within the population movement. In a letter to the editor of *Family Planning Perspectives*, Philip D. Harvey of the Population Service, Inc., Chapel Hill, North Carolina, argued, "In fact, the use of a 100 percent effective, 100 percent reversible (on demand) sterilant [in the water supply] is probably the most 'voluntary' method of birth and population control now under discussion. Such a measure would be no more coercive (or less humane) than water fluoridation." See "Sterilants in Water Supply: Coercive or Voluntary?" *Family Planning Perspectives* 2:1 (January 1971): 4.

Similarly, Don J. Young and Patricia Young Alverson argued two years earlier in a legal journal, "Our society relies on exhortation to prevent illegitimacy, but when exhortation fails and a girl has her second illegitimate child, it is time for a more realistic approach to the problem—court-ordered contraception." See Don J. Young, "Court-Ordered Contraception," *American Bar Association Journal* 55 (March 1969): 223–229.

25. Zero Population Growth and Negative Population Growth, as well as the anti-immigration movement that activists in ZPG and NPG helped organize later, need further scholarly attention. For a scientific discussion of ZPG, see "Z.P.G.," *Scientific American*, April 1971, 50. Catholic reaction to ZPG is found in Joseph H. Fichter, "ZPG: A Bourgeois Conspiracy?" *America*, August 19, 1972, 127, 88–90.

26. Richard M. Bowers to ZPG members, September 30, 1969, Population Council Papers (unprocessed), RA.

27. Bernard Berelson, Memorandum, May 14, 1969; Richard M. Bower to Bernard Berelson, June 8, 1969; Frederick Keppel to John D. Rockefeller 3rd, May 8, 1969, Population Council Papers (unprocessed), RA.

28. Marston Bates, *A Jungle in the House* (New York, 1970); Edgar Chasteen, "The Case for Compulsory Birth Control," *Mademoiselle*, January 1970, reprinted in Callahan, *The American Population Debate*, 274–297.

29. Chasteen, "The Case for Compulsory Birth Control," 275, 277, 278. Similarly, Melvin M. Ketchel, a proponent of placing contraceptive agents in public water supplies, declared, "Ultimately, the question of government control comes down to the question of whether it is necessary. If the population growth rate presents no serious problem, the government ought not to intrude. But if it adversely affects the common welfare—as a rapid growth rate surely does—and it cannot be lowered by voluntary means, then it is necessary and proper for the government to take action." Ketchel, "Should Birth Control Be Mandatory?" 70.

30. Bernard Berelson to files, July 28, 1970, Population Council Papers (unprocessed), RA.

31. Frank Notestein to Bernard Berelson, February 25, 1971, Notestein Papers, Box 8, Princeton University.

32. Frank W. Notestein to Donald A. Collins, November 3, 1969, Population Council Files, RA.

33. Frank Notestein, "Zero Population Growth: What Is It?" *Family Planning Perspectives* (June 1970), reprinted in Callahan, *The American Population Debate*, 31–43.

34. For labor's criticism of overpopulation, see Frank Pollar, "Trends in U.S. Population," *AFL-CIO American Federationist* (June 1970), reprinted in Callahan, *The American Population Debate*, 55–67. For Wattenberg, see "The Nonsense Explosion," *New Republic*, April 4, 1970, reprinted in Callahan, *The American Population Debate*, 96–109; and Donald J. Bogue, "The End of the Population Explosion," 7 (Spring 1967): 11–20.

35. Judith Blake, "Population Policy for America: Is the Government Being Misled?" *Science*, May 2, 1969, 522–529, reprinted in Callahan, *The American Population Debate*, 298–324.

36. Oscar Harkavy, Frederick S. Jaffe, and Samuel M. Wishik, "Family Planning and Public Policy: Who Is Misleading Whom?" *Science*, July 25, 1969, 367–373.

37. For a detailed list of people considered for the commission, see a lengthy memorandum prepared by Harris Huey to Chester E. Finn Sr., December 23, 1969, John D. Rockefeller 3rd papers (unprocessed), RA. Interestingly, most of Rockefeller's initial list of possible nominees did not appear among the final commission nominees. Interestingly, primarily at the urging of Moynihan's assistant Chester Finn, two Catholics were considered for appointment to the commission, Father James T. McHugh and John Francis Noonan, the latter a legal scholar who had served as a consultant on the Vatican's birth control commission. See Ronald Freedman to John D. Rockefeller 3rd, October 1, 1969, John D. Rockefeller 3rd Papers (unprocessed), RA.

For a secondary account of the politics involved in the formation and outcome of the commission, see Charles F. Westoff, "The Commission on Population Growth and the American Future: Origins, Operations, and Aftermath," in *Sociology and Public Policy: The Case of Presidential Commissions*, ed. Mirra Komorovsky (New York, 1975), 43–60.

38. Members of the commission included Lawrence Arnett, president of the Arkansas Association of State Colleges; Dr. Joseph D. Beasley, chair of family health and population, Tulane University; David Bell, former director of the Bureau of the Budget and vice president at the Ford Foundation; Bernard Berelson, Population Council; Representative John Blatnik; Arnita Young Boswell, social worker; Margaret Bright, professor of public health; Marilyn Jane Brant (Mrs. Otis Chandler), publisher of the *Los Angeles Times*; Paul Bertau Cornely, professor at Howard University; Senator Alan Cranston; Otis Dudley Duncan, University of Chicago sociologist; John Nel Erlenborn, lawyer; Antonia Luis Ferre, Puerto Rican businessman; Joan Flint, civil rights activist from Oklahoma; R. V. Hansberger, businessman; David Gale Johnson, Harvard University economist; Grace Olivarez, OEO director from Phoenix, Arizona; Senator Bob Packwood; James Rummonds, student at Stanford University; Stephen Salyer, student at Davidson College; Howard D. Samuel, vice president of Amalgamated Clothing Workers of America; and George David Woods, investment banker.

39. David K. Lelewer to John D. Rockefeller 3rd, December 3, 1971, David Lelewer Papers, Box 1, RA.

40. Paul B. Cornely, "Statement for the President's Commission on Population Growth and America's Future," December 6, 1971, John D. Rockefeller 3rd Papers (unprocessed), RA.

41. Joan Flint to Bernard Berelson, March 23, 1972, Berelson files, Population Commission, Population Council Papers (unprocessed), RA.

42. Paul Ehrlich to John D. Rockefeller 3rd, August 6, 1971, John D. Rockefeller 3rd Papers (unprocessed), RA.

43. Bernard Berelson to Population Commission, December 20, 1971, Berelson Papers, Commission on Population File, RA.

44. Summary of Commission Meeting, January 21–22, 1971, Records of the Commission on Population Growth and the American Future, RG 220, Box 3, NA, Washington, D.C.

45. Among the sixty-five separate bills introduced in Congress calling for revisions of the Immigration Act, four were the most important: HR 2328, HR 1523, HR 7466, and S. 1373. These bills set limitations from 260,000 to 320,000 people. David K. Lelewar to John D. Rockefeller 3rd, October 14, 1971, John D. Rockefeller 3rd Papers (unprocessed), RA.

46. Paul B. Cornely, an African-American commissioner, argued that the issue showed that "this country has totally neglected the problems of Blacks, Mexican-Americans, and Native Americans. Why should job opportunities go to immigrants and their descendants, while our own citizens are going hungry, ill cared for, and unemployed? . . . Is not it about time that we turned the Statue of Liberty with its compassionate admonition so that the promised land would become a reality to the people who were born here?" He maintained that it would be unfair to ask Americans to limit their numbers of children, when at the same time "we are permitting large numbers of immigrants to add to our population each year."

Unfortunately, detailed minutes of the commission meetings were not included in the final archival record of the Commission on Population Growth and the American Future, RG 220, NA. A sporadic record is found in the John D. Rockefeller 3rd Papers at the Rockefeller Archives.

Paul B. Cornley, "Statement for the President's Commission on Population Growth and America's Future," December 6, 1971; and a supporting letter by David K. Lelewer to John D. Rockefeller 3rd, December 3, 1971, John D. Rockefeller 3rd Papers (unprocessed), RA.

47. Summary of Commission Meeting, October 19–20, 1970, Records of the Commission on Population Growth and the American Future, RG 220, Box 3, NA.

48. Howard D. Samuel to Commission, October 12, 1971; and Dianne Wolman to Commission, October 12, 1971, Records of the Commission, RG 220, Box 5, NA.

49. Charles Westoff to John D. Rockefeller 3rd, April 12, 1971, David Lelewer Papers, Box 1, RA.

50. Summary of Commission Meeting, October 18–19, 1971; and Summary of Commission Meeting, August 15–16, 1971; Records of Commission on Population Growth, Box 5, NA.

51. Summary of Meeting of December 21–22, 1970, Records of Commission on Population Growth, Box 5, NA.

52. He invited his nephew, Nelson's son, Steven Rockefeller, a professor of philosophy at Middlebury College, to submit a position paper entitled "Legalized Abortion and Social Values." The young Rockefeller agreed with his uncle that abortion should "not be thought of as a form of birth control. . . . It should be thought of only as a last resort when other methods have failed." With "better" contraceptive methods, he believed, "abortion will gradually become less and less necessary." Still he worried about the general affects that legalized abortion would have on American "social attitudes toward human life and more specifically toward the taking of human life. Any dulling of the sense of the sacredness of the individual person is a threat to the health of a free society which is necessarily based on respect for the individual. . . . Abortion has the potential of increasing toleration of other forms of killing human life for the sake of some apparent good." In the end, after a careful wringing of hands, Stephen Rockefeller came out in favor of legalized abortion, but in doing so he raised an astute question, especially in light of the subsequent acrimony created by the abortion debate. He asked, unless "our environmentally unsound habits of consumption and our materialistic growth ethic are addressed . . . why muddy the waters by getting into a debate on values?" Steven Rockefeller to John D. Rockefeller 3rd, September 13, 1971 and September 3, 1971, John D. Rockefeller 3rd Papers (unprocessed), RA.

For an interesting look at Steven Clark Rockefeller and the next generation of Rockefellers, see Kathleen Telsch, "The Cousins: The Fourth Generation of Rockefellers," *New York Times Biographical Service*, December 30, 1984.

53. Paul B. Cornely, "Statement for the President's Commission on Population Growth and America's Future," December 6, 1971, John D. Rockefeller 3rd Papers (unprocessed), RA.

54. "Dissenting Statements," February 4, 1972, Bernard Berelson Papers, Box 38, RA.

55. Ibid.

56. Summary of Commission Meeting, November 29–December 1, 1971, Records of the Population Commission, Box 6, RG 220, NA.

57. An excellent overview of the report is provided in Richard Lincoln, "Population and the American Future: The Commission's Final Report," *Family Planning Perspectives* 4:2 (April 1972): 10–22.

58. David Lelewar, a Rockefeller family consultant, wrote Rockefeller 3rd, "Carol Foreman and I, your amateur political advisors, strongly urge you that the Democratic and Republican National Committees be approached by the Commission to assure that the convention delegates give consideration to population as they go about the task of formulating their platforms." David K. Lelewer to John D. Rockefeller 3rd, April 12, 1972, John Rockefeller 3rd Papers (unprocessed), RA.

59. Press Release, U.S. Catholic Conference, "Catholic Official Says Population Commission Has Entered Ideological 'Valley of Death,' " March 15, 1972, John D. Rockefeller 3rd Papers (unprocessed), RA.

60. U.S. Catholic Conference, "Catholic Official Says Population Commission Has Entered into an Ideological 'Valley of Death,'" March 15, 1972, John D. Rockefeller 3rd Papers (unprocessed), RA.

61. John D. Rockefeller 3rd to Rev. Theodore Hesburgh, March 1, 1972; Ted Hesburgh to John D. Rockefeller 3rd, March 6, 1972; John D. Rockefeller 3rd to Theodore Hesburgh, May 11, 1972; Theodore Hesburgh to John D. Rockefeller 3rd, May 17, 1972; and John D. Rockefeller 3rd to Bishop Bernardin, May 16, 1972, John D. Rockefeller 3rd Papers (unprocessed), RA.

62. "Pro-Abortion Policy on the Population Panel Opposed 5–1," *New York Times*, May 11, 1972.

63. Mrs. T. W. Hodges to John D. Rockefeller 3rd, May 22, 1972, Commission on Population, Box 8, RG 220, NA.

64. John D. Rockefeller 3rd to Katherine Graham, April 4, 1972; and John D. Rockefeller 3rd to John B. Oakes, April 7, 1972; John D. Rockefeller 3rd Papers, (unprocessed), RA.

65. John D. Rockefeller 3rd to Cynthia Wedel, April 7, 1972, John D. Rockefeller 3rd Papers (unprocessed), RA.

66. Cynthia Wedel to John D. Rockefeller 3rd, April 20, 1972, John D. Rockefeller 3rd Papers (unprocessed), RA.

67. John D. Rockefeller to President Richard M. Nixon, April 7, 1972; and John D. Rockefeller to Daniel Patrick Moynihan, April 11, 1972; John D. Rockefeller 3rd Papers (unprocessed), RA.

68. Nixon's Catholic strategy needs further exploration by historians and political scientists. A good beginning point, however, is found in Thomas B. Littlewood, *The Politics of Population Control* (Notre Dame, Ind., 1977), 107–132; and Theodore White, *The Making of the President* (New York, 1973), 51–52, 242–244. Mary T. Hanna, *Catholics and American Politics* (Cambridge, Mass., 1979), is useful on the demographics of Catholic voters.

69. Quoted in White, *The Making of the President*, 51.

70. Richard Nixon, "Remarks at the Annual Convention of the National Catholic

Education Association in Philadelphia, Pennsylvania, April 6, 1972," in *Public Papers of the Presidents of the United States: Richard Nixon, 1972* (Washington, D.C., 1974), 516–523; White, *The Making of the President*, 243–244.

71. Richard M. Nixon, "Statement by the President on the Report of the Commission on Population Growth and the American Future," May 5, 1972, in *Public Papers of the Presidents: Richard M. Nixon*, 576–577.

72. Quoted in White, *The Making of a President*, 244. A analysis of the subsequent election in New York is found in "The New York Campaign," *National Journal*, November 28, 1972, 1676–1678.

73. John Ehrlichman, "Office Notes, May 5, 1972, Phone Call to John D. Rockefeller 3rd," Ehrlichman Papers, Box 6, NA. In the previous spring, Nixon had reversed abortion policy in military hospitals to correspond with the laws of states where military bases were located. This conformed to his belief that the states should regulate abortion laws. In issuing this new directive he added, "From personal and religious beliefs I consider abortion an unacceptable form of population control. Further, unrestricted abortion policies, or abortion on demand, I cannot square with my personal belief in the sanctity of human life—including the life of the yet unborn. For, surely, the unborn have rights also, recognized in law, recognized even in principles expounded by the United Nations." Richard Nixon, "Statement About Policy on Abortions at Military Base Hospitals in the United States," April 3, 1971, *Public Papers of the Presidents: Richard M. Nixon, 1971* (Washington, D.C., 1972), 500.

74. The argument that issues did not play a significant role in the election is found in Seymour Martin Lipset and Earl Raab, "The Election and the National Mood," *Commentary*, 63, (January 1973): 43. Contrary to this view, Jeanne Kirkpatrick maintains that McGovern was hurt by the "three As"—amnesty, acid, and abortion—while Rosenthal found the hidden issue of race was critical to the outcome. See Jeanne Kirkpatrick, "The Revolt of the Masses," *Commentary*, 63, (February 1973): 60; and Jack Rosenthal, "The Secret Key Issue: Study of Polls Shows Racial Attitudes Critical with Nixon Gainer," *New York Times*, November 7, 1972. Background on Nixon's campaign strategy is found in Proinsias Mac Aonghusa, "Nixon on the Shamrock Trail," *New Statesman*, October 9, 1970, 442; "Report: Far Ahead in Polls," *National Journal*, October 28, 1972, 1655–1662. Also "Outlook '73," *National Journal*, November 11, 1972, 1727–1736; and "Continuity of U.S. Leadership," *U.S. News and World Report*, November 20, 1972, 12–18.

75. This analysis draws from Arthur H. Miller, Warren E. Miller, Alden S. Raines and Thad A. Brown, "A Majority Party in Disarray: Policy Polarization in 1972," unpublished paper, Library of Congress, Washington, D.C., 1972.

The importance of policy issues in determining voting behavior is analyzed by Gerald M. Popper, "From Confusion to Clarity: Issues and American Voters, 1956–1968," *American Political Science Review* 66 (June 1972): 415–428; Richard W. Boyd, "Popular Control of Public Policy: A Normal Vote Analysis of the 1968 Election," *American Political Science Review* 66 (June 1972): 429–449.

76. John D. Rockefeller 3rd, Announcement of Citizens' Committee, July 31, 1972; and "Citizens' Committee on Population and American Future" (n.d., 1972?), Rockefeller 3rd Papers (unprocessed), RA.

77. Initially the commission sought to purchase an hour of prime time on commercial television through privately raised funds, but when the networks refused to grant complete editorial autonomy, a complaint was brought before the FCC charging them with being unresponsive to public service. In the end the film was made by an independent producer and shown on national television. The White House subsequently exerted pressure on HEW to prevent it from circulating the film. Westoff, "The Commission on Population Growth and the American Future," 58. Also Carol T. Foreman to Bernard Berelson, October 26, 1973, Bernard Berelson Papers, Organization File (unprocessed), RA.

78. Carol T. Foreman to Bernard Berelson, October 26, 1973, Berelson Papers, Organization File (unprocessed), RA.

79. Bernard Berelson to Carol T. Foreman, November 1, 1973, Berelson Papers, Citizens' Committee on Population, Organization File (unprocessed), RA.

80. Carol T. Foreman to Bernard Berelson, October 26, 1973, Berelson Papers, Organization File (unprocessed), RA.

81. Charles F. Westoff to Commission, June 8, 1972, Berelson Papers, Westoff Folder (unprocessed), RA.

82. The Social Security amendments of 1972 are discussed by Jeannie I. Rosoff, "The Future of Federal Support for Family Planning Services and Population Research," *Family Planning Perspectives* 5:1 (Winter 1973): 7–18. Also Jeannie Rosoff, "Medicaid, Past and Future," *Family Planning Perspectives* 4:3 (July, 1972), 26–33; Donald Fisher and Jeannie Rosoff, "How States Are Using Title IV–A to Finance Family Planning Services," *Family Planning Perspectives*, 4, (October, 1972), 31–43; and Joseph Goldman and Leonard S. Kogan, "Public Welfare and Family Planning," *Family Planning Perspectives* 3:4 (October, 1971), 19–31.

For relevant government documents, see U.S. Congress, House Committee on Ways and Means, *First Annual Report of the Department of Health, Education, and Welfare on Services to AFDC Families* (Washington, D.C., 1970); U.S. Congress, Senate Committee on Finance, *Report on HR 175550*, December 11, 1970, (Washington, D.C., 1970). Also "Welfare Reform Deleted from Social Security Bill," 28, *Congressional Quarterly Almanac* (1972): 899–914.

83. PL 92–345.

84. "Major Congressional Action," *Congressional Quarterly Almanac* (1972): 192–193.

85. U.S. Senate, *Family Planning and Population Research Amendments of 1973: Hearings Before the Special Subcommittee on Human Resources of the Committee on Labor and Public Welfare* (Washington, D.C., 1973), 47–61.

86. "Twelve Health Programs Extended Through Fiscal 1974," *Congressional Quarterly Almanac* (1973), 489–493. Also "President Nixon's Message on Fiscal 1973 Budget," *Congressional Quarterly Almanac* (1972), 1–4.

87. See Rosoff, "The Future of Federal Support for Family Planning Services," 7–18, especially 12–13; Frederick Jaffe, Joy G. Dryfoos, and Marsha Corey, "Organized Family Planning Programs," *Family Planning Perspectives* 5:2 (Spring 1973): 73–79, which provides an overview of family planning; and Gerald Sparer, Louise M. Okada, and Stanley Tillinghast, "How Much Do Family Planning Programs Cost?" *Family Planning Perspectives* 5:2 (Spring 1973): 100–103, which provides a breakdown of Medicaid costs.

88. Littlewood, *The Politics of Population Control*, 107–133.

89. Frederick S. Jaffe and Phillip Cartwright, "Short-Term Benefits and Costs of U.S. Family Planning Programs, 1970–1975," *Family Planning Perspectives* 9:2 (March/April 1977): 77–81.

90. Robert H. Connery and Gerald Benjamin, *Rockefeller of New York: Executive Power in the State House* (Ithaca, N.Y., 1979), 94–95.

91. Joan C. Robbins to John D. Rockefeller 3rd, September 7, 1973, John D. Rockefeller 3rd Papers (unprocessed), RA.

92. For a detailed discussion of this debate, see Barbara Hinkson Craig and David M. O'Brien, *Abortion and American Politics* (Chatham, N.J., 1993), especially 109–119. This remains, in my opinion, by far the best book on the politics of abortion for its objectivity and insightful analysis.

93. Rockefeller was especially pleased to learn that Congressman Robert Drinan, S.J. (D-Massachusetts) had worked behind the scenes to help defeat the Bartlett amendment. Drinan reported to Harriet Pilpel, "By the time that you get this you certainly will have heard that the Bartlett amendment was dropped from the conference report. I

can take at least a little credit for that minor victory over the powers of darkness." He noted, "I must say that the so-called right to life movement attracts an extraordinary large number of arrogant individuals." Robert Drinan to Harriet Pilpel, November 26, 1974, John D. Rockefeller 3rd Papers (unprocessed), RA.

94. Bernard Berelson to Daniel Callahan, June 14, 1969; and Bernard Berelson to Mrs. Derek Bok, June 7, 1971; Berelson Papers, Chronological files 1968–1971, RA.

95. Frank Notestein to Bernard Berelson, August 26, 1971, Frank Notestein Papers, Box 10, Princeton University.

96. Frank Notestein to Bernard Berelson, February 8, 1973, Frank Notestein Papers, Box 10, Princeton University.

97. Bernard Berelson to Robert C. Bates, April 2, 1971, Rockefeller Brother Fund Papers, Box 210, RA.

98. Interestingly, only Raymond Ravenholt from AID remained optimistic that family planning programs were working, especially, he believed, if abortion became an acceptable instrument of population control. Dismissing concerns that family planning programs were not working, he told the group that he was moving ahead on a "new way" of solving the population problem by "seeding" throughout his work "advanced fertility clinics that would do the job" through "abortion, sterilization, infertility, contraception, and the rest, at a high level of technology." Bernard Berelson to Files, June 27, 1972, Berelson Files, Population Council Papers (unprocessed), RA.

99. Bernard Berelson to files, October 31, 1973, Berelson Files, Population Council Papers (unprocessed), RA.

100. Bernard Berelson to file, April 18, 1973, Berelson Files, Population Council Papers (unprocessed), RA. Similar expressions that family planning was not working were found at a Rockefeller Foundation conference held at Bellagio, Italy, on May 10–12, attended by major donors, including representatives from the Ford Foundation. See Memorandum, "Priorities for Work on the World Population Problem: Bellagio III, June 1973," Oscar Harkavy File, FA.

101. Charles Westoff to John D. Rockefeller 3rd, September 17, 1974; and Stephen L. Salyer to John D. Rockefeller 3rd September 30, 1974, Joan Dunlop Papers, Box 8, RA.

102. Joan Dunlop, Interview with author, New York City, April 3, 1997.

103. Joan Dunlop to John D. Rockefeller 3rd, May 2, 1974, John D. Rockefeller 3rd Papers (unprocessed), RA.

104. Pierre Pradervand, "Realistic Approaches to the Acceptance of Family Planning in Africa," John D. Rockefeller 3rd Papers (unprocessed), RA.

105. Joan M. Dunlop to John D. Rockefeller 3rd, July 23, 1974, John D. Rockefeller 3rd Papers (unprocessed), RA.

106. Joan Dunlop to John D. Rockefeller 3rd, April 19, 1974, John D. Rockefeller 3rd Papers (unprocessed), RA.

107. Stephen L. Salyer to John D. Rockefeller 3rd, August 8, 1974, John D. Rockefeller 3rd Papers (unprocessed), RA.

108. Quoting Berelson, Joan Dunlop to Porter McKeever, Jack Harr, Steve Salyer, July 15, 1974, John D. Rockefeller 3rd Papers (unprocessed), RA.

109. Joan M. Dunlop to John D. Rockefeller 3rd, July 23, 1974; Bernard Berelson to John D. Rockefeller, July 22, 1974; Bernard Berelson to John D. Rockefeller 3rd, n.d. (July 1974?); John D. Rockefeller 3rd Papers (unprocessed), RA.

110. Frank Notestein to Bernard Berelson, April 27, 1971, Notestein Papers, Box 8, Princeton University.

111. Rockefeller had prevented the appointment of William Draper as chair of the U.S. contingent. Draper was instead made a member of the five-person delegation that included Philander Claxton, special assistant for population to Secretary of State Henry

Kissinger; Governor Russell W. Peterson; Patricia Hutar, U.S. representative on the
UN Commission on the Status of Women; and Caspar Weinberger. Two congressional
advisers to the delegation were Representative Edith Green of Oregon and Senator
Charles Percy of Illinois. For opposition to William Draper becoming chairman of the
delegation, see Joan Dunlop to John D. Rockefeller 3rd, May 31, 1974, John D.
Rockefeller 3rd Papers (unprocessed), RA.

112. Documentation of the World Population Plan of Action and various speeches
of the American delegation are found in "United Nations World Population Conference Held at Bucharest," *Department of State Bulletin* 71 (September 30, 1974):
429–453. A detailed discussion of the Bucharest conference is found in Jason L. Finkle
and Barbara B. Crane, "The Politics of Bucharest: Population, Development, and the
New International Economic Order," 1, *Population and Development Review* (September
1975): 87–114.

113. John D. Rockefeller 3rd, "Population Growth: The Role of the Developed
World," John D. Rockefeller 3rd Papers (unprocessed), RA.

114. Quoted at length in Marcus F. Fanda, *Reactions to America at Bucharest*
(American Universities Field Staff Report, September 1975), (Pasadena, Calif., 1975),
especially 5–7. Also "United Nations World Population Conference Held at Bucharest," 1–25.

Interestingly, Rockefeller and Berelson had met two years earlier with the Chinese
ambassador to the United States, Huang Hua, concerning family planning in China.
Rockefeller left the meeting favorably impressed with China's family planning program.
Huang Hua reported that the Chinese government was trying to achieve population
control through propaganda and by providing free contraceptives in high-density population areas. Rockefeller was told that in areas with low population density or where
national minorities lived, the Chinese government did not "push" population control
programs. Bernard Berelson to Files, November 1, 1972, Berelson Files, Population
Council Papers (unprocessed), RA.

115. Quoted, in Franda, *Reactions to America at Bucharest*, 9.

Chapter 6

1. Jason L. Finkle and Barbara B. Crane, "The Politics of Bucharest: Population,
Development, and the New International Economic Order," *Population and Development
Review*, 1, (September 1975): 87–110, especially 101–110.

2. Frank Notestein to Frederick Osborn, "Uninhibited Notes on Bucharest—Not
for Publication," September 12, 1974, Frederick Osborn Papers, APS.

3. Donald Warwick to Joan Dunlop, November 12, 1974, Joan Dunlop Papers, Box
8; and Bernard Berelson to John D. Rockefeller 3rd, January 4, 1978, with attached
memorandum, Joan Dunlop to John D. Rockefeller 3rd, Joan Dunlop Papers, Box 8,
RA.

4. Robert C. Bates to Rockefeller Fund Files, October 2, 1974, Rockefeller Brother
Fund Files, Box 210, RA.

5. Ravenholt is quoted in David Heaps, "Report on the Population Council Prepared for the Ford Foundation," December 1973, Population Council Files (unprocessed), RA.

6. Mrs. Cordelia Scaife May to John D. Rockefeller 3rd, November 7, 1974, John
D. Rockefeller 3rd Papers (unprocessed), RA.

7. Cordelia Scaife May to John D. Rockefeller 3rd, November 24, 1974, John D.
Rockefeller 3rd Papers (unprocessed), RA.

8. For a detailed report on the Ford Foundation's population program, see David
Heaps, "Report on the Population Council Prepared for the Ford Foundation," December 1973, Population Council Files (unprocessed), RA.

9. Oscar Harkavy, "Foundation Population Strategy for the Next Five Years," November 29, 1974; and Oscar Harkavy to David E. Bell, September 20, 1974, Oscar Harkavy Files, FA.

10. David Heaps, "Report on the Population Council prepared for the Ford Foundation," December 1973, Population Council Files (unprocessed), RA.

11. Joan Dunlop to John D. Rockefeller, April 29, 1975, Box 8; Joan Dunlop to John D. Rockefeller 3rd, September 24, 1974, Joan Dunlop Papers, Box 10, RA.

12. Joan Dunlop to Files, September 27, 1974, John D. Rockefeller 3rd Papers (unprocessed), RA.

13. Joan Dunlop to John D. Rockefeller 3rd, September 24, 1974, Joan Dunlop Papers, Box 10, RA.

14. Gerald O. Barney and Robert C. Bates to Rockefeller Brothers Fund, April 1, 1975, Rockefeller Brothers Fund Files, Box 88, RA.

15. Dunlop's views are summarized in Gerald O. Barney to Rockefeller Brothers Fund Files, March 24, 1975; and Gerald O. Barney and Robert C. Bates to Rockefeller Brothers Fund, April 1, 1975, Rockefeller Brothers Fund Files, Box 88, RA.

16. Jack Bresan, "Recommendations on George Zeidenstein," July 31, 1975, John D. Rockefeller Papers (unprocessed), RA.

17. Population Council, Press Release, October 22, 1975, Rockefeller Brothers Fund Papers, Box 88, RA.

18. George Zeidenstein, "Future Direction of the Population Council," presented to the board of Trustees Annual Meeting, June 8 and 19, 1976, John D. Rockefeller 3rd Papers (unprocessed), RA.

19. Gerald O. Barney to Rockefeller Brothers Fund files, March 9, 1976, Rockefeller Brothers Fund Papers, Box 88, RA.

20. John T. Noonan to John D. Rockefeller 3rd, November 10, 1976, John D. Rockefeller 3rd Papers (unprocessed), RA.

21. Population Council, *The Population Council Annual Report 1978* (New York, 1978), 18.

22. Joan Dunlop to John D. Rockefeller 3rd, May 5, 1977, John D. Rockefeller 3rd Papers (unprocessed), RA.

23. These were Carmen A. Miro, a Brazilian demographer; Vina Mazumdar, chair of women's studies at the Indian Council of Social Science Research, New Delhi, India; Akin L. Mobogunje, a geographer from the University of Ibadan, Nigeria; Jose Pinotti, a Brazilian obstetrician; Masri Sinarimbun, director of the Population Institute in Indonesia; and Salvador Zubiran, director of the National Institute of Nutrition, Mexico City, Mexico.

24. Population Council, *The Population Council Annual Report 1978*, 23–31, especially 23–26.

25. Ibid., 127–131.

26. In an interview with the author, Joan Dunlop placed great importance on the influence the Rockefeller children had on their father and uncle. Interview, Joan Dunlop with author, April 3, 1997. Also Peter Collier and David Horowitz, *The Rockefellers: An American Dynasty* (New York, 1976), especially 528 and 588–606.

27. John D. Rockefeller 3rd, "No Retreat on Abortion," *Newsweek*, June 21, 1976, 11.

28. William Carmichael, "Report on the Foundation's Past Work on Abortion and Proposals Currently Under Consideration," September 9, 1981, FA.

29. Foundation support for the proabortion movement is detailed in a lengthy memorandum by Joan Dunlop, "Foundation Support for Abortion, 1973–1977" (n.d.), Joan Dunlop Papers, Box 1, RA. In this memorandum, Dunlop reviewed the extensive giving to proabortion causes by philanthropic foundations and specific donations of each organization, including the Cabot Charitable Trust, Massachusetts; the Commonwealth

Fund; the Maurice Falk Medical Fund; the Ford Foundation; the General Services Foundation, Illinois; the Grant Foundation of New York; the Luke B. Hancock Foundation of California; the McKnight Foundation of Minnesota; the Eugene and Agnes E. Meyer Foundation of Washington; the Louise L. Ottinger Charitable Trust of New York; the Theodore Parker Foundation of Massachusetts; the Rockefeller Brothers Fund; the Rockefeller Foundation; the Stern Fund of New York; and the Wallace Eljebar Fund of New York.

An interesting example of Rockefeller's giving in conjunction with other foundations was his "one-time" gift of $100,000 to the Alan Guttmacher Institute in 1978 to keep the institute running. This gift, was in addition to the Rockefeller's regular annual donation of $25,000. The Kellogg Foundation and the Rockefeller Brothers Fund also provided grants. In 1978 the annual budget of the Alan Guttmacher Institute was $2.9 million, including grants from the Gund Fund ($300,000); the Rockefeller Brothers Fund ($25,000); the Rockefeller Foundation ($25,000); the Mott Foundation ($30,000); the Packard Foundation ($10,000); PPWP ($121,000); and IPPF ($50,000). See John D. Rockefeller 3rd to Frederick Jaffe, March 1, 1978; and Joan Dunlop to John D. Rockefeller 3rd, February 13, 1978; Joan Dunlop Papers, Box 1, RA.

30. In 1970 the Ford Foundation provided a $500,000 grant to SIECUS. Rockefeller believed that his support for SIECUS was important because it showed his commitment to "the movement in general" and to Mary Calderone in particular. In 1970 he contributed $50,000 to SIECUS, followed by annual contributions of $25,000 in subsequent years, as well as a $50,000 gift in 1970. See John D. Rockefeller 3rd to Mary S. Calderone, February 26, 1970, Box 2; Undated memorandum, "Contributions 1970, John D. Rockefeller 3rd," Joan Dunlop Papers, Box 3, and David K. Lelewer to John D. Rockefeller 3rd, June 9, 1972, Box 3, Joan Dunlop Papers, RA. Contributions to the PPFA project in New York City are recorded in an undated memorandum, "JDR Giving," Joan Dunlop Papers, Box 3, RA.

31. Elizabeth J. Roberts, "Aspects of Sexual Learning," December 22, 1977, Joan Dunlop Papers, Box 3, RA.

32. Elizabeth J. Roberts to John D. Rockefeller 3rd, January 6, 1975, Joan Dunlop Papers, Box 3, RA.

33. A history of sex education in America awaits serious attention by scholars, but a wealth of primary materials can be found in the Rockefeller Archives and the Mary Calderone papers.

Included on the advisory board were Bert Brim, president of the Foundation for Child Development; Joan Cooney, executive director of the Children's Television Workshop; John Gagnon, professor of sociology at State University of New York at Stony Brook; George Gerbner, director of research on violence on television for NIMH at the Annenberg School of Communications; Stephen Hersh, chief of the Center for Studies of Children and Family Mental Health for NIMH; Stephen Hess, senior fellow at the Brookings Institution; Jerry Rosow, Exxon Corporation; Eli Rubinstein, professor of psychiatry at State University of New York at Stony Brook; Harold Stevenson, professor of psychology at University of Michigan; and Homer Wadsworth, director of the Cleveland Foundation. Elizabeth J. Roberts to John D. Rockefeller 3rd, January 6, 1975, Joan Dunlop Papers, Box 3, R.A.

The project kept a careful eye on recruiting other public figures to the board. Typical in this respect, Elizabeth Roberts reported to Dunlop that she was seeking ways to involve journalist John McNeil in the project. "I have learned," she wrote, "that John McNeil is very, very good in church and homosexuality in general." Although there is no evidence that John McNeil became involved in the project, this attention to "who stood where" in public circles was indicative of the desire to win over influential people in public affairs. Elizabeth Roberts to Joan Dunlop, December 23, 1976, Joan Dunlop Papers, Box 5, RA.

34. There is extensive correspondence on this film in Joan Dunlop's papers. Of particular relevance is Joan Dunlop to Fred Taylor, May 23, 1977; Joan Dunlop to Leonard Mayhew, April 4, 1997; Jean T. Mulcahy to Patricia Hewitt, May 25, 1977; Margaret Mead to John D. Rockefeller 3rd, January 21, 1977; and Lucy Phenis to Friends of Adair Film (n.d.); Joan Dunlop Papers, Box 11, RA.

35. Especially interesting in regard to public education was a memorandum written by Joan Dunlop directed to Rockefeller's attention. After outlining a funding strategy for Rockefeller's donations to abortion rights groups, Murray turned her attention to the public context to ensure that the right to abortion could be exercised. "Creating acceptance for the practice of abortion is, in my view, an unending struggle," she wrote. "Abortion is a negative activity. Just as people do not want to think of other surgical procedures until they need them, so people will think even less of abortion. Furthermore, there is a loss of abortion that cannot be denied, and I believe it is feared a little like death. . . . but fear and loathing can be lessened through education and understanding and a realization of the ordinariness of any feared activity (everybody has to die, for example, or x number of people last year had neurosurgery, or 1 million women last year had abortions). Here again, then, I think that a quiet steady public education campaign is in order." Joan Dunlop to John D. Rockefeller 3rd, "Abortion Strategy and Future Funding," April 19, 1977; and Anne Murray to Joan Dunlop, April 1, 1977, Joan Dunlop Papers, Box 3, RA.

36. Joan Dunlop, Grant Making in Abortion, 1973–1978 (n.d.), Joan Dunlop Papers, Box 3, RA.

37. For support of this retreat sponsored by the feminist caucus of the Democratic party in Minnesota, see Joan Dunlop to Koryne Horbal, June 15, 1978, Joan Dunlop Papers, Box 10, RA.

38. John D. Rockefeller 3rd to Nelson Rockefeller, September 1, 1976, Joan Dunlop Papers, Box 3, RA.

39. Vicki Z. Kaplan to Bea Blair, October 23, 1974, Joan Dunlop Papers, Box 10, RA.

40. Joan Dunlop to the Files, January 29, 1976, Joan Dunlop Papers, Box 10, RA.

41. Joan Dunlop to John D. Rockefeller 3rd, April 17, 1978; and Joan Dunlop to Fred Taylor, April 19, 1978, Joan Dunlop Papers, Box 1, RA.

42. For example, in 1978 the project received $60,000 from John Rockefeller 3rd; $15,000 from the Playboy Foundation; $10,000 from the Needmore Foundation; $5,000 from the J. M. Kaplan Fund; $5,000 from the Ottinger Charitable Trust; $5,000 from the Joe and Emily Lowe Foundation; $2,500 from the Bydale Foundation; and $2,500 from Mrs. Richard Chasin, as well as $150,000 from the Ford Foundation. Aryeh Neier to John D. Rockefeller 3rd, April 10, 1978, Joan Dunlop Papers, Box 1, RA.

43. This language emerged in a lengthy correspondence shared with Joan Dunlop with William Ruder concerning a speech given by Rabbi Seymour Siegel, a theologian at the Jewish Theological Seminary, at the right-to-life convention in 1976. Rudder told Dunlop that "the problem is that the Right to Life leadership gets its support of intellectuals like Dr. Siegel—uses their thinking and their statements to legitimize their position—and then goes on to approach the public on a rabble-rousing and hysterical basis. It's a neat combination." William Ruder to Joan Dunlop, July 27, 1976; David Finn to Dr. Seymour Siegel, July 14, 1976; and Seymour Siegel to David Finn, July 7, 1976; Joan Dunlop Papers, Box 3, RA.

44. Carol T. Foreman to John D. Rockefeller 3rd, August 20, 1973, Joan Dunlop Papers, Box 3, RA.

45. Overall, Rockefeller gave $462,400 to proabortion groups from 1973 to 1978. Joan Dunlop to John D. Rockefeller 3rd, February 5, 1975; and "JDR 3rd Grant Making in Abortion 1973–1978," February 28, 1978; Joan Dunlop Papers, Box 3, RA.

46. David K. Lelewer to John D. Rockefeller 3rd, January 12, 1970, Box 10, Joan Dunlop papers, RA. Callahan also received support from the Ford Foundation. See William Carmichael, "Report on the Foundation's Past Work on Abortion and Proposals Currently Under Consideration," September 9, 1991, Subject files, FA.

47. James T. Burtchaell to John D. Rockefeller, June 21, 1976; Peter Johnson to the Files, September 30, 1976; and John D. Rockefeller 3rd to Father Burtchaell, October 14, 1976, Joan Dunlop Papers, Box 3, RA.

Later, William Liu, chair of the Department of Sociology at the University of Notre Dame, told Rockefeller that his instincts about Burtchaell were correct and that he was "vehemently against abortion." Liu recommended that Rockefeller talk to David Solomon, a philosopher at Notre Dame, and Charles Curran at Catholic University, as well as George Schuster, "who is quite liberal," having been "radicalized by women at Hunter University." Selinda A. Melnik to Joan Dunlop, September 9, 1976, Joan Dunlop Papers, Box 3, RA.

48. Selinda Melnik to Joan Dunlop, August 18, 1975, Joan Dunlop Papers, Box 10, RA.

49. Selinda Melnik to Joan Dunlop, August 31, 1976, Dunlop Papers, Box 10, RA.

50. Joan Harriman, "Alternative Counseling Center: Two Year Pilot Project, January 1, 1976 to January 1, 1978" (January 1, 1978), Joan Dunlop Papers, Box 10, RA.

51. Selinda Melnik to Joan Dunlop, August 31, 1976; and Selinda Melnik to Joan Dunlop, January 5, 1976, Joan Dunlop Papers, Box 10, RA.

52. Dunlop to John D. Rockefeller 3rd, January 23, 1978; and Joan Dunlop to Joan Harriman, February 1, 1978, Joan Dunlop Papers, Box 10, RA.

Although Catholic Alternatives enlisted a number of notable Catholics on its board (including Rosemary Ruether, a leading feminist Catholic theologian; Dr. Edward Hughes, director for health services at Northwestern University; and Dr. Margaret Maxey, professor of bioethics at the University of Detroit), the number of Catholics acceptable to CCFC or willing to serve proved quite small. For example, Joan Harriman, the president of CCFC, ruled out appointing Father Andrew Greeley, a prominent Catholic sociologist, to the advisory committee because "he is on an ego trip." So desperate was the organization to find well-known Catholics that they considered inviting Gloria Steinhem, editor of *Ms.*, and author and longtime left-wing activist Lillian Hellman to the board because they had been "raised Catholic." Few within the Catholic Church, or, for that matter, the proabortion movement, would have considered either Catholic. Selinda Melnik to Joan Dunlop, August 31, 1976, Box 10, Joan Dunlop Papers, RA.

53. Joan Dunlop to John D. Rockefeller 3rd, August 11, 1972, Joan Dunlop Papers, Box 2, RA.

54. Joan Dunlop to John D. Rockefeller 3rd, April 10, 1978, Box 1; and Joan Dunlop to John D. Rockefeller 3rd, August 10, 1977, Joan Dunlop Papers, Box 3, RA.

55. Stanley Henshaw, "Induced Abortion: A Worldwide Perspective," *Family Planning Perspectives* (1965), 5, quoted in Barbara Hinkson Craig and David M. O'Brien, *Abortion and American Politics* (Chatham, N.J., 1993), 77. Craig and O'Brien provide a thorough overview of abortion politics on the state level. Also Alan Guttmacher Institute, *Abortion 1974–1975: Need and Services in the United States, Each State and Metropolitan Area* (New York, 1976).

56. These figures are cited in Craig and O'Brien, *Abortion and American Politics*, 78.

57. For example, Alabama, Arkansas, Georgia, Hawaii, Idaho, Indiana, Kentucky, Maine, Maryland, Minnesota, Mississippi, Missouri, Montana, Nebraska, Nevada, New York, North Carolina, South Carolina, Tennessee, Texas, Utah, Virginia, Washington, and Wyoming required licensed physicians to perform abortions in licensed clinics or hospitals. All of these states, with the exception of Alabama, Maryland, Montana, New York, North Carolina, and Texas, required reports to public health authorities.

In addition, California, Delaware, Illinois, South Dakota, and Wisconsin had reporting requirements. Similarly, a number of states attempted to ban advertising for abortions, but the Supreme Court ruled that advertising was protected under the First
Amendment in *Bigelow v. Virginia* and *Carey v. Population Services International* (1977).

Viability regulations were also imposed by requiring physicians to try to save the life
of an aborted fetus. Regulations of this nature were passed by state legislatures in
Louisiana, Pennsylvania, and Utah. The strictest such regulation was enacted by the
Missouri state legislature in 1969. When this was overturned by the Burger Court, the
Missouri legislature enacted an abortion law in 1974 requiring, along with reporting
and record keeping of abortions, spousal consent, and unwed minor parental consent,
that physicians preserve the life and health of the fetus. A similar act was enacted in
Pennsylvania. Although the Missouri and Pennsylvania acts were overturned, several
states, including Arizona, Arkansas, Illinois, Minnesota, North Dakota, Oklahoma,
Utah, and Wyoming, kept their statutes intact, although unenforced.

Spousal and parental consent and notification measures were enacted in thirty-four
states, with various degrees of legal success and enforcement. Although spousal consent
regulations were overturned by the court, nine states continued to maintain spousal
consent. The court upheld parental consent or "judicial bypass" regulations in a series
of decisions designed to clarify the intent of *Roe*. Public funding of abortion became an
even more contentious issue. By 1989 only thirteen states did not have any restrictions
on public funding, while thirty-seven states provided public funding in cases of rape,
incest, or to save the woman's life. See Craig and O'Brien, *Abortion and American Politics*,
78–96.

58. Ibid., 96.

59. This followed from the logic of *Roe v. Wade* (1973) and *Doe v. Bolton* (1973). *Roe*
and *Doe* specifically addressed Texas and Georgia laws prohibiting abortion except for
"the purpose of saving the life of the mother" (Texas) and where "pregnancy would
endanger the life of the pregnant mother or would seriously and permanently injure her
health" (Georgia). In finding that the Texas and Georgia laws violated the due process
clause of the Fourteenth Amendment, the broad scope of the Court's constitutional
interpretation invalidated abortion laws in forty-six states. The Court's ruling, however,
set standards that allowed the state to have a "compelling" interest in preserving the life
of a viable fetus in the later stages of pregnancy. The Court upheld a fundamental right
of women to have an abortion. In the first trimester of pregnancy this right, based on
the doctrine of privacy, remained absolute, leaving the decision to have an abortion the
pregnant woman's alone, in consultation with a physician. At the end of the first
trimester the state had an "important and legitimate interest in the health of the mother," and having this "compelling" interest the state could "regulate the abortion procedure to the extent that regulation reasonably relates to preservation and protection of
maternal health." In the final third trimester, the Court found that state interest in preserving the life of the possibly viable fetus was compelling, which allowed for the state
to impose certain restrictions and regulations, provided they did not conflict with the
general right of the woman to legalized abortion. For a superb account of Court rulings, see Gerald N. Rosenberg, *The Hollow Hope: Can Courts Bring About Social Change?*
(Chicago, 1991), 173–201.

60. This discussion of the federal abortion policy in Congress and the White House
relies heavily on Karen O'Connor, *No Neutral Ground? Abortion Politics in an Age of Absolutes* (Boulder, Colo., 1996), and on Craig and O'Brien, *Abortion and American Politics*.

61. Ford's veto was overturned when a strange alliance was formed with liberals
such as Representative Bella Abzug (D-New York), who because of their commitment
to maintain spending levels in the appropriations bill joined antiabortion congressmen
such as Hyde. An important understanding of the politics of the Hyde amendment during this period is found in Joyce Gelb and Marian Lief Palley, "Women and Interest

Group Politics: A Comparative Analysis of Federal Decision Making," *Journal of Politics* 41 (May 1979): 362–392, especially 375–377.

62. Ford remained steadfast in his support of Rockefeller during his nomination hearings, even though four Roman Catholic bishops testified against him. See Connie Paige, *The Right to Lifers: Who They Are; How They Operate; Where They Get Their Money* (New York, 1983), 63.

63. Party platforms quoted in full in O'Connor, *No Neutral Ground?* 73.

64. Quoted in ibid., 74.

65. Following the enactment of New York's abortion law in 1970, McCormack joined other antiabortionists in organizing a statewide antiabortion movement. Most of these activists came from decidedly apolitical backgrounds. Their first foray into politics came in 1970 when they ran two candidates in the Democratic primary for governor and the Fifth Congressional District against Democratic incumbent Alard Lowenstein. Although both antiabortion candidates were unsuccessful, antiabortionists claimed credit for helping Norman Lent, a Repub-lican, defeat Lowenstein. Following the election, McCormack declared, "Even though we lost the election, we felt we had been successful." This success led McCormack's group to work actively for Barbara Keating, the New York Conservative party's candidate for the U.S. Senate, in 1974. This early political experience convinced antiabortionists that electoral politics was more fruitful than traditional lobbying. In the 1976 campaign, McCormack ran as a Democrat in the presidential primaries, receiving 238,000 votes in eighteen primary states, acquiring twenty-two convention delegates. This modest success led McCormack and her followers to organize the Right to Life party to voice the antiabortion position, regardless of other issues or party attachments. Following the election, the Right to Life party became increasingly separatist, refusing to work within the two-party system. This separatism created a schism in the movement, eventually leading the National Right to Life Committee to denounce McCormack and her followers as ideologically rigid. Quoted in Robert J. Spitzer, *The Right to Life Movement and Third Party Politics* (New York, 1987), 59, 50–80; O'Connor, *No Neutral Ground?* 71–73.

66. John D. Rockefeller 3rd, September 1, 1976; Jimmy Carter to John D. Rockefeller 3rd, September 22, 1976; John D. Rockefeller 3rd to William Friday, September 1, 1976; Box 2, Joan Dunlop Papers, RA.

67. *Maher v. Roe* (1977); *Beal v. Doe* (1977); and *Poelker v. Doe* (1977).

68. Joseph Califano, *Governing America: An Insider's Report from the White House and the Cabinet* (New York, 1981).

69. Joan Dunlop to John D. Rockefeller 3rd, August 10, 1977, Box 3, Joan Dunlop Papers, RA.

70. Included among those who switched their positions were a number of prominent liberals, including Frank Church (D-Idaho), Lawton Chiles (D-Florida), Hubert Humphrey (D-Minnesota), Edward Kennedy (D-Massachusetts), Patrick Leahy (D-Vermont), and Edmund Muskie (D-Maine). They were joined by moderates such as Sam Nunn (D-Georgia) and Howard Baker (R-Tennessee).

71. Quoted in Califano, *Governing America*, 74.

72. *Congressional Record, House*, 95th Cong., 2nd sess., 1978, 17266–17274; also quoted in Craig and O'Brien, *Abortion and American Politics*, 127.

73. Quoted in Craig and O'Brien, *Abortion and American Politics*, 128.

74. Ibid., 132.

75. A study published in the *New England Journal of Medicine* reported that in 1972 23.0 percent of all women having abortions were nonwhite, while by 1976 this had increased to 32.2 percent. The number of unmarried women increased from 70.3 percent to 73.9. See Lawrence R. Berger, "Abortion in America: The Effects of Restrictive Funding," *New England Journal of Medicine* 298:26 (June 29, 1978): 1474–1477.

76. "Family Planning, Crib Death Funds Authorized," *Congressional Quarterly—Weekly Report* 36 (August 5, 1978): 2063–2065.

77. Initial opposition to the bill came from the National Child Welfare League, Zero Population Growth, the Women and Health Roundtable, as well antiabortion groups that worried that counselors might promote abortion. See "Interest Groups Are Seeking Modifications in Pregnancy Prevention and Care Bill," *Congressional Quarterly—Weekly Report* 36 (August 26, 1978): 2248–2250. Also Califano, *Governing America*, 71.

78. Berger, "Abortion in America," 1476.

79. Joyce Gelb and Marian Lief Palley, "Women and Interest Group Politics: A Comparative Analysis of Federal Decision Making," *Journal of Politics* 41 (May 1979): 377. Also see David Brody and Kent Tedin, "Ladies in Pink: Religion and Political Ideology in the Anti-ERA Movement," *Social Science Quarterly* 57 (March 1976): 72–82.

80. Quoted in Gelb and Palley, "Women and Interest Group Politics," 379.

81. John Ensor Harr and Peter Johnson, *The Rockefeller Conscience: An American Family in Public and in Private* (New York, 1991), 463–553.

82. Roger Williams, "The Power of Fetal Politics," *Saturday Review*, June 9, 1979, 12–15.

83. There is a rich literature on the emergence of the new Christian Right in recent American politics. For a selective reading of this literature, see David H. Bennett, *The Party of Fear: From Nativist Movements to the New Right in American History* (Chapel Hill, N.C., 1988); Steve Bruce, Peter Kivisto, and William H. Swatos Jr., *The Rapture of Politics* (New York, 1995); Matthew Moen, *The Christian Right and Congress* (Tuscaloosa, Ala., 1992); Robert Liebman and Robert Wuthnow, *The New Christian Right* (New York, 1983); James Davison Hunter, *Cultural Wars: The Struggle to Define America* (New York, 1991); Clyde Wilcox, *Onward Christian Soldiers? The Religious Right in American Politics* (Boulder, Colo., 1996); Michael D'Antonio, *Fall from Grace: The Failed Crusade of the Christian Right* (Boston, 1989); Alan Crawford, *Thunder on the Right* (New York, 1980); and David Bromley and Anson Shupe, *New Christian Politics* (Macon, Ga., 1984). Of importance in understanding the extreme right is Seymour Lipset and Earl Raab, *The Politics of Unreason* (New York, 1970). Also, the first emergence of the religious right in the anti-ERA movement is examined in David W. Brody and Kent L. Tedin, "Ladies in Pink," 564–575.

84. In a close examination of abortion attitudes published shortly before the 1980 election, Lucky M. Tedrow and E. R. Mahoney found that there were "substantial differences between Catholic and Protestant approval of abortion, with Protestants more approving than Catholics," even though there was a sharp movement toward approval among Catholics beginning in 1973, inversely related to church attendance. Also of note, they found that by 1976 there was a trend of increased approval among males, while females were "still experiencing a conservative trend." Lucky M. Tedrow and E. R. Mahoney, "Trends in Attitudes Toward Abortion: 1972–1976," *Public Opinion Quarterly* 43 (Summer 1979): 181–89, especially 188, 184.

85. Clyde Wilcox, *God's Warriors* (Baltimore, 1992); and Duanne Murray Oldfield, *The Right and the Righteous: The Christian Right Confronts the Republican Party* (Lanham, Md., 1996). Also Kenneth D. Wald, Dennis E. Owen, and Samuel S. Hill Jr., "Evangelical Politics and Status Issue," *Journal for the Scientific Study of Religion* 28:1 (1989): 1–16. Steve Bruce, *The Rise and Fall of the Christian Right* (Oxford, 1988), argues against status explanations in explaining the new Christian Right.

86. Patrick Buchanan, *Conservative Votes, Liberal Victories: Why the Right Has Failed* (New York, 1975); and William Rusher, *The Making of the New Majority Party* (Ottawa, 1975). The implications of this New Right agenda from a critical conservative position is found in Crawford, *Thunder on the Right.*

87. Michele McKeegan, *Abortion Politics: Mutiny in the Ranks of the Right* (New York, 1992), 1–23.

88. Useful on state antiabortion activity is Michael Margolis and Kevin Neary, "Pressure Politics Revisited: The Anti-Abortion Campaign," *Policy Studies Journal* 8 (Spring 1980): 698–716.

89. Quoted in Williams, "The Power of Fetal Politics," 12.

90. Michael Johnston, "The 'New Christian Right' in American Politics," *Political Quarterly* 53:2 (April–June 1982): 181–199.

91. Religiosity proved critical in predicting antiabortion and proabortion positions, as well as attitudes toward the ERA. Surveys showed increased polarization in the electorate (the proportion of people with perfect liberal scores increased, while those with perfect conservative scores declined). Moreover, detailed analysis of survey data showed that abortion was critical in mobilizing conservatives, while *no* support was found in the data for the hypothesis that conservatism emerged specifically around feminist issues associated with the ERA. The trend toward conservatism among certain voters first coincided with the abortion debate in the late 1960s. Pamela Johnston Conover, "The Mobilization of the New Right: A Test of Various Explanations," *Western Political Quarterly* 36 (December 1983): 632–649; Carol Mueller, "In Search of a Constituency for the 'New Religious Right,' " *Public Opinion Quarterly* 47 (Summer 1983): 213–229, especially 220–222. Mueller found that many Christian activists supported a number of feminist issues, including female participation in the workplace and politics. Also useful is Clyde Wilcox and Leopoldo Gomez, "The Christian Right and the Pro-Life Movement: An Analysis of Sources of Political Support," *Review of Religious Research* 31:4 (June 1990): 380–388.

92. This division between Falwell's Moral Majority and Pat Robertson's Christian Coalition is developed more fully in Wilcox, *Onward Christian Soldiers?*

93. During the campaign, the New Right and the Christian Right further flexed their muscles by targeting the "Deadly Dozen"—a hit list of congressional supports of abortion rights. Five of these proabortion Democratic senators went down in defeat. Antiabortion activists poured millions of dollars into the congressional campaign. In addition, the antiabortion Life Amendment Political Action Committee endorsed sixteen Republicans and five Democrats running for the Senate, as well as seventy-eight Republicans and forty-four Democrats for the House. Proabortion groups counterattacked by pouring funds into the campaigns of congressional candidates who supported abortion rights. Although economic and other issues largely determined the outcome of these elections, expressed in the strong anti-Carter vote revealed in the exit polls, antiabortionists claimed victory. Lou Cannon, *President Reagan: The Role of a Lifetime* (New York, 1991); and Rowland Evans and Robert Novak, *The Reagan Revolution* (New York, 1981). The turn to the right in the Republican party is discussed by Gillian Peele, *Revival and Reaction: The Right in Contemporary America* (Oxford, 1984).

94. An excellent legislative summary of congressional actions on abortion is found in Edward Keynes, "Abortion," in *The Encyclopedia of the United States Congress*, vol. 1, ed. Donald C. Bacon, Roger H. Davidson, and Morton Keller (New York, 1995), 1–2. Also see Edward Keynes, with Randall K. Miller, *The Court vs. Congress: Prayer, Busing, and Abortion* (New York, 1989), 244–312; and Laurence H. Tribe, *Abortion: The Clash of Absolutes* (Cambridge, Mass., 1990).

95. Craig and O'Brien, *Abortion and American Politics*, 137–147, especially 140.

96. Meanwhile, eighteen other proposed constitutional amendments had been introduced in Congress.

97. *Congressional Quarterly Weekly Report*, December 19, 1981, 2526. Also Timothy Noah, "The Right-to-Life Split," *New Republic*, March 21, 1981, 7–9.

98. Senate Judiciary Subcommittee on the Constitution, *Hearings, Constitutional Amendments Relating to Abortion*, 97th Cong., 1st sess., October 5, 14, 19, November 4,

5, 12, 16, and December 16, 1981. Voting for the bill were two Democrats, Joseph Biden (Delaware) and Dennis DeConcini (Arizona), and eight Republicans, Orrin Hatch (Utah), Strom Thurmond (South Carolina), Alan Simpson (Wyoming), Paul Laxalt (Nevada), Robert Dole (Kansas), Charles Grassley (Iowa), Jeremiah Denton (Alabama), and John East (North Carolina). Opposing the amendment were Democrats Edward Kennedy (Massachusetts), Robert Byrd (West Virginia), Patrick Leahy (Vermont), Max Baucus (Wyoming), Howard Metzenbaum (Ohio), and two Republicans, Arlen Specter (Pennsylvania) and Charles Mathis (Maryland). For quotation and vote, see Craig and O'Brien, *Abortion and American Politics*, 141. They mistakenly identify Joseph Biden as a senator from Maryland.

99. *Congressional Quarterly Weekly Report*, September 4, 1982, 2202, quoted in Craig and O'Brien, *Abortion and American Politics*, 145.

100. When Congress reconvened in June 1983, following major defeats for Republicans in the 1982 midterm elections, the reintroduced Hatch amendment was defeated in a Senate vote of 49 to 50 (eighteen votes short of the two-thirds constitutionally required for passage). In the end, economics within the Reagan administration had won over the social issues. Proabortionists acclaimed Packwood a hero. A decade later, however, when it was revealed that he had sexually harassed female members of his staff and supporters, he was forced to resign from the Senate in October 1995.

101. The following discussion of antiabortion activity within the Reagan administration relies on Connor, *No Neutral Ground?* 81–111. Also on the 1984 election see Keith Blume, *The Presidential Election Show: Campaign 84 and Beyond the Nightly News* (South Hadley, Mass., 1985); and Jonathan Moore, ed., *Campaign for President: The Managers Look at the '84 Election* (Dover, Mass., 1986); and Stephen D. Johnson and Joseph B. Tamney, "The Christian Right and the 1984 Presidential Election," *Review of Religious Research* 29 (December 1985): 124–133.

102. Still, fifteen states and the District of Columbia continued to provide abortion funding for poor women.

103. Reagan's cut in Title X funds was challenged in court but upheld in *Rust v. Sullivan (1991)*. See "U.S. Supreme Court Considers New Title X Regulations," *Family Planning Perspectives* 23:1 (January/February 1991): 38–40; and "Court Upholds Title X Ban on Abortion Information," *Family Planning Perspectives* 23:4, (July/August 1991): 175–181.

104. In FY1981 Family Planning Service under Title X expenditures were $161,671,000; they fell to $124,174,000 in FY1982 and $124,088,000 in FY1983, and then rose to $140,000,000 in FY 1984 and $142,500,000 in 1985. At the same time, funding for the National Institute of Child Health and Human Development (NICHD) increased in Reagan's first term from about $83 million in FY1982 to $105 in FY1985, the bulk of research going to fertility research. Funding for the Maternal and Child Health Block Grants rose slightly from $454 million in Carter's last year to $478 million, even though Reagan requested deeper cuts. Nadine Cohodas, "Federal Abortion Alternatives Cut by Reagan Administration," *Congressional Quarterly Weekly Report*, November 17, 1984, 2949–2955.

105. Expressing bewilderment, Representative Henry A. Waxman (D-California) declared, "I have always found it incredible that an administration opposed to abortion would also oppose family planning—which is the only federal program that could directly help reduce the number of unwanted pregnancies." The administration defended its cuts as a strategy to improve family planning by turning programs back to the states. As one Reagan official said, "It is the administration's view that some categorical service programs such as family planning and maternal-child health programs are best administered by the states through block grants." These cutbacks in family planning programs outraged activists. PPFA in New York City ran a full-page newspaper ad featuring a diaphragm floating through a galaxy. "When it comes to birth control, our

technology isn't exactly space age," the caption read. Quoted in Cohodas, "Federal Abortion Alternatives Cut by Reagan Administration," 2949–2950.

106. These included the appointment of Rex R. Lee, a Mormon professor of law from Brigham Young University, as his solicitor general. He appointed Dr. C. Everett Koop, a pediatrician and cofounder of Christian Action Council, as his surgeon general. And former head of the Life Amendment Political Action Committee, Donald Devine, became head of the Office of Personnel Management. Another antiabortion activist, James Mason, was appointed director of the Centers for Disease Control. Majorie Mecklenburg, the National Right-to-Life Committee, became head of Title X family planning program.

107. For a detailed account of the struggle between Congress and the Reagan administration, especially on international family planning matters, see McKeegan, *Abortion Politics.*

108. Reagan-appointed federal district judges subsequently proved more antiabortion in decisions than were Carter-appointed judges. See Steve Alumbaugh and C. K. Rowland, "The Links Between Platform-Based Appointment Criteria and Trial Judges' Abortion Judgments," *Judicature* 74:3 (October/November 1990): 153–162.

109. Charles Fried, *Order and Law: Arguing the Reagan Revolution—A Firsthand Account* (New York 1991), 57.

110. Judge Sandra Day O'Connor quotation is found in O'Connor, *No Neutral Ground?* 97, 94–102. See also McKeegan, *Abortion Politics,* 173–191.

111. Fried, *Order and Law,* 77.

112. Ibid., 77–81.

113. Robert Bork, *The Tempting of America: The Political Seduction of the Law* (New York, 1990), 291. Also Herman Schwartz, *Packing the Courts: The Conservative Campaign to Rewrite the Constitution* (New York, 1988).

114. Indicative of attitudes within the membership of the National Right-to-Life Committee was a survey reported in *Family Planning Perspectives* that found that seven in ten NRLC members favored legal abortion if the pregnant woman's life would otherwise be in danger. Donald Granberg, "The Abortion Activists," *Family Planning Perspectives* 13:4 (July/August 1981): 157–163, especially 158. This suggests greater contrasts with membership found in more militant antiabortion groups, although detailed studies of these groups need to be conducted.

115. On the 1988 presidential campaign, see McKeegan, *Abortion Politics,* 147–176.

116. Quoted in O'Connor, *No Neutral Ground?* 117.

117. Ibid., 119–120.

118. Craig and O'Brien provide a good discussion of the *Webster* decision in *Abortion and American Politics,* 197–243. Also O'Connor, *No Neutral Ground?* 119–142.

119. Quoted in O'Connor, *No Neutral Ground?* 133.

120. An excellent and well-balanced appraisal of the decision is found in Randall D. Eggert, Andrew J. Klinghammer, and Jeanne Morrison, " 'Of Winks and Nods': *Webster's* Uncertain Effect on Current and Future Abortion Legislation," *Missouri Law Review* 55:1 (Winter 1990): 163–217.

121. McKeegan, *Abortion Politics,* 158–159.

122. The editors of the conservative and influential religious journal *First Things* denounced the decision as analogous to the infamous *Dred Scott* decision in 1857 that claimed to "resolve" a passionate dispute in a nation divided. "Abortion and a Nation at War," *First Things* 26 (October 1992): 9–13.

123. In 1991 the Alan Guttmacher Institute provided a detailed and fascinating analysis of family planning expenditures over the decade. In FY1990 federal and state governments spent $504 million to provide contraceptive services and supplies, with Medicaid accounting for all public funds spent on contraceptive services and Title X

providing 22 percent, and federal block grants another 22 percent. State government accounted for the remaining 28 percent. Since 1980, however, the proportion of public contraceptive expenditures contributed by Title X fell virtually in half, while state expenditures nearly doubled. Family planning services under Medicaid rose sharply, especially beginning in 1987, largely due to the increased number of program recipients, especially recipients under sixty-five years. Moreover, expenditures on the federal and state levels increased for sterilization services, rising to $95 million by 1990. Most of the federal expenditures for sterilization came through the Medicaid program. The Hyde amendment, implemented in 1977, dramatically reduced federal expenditures for abortion. Title X expenditures for contraceptives services and supplies went to seventy-seven grantees, including thirty-seven state health agencies and forty agencies such as family planning councils and Planned Parenthood affiliates. See Rachel Benson Gold, "Public Funding of Contraceptive, Sterilization and Abortion Services, Fiscal Year 1990," *Family Planning Perspectives* 23:5 (September/October 1991): 204–211.

124. "A Republican God," *Christianity Today*, October 5, 1992, 50–52; "Evangelicals Offer Uneasy Support to Bush," *Christianity Today*, April 6, 1992, 84–85; and "Bush Solidifies Support with Pro-Lifers," *Human Events*, May 2, 1992, 3–4.

125. Quoted in "Abortion Case Adds an Edge to the Election," *New York Times*, January 26, 1994, 4: 1–2.

126. National Election Study (1992), cited in O'Connor, *No Neutral Ground?* 151.

127. Alan I. Abramowitz, "It's Abortion, Stupid: Policy Voting in the 1992 Presidential Election," *Journal of Politics* 67:1 (February 1995): 176–185, especially 176, 178.

The abortion issue continued to play an important role on the state level. Clyde Wilcox, Elizabeth Adell Cook, and Ted G. Jelen showed that abortion was a "significant predictor of voter choice" in exit polls in ten state elections in 1989 and 1990. Clyde Cook, Ted Jelen, Elizabeth Wilcox, "Issue Voting in Gubernatorial Elections: Abortion and Post-*Webster* Politics, *Journal of Politics* 56:1 (February 1994): 187–199.

128. David M. O'Brien, "Clinton's Legal Policy and the Courts: Rising from Disarray or Turning Around and Around?" in *The Clinton Presidency: First Appraisals* ed. Colin Campbell and Bert A. Rockman. (Chatham, N.J., 1996), 126–162, especially 152. Also American Civil Liberties Union, "The 104th Congress's Assault on Reproductive Rights," Press Release (April 28, 1997).

RU 486 created controversy from the outset. Proabortion groups greeted the drug as a technological breakthrough that promised to end the debate. Antiabortionists denounced the drug as another example of the further demeaning of life. Behind much of this rhetoric lay serious misunderstandings of the medical effects of the drug. Tests showed potential benefits of RU 486 as a safe and effective abortion procedure when used correctly, potentially offering women a less stressful abortion decision than surgery, while avoiding the risks of perforation and scarring to the uterus associated with surgical abortion. RU 486 tests also revealed many potentially serious side effects. The drug frequently induced prolonged menstrual-like bleeding lasting anywhere from a few days to a few weeks. This bleeding occurred whether the fetus was expelled completely or unexpelled tissue remained in the uterus, thereby requiring medical supervision in taking the drug. Furthermore, the efficacy of RU 486 after eight weeks of pregnancy remained uncertain. Tests also revealed a potential risk of fetal damage caused by improper use of RU 486. The legal ramifications of these tests are discussed by Eric M. Haas, "*Webster*, Privacy, and RU486," *Journal of Contemporary Health Law and Policy* 6 (Spring 1990): 277–295.

Etienne-Emile Baulieu, an endocrinologist and director of the National Institute of Health and Medical Research, developed RU 486 in the early 1980s. He discusses his work and makes a case for the pill in his book, *The "Abortion Pill": RU486, A Woman's Choice* (New York, 1996).

129. This summary of Clinton's proabortion agenda draws from O'Connor, *No Neutral Ground?* 146–153.

130. Of this total of $715 million, 77 percent ($554 million) came from the federal government. The single largest source of public funds was Medicaid, providing $331 million, or 46 percent of the total expenditures for contraceptive services and supplies. In 1994 an estimated 2.2 million women received public-supported family planning services, including contraceptive services and supplies and sterilization, under the Medicaid program. Medicaid provided the major part of federal expenditures for sterilization.

State expenditures remained higher than the other federal programs, including Title X of the Public Health Service Act, maternal and child health block grants, and social service block grants. The Title X program awarded family planning-specific grants through its ten regional offices to a variety of public and private agencies. In 1994 forty-four of those grants went to state government agencies and forty-one went to nonstate agencies, including regional family planning councils, Planned Parenthood affiliates, and public and community health services. In 1994 Congress appropriated $181 million for this program, compared with $150 million in 1992, an increase of 21 percent. Maternal and child health block grants go exclusively to state government agencies. Between 1992 and 1994, public expenditures for sterilization rose by 7 percent, substantially less than the 46 percent increase recorded between 1990 and 1992. Terry Sollom, Rachel Benson Gold, and Rebekah Saul, "Public Funding for Contraceptive, Sterilization and Abortion Services," *Family Planning Perspectives* 28:4 (July/August 1996): 167–173. I would like to thank the research staff at the Alan Guttmacher Institute in Washington, D.C., for providing this article and other data on family planning in the Clinton administration.

131. Full statistics on violence are found in National Abortion Federation, "Incidents of Violence and Disruption Against Abortion Providers," Press Release, July 1995, cited in O'Connor, *No Neutral Ground?* 162–163.

132. FACE passed the House by a 241 to 174 vote and the Senate by a 69 to 30 vote. See Connor, *No Neutral Ground?* 158–169.

133. The importance of the Christian Right in this election is discussed by John C. Green et al., "Evangelical Realignment: The Political Power of the Christian Right," *Christian Century*, July 5–12, 1995, 676–679. Also, for the relationship between traditional Catholics and the Christian Right, see Rob Boston, "Marriage of Convenience," *Church and State* 47:3 (May 1994): 7–10.

134. O'Connor, *No Neutral Ground?* 170.

135. Terry Sollom, "State Actions on Reproductive Health Issues in 1994," *Family Planning Perspectives* 27:2 (March/April 1995): 83–87. This article provides an excellent overview of abortion law and policy on the state level.

136. Charles E. Cook, "Partial-Birth Betrayal: Democrats Seething as Activist Admits Lie," *Roll Call*, February 27, 1997, 8. For a detailed legislative history of partial-birth legislation, see Library of Congress, Electronic Legislative Database, "Legislative History of H.R. 1833" (1997).

137. Christopher Wolfe, "Abortion and Political Compromise," *First Things* (June/July 1992), 22–29.

Conclusion

1. Peter Bachrack and Elihu Bergman, *Power and Choice: The Formation of American Population Policy* (Lexington, Ky., 1973).

2. For an excellent discussion of international family planning policy in the United States, see John Sharpless, "World Population Growth, Family Planning, and American Foreign Policy," in *The Politics of Abortion and Birth Control in Historical Perspective*, ed. Donald T. Critchlow, (University Park, Pa., 1996), 72–102.

3. This sharp decline in the rate of population growth averted the disasters that had been predicted by authors such as Guy Irving Burch, Fairfield Osborn, and William Vogt, and later by Paul Ehrlich. Writing in 1968, Ehrlich warned that hundreds of millions of people would starve to death because of overpopulation in the 1970s. Paul R. Ehrlich, *The Population Bomb* (New York, 1968). An excellent article on changes in demographic thinking is D. Hodgson, "Orthodoxy and Revisionism in American Demography," *Population and Development Review* 14 (1988): 170–173.

4. John Bongaarts and Judith Bruce, "Internation Population Trends and Policy Choices" (paper delivered at Woodrow Wilson International Center for Scholars, Washington, D.C., February 4, 1997); and Barbara Crossette, "How to Fix a Crowded World: Add People," *New York Times*, November 2, 1997.

5. Sub-Saharan Africa and some areas in the Middle East, South Asia, and West Africa continued to experience high rates of population growth. The rapidly growing population in Asia and Africa means that the composition of the world will change dramatically. In 1950 about a third of the world's population lived in the North America and Europe, but with rapid population growth occurring in Asia and Africa, the proportion will drop to 10 percent. Bongaarts and Bruce, "International Population Trends and Policy Choices."

6. Ibid.

7. For a critical assessment of the problems of overpopulation, see George D. Moffett, *Critical Masses: The Global Population Challenge* (New York, 1994). Also "Battle of the Bulge," *The Economist*, September 3, 1994, 23–25; John Bongaarts, "Can the Growing Human Population Feed Itself," *Scientific American*, March 1994, 18–24; and Bongaarts, "Population Policy Opinions in the Developing World," *Science*, February 11, 1994, 771–775. Credit for government intervention in reducing the rate of global overpopulation is found in Bongaarts and Bruce, "Internation Population Trends and Policy Choices." The most forceful criticism of population control is found in the work of Julian Simon, including *Population Matters: People, Resources, Environment, and Immigration* (New Brunswick, N.J., 1990); *The Ultimate Resource* (Princeton, N.J., 1981); and Julian Simon and Herman Kahn, *The Resourceful Earth* (New York, 1984). Also see William McGurn, "Population and the Wealth of Nations," *First Things*, December 1996, 22–25. Congressional cutbacks in U.S. international population programs are detailed in Barbara Crossette, "U.S. Aid Cutbacks Endangering Population Programs, U.N. Agencies Say," *New York Times*, February 16, 1996, 6.

8. Phillips Cutright and Frederick Jaffe, *Impact of Family Planning Programs on Fertility: The U.S. Experience* (New York, 1977).

9. Edward E. Berkowitz, *America's Welfare State:* (Baltimore, 1991); James T. Patterson, *America's Struggle Against Poverty, 1900–1980* (Cambridge, Mass., 1981); Michael Katz, *The Undeserving Poor: From the War on Poverty to the War on Welfare* (New York, 1989); Daniel Levine, *Poverty and Society: The Growth of the American Welfare State in International Comparison* (New Brunswick, N.J., 1989); and Henry Aaron, *On Social Welfare* (Cambridge, Mass., 1980).

10. Terry Sollom, Rachel Benson Gold, and Rebekah Saul, "Public Funding for Contraceptive, Sterilization and Abortion Services, 1994," *Family Planning Perspectives* 28:4 (July/August 1996): 166–173.

11. David Popenoe, *Life Without Father* (New York, 1996), 6, 229. Also, U.S. Department of Health and Human Services, *Vital Statistics of the United States, 1991*, vol. 1, *Natality* (Washington, D.C., 1993).

12. Kristin Luker, *Dubious Conceptions: The Politics of Teenage Pregnancy*, (Cambridge, Mass., 1996). Also Maris Vinovskis, *An "Epidemic" of Adolescent Pregnancy? Some Historical and Policy Considerations* (New York, 1988).

13. Luker, *Dubious Conceptions*, 192.

14. Popenoe, *Life Without Father*, 8–10. He cites Sara S. McLanahan, "The

Consequences of Single Motherood," *The American Prospect* 18 (1994): 48–58; Sara McLanahan and Gary Sandefur, *Growing Up with a Single Parent* (Cambridge, 1994); and Elaine Ciulla Kamark and William A. Galson, *Putting Children First: A Progressive Family Policy for the 1990s* (Washington, D.C., 1990).

15. David Blankenhorn, *Fatherless America: Confronting Our Most Urgent Social Problem* (New York, 1995), 1–5.

16. Patrick F. Fagan, "Social Breakdown in America," in *Issues '96: The Candidate's Briefing Book*, ed. Stuart Butler and Kim Holmes (Washington, D.C., 1996), 163–195, especially 189–190. He cited U.S. Department of Health and Human Services, Office of Adolescent Programs, *Final Report O.A.P.P., 1985–1990* (Washington, D.C., 1990).

17. In 1996 Susan V. Berresford became president of the Ford Foundation. She told reporters that while the Ford Foundation would stay focused on its longtime interests of poverty, inequality, governance, arts, and education, the foundation wanted to explore the role of religion and the media in American civic life. Karen W. Arson, "Ford Foundation Gets New Leader, New Style," *New York Times*, February 14, 1996, 9.

18. An important source for the founding of FAIR can be found in the oral history collection housed in the Washington, D.C., headquarters of FAIR. Also, an important discussion of FAIR, on which this discussion relies heavily, is found in David H. Bennett, *The Party of Fear: The American Far Right from Nativism to the Militia Movement*, rev. ed. (New York, 1995), 369–372. It is important to note that Bennett describes FAIR as "liberal restrictionists" and not nativists. I want to thank FAIR for allowing me full access to its oral history collection in Washington, D.C.

19. "A Champion for Choice," *Ms.*, September/October 1996, 43–44.

20. "A Scrapper for Planned Parenthood," *Ms.*, July/August 1996, 17.

21. H. Thorpe, "Gloria Feldt," *Texas Monthly*, September 1996, 24, 122–123, 174. Feldt is quoted on page 174.

22. Susan Faludi, *Backlash: The Undeclared War Against Women* (London, 1992).

23. James Davison Hunter, *Cultural Wars: The Struggle to Define America* (New York, 1991).

24. James Davison Hunter and Joseph E. Davis, "Cultural Politics at the Edge of Life," in *The Politics of Abortion and Birth Control in Historical Perspective*, ed. Donald T. Critchlow (University Park, Pa., 1996), 103–127, especially 106. The intractable nature of this debate is captured in two books published in 1993. Patricia G. Miller, *The Worst of Times* (New York, 1993), interviewed fifty people who had experienced or performed illegal abortions before *Roe v.Wade*. Marvin Olasky, *Abortion Rites: A Social History of America* (Wheaton, Ill., 1993), studied abortion in the eighteenth and nineteenth centuries from an antiabortion perspective.

25. Nancy J. Davis and Robert V. Robinson, "Are Rumors of War Exaggerated? Religious Orthodoxy and Moral Progressive in America," *American Journal of Sociology* 3 (November 1996): 756–787.

26. Paul DiMaggio, John Evans, and Bethany Bryson, "Have Americans' Social Attitudes Become More Polarized?" *American Journal of Sociology* 3 (November 1996): 690–75.

27. "U.S. Religious Groups Vary in Patterns of Method Use But Not in Overall Contraceptive Prevalence," *Family Planning Perspectives* 23:6 (November/December 1991): 288–290.

28. Tom W. Smith, "Adult Sexual Behavior in 1989: Number of Partners, Frequence of Intercourse and Risk of AIDS," *Family Planning Perspectives* 23:3 (May/June 1991): 102–107.

29. I would like to thank Clyde Wilcox, a political scientist at Georgetown University, for sharing his analysis of data drawn from the General Social Survey (1997).

30. Smith, "Adult Sexual Behavior in 1989," 102, 106.

Index

Donald T. Critchlow is the founding editor of the *Journal of Policy History*, an interdisciplinary quarterly concerned with the application of historical perspectives to public policy studies. He has taught at a number of universities in the United States and internationally, including Hong Kong University (1997–98) and Warsaw University (1988–89). He received his doctoral degree in History from the University of California, Berkeley. He is the author and editor of a number of books on history and public policy in the United States.